Duke University Press DURHAM AND LONDON 2014

Paige A. McGinley

Staging the Blues

FROM TENT SHOWS TO TOURISM

All rights reserved
Printed in the United States of America on acid-free paper ∞
Designed by **Natalie F. Smith**
Typeset in Chaparral by **Graphic Composition, Inc.**

Library of Congress Cataloging-in-Publication Data
McGinley, Paige A.
Staging the blues : from tent shows to tourism / **Paige A. McGinley.**
pages cm Includes bibliographical references and index.
ISBN 978-0-8223-5731-5 (cloth : alk. paper)
ISBN 978-0-8223-5745-2 (pbk : alk. paper)
1. Blues (Music) —History and criticism. 2. Performance practice
(Music) —Southern States—History—20th century. I. Title.
ML3521.M33 2014   781.64309—dc23 2014006956

This book was published with the assistance of
The Frederick W. Hilles Publication Fund of Yale University.

Cover art: Sister Rosetta Tharpe (1915–1973) at the London
Palladium in 1964. Pictorial Press Ltd. / Alamy.

© 2014 DUKE UNIVERSITY PRESS

Contents

Acknowledgments, vii

Introduction
Beale on Broadway, 1

ONE   **Real Personality**
The Blues Actress, 31

TWO   **Theater Folk**
Huddie Ledbetter On Stage, 81

THREE   **Southern Exposure**
Transatlantic Blues, 129

FOUR   **Highway 61 Revisited**
Blues Tourism at Ground Zero, 177

Notes, 221
Bibliography, 257
Index, 271

My first debt of gratitude is to the performers, living and dead, whose works infuse these pages, and whose creativity, professionalism, and humor I hope to have at least partially captured. Likewise, this work would not be possible without some of the pioneering scholarship produced in the last ten years by scholars of black performance, popular music, and theater history, particularly Daphne A. Brooks, Jayna Brown, David Savran, and Gayle Wald.

Most of this book was written during my time at Yale University, which generously supported my work with a Morse Fellowship in the year 2010–11. The Frederick W. Hilles Publication Fund of Yale University also aided in bringing this book to fruition. My colleagues and students, graduate and undergraduate alike, in theater studies, American studies, and African American studies challenged every bit of my thinking in the best possible way; I could not have asked for a better set of interlocutors at such a crucial time. Hazel Carby, Glenda Gilmore, Matthew Frye Jacobson, Steve Pitti, Marc Robinson, and Laura Wexler all read and commented on portions of the manuscript. Jonathan Holloway did, too; his suggestion that we team-teach a graduate seminar together allowed me to refine some of the book's arguments in conversation with him and a fantastic group of students. Elizabeth Alexander, Toni Dorfman, Jackie Goldsby, Alicia Schmidt-Camacho, and Michele and Robert Stepto provided lively meals and warm mentorship just when I needed them most. Ryan Davis, Helen Jaksch, and Jamie Kallestad were cheerful and able research assistants, and May Brantley and Alexa Schlieker graciously stepped in to provide eleventh-hour assistance. I extend a heartfelt thanks to Joseph Roach. He has been a fierce and unwavering advocate for this work, and his scholarship on circum-Atlantic performance has profoundly influenced my own. I also thank my colleagues at Washington University in St. Louis, particularly Iver Bernstein, Rob Henke, Bill Maxwell, Jeffrey McCune, Mark Rollins, Henry Schvey, and Julia Walker. I'm so grateful for their support of my scholarship, for their warm welcome when I arrived in 2014, and for their curation of lively intellectual communities in both Performing Arts and American Culture Studies.

It feels impossible to adequately thank one's teachers. Arthur Feinsod and Katharine Power whetted my appetite for theater and for scholarship; their example led me to contemplate a career in academia, something I never would have considered without their prompting. As with so many of the most important and rewarding pieces of my adult life, the seeds of this project were sown in Providence, Rhode Island. I hope that John Emigh, Spencer Golub, Don Wilmeth, and Patricia Ybarra, all of whom nurtured my intellectual and professional development in the early days of this project, can see their profound influence at work in these pages. I express special thanks to Rebecca Schneider, my graduate advisor and friend, who brought me along, intellectually and institutionally. I am grateful to her for setting the bar so high and for the many hours she spent helping me expand my thinking and hone my writing.

Scholars beyond my home institutions have also contributed to this book's development in significant ways. Patrick Anderson, Robin Bernstein, Daphne A. Brooks, E. Patrick Johnson, Ric Knowles, Josh Kun, Jill Lane, Eng-Beng Lim, Ana Puga, Ramón Rivera-Servera, Mariellen Sandford, Richard Schechner, and Harvey Young all read and commented on various portions of the manuscript. Kate Elswit invited me to present material on *The Blues and Gospel Train* at the Centre for Research in the Arts, Social Sciences, and Humanities at the University of Cambridge. I always look forward to thinking out loud and at length with Joel Anderson and Louise Owen. In the course of one conversation, Nick Ridout asked the key question that changed the trajectory of the book. I also thank Martyn Bone and Brian Ward, who hosted an extraordinarily productive meeting, "Creating and Consuming the South," at the University of Copenhagen, for which I developed much of the material in chapter 1.

An earlier version of part of chapter 2 appeared in "The Magic of Song!," in *Performance in the Borderlands*, edited by Ramón Rivera-Servera and Harvey Young (Palgrave Macmillan, 2010), and portions of chapter 4 originally appeared in "Highway 61 Revisited," *TDR* 51, no. 3, 2007.

Many librarians, musicians, critics, and fans shared sources that I did not know existed, granted me interviews, and pointed me in new directions. I am grateful to them all, particularly Todd Harvey and the staff of the American Folklife Center at the Library of Congress; Greg Johnson and the staff of the Blues Archive at the University of Mississippi; Louise

Bernard, Nancy Kuhl, and the staff of the Beinecke Rare Book and Manuscript Library at Yale University; and the cheerful and helpful staffs of the New York Public Library for the Performing Arts, the Dolph Briscoe Center for American History at the University of Texas, and the Carnegie Public Library in Clarksdale, Mississippi. Conversations with Sam Carr, Johnnie Hamp, C. P. Lee, Matthew Norman, Kim Massie, George Messenger, Joe and Dorothy Middleton, Bill Talbot, Frank Ratliff, John Reynolds, and Roger Stolle were similarly invaluable.

Working with Duke University Press has been a great pleasure. Ken Wissoker's enthusiasm for the project has been matched only by the wisdom of his editorial advice. Elizabeth Ault and Danielle Szulczewski shepherded the book through review and production and answered my many questions with alacrity and warmth. I am deeply beholden to the two anonymous readers whose detailed comments on and criticism of the manuscript encouraged me to clarify and strengthen the book's arguments at a critical point in its development.

Many friends, among them Christian DuComb, Christine Evans, Jeff Foye, Jocelyn Foye, Elise Morrison, Caitlin Nye, and Ken Prestininzi, patiently listened to my monologues about the book and provided joyous respite from its trials. John and Shannon Mackey have buoyed and nourished me over many evenings of food, wine, and conversation. Molly Brunson, Bella Grigoryan, Katie Lofton, and Sam See were, and remain, my New Haven family. Matthew Glassman, Megan Shea, and I have been on this road together longer than seems possible.

Words can do little to express my gratitude to my large and loving family of Camps, Tices, Stephenses, Kavanaghs, and McGinleys. My siblings and their spouses—Laura, Will, Paul, and Julia—have always offered unconditional love and acceptance. My parents, Carol K. McGinley and Paul A. McGinley, lovingly encouraged me throughout my very long education, and never let me forget how much they prized curiosity, debate, and inquiry. Wayne T. Stephens and Shirley Coffey have both graced my life with their love and laughter. Melissa and Vicki Camp welcomed me with open arms into the warmth of their family.

In the years that I have been writing this book, Pannill Camp and I have built a life together—a journey that has offered richer rewards than any book. Pannill's intellectual companionship, reserves of patience, and capacity for laughter have immeasurably enriched my life. I dedicate this book to him.

Every Tuesday and Thursday night, hundreds gather at Beale on Broadway, a blues bar and music venue located in the shadow of Busch Stadium in downtown St. Louis, Missouri. Only partially shielded from the heat and the rain by a corrugated tin roof, patrons crowd around wobbly wooden tables and perch on green plastic lawn chairs, many of which end up pushed aside when the dancing begins in earnest. The bartender pours gin in plastic cups; the occasional delivery of takeout food serves as a proxy for an in-house kitchen. The outdoor stage, with its wooden planks and kitschy Southern-themed décor, was designed by the owner, Bud Jostes, to resemble "a rickety front porch in the Mississippi Delta," that place famously described by Alan Lomax as "the land where the blues began."[1] From this outdoor patio one can see the Union Pacific tracks in the middle distance. As if employed to complete the mise-en-scène, freight trains rumble by from time to time, on their way from Memphis to Chicago, perhaps.

The domesticity of the stage set suggests that these performers are talented down-home amateurs, rather than paid professionals. The crowd—an unusually heterogeneous group in this strikingly segregated city—has come to see and hear Kim Massie, a self-identified and crowd-confirmed "St. Louis diva." Massie, who is black, sings in churches and in musicals at local theaters, but she is best known as a cover artist. With her band, the Solid Senders, Massie twice-weekly thrills audiences with her uncannily precise imitations of black female singers and their most iconic songs: Etta James ("At Last"), Georgia White ("I'll Keep Sitting on It [If I Can't Sell It]"), Dinah Washington ("Evil Gal Blues"), Aretha Franklin ("[You Make Me Feel like a] Natural Woman"), and Whitney Houston ("I Will Always Love You"). Massie's repertoire is imaginatively extensive, however, and she also covers songs originally popularized by men, including B. B. King's "The Thrill Is Gone" and Led Zeppelin's "Whole Lotta Love." Massie not only exhibits musical mastery of material usually associated with other singers but also assumes the characteristic gestures and recognizable physical attitudes of the songs' past performers. Massie's performance of "I Will Always Love You," for example, captures both the delicate and determined long counts of the word *I* and the familiar tilting upward of the head, a sweeping backward of the right arm—a physical integration of singing with longing that is so very Whitney, a choreographic reanimation offered up as poignant tribute.

While some cover singers attempt to interpret their songs anew, moving "beyond" the copy to showcase their own originality, Massie's exactitude embodies a moving homage to performers passed and past. "I try to mimic whatever it is that I admire," she says.[2] Her uncanny embodiment of the gestural and affective repertoires of singers from the 1920s to the end of the twentieth century stages a living and lively genealogy of black female song as it has passed through and shaped theater, radio, and live concert events. Even if an audience does not know Georgia White's "I'll Keep Sitting on It (If I Can't Sell It)," Massie's very funny and suggestive routine provides context, placing the song and the singer—then and now—within a recognizable tradition of cabaret entertainment. Massie leaves no double entendre unexploited: sing-speaking the lyrics to the audience ("You can't find a better pair of legs in this town/And a back like this, not for miles around!"), she performs an elaborate choreographic routine of standing up and sitting down on a chair—ostensibly the subject of the song—while offering herself as a living likeness of some nearly lost bits of black vaudeville theater and classic blues performance.

As a cover singer, Massie reanimates collective cultural memory; she also revises histories and memories long gone unquestioned, such as when she covers Led Zeppelin's "Whole Lotta Love," a perennial crowd favorite. Massie bears little physical resemblance to Robert Plant, but she assumes his vocal affect with absolute precision, even as she slows down the tempo of the song to turn up its soulful volume. Taking on Plant's gestural repertoire of hip swivels and sexual guarantees ("I'm gonna give you my love"), Massie's performance *corrects the record* by calling received narratives of music history into question. As Massie keeps pace with the driving electric guitar, Plant seems to converge with the sexual frankness of Gertrude "Ma" Rainey, whose "Daddy, won't you shave 'em dry?" seems a fitting prelude for "Shake it for me/I wanna be your backdoor man." Pointing to the history of British borrowing of African American musical traditions while simultaneously recuperating the queer life of early women's blues, Massie corporeally reanimates a tradition of theatrical women's blues often effaced by histories of British blues and rock—a tradition that this book places at the center of blues' performance history.

In a city well known as a historically important destination and transfer point for Southern black migrants, Massie excavates embodied histories of blues performance in a location that is anything but singular. Evoking Memphis's Beale Street, Mississippi's Delta, and New York's Broadway, the Beale on Broadway porch-stage is a geographic palimpsest—a sedimentation of various musical places and an imagined archetypal blues scene that conflates the front porch and the proscenium architecture of the theatrical stage. Channeling Delta imaginaries, this porch-stage points, indexically and poetically, to histories and memories of Southern black migration, road-show itineraries mapped along railway lines, and transatlantic tours; its familiarity suggests its potential to body forth performances of the past. Aware of her reputation as a tourist attraction, as well as the venue's proximity to the business district, Massie often starts up an enthusiastic call-and-response, prompting some in the crowd to shout out the names of their hometowns. Chicago, Houston, Tokyo: against the backdrop of train tracks, the exclamations of these dislocated travelers nightly reshape Beale on Broadway as a modern-day roadhouse, a site of comings and goings, of arrivals and departures, where contemporary leisure tourism and business travel echo the migrations and relocations that were the founding conditions of the blues songs Massie now sings.

Like the early twentieth-century blueswomen whose repertoires she has mastered, Massie gives a performance that is shaped by decades of interplay between blues performance and the architectures, devices, and practices—the trappings—of the popular theater.[3] It is this theatrical genealogy of blues performance that is the subject of this book. Conventional tracings of the origins and histories of blues often marginalize or sidestep histories of theatrical practice that have buttressed blues' stage life. Recognizing the instability of Eurocentric generic distinctions between music, dance, and theater, this book seeks to recover the theatrical histories of blues—both in the period of "classic" blues of the teens and twenties, and throughout the twentieth century—and place them center stage. I have not attempted to write a comprehensive account of blues and its intersections with theatrical histories and devices; indeed, the capacious variety of the music known as blues and the difficulties of genre formation make such a task impossible. Instead, I trace a linked but discontinuous genealogy of theatrical blues performance, highlighting its early emergence in the touring tent show and exploring the way theatrical conventions and debates have remained at the heart of blues performance practice in the decades since. By charting the theatrical roots and routes of a musical form that leads us, among other places, to the contemporary performances of Massie, this study analyzes the most "authentic" of black vernacular musical forms, revealing the theatrical histories and practices at the heart of blues as both genre and cultural product.

It may seem as though the front-porch-styled stage at Beale on Broadway, like the stages at the well-known chain House of Blues, represents something of a Disneyfication of blues—a late-capitalist fiction that bears no resemblance to the "real thing." But such a claim only holds water if we neglect the intensely intertwined histories of blues performance and the popular theater—histories that throw into question the premise that the "real thing" ever was. Far from descending from authenticity into theatricality, black vernacular blues have moved in tune and in time with theatrical conventions since the moments of their earliest emergence. But this early conjunction between blues and theater is haunted by sinister histories. A "shack," a bale of cotton, a bottle of liquor, a fence line, a front porch: these are the trappings of an imagined Southern life and landscape, bequeathed in large part by scenic conventions of blackface minstrelsy and nineteenth- and twentieth-century pastoral fantasies of the South. To put it another way: a pastoral tradition of "staging the South"—a performance genealogy, largely authored by whites and traceable from the early days of antebellum minstrelsy through the songs of Stephen Foster, from Tom shows and plantation musicals to melodramas of stage and screen—constitutes the milieu in which theatrical stagings of the blues often were and are presented and received. It is a milieu in which white producers, audiences, and cultural brokers have demonstrated a possessive investment.[4]

The staging of the imagined South is not "just" a scene but a set of relations, an architectural and perceptual matrix where ideology and representation meet. To look at the choreographies, costumes, and scenic design of blues performance may seem a bit of an afterthought—a project secondary to the "real" work of musicological or lyrical analysis, of which there is comparatively little of in this book. Surely we might dismiss these props, costumes, and choreographies as simple adornment, meant to either enliven a bare stage or solve practical concerns, such as seating for the musicians. And yet it is the pervasiveness of these trappings that makes them distinctly worthy of attention: their ubiquity has produced their invisibility. I am interested in what happens when we subject the mise-en-scène of blues performance to critical analysis, and how such analysis might transform our understanding of the relationship between blues and the popular theater. In the pages that follow, I turn my attention to the performances of musicians that have been enframed by the devices and practices of the theater. This book traces the circulation of these theatrical effects and examines them for what they reveal, not only about the cultural histories of blues performance but also the unspoken assumptions about Southernness, race, and performance that govern the reception of blues, past and present. It follows, then, that the *stage* or *staging* of blues that I describe signifies multiply and refers to the wooden planks of the front-porch music venues as well as the perceptual imposition of a theatrical frame that isolates an event *as* performance. While these stages, these scenarios, are not always identical in form or function, they share enough in common that they are easily recognizable and often instantly evocative of an imagined Southern landscape of plantation labor and racialized poverty. Notable for their constancy as well as their iterability and mobility, these scenarios reappear across space and time, erupting in new cultural moments and media, even as they hearken back to an imagined referent of the Old South.[5]

The theatrical conventions of staging the South are inseparable from the region's designation as "scenic" by everything from tourist pamphlets to Southern Agrarian literature, a designation that, frequently, reinscribes the aesthetics and the politics of the pastoral. To speak of the South's scenic qualities is always to keep alive multiple meanings of the word: "of or belonging to the stage," a usage that stretches back to the seventeenth century; "of or belonging to natural scenery," a nineteenth-century innovation; and "applied to a road that has been planned and landscaped so as to provide fine views," first recorded in 1914.[6] The scenic multiplicity of the South, as a place given to be both visually and theatrically consumed, brings to mind Shreve's exclamation in *Absalom, Absalom!*: "Jesus, the South is fine, isn't it. It's better than the theater, isn't it."[7] For the Canadian Shreve, the South—what the historian Jennifer Greeson calls "an internal other" to the nation—is more theatrical than the theater itself, more scenic than the stage.[8] But for all that it shows, the scene also occludes. It is shadowed by other scenes—of enslavement, poverty, and environmental degradation. The paraphernalia of the scenic South all too often entraps, producing an overdetermined stage arrangement that links land and landscape, forced labor and musical performance.

But does the deployment of theatrical devices—the costume of the criminal, the mise-en-scène of pastoral contentment—always yoke "innocent amusements" to violence?[9] Put another way, do trappings always equal entrapment? The performers in this book—among them Sister Rosetta Tharpe, Bessie Smith, Rainey, and Huddie Ledbetter (known to many as Lead Belly)—stepped into scenic environments of front porches and bales of hay, bringing with them their training, their repertoires, and what the critic and scholar Paul Oliver calls the "conscious artistry" that characterizes theatrical blues.[10] While I am interested in the iterability of the mise-en-scène of blues performance, including its transnational repetitions and persistent performativity, an exclusive focus on these repetitions across space and time runs the risk of taking our eyes off the creative power of the artist, who is always working *with and within* the mise-en-scène of the stage. To make use of the devices of the theater necessarily means to risk the instability of audience reception and the unpredictability of fellow performers' adjustments, night after night. Keeping this variability in mind, I track the deployment of these theatrical devices, but I also track the bending of their implied rules and the double codings that emerge when performers take these devices into their own hands. This struggle over theatrical signification—a struggle that often played out between black performers and white producers—is an ever-present backdrop to many of the live performances examined in this book.

The performance histories explored here are shaped, in part, by their proximity to racial violence, by small acts of resistance to violence, and by ambiguous acts that, because they took place within the proscenium arch of the stage, were, and are, difficult to interpret. The variety format of many of the performances explored here makes it particularly challenging to identify acts of full-scale resistance; as Jayna Brown has noted, the malleability of the (often unscripted) variety act sometimes makes it "impossible to prove in which directions the artists may have gestured." But the evanescence of variety also offered its performers some room in which to move, to occasionally express a hidden transcript that made visible, if only momentarily, the conditions of oppression and the demands of hypervisibility placed upon the black body. Brown continues: "Some aspects of the revue form encourage a space of dialogic interchange and public critique. . . . Constant improvisation, versioning, and multi-signification were possible in this space."[11] Such constant reworkings allowed for the tailoring of acts to specific audiences, and, indeed, different audiences may have read the same performance action in different ways.[12] What seemed to be acquiescence to some may have read as refusal to others; many of the performers explored here found a way to inhabit racialized types and to simultaneously—by the grain of the voice, by the corporeal insinuations of the body—disturb the smooth finish of these all-too-familiar representations.

That blues emerged, in large part, within a theatrical tradition of Southern black entertainment—both in the vaudeville theaters of cities such as Memphis, Jacksonville, and Indianapolis and in the tented minstrel shows that toured to towns such as Clarksdale, Mississippi, and Columbus, Georgia—is a key premise of this book, but it is one that is all too frequently marginalized in blues scholarship. This sidelining of the role of popular theater in early blues has an impact on the narration of the history of this performance form: what is attended to and what is left out (there are few detailed assessments of blues singers' costumes, for example). While it is not my intention to establish a new master narrative about a performance form as difficult to define and sundry as "blues," I do aim to shift an understanding of blues performance and its histories by treating its relationship to theatrical practices as central, rather than secondary. If the theatrical history of blues is established as fact, why is it so frequently mentioned only as an aside? Certainly one issue is methodological: accessing and analyzing recorded performances is perceived to be more straightforward, methodologically speaking, than assessing the rural tent show proceedings, which leave behind few scripts and little photographic evidence. But there are other factors at play—one of which is an exceptionally prevalent "cult of authenticity," evocatively described by Benjamin Filene as "a thicket of expectations and valuations" that has historically informed blues' production and reception, especially since the revival period of the 1950s and 1960s, when widespread white attention to the blues intensified and blues histories and criticism were written in earnest.[13] As Filene notes, the concept of authenticity grew nearly intractable roots during the middle of the twentieth century, when cultural brokers—critics, record producers, managers, and other intermediaries—labored to establish American blues music and musicians as authentic and, therefore, valuable. Nowhere else was the notion and performance of so-called authenticity more hotly debated than in the world of blues fandom, scholarship, and musicianship.

The irony is that as midcentury artists and critics assiduously worked to establish blues' singularity, blues was already in a state of revival, in a moment of repetition and revision, already "again." In these and the decades that followed, Jeff Beck, Jimmy Page, Eric Clapton, and Mick Jagger took center stage, identifying themselves as heirs to an African American musical tradition with which few white Americans were familiar. Simultaneously, folk revivalists embraced blues, and Alan Lomax released album after album of his recordings; the political economy of revival came to depend, increasingly, on a paradox that can only be described as theatrical: repetition that labored under the illusion of the first time. Fans, critics, and scholars of this period doggedly advanced a rhetoric of authenticity—an arbitration of musicians according to whether or not their blues were real. But such debates, though explosive during the midcentury, were not new. Decades before the blues and folk revivals, folklore scholars had already effectively expunged theatrical histories of blues music from the record, as Lynn Abbott and Doug Seroff have demonstrated in their analysis of Howard Odum's recordings in Georgia and Mississippi in the early twentieth century. Odum rejected the theater, maintaining that his work "was not concerned with songs performed on the professional stage" and segregated stage performance from "informal" singing that took place "within the 'folklife' of indigenous black southern communities."[14] Yet Odum's recordings belie his separation of the theatrical from daily life and demonstrate the impossibility of keeping ragtime, coon songs, and other theatrical influences *out* of folk blues. I shall further explore this antipathy between folklore and theater—and folklore studies and theater studies—in chapter 2.

Not all musicians resisted the designation of "theatrical": speaking to Val Wilmer in the 1960s, Sister Rosetta Tharpe, one of the great blues, gospel, and rock-and-roll singers of the twentieth century, proclaimed: "Blues is just the theatrical name for gospel."[15] Tracing a genealogy of popular music, Tharpe invoked theatricality as particular to blues, and, by extension, to rock and roll. Tharpe's own performance style reflected her claim: on stage, she distinguished herself with an ever-changing array of wigs, glittery costumes, and, most important, her shining-white Gibson electric guitar, which she played with flamboyant virtuosity. Tharpe's frank embrace of theatrical elements (costumes and wigs that enabled protean transformation, an identifiable shift to a stage persona, and a highly energetic performance style that was brazenly conscious of itself *as* performance) and her performed citations of her actress-singer forbearers, Rainey and Bessie Smith, make it easy to identify her celebrated style as theatrical. But critics and audiences alike have often condemned the deployment of theatrical elements by blues musicians, especially the so-called authentic pioneers. In a 1964 review of performances of Howlin' Wolf and Sonny Boy Williamson, Oliver took both performers to task for indulging the (unnecessary, to his mind) trappings of stage performance. His critique of Williamson decried the singer's costume: "[Williamson] now affects a Harlequin suit of grey and black alternating and gloves, umbrella, and a derby hat. It is an ensemble that doesn't really add anything to the performance." Meanwhile, he skewered Howlin' Wolf's performance style by claiming that "Howlin' Wolf is an actor, and just about the biggest ham actor on the stage."[16]

But clothes on stage are always a costume: whether a performer wears a "Harlequin suit" or overalls, whether the "theatrical" Tharpe swings her guitar or the "authentic" Mississippi John Hurt hunches silently over his, corporeal practices and material objects on stage can never *not* signify. Though he has repeatedly drawn attention to the fact of blues' emergence in the popular theater, Oliver's review is representative of a more widespread antitheatricalism in blues criticism, which dismisses the theatrical trappings of blues performance as secondary, feminized, derivative, or affectively excessive.[17] This approach to blues performance has extended to blues scholarship, which tends to emphasize recordings at the expense of the live. Even when specific live performances are discussed, these analyses often tend to marginalize the scenic and choreographic dimensions, prioritizing the musical content and providing little analysis of costume, set, or gestural choices. And while the history of antitheatrical prejudice invites us to place the bona fide and transparent authentic in contradistinction to the imitative and debased theatrical, this work extends the much-needed exploration of the theatrical histories and presents of blues performance. Extending the premise that authenticity is produced theatrically, on stage, in the context of the performance event, my analysis works to eradicate the binary relationship between theatricality and authenticity that has governed much popular and scholarly blues criticism and emphasizes, instead, theatricality's and authenticity's intertwined and interdependent stage histories.

"THE DEVIL'S MUSIC"

Long before white midcentury fans and critics dedicated themselves to policing authenticity, black aversion to blues performance manifested in religious, class, political, and regional terms; throughout the twentieth century, blues, especially theatrical blues, were alternately understood as immoral, lowbrow, too minstrelesque, or simply too Southern. If there is one phrase that is synonymous with blues, a kind of shorthand expressive of both blues' spiritual peril and transgressive thrill, it is *the devil's music*. In his autobiography, *Father of the Blues*, W. C. Handy famously recounted his parents' horror at his purchase of a guitar:

> I waited in vain for the expected congratulations. Instead of being pleased, my father was outraged. "A box," he gasped, while my mother stood frozen. "A guitar! One of the devil's playthings. Take it away. Take

it away, I tell you. Get it out of your hands. Whatever possessed you to bring a sinful thing like that into our Christian home?" . . . My father's mind was fixed. Brought up to regard guitars and other stringed instruments as devices of Satan, he could scarcely believe that a son of his could have the audacity to bring one of them into his house.[18]

Handy's description of his parents' revulsion at the sight of the guitar crystallizes what, for many performers, was a paradigmatic moment of attempted dissuasion from blues by their ministers, teachers, and parents. For many, especially early twentieth-century Christian Southerners like Handy's parents, their aversion to the devil's music came from deep-seated beliefs in the potent reality of Satan and a religious suspicion of stringed instruments. Though religious mistrust of blues persists today, particularly in the rural South, musicians and fans, powerfully influenced by the tale of Robert Johnson, have taken up the devil's music with pride, using the phrase to entitle books, albums, and even stage musicals.[19] But the phrase does not fully account for some black people's antipathy to blues, especially when one considers that the historical relationship between black secular and sacred music is decidedly more complex—and the line between the two more blurry—than "the devil's music" allows. Indeed, by exploring blues songs in church and the crossover of many musicians who recorded both blues and gospel, Lawrence Levine has demonstrated that the "barriers" between sacred and secular music were "never complete."[20]

While many Christians, particularly Southern Christians, singled out blues for condemnation in the interwar period, many of its musicological tropes found their way into gospel music—and vice versa—during this time. Thomas A. Dorsey, known as the father of gospel music, began his career as a pianist and arranger for Rainey and toured with her for nearly four years; Tharpe, a foundational innovator in both blues and rock, was primarily known as a gospel singer; Kim Massie, like many contemporary performers, sings both sacred and secular music, in church and at the club. If the devil's music tells only part of the story, how else to account for black intellectual and popular resistance to blues performance? Though a rhetorical division between secular and sacred black music at times held firm, this demarcation often had as much, if not more, to do with the environmental and sociological frames around the music's performance than it did with musicological distinctions. As Dorsey explained of the teens, "Well, blues was in, but the people were not accepting them. They said it was something bad. But it wasn't nothing wrong with the blues, it was just the places where they was playin' 'em in!"[21] In other words, more problematic than the music itself were the venues of performance and what went on there: the drinking and dancing of juke joints, rent parties, and barrelhouses and the sensual titillation of the popular theater presented a critical threat to public morality and Christian living.

Nearly a century before Jonas Barish's influential analysis of antitheatrical prejudice in Euro-American history, W. E. B. Du Bois was exploring the Christian aversion to both popular theater and popular music from an African American perspective. The place of amusement and entertainment was a central issue in turn-of-the-century black public debate for several reasons—religious, political, and representational. In addition to the moral skepticism that greeted popular blues and popular theater, the question of how to respond to the denigrating practices of blackface minstrelsy engendered a protracted conversation—sometimes explicit, sometimes implicit—between black public intellectuals, political leaders, critics, and artists about black participation in popular entertainment, particularly stage entertainments.

The concurrency of black performers' politically ambiguous appropriation of the minstrel mask and the beginnings of theatrical blues performance shaped early twentieth-century intellectuals' ambivalence about both popular theater and popular music. Racialized performances by both enslaved persons and blackface minstrels during the antebellum period, more than half a century before the emergence of blues music, laid the groundwork for an antitheatrical distrust of popular performance. Saidiya Hartman's detailed account of the compulsory performances demanded of enslaved persons—the coffle, the coerced gaiety at the slave market, the display of bodies on the auction block—demonstrates in horrific detail the abuses of theatricality turned against an entire people. Nineteenth-century theatrical conventions, particularly the sadistic mockeries of blackface minstrelsy and the insidious trope of the singing and dancing slave, further underscored the compromised and compromising dimensions of black theatricality before and after the Civil War. It is no wonder, then, that the black intelligentsia of the early twentieth century, though supportive of "high" art, looked upon the emergent black entertainment industry, with its close proximity to minstrelsy, with some degree of trepidation.

The sheer dominance of the legacy of blackface minstrelsy meant that any and all African Americans in early twentieth-century public life, particularly those who appeared on the stage, inevitably performed in relation to this theatrical history. Sometimes the relation was direct: performers in tent shows were referred to and described themselves as minstrels, regularly covered their faces in black makeup, and performed comic chicken-stealing scenes, much to the delight of black and white audiences. At other times, blackface minstrelsy operated in a more ghostly fashion: barely visible, but present just the same. In Houston Baker Jr.'s words, "it was in fact the minstrel mask as mnemonic ritual object that constituted the *form* that any Afro-American who desired to be articulate—to speak at all—had to master during the age of Booker T. Washington"—and, arguably, beyond.[22] And, indeed, the relationship between black performers and the brutal history of their ventriloquized stage life preoccupied critics of early twentieth-century entertainment, such as Sylvester Russell, whose columns for the *Indianapolis Freeman* regularly, if implicitly, posed the question: how can—and should—a black performer speak from the stage? Performers explored in this book, such as Bessie Smith, Ledbetter, and Cousin Joe, reckoned with this very question, attempting to navigate minstrelsy's vicious hangover, which remained very much in evidence throughout twentieth-century blues performance. As Baker suggests, the mastery of (the minstrel) form may not have been pleasant or palatable, but from time to unpredictable time, it provided the performer the privacy of masquerade—a space of concealment from which to speak, "float[ing] like a trickster butterfly to sting like a bee."[23] The performers who populate these pages—especially those who lived and worked in an era when blackface was still a popular practice—did not shy away from the musical and theatrical pleasures of the minstrel form, even as they sometimes attempted to steer their performances away from its debasements. At the same time, however, we would do well to heed Kevin Gaines's suggestion that "black cultural expression, while in part contained within the mass cultural industry of minstrelsy, might bear an anterior or independent relationship to it."[24] While Gaines's analysis is historical, it also operates as an incisive reminder to the contemporary critic: while performers at times navigated their proximity to blackface minstrelsy in pointed and particular ways, modifying minstrelsy may not have always been their central project, or even a significant concern.

Theater was a problematic site for the New Negro–era project of uplifting the race; often African American artists and critics left the entire medium of theatrical performance out of their oeuvres and polemics, turning instead to photography and literature in order to produce fully realized portraits of black respectability.[25] While artists and intellectuals advocated for more complete and richly textured representations of African American life in every medium, theater was, in many ways, the thorniest site: arguably, it was the site where the indulgence of black stereotypes had been most explicit.[26] Literature and visual art had produced more than their fair share of retrograde and pastoral visions of the South, but theater's pleasure, comedy, and instability of meaning making and reception challenged many efforts to secure the script of black respectability.[27] But for a handful of prominent New Negro intellectuals, the derogatory stereotypes of blackface minstrelsy demanded to be deposed from within minstrelsy's own medium. Furthermore, these figures, among them Du Bois, Sterling A. Brown, and James Weldon Johnson, did not see black theatrical efforts as incompatible with, in Gaines's words, "the struggle for a positive black identity in a deeply racist society, turning the pejorative designation of race into a source of dignity and self-affirmation through an ideology of class differentiation, self-help, and interdependence."[28]

"The Problem of Amusement," a speech delivered by Du Bois in 1897 at the Hampton Normal and Agricultural Institute (later published in the school's *Southern Workman*), offers a compelling and broadening supplement to the notion that Du Bois, who popularized the concept of the talented tenth, was generally hostile, or at least indifferent, to all things popular.[29] In the speech Du Bois assesses not just popular theater but recreation in general, and its significance for young people. "There is nothing incompatible," he argues, "with wholesome amusement, with true recreation." Amusement was not to be pursued for its own pleasure, however, but for the finer effects that it allowed: "For what is true amusement, true diversion, but the re-creation of energy which we may sacrifice to noble ends, to higher ideals." Du Bois identifies the black Christian rejection of amusement as originating in English Protestant austerity, particularly in the Methodist and Baptist churches. "Transported to America," he claims, "this religion of protest became a wholesale condemnation of amusements, and a glorification of the ascetic ideal of self-inflicted misery." Despairing over a "fusillade of 'don'ts'" addressed to young people, Du Bois mounts a spirited defense of amusement, proclaiming: "I have long noted with silent apprehension a distinct tendency among us to depreciate and belittle and sneer at means of recreation, to consider amusement as the peculiar property of the devil, and to look upon even its legitimate pursuit as time wasted and energy misspent."[30] Amusement, Du Bois concludes, is as necessary and as natural as the pause between two heartbeats.

Du Bois continued to develop these ideas, suggesting in later years that amusement, particularly theater, could be channeled into the broader project of African American uplift. In his essay "Krigwa Players Little Negro Theatre: The Story of a Little Theatre Movement" (1926), Du Bois argues that "a new Negro theatre is demanded," one in which the Negro character "emerge[s] as an ordinary human being with everyday reactions," as opposed to being represented as a minstrel figure, designed to appeal solely to the desires of a white audience.[31] Du Bois had already ventured into theater artistry himself; his massive 1913 *The Star of Ethiopia* employed spectacle, music, and hundreds of performers to stage a pageant of black history that celebrated transnational connections to Africa and the black diaspora throughout the Americas. But while he advocated for moderation in all things, Du Bois nonetheless revealed a preference for "art" over "amusement," and certain kinds of art over others, reflecting a broader New Negro preoccupation with the distinction between art and entertainment, a distinction frequently drawn along regional and class lines. While occasionally expressing tolerance for ragtime, blues, and jazz, both Du Bois and Alain Locke nevertheless preferred the spiritual, which had been swiftly anointed by the former as "the most beautiful expression of human experience born this side of the seas" and by the latter as "the most characteristic product of the race genius."[32] The distinction drawn by Du Bois between musical art and entertainment is instructive: writing in *The Souls of Black Folk*, Du Bois proclaimed "Negro 'minstrel' songs, many of the 'gospel' hymns, and some of the contemporary 'coon' songs" to be "debasements and imitations" of the sorrow songs that gave "true" voice to black Americans. According to Du Bois, popular songs were theatrical copies—"debasements and imitations"—of the "real thing" that were sorrow songs.[33]

For Du Bois, and for many other intellectuals of the day, realism and historical drama were the privileged forms of the new black theater. Musical comedy, with its proximity to minstrelsy and to the popular, was more difficult to swallow. James Weldon Johnson, a frequent collaborator with numerous musical-theater artists, including his brother, J. Rosamond Johnson; Bob Cole; Paul Laurence Dunbar; Will Marion Cook; George Walker; Bert Williams; and Aida Overton Walker, made the advancement and preservation of black musical comedy one of the causes of his life. Though primarily known as a literary author, Johnson wrote several opera libretti and worked as a Tin Pan Alley songwriter. A passionate lifelong theatergoer and critic, Johnson amassed a huge collection of reviews, playbills, photographs, and other ephemera relating to black theater both uptown and downtown, collating these into four large scrapbooks, each entitled "The Stage." Taken together, these scrapbooks paint a lively picture of black theater in New York in all its forms, from the vaudeville-inspired work created by Cole, both Johnson brothers, Williams, and Walker in the late nineteenth and early twentieth centuries, to the "exile" of black theater from downtown and the concomitant development of a Harlem-based theater in the 1910s, to the watershed 1917 production of Ridgely Torrence's *Granny Maumee*, *The Rider of Dreams*, and *Simon the Cyrenian*, which featured actors from the Negro Players company, to star vehicles for Ethel Waters (*Africana*) and Florence Mills (*Dixie to Broadway*) in the 1920s, to the groundbreaking *The Green Pastures* of 1930. These scrapbooks, in turn, form the research corpus for Johnson's major published contribution to black theater history: *Black Manhattan*. In *Black Manhattan*, his comprehensive history of black life and culture in New York, Johnson dedicates significant time and energy to exploring the transformations in black theatrical culture in the early decades of the twentieth century. He does so in a way that is broadly inclusive of both "high" and "low" forms, and he embraces popular music to a greater degree than many of his predecessors. Identifying the 1890s *Creole Show* as the beginning of a "line which led straight to the musical comedies of Cole and Johnson, Williams and Walker, and Ernest Hogan," Johnson charts a course for black theater history: from minstrelsy to black musical comedies that were performed before primarily white audiences to the development of a Harlem-based theater, where the black artist "found himself free from a great many restraints and taboos that had cramped him for forty years. . . . For the first time [black artists] felt free to do on the stage whatever they were able to do."[34]

Johnson was one of the early members of the Harlem intelligentsia to speak out in praise of the blues. He chronicled their emergence in *Black Manhattan*, placing them on par with the spirituals that Du Bois and Locke had elevated to the exclusion of other forms: "1912 was also the year in which there came up out of the South an entirely new genre of Negro songs, one that was to make an immediate and lasting effect upon American popular music; namely, the blues. These songs are as truly folk-songs as the Spirituals, or as the original plantation songs, levee songs, and rag-time songs that had already been made the foundation of our national popular music. . . . It is from the blues that all that may be called *American music* derives its most distinctive characteristic."[35] In a review of Handy's *Blues* a few years earlier, Johnson had similarly championed the form, while bemoaning the fact that black folk rarely received credit for many of their most significant cultural contributions, such as social dance and secular music, which had been unceremoniously co-opted by white composers for black-face minstrel tunes. "But the tide has set in the other way," he remarks, positioning himself as one who would redeem and chart the significance of black popular entertainment.[36] Though his rhetoric was evenhanded and noncombative, Johnson had delivered the chink in the armor to the bourgeois bulwark against blues.

An enormous wave of Southern migrants settled in Harlem in the 1920s, making rent parties and cabaret culture a way of life for the newly arrived and, eventually, bohemian whites. Concerned about the rapid transformation of Harlem, many members of the black intelligentsia bemoaned "a moral and spiritual crisis among younger black migrants, as well as a crisis regarding their own cultural authority."[37] The antipathy toward cabaret entertainment and blues was not only moral and spiritual but also class and region based, as urbanity began to be seen as a crisis for the Southern black migrants who could not navigate the seductions of the city, and toward whom much of the city's burgeoning entertainment industry was directed. Furthermore, blues and cabaret seemed to stand in opposition to the morality of the aspirational middle classes: blues' celebration of the pleasures of alcohol during a period of Prohibition, its assertion of a right to sexual pleasure, including same-sex desire, and its embrace of leisure instead of (morally improving) labor all countered uplift ideology, queering the Harlem Renaissance—for some, beyond recognition.[38]

Wallace Thurman, Langston Hughes, and their peers determinedly sought to refigure this narrative of decline. In "The Negro Artist and the Racial Mountain," Hughes seized on the opportunity to skewer the "Nordicized Negro intelligentsia" who rejected "the blare of Negro jazz bands and the bellowing voice of Bessie Smith singing the Blues"; for Hughes, celebrating blues and incorporating its rhythms into *Fine Clothes for the Jew* and *The Weary Blues* enabled a critique of the normative class and sexual orientations of uplift ideology.[39] In "Negro Artists and the Negro," an essay published in *The New Republic* in 1927, Thurman summed up the intervention that he, Zora Neale Hurston, Richard Bruce Nugent, Aaron Douglas, Gwendolyn Bennett, John P. Davis, and Hughes made with their 1926 publication of *Fire!!*, a new literary journal for "younger Negro artists." Of the journal, Thurman wrote, "It was not interested in sociological problems or propaganda"—a direct challenge to representative Du Boisian works *The Philadelphia Negro* and "Criteria for Negro Art." "Its contributors," Thurman went on, "went to the proletariat rather than to the bourgeoisie for characters and material. They were interested in people who still retained some individual race qualities and who were not totally white American in every respect save color of skin."[40] Though only one issue of *Fire!!* was published, its polemic signaled a sea change in the understanding of blues and popular theatrical performance as central to New York cultural life at the heart of the Jazz Age. While Hughes hailed the blues as a proletarian form, Hurston celebrated blues and popular entertainment as distinctly Southern. Raised in Florida and deeply immersed in fieldwork in the rural South, Hurston criticized those who rejected blues: "I met the type which designates itself as 'the better-thinking Negro.' I was thrown off my stride by finding that while they considered themselves Race

Champions, they wanted nothing to do with anything frankly Negroid. . . . The Spirituals, the Blues, *any* definitely Negroid thing was just not done."[41] It was Hurston's work—in her critical writings on folklore and in her theatrical revue *The Great Day* (explored in chapter 2)—that suggested that blues might not simply be a symbol of urban decay and decline but a remembering of a rural life and landscape left behind. And she had some measure of persuasive success: "Dr. Locke . . . had opposed [*The Great Day*] at first. . . . To his credit, he has changed his viewpoint."[42]

THE PROBLEM OF ORIGINS

In an early scholarly study of "downhome" blues, the ethnomusicologist Jeff Todd Titon articulates the difficulty of determining the origins of blues: "Finding evidence to support a theory of blues origins is so problematic that one becomes impatient with guesswork and is tempted to agree with [the *Urban Blues* author Charles Keil] that those who seek the origins of blues are sticking their heads in the sand."[43] And yet a great deal of early blues scholarship was concerned with exactly these questions of origin. Scholars such as Titon, William Barlow, Oliver, Lawrence Levine, and Amiri Baraka have significantly and variously advanced our understanding of blues' emergence in the late nineteenth and early twentieth centuries.[44] Growing out of the vaudeville and ragtime tunes of popular entertainment and the work songs that regulated black labor in the unreconstructed Jim Crow South, blues was, from its beginnings, a hybrid form, musically and generically indebted to a variety of early influences: male and female, rural and urban. Rather than institute a new narrative of origin, it is the relentless *pursuit* of origins, rather than their essences, that I wish to interrogate here. What blinders have pursuits of singular origin produced? And what insights are possible when one examines the scholarly and popular investments in specific narratives of origin?

Building on tenets of poststructuralism, scholars in the field of performance studies have offered useful critiques of the Western obsession with origins and the productive difficulty the human activity of performance poses to a unitary concept of origin. Performance itself, a medium rooted in mimetic action and repetition, offers a rejoinder to the privileging of authentic originals; it is, in Rebecca Schneider's words, "indiscreet, non-original, relentlessly citational, and remaining."[45] Repetition, rather than the singularity of authenticity or origin, is a key characteristic of performance and its analysis. Yet performance is a paradoxical thing: composed always in repetition, it behaves as if (and spectators often behave as though) "something else . . . preexists it."[46] The presumed origin, though, is always elusive; performance propagates copies without originals. The pursuit of presumed origins is, as Joseph Roach provocatively argues, "a voyage not of discovery but of erasure."[47] Tracing origins, especially of a performance form documented by fraught and incomplete archival evidence and burdened with racism and neglect, inevitably erases as much as it preserves. And while performance theory enables a Foucauldian- and Derridean-inspired critique of the obsession with origins that has governed so much early blues scholarship, blues itself already offers its own riposte: the formal structure of an A–A–B lyric is always already doubled. Repetition and revision—or "rep and rev," as Suzan-Lori Parks calls it—are the foundational elements of a twelve-bar blues; "never for the first time," these performances are always "for the second to the nth time."[48]

This study, then, is organized as a genealogy. It does not attempt to determine a singular point of origin for blues nor does it narrate an unbroken series of events generated by sequential causes and effects.[49] Rather, the genealogy isolates scenes of blues' theatricality as socially, politically, and economically produced, "record[ing] the singularity of events outside of any monotonous finality," and historicizing those feelings, tropes, and scenarios that masquerade as universal, or that seem to be outside of history.[50] By examining discrete performances of theatrical blues, this book traces decisive shifts in the uses and abuses of theatrical scenarios of blues travel, without shoehorning its analyses into a "discourse of the continuous." A genealogical pattern of descent—a means of tracing links between events that are connected not by direct chains of causation but by accident, rupture, and discontinuity—emerges as the most effective way to examine this performance history, a history that is fundamentally *embodied*. The "acts of transfer" that characterize performance transmission are primarily contingent on embodied acts of imitation, repetition, and revision that are traceable through a descent model, one that constructs the connective tissue between the discontinuous studies that make up this book. Descent "attaches itself to the body" and foregrounds the practices of moving bodies: the tent-show tours, black migrations, and cultural-tourism routes that participate in the transmission of images, lyrics, themes, and scenarios that attach themselves to bodies in motion.[51]

OFF-THE-RECORD PERFORMANCE

It is undeniable that the story of blues' emergence is parallel to—and sometimes conjunctive with—the emergence of recording technologies and economies. As the phonograph industry and the (race) record industry became widespread, supplanting and eventually surpassing the sheet-music industry, and as portable recording technologies became more widely available to researchers, folklorists, and archivists, blues was constituted as an object to be sold, collected, archived, and marketed. An instructive paradoxical attitude toward live performance pervades blues fandom and scholarship. On the one hand, music magazines fetishize attendance at live blues performances; the claim "I was there" stands as evidence of unmediated access to a music's essence. On the other hand, blues scholarship has had a tendency to neglect the live scene as a site of specific investigation. Recordings are routinely used as a primary source of evidence, overlooking a live-performance scene that includes visual elements, architectural frames, and, especially, audiences. As Christopher Small has economically put it: "Music is not a thing at all but an activity, something that people do."[52] Records tend to be thought of as *records*, as immutable and objective archival documents of musical history. Yet such an approach sometimes fails to appreciate that the process of recording was inflected with raced, gendered, and economic hierarchies, as well as a massive decontextualization of music making from the environment in which it was often performed. One only need imagine Rainey singing into a phonograph (something she had never done) in rural Wisconsin (a place she had never been), separated from her adoring tent-show audiences (who were anything but passive), to speculate on the enormous changes, musical and otherwise, that the recording scene wrought. Records do not tell the whole story. As Elijah Wald makes clear in his account of blues as a popular, commercial form, early records, especially, were a by-product of show-business success; passed down to us today as primary sources, they are, more accurately, secondary documents made in response to performance successes, like sheet music. Though we may see these records as foundational, it was the repertoire of live performance, Wald suggests, that was the primary site of blues entertainment in the early decades of the twentieth century. Exclusively focusing on recordings results in a neglect of all the music that went unrecorded, in part because record companies or folklorists deemed it too white, too Northern, too commercial, too ragtime, or too popular.[53] The performance scenes of dances, tent shows, vaudeville theaters, and juke joints also go unacknowledged by many recordings. As Wald indicates, relying too heavily on records produces a skewed historical analysis of blues. Lynn Abbott and Doug Seroff similarly argue that the history of recorded blues provides only a partial account of blues' varied performance histories:

Phonograph records have long been the major jumping-off point for blues and jazz scholarship. . . . Old recordings are relatively easy to access, certainly a more convenient and enjoyable reference tool than old newspaper accounts or oral histories, and more familiar to the general public. However, far too much focus on the commercial recording industry has distorted the prevailing concept of the history of American popular music. It seems to be accepted as a matter of faith that mainstream America was first introduced to blues through the medium of phonograph records. But long before blues records became available, the compositions of W.C. Handy and other blues writers were repeatedly performed in street parades and on circus lots in countless locations throughout every inhabited part of the United States and much of Canada. Generally speaking, white America was introduced to the blues by sideshow annex bands of the World War I decade.[54]

This is not to say that records cannot offer any information about the live scene of performance; furthermore, explorations of the conventions and innovations of live blues must resist fetishizing these performances as any more authentic, true, or pure than their recorded counterparts.

While music plays an important role in my analysis, this book is often more directly focused on the sets, costumes, and choreographies of sometimes avowedly stagey performances. Though I make use of recordings, I aim to recenter the role of live performance in blues scholarship and to use the methodologies of theater history and performance studies to both reconstruct and interpret the live-performance event.[55] Performance, as Small notes, "does not exist in order to present musical works, but rather, musical works exist in order to give performers something to perform."[56] These aspects of blues' stage scenarios can be accessed musically (such as by carefully listening for dance breaks that masquerade as musical interludes) and by turning to archival sources, particularly press accounts, the form of which demanded that the journalist or critic communicate visual and sonic elements to an absent reader. A great deal of information about the early performance, circulation, and dissemination of blues acts, for example, is contained within the pages of the *Indianapolis Freeman*. Its influential column The Stage, which published reports filed by traveling companies, facilitated communication among performers working in such diverse stage idioms as musical comedy, tent shows, vaudeville, and ragtime. These entertainers, male and female, developed their repertoires through models of reciprocal exchange and imitation.

Though Rainey claimed to have incorporated blues singing into her stage act as early as 1902, the earliest published account of blues being sung in a public setting appears in a 1910 newspaper description of the black vaudeville performer Johnnie Woods's act at the Airdrome Theater in Jacksonville, Florida. Trained on the medicine-show circuit, Woods was celebrated for his skills as a female impersonator, buck-and-wing dancer, and, most significantly, ventriloquist. Inspired by the Punch and Judy shows he had seen in his youth, Woods, dressed in a fine, light-colored suit, performed a popular ventriloquist act that climaxed in "Henry," a black dummy clad in a conductor's cap and a checked suit, getting drunk and singing the blues.[57] This first published description of theatrical blues singing was reported in the *Indianapolis Freeman*, with blues emerging as a performance form first and foremost: the 1910 account of Woods's act was published two years before Handy, the self-nominated "Father of the Blues," published the first piece of sheet music with *blues* in the title, and ten years before Mamie Smith became the first black woman to record blues for Okeh Records.[58] Inscribed texts—sheet music or pressed wax—make up only some of the body of evidence that provides contemporary access to early twentieth-century blues music. The story of Johnnie Woods and Little Henry underscores the lively theatrical environment of off-the-record blues performance that remains and the bodies that evidence themselves in memory and ephemera, in apocryphal tales and archival traces. These traces—photographs, columns, reviews, pamphlets, advertisements, and gossip—constitute, in part, the evidentiary corpus of this book, assisting in the reconstruction of the live-performance scenes of theatrical blues singing, events that, by virtue of their assessed ephemerality, have largely—though not completely—evaded historical preservation.

GENDERING GENRES

In the account of the ventriloquist and his dummy, theatrical blues materializes as a throwing of the voice, a deliberate disorientation that engendered confusion about the "real" source of sound. Early blues singing manifested an analogous throwing of the voice, but one with a more disturbing cast, rife with appropriation. Gravitating toward black popular song and imitations of black vernacular music popularized by blackface minstrelsy, white theatrical entertainers such as Sophie Tucker, May Irwin, and Claire Vance made a name for themselves as blackfaced "shouters" of "coon songs." These ragtime-inspired tunes, many of them written by black composers, were prominent on vaudeville stages beginning in the late 1890s. In reference to these white women, the press dubbed Bessie Smith, Rainey, and Clara Smith "up-to-date coon shouters."[59] Together these black and white women gave rise to what Daphne A. Brooks has named "sonic blue(s)face performance," "a vocal phenomenon . . . that had a ground-shifting impact on the histories of how we sound race and how we racialize sound in the contemporary popular imaginary."[60] While the continued power of Bessie Smith and Rainey (and the concomitant fading away of Vance, Irwin, and Tucker) has been described as "the triumph of the real over the false," blues performance from its beginnings has been a mélange of mimicry, a device of mistaken identity and masquerade, a scene where *who is singing* is forever in doubt.[61] This scene stages an unstable relationship between the *I* of the songs' first-person narration, the onstage singer, and the performer presumed to be (behind) the mask. Though ventriloquist blues acts were relatively rare, the tale of Woods's bluesy ventriloquism is redolent of theatrical blues in general, especially the tension between performer and persona and the pliability of its first-person *I* employed in so many blues lyrics.[62] This tension between performer, persona, and the first-person narrator will materialize several times in the pages that follow, especially in the analyses of the classic blues-singer-as-actress and Ledbetter's complex relationship to his stage name, Lead Belly. What's more, many of the most prominent blues performers had years of theatrical experience among them: Bessie Smith transitioned from vaudeville star to film actress; Waters starred in *As Thousands Cheer* (1933), and numerous other productions; Alberta Hunter played the lead in *Showboat* in London in 1928; and Sonny Terry and Brownie McGhee, whose performance in *The Blues and Gospel Train* will be explored in chapter 3, were in the original Broadway cast of *Cat on a Hot Tin Roof*.

Blues performers, then, were quite accustomed to inhabiting a persona on stage. This instability of persona was especially challenging to those critics, fans, and scholars who wished to emphasize the autobiographical authenticity of the blues artist; as a result, theatrical blues, often performed by women, were covered up and covered over, their status as a central genealogical line in blues performance minimized and maligned. As Elijah Wald has persuasively demonstrated, performances of "authentic" blues often emerged as a response to the demands of the record producers, folklorists, and scholars who demanded songs and styles that conformed with preconceived notions of blues as primitive folk music, linked directly to its African roots. But the theatricality of blues performance has remained ever present, despite attempts to suppress it.

While there is no doubt that the musical innovations of the male laborers of East Texas and the Mississippi Delta in the 1890s were extraordinarily significant, this book contests historiographical narratives that position the female singers of the "classic" blues as either derivative or debauched imitators, on the one hand, or manipulated victims of the culture industry, on the other. In the face of narratives that suggest otherwise, it is difficult yet necessary for us to imagine a comprehensive history of the blues that positions Rainey and Bessie Smith, and others like them, as originators and as innovators. Attending only to the chronology of records is misleading. Rainey and Smith, for example, are most often discussed in terms of their late 1920s recordings; as a result, they seem to follow behind the innovations of Delta bluesmen, whose music is sometimes ahistorically collapsed with the distinctly different field hollers of agricultural workers and the call-and-response songs of convict laborers. But Rainey was born in 1886, before Big Bill Broonzy (1893), Charley Patton (1891), and Son House (1902). Bessie Smith was also a contemporary, born in 1894; both women began their performance careers in their teens, and they sang and composed blues years ahead of their male colleagues. Indeed, their touring was largely responsible for disseminating these innovations in the first place.[63] To position Smith and Rainey as innovators means to embrace the fact that blues was developed by "pros, not primitives," and that blues was, from its beginnings, a commercial, theatrical form.[64] While folklorists such as John Lomax preferred to hear the blues as a pure folk expression—set apart from radio, theatrical entertainment, and the corrupting influence of popular culture—the emerging black theatrical entertainment industry and so-called folk musical expressions were intricately intertwined. Regular reports in the *Indianapolis Freeman* demonstrate that what Barlow calls the "tentacles of the American entertainment industry" abundantly extended throughout the rural South, especially the Mississippi Delta, from the very beginning of the twentieth century.[65]

The gendering and "genre-ing" of blues performance has produced a series of binaries that has governed its analysis. While the details vary, many classifications of early twentieth-century blues establish two categories, "Country" or "Downhome" blues, and "Classic" or "Vaudeville" blues:

Country Blues	Classic Blues
Male	Female
Rural	Urban
Authentic	Theatrical
Folk	Commercial
Pure	Hybrid

Hazel Carby has summed up the impact of this binary classification as follows:

> The field of blues history is dominated by the assumption that "authentic" blues forms are entirely rural in origin and are produced by the figure of the wandering lone male. Thus the formation of mythologies of blues masculinity, which depend on this popular image, has obscured the ways in which the gendering of women was challenged in the blues. The blues women of the twenties, who recorded primarily in urban centers but who employed and modified the full range of rural and urban blues styles, have come to be regarded as professionalized aberrations who commercialized and adulterated "pure" blues forms.[66]

As Carby notes, the privileging of "mythologies of blues masculinity" results in the debasement of female blues singers. The fact that "classic blues" were sung primarily, but not exclusively, by women in a popular theatrical context is another strike against them.[67] As I suggested, the antitheatrical prejudice that pervades cultural histories of blues is profoundly gendered, and it accounts not only for the twin dismissals of "women's blues" and "theatrical blues" but also for their amalgamation: theatrical blues, even when not sung by women, *become* feminized. Oliver's review of Williamson's performance, cited earlier, skewers the elegantly costumed performer for being "affected" and also, implicitly, effete.

These binary categories are not only inadequate; they are detrimental. The gendering of binary categories such as "downhome" and "vaudeville"—and the assignation of value to these categories—makes it all too easy to downplay the political, cultural, and artistic contributions of theatrically trained female blues performers. Despite the existence of male theatrical entertainers, such as Johnnie Woods, and female downhome blues singers, such as Memphis Minnie, the male-rural and female-urban dichotomies remain deeply difficult to dislodge. Though Titon ultimately organizes his analysis around these categories, in *Early Downhome Blues* (one of the earliest musicological and cultural-historical analyses of Delta blues) he is very careful to note their instability and regularly highlights their points of overlap. For example, Titon points out that the songs sung at Saturday-night dances in the Delta were just as diverse as the repertoire sung in the tent shows: coon songs, minstrel songs, blues, and ragtime.[68] Titon reminds his readers that blues is constituted as an object by institutional power—by race record producers, by scholars and folklorists, and by chambers of commerce bolstering their tourist economies. The scene of live performance was—and is—much less generically rigid and always more fluid than musicological definitions suggest, and yet the categories themselves have remained nearly unshakeable.[69] This is not to say that there are not important cultural and musicological differences between the blues of, say, Patton and Hunter. But these distinctions are partially undone when we consider that musicians of both the downhome and vaudeville varieties were neither geographically static nor bound to the regions of their birth; they were constantly on the move. They had ready access to records of all kinds, and they also, quite literally, *crossed paths*. This book, therefore, considers blues not as a local or static phenomenon but as a migratory one: if "downhome" is a state of mind, it is a home on the road.

MAPPING A ROUTE

The materiality and the conventions of the theater were, and have remained, central to the staging of migration and travel that many blues performances enact. This study traces both the circulation of the mise-en-scène of the blues scenario and the figures who populated these stages. These figures—among them the blues actress, the convict turned folk hero, the touring professional, and the pilgrim tourist—were not characters in a psychological or naturalistic sense, but, rather, they were representative surrogates for the diasporic, migratory, and touristic travels of millions, both past and present. Circulating and reappearing across space and time, they pointed to the process and material realities of circulation itself: the circum-Atlantic trade in raw material, refined goods, and human capital that has characterized modernity. While managers and producers of these theatrical events deployed scenic fantasies of "the South," individual performers attempted—with some success—to make the displacements that haunted these landscapes visible and audible.[70] Laying bare the often hidden histories of forced and chosen migration that haunt the American open road, these performers intimated that the mythology of the free traveler was—and is—deeply dependent on the performed memories of those whose mobility was limited, compromised, or compulsory.

The thrill of the open road has historically shared a lane with a silent—and silenced—partner. In his 1986 travelogue chronicling his quest for "astral America," the French intellectual-turned-tourist Jean Baudrillard found what he pursued: an amnesic experience of the open road that celebrated the unencumbered mobility of the traveler. He jubilantly describes his car "gliding down the freeway, smash hits on the Chrysler stereo."[71] But there is another side to the rhetorics of freedom, progress, and autonomy that govern imaginings of the open road: the Trail of Tears and the legacy of Indian removal, the dust-bowl migrants and the failed farm policies that devastated a generation, and a sustained history of black displacement, from the Middle Passage to the Great Migration, from the auction block to Hurricane Katrina. These "shadow texts" of heroic American travel narratives suggest the ambivalence of the road-trip romance and reveal the forgetting of diasporic and genocidal histories at the heart of these triumphant narratives.[72] Far from being an exclusively contemporary phenomenon, though, this slippage between migration, the musician's tour, and recreational tourism is typical of many of the performances that I examine in the book, where migratory histories set in motion by forced removal refuse to disappear.

The Mississippi Delta, a crossroads for the touring tent shows which flooded the area at harvest time, served as a locus of repertoire development and exchange among traveling entertainers and itinerant agricultural laborers during the first half of the twentieth century. A frontier state as much as a Southern one, Mississippi's agricultural economy was not developed until the late nineteenth century, and its field hollers and work songs are often described as direct forerunners of the blues. Mississippi is where this book begins and ends, but Mississippi is only one geographic point of origin for a polygenetic music that seems to have simultaneously developed in the Delta, in East Texas, in Missouri, and in the Piedmont. Significantly, however, Mississippi—and the Mississippi Delta, in particular—appears again and again as a *mythical* point of origin and as inspiration for the mise-en-scènes of the performances I examine in this book; as a frame of mind, Mississippi's musical, racial, and political legacies are never far from the performances analyzed here. But this book is more concerned with routes than roots, focusing on the actual and imagined racial and sonic mappings that are effected by blues performance's circulation, together with its material and mythical transmission and reinvention. Accordingly, the itinerant structure of this book is spatial as well as temporal, mirroring the historic circulation of blues scenarios from the tent shows of Mississippi to the cabaret stages of New York to the television studios of Northern England to sites of memory in Mississippi.

Each chapter of the book focuses on a transformational crossroads, a moment when blues underwent a major shift or reorientation in terms of performance, reception, circulation, or dissemination. Each chapter deeply dives into a key performance or series of performances at the heart of that crossroads, exploring the role of the actress in classic women's blues in the teens and twenties (chapter 1), Ledbetter's vaudeville-inspired performance career and his collision course with folkloric theatrical thinking (chapter 2), the transatlantic circulation and translation of blues during the revival of the late 1950s and early 1960s (chapter 3), and the embrace of tropes of theatrical reenactment by the blues tourism industry in the 1990s and 2000s (chapter 4).

The first two chapters examine paradigmatic cases of theatrical blues in the interwar years when many black Southerners, threatened by economic insecurity and vigilante violence, headed north bringing their music with them, transforming the demographics and daily life of cities like New York, St. Louis, and Chicago. Southern blues performers, many of them women, represented this travel in their stage acts. Singing, dancing, and shticking in the vaudeville houses of the burgeoning Theater Owners Booking Association (TOBA) circuit, they provided many audience members of the teens and early twenties with their first exposure to blues singing. These artists also performed on the tented platforms of touring minstrel shows, where "wooden boards on a folding frame served as the stage" and "the footlights were Coleman lanterns"; in both these indoor and outdoor arenas, they were some of the first artists to widely popularize blues throughout the black South.[73] In chapter 1, I extend my critique of the gendered dimension of blues historiography, where "authentic" bluesmen are often celebrated at the expense of "theatrical" female blues singers, who disseminated blues within the context of black popular theatrical entertainments: minstrelsy, vaudeville, and touring tent shows. I focus my investigation on the careers and performances of two classic blues singers, Rainey and Bessie Smith. These women, particularly through their glamorous costuming, fashioned a new model of Southern womanhood, one that pushed back against the Topsy and mammy figures that dominated stage representations of black women. Their performances staged the South as a place of departure and return, their traveling blues simultaneously representing both migration and the theatrical tour. Though these are women whose names we know, they stand in as surrogates for the many performing women of this period whose names and lives are unknown to us. This chapter makes extensive use of the *Indianapolis Freeman* and illuminates the role played by blues performers within a set of debates about the so-called proper conventions of stage performance by black actors. These debates, chronicled in the *Indianapolis Freeman* by Aida Overton Walker, the actress and dancer, and Sylvester Russell, the critic, demonstrate the significance of the theater for the uplift movement and the threat that working-class blues posed to the bourgeois respectability to which black actors often aspired.

Chapter 2 is organized around the performance career of Ledbetter, better known as Lead Belly, a Louisiana songster who absorbed and reinvented the music and dance of the blueswomen of the teens. While contemporary scholarship on Ledbetter generally focuses on the few years during the 1930s that he toured under the management of John and Alan Lomax (two men with their own vexed relationship to the theater), this chapter advances a more comprehensive analysis of Ledbetter's long career, which sustained the theatrical traditions of blues' "classic" period in spite of the increasing demands for authenticity by folklorists and, later, revivalists. Ledbetter's relationship with the Lomaxes emerges as a paradigmatic example of the uneasy relationship between "the folk" and those writers and academics who endeavored to present and represent black vernacular folklore to Northern urban audiences. Finally, this chapter offers a reconsideration of earlier assessments of Ledbetter as apolitical, and of the role played by theatrical blues in the pursuit of racial and economic justice by cultural-front artists in the late 1930s and early 1940s.

In the postwar years, the Southern system of sharecropping underwent a radical shift: planters overhauled the industry by introducing the mechanical cotton picker. This change resulted in massive unemployment and continued dissatisfaction for black workers, triggering an additional wave of the Great Migration. At the same time, blues gained new audiences in the United States and Europe in the 1950s and 1960s. The revival of previously neglected musicians and the adoption of blues by white performers such as the Yardbirds resulted in an increased emphasis on authenticity, an authenticity frequently produced by theatrical means. The blues travel of many migrants began to be replaced by the tour as American blues stars spent more and more of their time performing in Europe. Chapter 3 examines some of the unique shifts in blues performance that occurred during this period of transatlantic exchange, particularly the use of theatrical practices and devices to translate the content of African American blues to an audience largely unfamiliar with its musical, theatrical, and political traditions. By exploring the performance of blues on stage and on television, this chapter provides a close reading of the 1964 live show and television program *The Blues and Gospel Train*, a site-specific event held at an abandoned train station decorated with the props of Southern detritus. A landmark event that presented Muddy Waters, Sister Rosetta Tharpe, Sonny Terry, Brownie McGhee, and Cousin Joe to an audience of Mancunian teenagers, *The Blues and Gospel Train* crystallized the stakes of theatrical translation during the blues revival. While the arrival of blues in England is most often championed for the influence the music had on soon-to-be-famous British musicians, I emphasize the local significance of these transatlantic tours, and examine *The Blues and Gospel Train* within the specific historic, cultural, and economic contexts of Manchester.

The final chapter of the book explores the late twentieth- and early twenty-first-century blues tourism industry of Mississippi Delta towns. In the context of the Clarksdale tourist economy, the theatricality that pervaded earlier iterations of blues performance leaps to the body of the tourist, who is invited to immerse himself or herself in an in situ performance environment. Throughout the Delta, tourist trails draw on living history and theatrical reenactment practices, encouraging visitors to walk in the footsteps of migrants. Accordingly, Clarksdale has staked its claim as the ground zero of blues music, not least because John Lee Hooker, Pinetop Perkins, and dozens of other blues musicians were born there. In the 1990s Clarksdale attempted to build up its local economy by turning its blues history into a tourist attraction: the Delta Blues Museum and the Sunflower Blues and Gospel Festival have since brought thousands of people to the region each year. The Shack Up Inn, a popular accommodation, opened on the site of the former Hopson Plantation, just outside town. Consisting of half a dozen "shotgun shacks" formerly inhabited by sharecroppers, the inn has updated these cabins with heat, electricity, and running water and made them available to travelers for around seventy dollars a night. I conclude the book by reading these and other "scriptive sites" of blues tourism as environments that invite white tourists to stage the blues in a period of late capitalism, remembering theatrical blues of the past, even while their own steps rewrite the history they consume.

Sometime after 1923, Gertrude "Ma" Rainey, already famous from decades of touring with various tent shows, as well as her more recent recordings for Paramount, became known for a stage entrance that gestured to her dual status as both a theatrical and recording star. Ruby Walker, who saw Rainey perform in a 1925 show in Birmingham that Walker attended with her aunt Bessie Smith, has provided the most complete account of this coup de théâtre. Near the conclusion of the variety evening that culminated in Rainey's act, the Wildcats Jazz Band assembled on stage; collectively, the audience began to call out "the Phaaantuhm." Walker initially assumed that this cry was a reference to *The Phantom of the Opera*, a newly released silent film enjoying widespread popularity at the time. But the call referred to Rainey herself. Her presence was duly conjured by the Wildcats Jazz Band's instrumental blues and the audience's enthused chant: "The Phaaantuhm! The Phaaantuhm!" The curtain rose, revealing a giant prop replica of a Victrola; a chorus dancer began to play a similarly outsized prop record on the phonograph. From inside the Victrola, not yet visible to spectators, Rainey began to sing her wildly popular "Moonshine Blues," its lyrics flaunting the strictures of Prohibition. At a climactic moment in the song, she emerged from the boxy set piece, glittering in a famously extravagant gown and jewels, to the great delight of her audience.[1]

Rainey's spectacular entrance mimicked her arrival in private homes by way of the Victrola, its fabulous stagecraft capturing the magic of the new technology of the phonograph, especially its disembodiment of sonic production.[2] The phonograph's ability to conjure absent voices was its most novel quality; the iconic trademark image for the Victor Talking Machine Company that frequently ran alongside advertisements for race records in the *Chicago Defender* featured a small dog, curiously sniffing into the external horn of a gramophone, investigating the source of the sound. This well-known logo, drawn from Francis Barraud's painting *His Master's Voice* (1899),

1.1 A dog hears "his master's voice" in this advertisement for the Victor Talking Machine Company. Warshaw Collection of Business Americana, Phonographs, Archives Center, National Museum of American History, Smithsonian Institution, Washington, DC.

represented phonograph advertising's exploitation of Victorian tropes of grief—namely, the return of the voice of the dead (see figure 1.1).[3] The dog recognizes the voice of his deceased master, thus revealing both the affective power of the talking machine and its power to resurrect those who have been (only temporarily) lost. Rainey's arrival scene, repeated nightly under tents and on indoor vaudeville stages, staged a thrilling resurrection; she was, on her terms, the phantom of the opera.

Though celebrated for its novelty, Rainey's dazzling entrance bore an uncanny resemblance to the performances some decades earlier of Henry "Box" Brown, a Virginia slave who made his escape by mailing himself to freedom in a crate in 1849. For years after, he commemorated his flight by reenacting his triumphant emergence from the box, marking his rebirth by singing. Touring on the British show circuit, Brown linked his "unboxing" to his newfound career as a mesmerist and conjurer, corporeally suturing his emergence from the box with the return of the dead, a connection further established by Samuel Rowse's 1851 lithograph, *The Resurrection of Henry Box Brown at Philadelphia* (see figure 1.2).[4] A theatrical echo of Brown's famed escape, unboxing, and theatrical stardom, Rainey's arrival scene dramatized the collapse of space and time enabled by recording technology; it also, inversely, emphasized the actual distance traveled by the performer—and by the enormous set piece—to the venue itself. The

1.2 *The Resurrection of Henry Box Brown at Philadelphia*, Samuel Rowse, 1851. Courtesy of the Virginia Historical Society.

mechanics of the tour and, implicitly, the labor required to transport the outsized Victrola were placed on display for an audience of eager spectators, many of whom had traveled their own lengthy distances to witness this theatrical display by a touring actress-singer. Night after night the Victrola act highlighted Rainey's fame as a touring entertainer, repeatedly establishing both her stardom and her geographic command.

While their recordings made them famous to the world, recognizing Rainey's and Smith's work as actresses, singers, dancers, and producer-entrepreneurs more accurately represents their careers in show business in the early decades of the twentieth century. Blues singing, or something like it, was likely a part of Rainey's early act—she told the musicologist John Wesley Work Jr. that she incorporated blues into her show in 1902—but until she recorded for Paramount in 1923, she was primarily known as a theatrical star, alternately described in the pages of the *Indianapolis Freeman* as an actress, singer, dancer, producer, wardrobe mistress, monologist, and comedienne.[5] Traveling troupes, such as the Rabbit's Foot Minstrels, the Georgia Smart Set, and Silas Green from New Orleans, were very much a presence in recreational life in the South, especially the Mississippi Delta, where blues emerged in the early decades of the twentieth century as both "vaudeville" *and* "downhome." Rainey's contralto belt and humorous treatment of rural subjects of interest, such as the dreaded but cunning boll weevil, cultivated a stage act of glamour and spectacle for a largely rural audience. Smith, Rainey's colleague and friendly rival, also came up as a performer on the vaudeville and tent-show circuits. While Smith ultimately spent more time in the urban Northeast than Rainey did, she toured the South regularly in tent shows, and she and Rainey toured together for a short time in the Rabbit's Foot Minstrels in 1915.

A full consideration of Rainey's and Smith's live theatrical blues careers prompts a recognition of the adjacency of popular theater and popular music in the early decades of the twentieth century and a reassessment of the classic blues tradition and its legacy. Close investigation of the itinerant performances of both Rainey and Smith, arguably the two most well-known theatrical blues stars of the teens and twenties, shows how their tours participated in the shaping of a black public during a period of enormous geographic, social, and cultural transition. Cumulatively appearing before audiences of many thousands, Smith's and Rainey's performances are legible within contemporary theatrical conventions and debates of their day, pushing back against representations of the South that had come to dominate theatrical practice and staging a counterpoint to black bourgeois performances of uplift. By manipulating—indeed, inventing—conventions of black stardom, Rainey and Smith styled themselves as actresses for particular ends. Their embrace of the role of actress allowed them not only to play with expressions of sexual and economic desire but also to fashion a model of black womanhood that was, above all, capable of protean transformation. Vigilant against the reductive aesthetics of dramatic realism and the assumptions about identity and authenticity it invited, these stars both invoked and undermined a persona of the self, highlighting the theatrical construction of the star on stage.

With the notable exceptions of Lynn Abbott and Doug Seroff's *Ragged but Right* and Peter Muir's *Long Lost Blues*, most key works on the emergence of blues treat the theatrical background of many blues musicians, especially female singers, as a footnote. But most American audiences, both black and white, became aware of blues in theatrical venues and in combination with theatrical entertainments—as one element of the traveling tent shows, circuses, vaudeville teams, and black minstrel entertainments that crisscrossed the United States, particularly the South and the Midwest, in the early decades of the twentieth century.[6] Tent shows were constantly on tour throughout the rural South, as were vaudeville acts and, sometimes, musical-comedy imports from Northern cities, such as George Walker and Bert Williams's *Abyssinia*. These vaudeville and musical-comedy acts traveled from theater to theater on what was to become the Theater

Owner's Booking Association (TOBA) circuit, while the tent shows were set up in outdoor sites in more rural environments. Though especially prominent in the teens and twenties, these tours began in the early years of the century and persisted, in the case of the Rabbit's Foot Minstrels, until 1950, even as other traveling road shows (particularly those with more urban routes) succumbed to the economic pressure of the Great Depression and the popularity and affordability of luxurious movie palaces.[7] Over the course of Rainey's and Smith's careers, the race-records industry powerfully segmented popular music from live performance, just as the burgeoning art-theater movement pried so-called legitimate theater away from the musically rich variety shows. Rainey, Smith, and countless others, however, kept theatrical performance and blues singing deeply integrated. One of the most popular and prominent of the tent shows was Tolliver's Smart Set, described by Abbott and Seroff as "a freewheeling variety show" that included blues singing in addition to wire walkers, trapeze artists, sketch comedians, and monologists. It was under Tolliver's big tent that Ma and Pa Rainey came to prominence as the "Assassinators of the Blues."[8]

Theatrical blues singing developed during a period when popular music and popular theater were deeply intertwined. As David Savran suggests, popular theater and black vernacular music (ragtime, swing, blues, and jazz) were seen as roughly equivalent and were performed in shared venues: the vaudeville house, the minstrel tent, and the cabaret. The shows on Benjamin Franklin Keith's circuit of theaters "undermined the distinction between music and theater"; its houses were architectural and conceptual sites where theater, broadly construed, and jazz, broadly construed, intersected in early twentieth-century performance.[9] Simultaneously, burgeoning art and little-theater movements felt the need to cement the superiority of their endeavors and to "defeat" jazz in order to become a "sanctuary for sacred art"; they did so by emphasizing the distinct characteristics of their "legitimate" theater and by quickly elevating the playwright Eugene O'Neill to the status of patron saint. This anxiety about art theater's legitimacy mirrored the fretful response of European classical-music aficionados to the threat of jazz. Not coincidentally, the unease about the hybrid aesthetics of "jazzed theater and theatricalized jazz" arose during a moment of widespread white concern about miscegenation more generally.[10] As massive demographic changes wrought by economic migrations brought urban whites and African Americans into contact in unprecedented numbers, racial hatred, lynching, and intimidation were one set of responses to perceived racial mixing and amalgamation; maintaining the so-called purity of art forms was another. But the overlap between theater and jazz was not just happening on New York stages, in Harlem nightclub floor shows, or in the vaudeville houses of the Keith circuit. The "big shows" of Tolliver's Smart Set and other tented performances of the Southern touring circuits were also sites of generic overlap between black vernacular music and popular theater. What Savran claims about the mostly white vaudeville of the Keith- and Albee-owned theater circuits was also true for black vaudeville and touring tent-minstrel shows, which, as a rule, combined the entertainments of bands, orchestras, and singers with monologues and comic skits. Thus, black theatrical entertainment and early women's blues share a tangled history: their performances took place on the same stages, often using the same actors, songs, and conventions.

Understanding these performance conventions requires an imaginative leap through—beyond—the familiar in-studio amplified recordings of the songs that circulate so widely today. The demands on a tent-show performer varied significantly from those placed on a singer in a recording studio. Live, unamplified tent-show and vaudeville singing relied on the power of the singer's voice and the expressivity of the dancer's body to address a crowd. The early recordings of both Rainey and Smith offer contemporary researchers not an exact replica of tent-show singing but vocal expression in the midst of modification, a compromised meeting point between the theatrical entertainer and the demands placed on her in the recording studio. Though these recordings transmit invaluable sonic information and affect, they provide imperfect evidence when it comes to live performance; these songs were acoustically, theatrically, and affectively distinct when performed in a tent or vaudeville show. The architectural and technological requirements of the recording studio—even prior to the introduction of the microphone—were very different from the physical conditions of the tent-show environment. In the early Paramount recordings that used an external horn, one can hear Rainey only somewhat successfully holding back the belt that made her audible to patrons in the last row of the theater. Due to technological limitations, her alto voice recorded far less well than the head voice of the more classically trained sopranos who would follow her. As microphone singing and electric recording became more widespread and technically refined, singing styles changed; the "crooning" enabled—even demanded—by microphone singing produced both the (apparently autobiographical) interior life of the singer and a sense of private intimacy with the listener that annihilated the space between self and other.[11] For the most part, listeners experienced these recorded performances in the privacy of their homes, either alone or with a small group of intimates.

The significance of dance and choreography to early blues is a profound example of a theatrical component to the genre that was repressed by the music industry's focus on mass production and circulation of records. If "railroad blues" were widely encouraged by record-industry executives, the songs privileged at live shows were ones that invited a particularly witty or complex bit of stagecraft or choreography. Songs with choreography or demonstrable action embedded in the lyrics (such as Rainey's beloved "Black Bottom" or Smith's "Cakewalking Blues") were, for obvious reasons, appealing to singer-dancers. "Moonshine Blues," the opening number that contained Rainey's famous entrance, offered the star the opportunity to swing her head "'round and around"; her audience could find her "wrigglin' and a-rockin', howlin' like a hound," as the band set the pace of the bouncing, rhythmic shifts. When Smith sings "Moonshine Blues" on record, it is a morose bereavement; for Rainey, the song is a dizzy, rhythmic celebration. "Here I'm upon my knees," she cried; as an experienced performer and skilled dancer, Rainey built plenty of opportunities for choreography and other theatrical bits into her songs. Sometimes a song organized an entire scene. The famed Thomas A. Dorsey, known as the father of modern gospel, toured with Rainey as the leader of her Wildcats Jazz Band in the mid-twenties. He described the mise-en-scène of the tours as extensive: "We carried about four trunks of scenery, of drops and things you could fold up there. And we'd have lightin' effects, the stage manager give 'em to us." Regarding the performance of "Stormy Sea Blues," he portrayed a scene that was suggestively operatic in scale: "She'd . . . do whatever what you do in a storm. The storm started to raging, you try to run here and run there, and get away, and you become excited. Oh, yeah, she had a good act there. Yeah, that was one of the best numbers on the show for a long time."[12]

ROAD SHOWS: THE THEATRICAL TOUR AND ITINERANT PUBLICS

Migration is the backdrop to the performances and the period that I explore in this chapter. Remaining cognizant of the migration narratives that are chronicled in blues lyrics, I focus my attention less on those who migrated from South to North and instead on the cultural experiences and productions of those who stayed behind, who did not move, or who moved within the South.[13] Statistics persuasively chart the epic scale of the Great Migration, the six to eight million who moved from the South to Steel Belt and northeastern cities, and the demographic, sociological, cultural, and economic shifts they engendered. These shifts are not to be underestimated, but we should not neglect to observe that the rural South remained home to millions of black residents. Though the percentage of black residents declined gradually during the first three decades of the twentieth century, the black population of Coahoma County, in the heart of the Mississippi Delta, fluctuated between 77 and 88 percent of the overall total population.[14] That is to say: in spite of mass migration, the rural South was home to a large and dynamic populace that, particularly before the widespread availability of the record player and movie houses, maintained its own distinct regional entertainment culture. One of my goals in this chapter is to draw attention to the forms of popular entertainment that were central to the life and leisure of the rural South—forms that, as we shall see in the chapters that follow, had long and vivacious afterlives, far beyond their local origins. No less modern than their urban counterparts, these traveling performers of tent shows and TOBA acts traversed a landscape infused by the possibility of a new life elsewhere, as well as the psychic rupture and loss engendered by the departure of loved ones. For those kin who remained in places such as Natchez, Yazoo City, and Rosedale, these traveling performers served a unique function in making migration visible and audible, providing aesthetic and affective parameters to a phenomenon impossible to conceive in its totality.

Rainey's and Smith's performances were frequently witty, sometimes literal representations of the travel endured—in all its libidinal pleasures and humiliating Jim Crow perils—not only by the narrator of the song but also by the touring performer herself. While Rainey's "music also invited her female audience to glimpse for themselves the possibility of equaling their men in this new freedom of movement," her songs also reflected on the hassles, poverty, and physical pain of life on the road.[15] These reflections frequently took the form of a bit of shtick that mimicked and commented on the travel of the star. Rainey reportedly described her performance of "Traveling Blues" as follows: "Baby, I come out on that stage, dressed down! I had on a hat and a coat and was carrying a suitcase. I put the suitcase down, real easy like, then stand there like I was thinkin'—just to let 'em see what I was about. Then I sing. You could jes' see them Jiggs wantin' to go some place else."[16] Perhaps Rainey arrived on stage with her actual personal suitcase, or perhaps it was a prop; the ambiguity of the suitcase, floating somewhere between real and fictional object, suggested the merging of real travel with its representation—something that theatrical blues singing did with regularity.[17] "Traveling Blues" is also notable for the fact that, like many other classic blues songs, it contains an internal bit of dialogue:

The ticket agent said, "Woman, don't sit and cry,"
The ticket agent said, "Woman, don't you sit and cry,
The train blows at this station but she keeps on passing by."

Rainey, especially, regularly sang duets with other performers. While Rainey sings all the lyrics on the recording, it likely that, in the live performance of this song, Pa Rainey or another performer took on the lines, and character, of the ticket agent.

Just as the *Indianapolis Freeman* aggregated news and gossip from touring performers, tent-show and TOBA blues acts operated as travelogues: reports from life on the road that knitted together a migratory black public through the embodied circulation of its singers. Hazel Carby, in particular, has reflected on the role of the female blues singer within the context of early twentieth-century migration, noting that the singer could serve as a cipher for audiences' varied desires, lyrically expressing both a wish to move and a longing for home.[18] In addition to speaking—or singing—on behalf of the audience, the blues singer often operated as a surrogate for the departed. Smith's "Far Away Blues," sung as a duet, is a haunting missive from two young women, perhaps sisters, who "wandered north to roam/Like birds." The repetition of the blues lyric is doubled by the women's performance of the duet, as one echoes the other, line after line. "We don't know why we are here," they sing, "but we're up here just the same/And we are just the lonesomest girls that's ever born." Communication from departed loved ones was unreliable at best; the women warn that "there'll come a day when from us you'll hear no news." A blues act, for some rural family members and loved ones, operated as an affective substitute, a stand-in that filled the absence left by departure.

The blues star represented more than migration; she embodied it for her adoring fans. The figure of the itinerant male agricultural laborer, who travels from town to town with his guitar in tow, is a familiar—indeed, emblematic—symbol of early twentieth-century black migration. Less iconic but no less significant, the male and female artists of the tent show were also migrant laborers; their work sites, however, were not the fields but the stage and the Saturday-night breakdown house. Though attendance at tent shows was purely recreational for their audiences, the performers were mobile professionals; women frequently joined touring companies as an economically promising alternative to agricultural or domestic employment.[19] Elijah Wald's fine revisionist history of blues makes the professionalism of the most successful musicians clear: "It is important to remember that most of the successful ['folk' or 'country' artists] were professional musicians, not farmers who played guitar on the side."[20] These itinerant entertainers, many of whom were female, made a career of traveling the South for decades, some of them nearly nonstop; rather than representing migration and movement from a distance, these workers participated in it.[21]

It would be a mistake, however, to assume that the mobility of the touring performer contrasted with the stasis of an economically and geographically immobilized audience. Contrary to stereotypes of the Mississippi Delta as an unchanging repository of the past and its people (assumptions advanced, in part, by folklorists of the 1930s and the revivalists of the 1960s), the Delta was home to a highly mobile and outward-looking population; unlike the southeastern states, which had been planting cotton since the antebellum period, the Delta had only been cleared of its forests and settled by black "pioneers" from the eastern United States in the later decades of the nineteenth century. Many of these recent arrivals established families, but their descendants remained for only a generation or two before moving on to Chicago or St. Louis.[22] Nor was the Delta culturally isolated; at all times, but particularly in the period before widespread phonograph and record ownership, touring shows were a primary site of reciprocal artistic exchange throughout the black South. Tours enabled the transmission, innovation, and reinvention of popular theatrical and musical practice between residents and visitors. Abbott and Seroff have demonstrated how lyrics, licks, and theatrical scenarios spread geographically as performers toured.[23] As a scene of encounter between local artists, audiences, and entertainers from out of town, the theatrical tour of tent-show or vaudeville performers was a mobile site of transmission between rural and urban musicians, both male and female, who continuously learned from and with each other.

The prevalence of the tent show, its conjunction with community dances and juke joint parties, and the constant travel of both male and female entertainment and agricultural laborers made the Mississippi Delta a lively site where performance skills, conventions, and material could be shared, traded, repeated, and revised. More than any other state, Mississippi was the geographic hub for touring entertainment, especially the tent shows that descended on its small towns. Listings in the *Indianapolis Freeman* indicate that tent shows arrived most regularly and reliably as the annual harvest concluded. A report filed by Max C. Elliott indicates that an astonishing eighteen shows performed in Clarksdale, Mississippi, in just one month in the autumn of 1917—this in a county of just over 34,000 in population.[24] The Rabbit's Foot Minstrels toured to towns such as Clarksdale, but also smaller hamlets, such as Rosedale, Mississippi, all between late

October and early December. The touring players who made their living on the enthusiasm of their audiences always took note of the lively theatrical performance culture in the Mississippi Delta. "Mississippi is some minstrel show state," marveled a correspondent for the Georgia Smart Set Minstrels in 1917.[25] With its dense population of black residents, the Mississippi Delta's demand for black entertainment is unsurprising. But the sheer quantity of tent shows that regularly drew crowds seemed to surprise even the performers themselves. Regular reports in the *Indianapolis Freeman* describe troupes encountering each other on the road, one leaving a tiny town the same day another arrived, or even multiple shows occupying the same small town for several days at a time. These reunions engendered a spirit of great competitive fun, and various performers filed hyperbolic reports describing "battles" and "clashes" between rival companies—the friendliness of their competition enabled by the sold-out crowds that continued to pour in, even when there were several shows a day for weeks at a time.[26] One could not live and labor in the Delta and remain untouched by this vibrant culture of traveling entertainment, music, and dance, especially if one were a professional musician. Jeff Titon persuasively describes the influence of Smith's recordings on the male Delta musicians, but it is also true that a young Smith regularly appeared on the stages of these Delta towns, singing a new form called blues.[27] While it would be challenging if not impossible to prove, it is difficult to imagine that Muddy Waters (who would become a performer in the Silas Green from New Orleans tent show), Charley Patton, or Robert Johnson—all residents of the Delta—would not have attended one of these shows or not have been present at the dances that often followed.[28]

The routes of the Southern tent shows and the geographically inflected performances of their blues singers charted the geographic and cultural shifts of communities in transition, staging the black South as a discrete region, with discrete audiences, characterized not only by its locales but also by violence, economic deprivation, and outward migration.[29] St. Louis, Chicago, Clarksdale, Jacksonville: the tour mapped a geography of a black South on both sides of the Mason-Dixon Line, chronicling its changing demographics and constructing a geographically widespread public, one held together by the travels of the itinerant performers, the warp and the woof of a transforming fabric of African American public life.[30] Through their travels, and the representation of these travels in songs, skits, and monologues, these performers mapped the geographic and cultural shifts of communities facing the fracturing pressures of migration and displacement. A quick glance at Smith's oeuvre shows it as a kind of cartographic tool, geographically identifying not just migrant destinations but also the places of the audience, the places of home: "Florida Bound Blues," "Chicago Bound Blues," "Beale Street Papa," "Black Mountain Blues," "St. Louis Blues," "Gulf Coast Blues," "New Orleans Hop Scop Blues." Prior to the circulation of recordings, stars such as Rainey and Smith, who traveled from one city to another, often overnight, were a fast and efficient form of cultural communication. To put it another way: while an Andersonian notion of "imagined community" depends on the circulation of common *texts*, the circulating bodies and voices of performers knitted together a geographically dispersed but affectively connected black Southern public.[31] The routes of the touring star linked migrants to their hometowns and linked those who stayed in place to the new homes of their brothers, sisters, husbands, and children—places where they might, one day, find themselves.

Migration risked—and often effected—the fragmentation of families and communities; a more widespread popular culture offered the promise of holding them together. Word of mouth and the black press spread expectation and seeded public behaviors: the audience at Rainey's Birmingham show eagerly joined in the proliferating ritual of calling out for "the Phaaantuhm."[32] Rather less centralized than the strictly controlled Keith and Albee vaudeville circuits, the tent shows' creation of a black public did not depend on audiences witnessing the exact same show; instead the creation depended on the star power of the performers themselves, who served as a kind of tether between one place and another and enabled rituals of communal audience adulation ("the Phaaantuhm"). Similar to the black female singers Farah Jasmine Griffin explores in her decisive essay "When Malindy Sings," Rainey's and Smith's theatrical singing served as a "hinge," capable of representing not only interracial harmony or political dissent but also the potential thrills and hazards of black migration and the reinvention and sustenance of communities on the move.[33] These stars corporealized as well as represented the changes in the racial geographies of the nation; traveling the highways and sound waves, these women's voices conjured forgotten and imagined corners of the nation for both white and black listeners. Declining to disclose autobiographical "truths" in interviews or memoirs and using theatrical trappings to play with the first-person narration of their lyrics, Smith and Rainey blurred the line between their onstage and offstage lives, and spoke for others as both surrogates and stars.

Rainey's cultural role in reflecting and crafting a migratory African American public is most evident in a source that is as aesthetically affective as it is suggestively ethnographic: Sterling A. Brown's poem "Ma Rainey" (1932).[34] In this possibly eyewitness account of Rainey's performance in a touring tent show in Missouri, Brown describes a performance scene that leaves few conventional archival traces but lingers tenaciously in poetic memory. Brown lived in Missouri in the 1920s and taught at Lincoln University in Jefferson City. During this time he immersed himself in local cultural events, many of them rural, including the many traveling shows that passed through the region.[35] The poem presents Rainey as a "high priestess" of black folk who invokes the audience members' communal identification and purges their pain through a cathartic moan.[36] Rainey's moan is the climactic sound of the poem, which is structured as a series of frames, each enclosing a more tightly nested scene; Rainey's stage performance is only the most narrowly enclosed object of the poem's examination. Taken as a whole, "Ma Rainey" produces a doubled scene of migration, representing the movement of both artist and audience toward and away from their place of mutual rendezvous. The poem begins with the travels of the crowds; when a tent show arrives "anywheres aroun'," people set out on the road, for a long journey by foot and by mule from "Cape Girardeau" and "Poplar Bluff" in Missouri. By calling out these place names, much as Rainey did in her show, Brown draws the reader's attention to the scenes of journey and arrival at the performance venue as a "nesting" context of the event itself.

Affixing the touring theatrical show to the journeys undertaken by the audience, Brown invites the reader to dialogically imagine these two scenes of travel and to generate a cognitive map of diasporic travel that positions these local events within a larger context of mass movements and migrations. In the poem Rainey and her audience are both on the road, only to meet at a particular time and place, where the performance architecture of the tent underscored the temporary nature of everyone's stay. Brown sounds out Rainey's appearance before her public as a scene of hospitality and taking leave, of departure and return, one that locates her "back" in the rural South ("Now you's back/Whah you belong"), if only temporarily. Brown juxtaposes Rainey's demanding touring schedule and the journeys of the audiences, who implore the star to "sing us 'bout de lonesome road," something they know all too well.[37] Brown concludes his third stanza with the trailing line "We mus' go . . ."; the ellipsis carries both Rainey and audience out of the tent, physically and psychically, "back" to the river settlements and lumber camps (temporary domiciles, all) from which they came. But the doubled scene of migration—the journey to the performance that intersected with that of the touring star—was redoubled yet again by Rainey's performance. As she called out the place names of St. Louis, Clarksdale, and levee camps, she sang of the "lonesome road," the road to Chicago or

New York or Detroit that beckoned to migrants seeking economic justice and personal safety. Brown's poem indicates the broader significance of the touring entertainer in an era of mass migration. The routes and roots of black migrants—and those who remained in place—were theatrically staged through the touring bodies of the female blues singers, who, in their travels and on the stage, corporealized practices of migration and histories and futures of black diaspora. In so doing, these actress-singers were key players in the knitting together of a Southern black public whereby practices and representations of travel, economic migration, and theatrical song tied together communities on the move.

MINSTRELSY, REALISM, AND CONFESSIONAL MODES

The first-person *I* that organizes so many lyrics of the blues songs of the teens and twenties is never exactly what it seems to be. That is, because of the theatrical frame of the variety show, and because the women that we today call singers were then primarily understood as actresses, the *I* does not function within stable parameters of authenticity or singular identity. Feminist scholars such as Angela Davis, Daphne Duval Harrison, and Hazel Carby have, quite significantly, drawn our attention to the way blues songs are manifestations of early twentieth-century black women's subjectivity, expressive sites of experience that have been marginalized in more traditional literary and historical archives. While I am not arguing against this model of reading, I do want to suggest that we remain aware of the way such approaches confer a rhetoric of authenticity upon a highly flexible, mobile, theatrical event, one in which the *I* signifies multiply and simultaneously—and does not always refer back to the self, or to one's own identity position. Even "the self" in these theatrical venues and situations is up for constant refiguring and revision, a reality that does not undermine the recovery of black women's subjectivity but instead suggests the imaginative and creative possibilities at the heart of such a project.[38]

These performers were always greater than their autobiographical *I*. A theatrical approach—as opposed to an approach that solely analyzes lyrical content, or one that exclusively listens to recorded song—necessarily puts the supposed singularity of the first-person *I* into question. To what extent did audiences understand Rainey's and Smith's performances as bits of music-theater, complete with scenario, characters, and narrative? To what extent did they understand their songs to be personally expressive? These two understandings of the blues queens' performances need not be mutually exclusive; indeed, the tension between blues as an expression of black women's subjectivity and blues as a theatrical creation authored by black women calls into question the bright line between the "public" world of theatrical presentation and the "private" world of interior life. Constantly undermining and exceeding the autobiographical *I*, Rainey's and Smith's first-person musical performances slipped between representation and testimony, reveling in a space of undecidability that both rendered their intimate lives as public and, at the same time, called all certainty about these disclosures into question.

Indeed, the double entendre—so characteristic of the blues actress's approach to meaning making—is a useful metaphor for thinking about how Rainey and Smith both are and are not on the stage. Just as a song such as "Kitchen Man," written by the Tin Pan Alley team of Andy Razaf and Maceo Pinkard, could be taken at face value as an expression of the narrator's love of her cook's food, it is quite clear that Madame Bucks's love for Dan, the kitchen man, goes beyond the culinary:

His jelly roll is so nice and hot
Never fails to touch the spot
I can't do without my kitchen man.

The doubleness of the double entendre breaks through in performance, as Smith rolls her *r*s and growls through the line "when I eat his donuts, all I leave is the hole." Built into the logic of the double entendre, and into the logic of theatricality, is the potential of deniability—the defensible claim that one is "only" putting on an act, or "only" singing about baked goods. The practice of such doubling sits at the very heart of theatrical performance, wherein, as Richard Schechner suggests, an actor is both "not Hamlet" and "not not Hamlet" and performs "in the field between a negative and a double-negative, a field of limitless potential, free as it is from both the person (not) and the person impersonated (not not)."[39]

The touring tent shows of the black South shared aesthetic and narrative elements with the emergent forms of black musical comedy in the urban North, but the two forms significantly diverged in both matters of dramaturgical structure and the relationship between actor and character. Comedians from the black minstrel tradition, such as Bert Williams and George Walker, joined forces with composers and lyricists, including Eubie Blake, Noble Sissle, Bob Cole, J. Rosamond Johnson, and James Weldon Johnson to develop the long-form narrative musical comedies *Bandanna Land*, *In Dahomey*, *Abyssinia*, *The Red Moon*, and, some years later, *Shuffle Along*.

Actresses (many of whom also sang blues in other settings) such as Aida Overton Walker, Florence Mills, Alberta Hunter, and Ethel Waters also found fame on New York stages in these musical comedies and were key artistic contributors to their development. In many of these shows, black theater artists reappropriated the mask of blackface and played within its performance constraints and conventions, signifying on them in a complex dance of parody and double consciousness.[40] By necessity and by strategy, many of these early twentieth-century performances worked within and against theatrical traditions of "staging the South"—a performance genealogy that is traceable from the early days of antebellum minstrelsy through the songs of Stephen Foster, from Tom shows and plantation musicals to melodramas of stage and screen, from Dion Boucicault's *The Octoroon* to D. W. Griffith's *The Birth of a Nation*. Shows such as the 1890 *The South before the War* bridged the genres of the minstrel show and the emergent plantation musical, as did the various Tom shows of the 1880s and 1890s. In the first decade of the twentieth century, versions of the plantation musical *Southern Enchantment* were hugely popular and toured widely. Later works, such as Will Marion Cook and Paul Dunbar's *In Dahomey* (1902), maintained some of the scenic appeal of their forerunners while also signifying, often quite comically, on the conventions they both exploited and spoofed. Coon songs were prevalent in both the North and South; the comedian Ernest Hogan became widely known for the ragtime tune "All Coons Look Alike to Me," while Ma and Pa Rainey frequently performed what the *Indianapolis Freeman* cites as "The Man in the Moon," but was most likely the white ragtime composer Fred Fischer's "If the Man in the Moon Were a Coon."

But if Rainey, Smith, and other early blues artists shared a great deal in common with their Northern counterparts in terms of source material and content, the trajectories of their artistic development were not the same; indeed, their formal responses to the racist dramaturgies set in motion by white antebellum minstrelsy were quite distinct. While Northern artists largely abandoned the variety format for long-form musical comedies complete with consistent characters and narrative developments, Southern tent shows continued to embrace the variety format and the olio of the nineteenth-century minstrel show. The Raineys, for example, were billed as "Blackface Song and Dance Comedians, Jubilee Singers, and Cake Walkers" long after such appellations had ceased in Northern theatrical circles.[41] Rather than exclude Southern tent shows and their stars from teleological narratives of the black entertainment industry, or characterize them as temporally behind the advancements of urban theatrical forms, however, we should read the Southern retention of the variety format as a formal strategy, one that embraced stardom and discontinuity over realism and consistency.

While frequently championed by advocates of uplift, realism also rhetorically accrued to nostalgic stagings of a static black past, which portrayed antebellum slave life as positively Edenic. This rhetoric of realism was particularly powerful in Billy McClain and Nate Salsbury's 1895 plantation reenactment *Black America*, a gigantic exhibition staged in Ambrose Park, Brooklyn, that erected "real cabins" and employed some five hundred "actual field hands from the Cotton Belt." *Black America* staged the South for an urban Northern audience—a reenactment that, in the words of Jayna Brown, building on the work of Lori Brooks, "re-version[ed] slavery as a prelapsarian innocence."[42] These discourses of the real ("real cabins" and "actual field hands") served to naturalize these representations of a black slave past. By refusing to acknowledge that the participants in these recreations were actors, the producers obscured the constructedness—and the fiction—of their historical reenactment. While this staging of the "authentic" South for Northerners produced an armchair imaginary of a region that many spectators did not know and would never visit, the Southern tent shows that Rainey and Smith performed in staged the South *in* the South, quoting representations of their region by outsiders and playing with their theatrical conventions. Rather than naturalize Southern nostalgia through discourses of authenticity and the real, Rainey's and Smith's live acts played *up* the staginess of their endeavor, revealing these pastoral Southern scenes as constructed fictions. Rainey and Smith's embrace of the role of the protean actress refused the naturalizing tendencies advanced by a rhetoric of authenticity. Instead, the women juxtaposed the pastoral with the urbane, nostalgic stasis with locomotion, and the mammy with the queen. To put it another way: they embraced the spectacle of an actress who refused to stay put.

BREAKING CHARACTER: UPLIFT AND THE TOURING ACTRESS

While journalists avidly covered blues actresses' spectacular stage performances, they also demonstrated a fascination with the spectacle of the actresses' mobility.[43] When Rainey arrived in Chicago, the critic Sylvester Russell devoted his column not to her music but to the details of her journey, describing how the star "arrived in the city early last week in her Mack motor car, in which she carries her entire company and band. She made the trip of over 1,000 miles from Charlotte, N.C., camping only two nights before her arrival in Chicago, on a special trip to make new records."[44]

The black press breathlessly covered the details of Rainey's travels. When Rainey bought a bus for her company, she signaled not only her own financial achievement but also what money could buy: protection from the indignities of Jim Crow lodging and services she and her company faced as they toured throughout the South. Though the *Chicago Defender* and other papers frequently discussed the inconveniences of life on the road when segregated facilities and accommodations were the norm, such fretting veiled greater threats that were often left unspoken, circulating only off-the-record. When Smith was killed in a car accident in 1937, however, the perils of being black and on the road in the Jim Crow South rose to the surface.

But how did fans see and hear the woman on stage before them? Davis proposes a model of identification, whereby Rainey "permitted her audience—especially the women who came out to see her—to partake vicariously of the experience of travel."[45] This model of identification implicitly understands the first-person *I* of Rainey's lyrics to be autobiographical. But given the theatrical frames that enclosed the act of blues singing, where dramatic character was frequently employed in various skits, sketches, and songs, the first-person narration of blues lyrics, when combined with theatrical trappings, often deflected attention away from the autobiographical experience of the singer. In such a setting, the confessional mode of the first-person *I* becomes only one strategy among many for building a character and staging a theatrical event. The performance and listening practices of the tent show, therefore, played a central role in allowing the performer to move between confessional autobiographical and expressive theatrical modes. The *theatrical* first person of many blues songs staged a scene of doubleness, where performer oscillated with narrator, and with dramatic character. As autobiographical figure, theatrical character, narrator, and surrogate, the "not I" and the "not not I" of Rainey's and Smith's first-person musical performances moved back and forth between representing their own travel and the travel of others, between representation and embodiment.

The policing of dramatic aesthetics that characterized early twentieth-century theatrical performance was intertwined with moral questions of character and behavior, particularly the character of actresses, whose profession had historically attracted misgivings. For some, black women's participation in the entertainment industry threatened uplift ideology's emphasis on the respectability and privacy of the bourgeois family unit; the black actress seemed doubly susceptible to defamation. But many Northern black actresses worked to reconcile the perceived split between a career in the theater and a life rich in moral character that uplifted the race.[46] In an attempt to reject the sexual slander that had historically defamed black women, they declared as acceptable only those performances of femininity that were modest and decorous. As Daphne A. Brooks has noted, the performances of late nineteenth- and early twentieth-century black women such as Aida Overton Walker, Pauline Hopkins, and Sissieretta Jones "balanc[ed] aesthetic passion with clear and purposeful commitments to racial uplift." Such performances "sharply contradicted competing images of debauched and demoralized black women in theatre" and "fused racial uplift with revised black female subjectivity at the dawn of a new century."[47] Walker, in particular, sought to establish theatrical life as an honorable profession for young black women. Her attempt to rescue actresses from accusations of disrepute comes through in the pages of Colored American magazine, where she published a lengthy article that aligned theatrical performance with the politics of respectability: "Some of our so-called society people regard the Stage as a place to be ashamed of. Whenever it is my good fortune to meet such persons, I sympathize with them for I know that [they] are ignorant as to what is really being done in their behalf by members of their race on the Stage."[48] In championing of the moral character of the actress, Walker walked a fine line, touting the artistic achievements and inherent respectability of a life on the stage, but warning women of dangerous elements, especially "the things we must avoid whenever we write or sing a piece of music, put on a play or sketch, walk out on the street or land in a new town." Walker reminds black female readers that, whether singing on stage, or walking across the street, they risk being a spectacle, and must be careful to maintain moral character at all times as they performed for their audiences.

Closely associated with the project of black uplift and respectability, dramatic character took on moral valences during this period. One influential black critic in particular attacked the question of dramatic character with missionary zeal: Sylvester Russell. A widely published and widely read critic, Russell, who reprinted Walker's reflection on the moral character of actresses in the pages of the Indianapolis Freeman, championed what he saw as morally appropriate bourgeois theatrical conventions and criticized the degrading practices of tented minstrelsy and black vaudeville. Aware of his role as an architect of a new industry, he wrote consistently and with bad temper on these topics. Russell covered both popular theater and popular music for the Indianapolis Freeman, and later for the Chicago Defender and the Pittsburgh Courier; a retired performer himself, he saw his criticism as an instrumental force in the evolution of black theater. Russell believed that black theater's evolution was strictly teleological; minstrelsy, burlesque, and tent shows were of the compromised past, while "genuine" musical comedy, art theater, and realistic drama represented the future.

Russell's impassioned criticism in the early decades of the twentieth century can be summed up in a question: to what extent is it allowable or preferable for a performer to *break character* in the midst of a play, sketch, or song? And, implicitly, what are the moral, classed, and representational stakes of doing so? In his columns Russell, who advocated using the legitimate stage as a part of a broader project of African American uplift, regularly excoriated performers for talking to the audience, introducing songs with prefatory remarks, and generally breaking character. When actors did not heed his commands, he became quite tetchy; in a review of Harrison Stewart's performance in the comedy *The Husband?*, Russell bemoaned Stewart's ignorance—as well as his own lack of influence:

> If Mr. Stewart were not a young performer who has come up within a period of at least five years of *Freeman* criticism, which reminded actors of the importance of addressing themselves in the play, instead of addressing the audience, when on the stage alone, there would be some excuse for the illegitimate features of Mr. Stewart's performance. It has been repeatedly explained so simply that a child could understand it. It was not the duty of [the director] to necessarily instruct him along this individual line, nor could Mr. Stewart be well excused from the same course of criticism that has passed through the ranks of nearly all the best colored comedians on the boards. White comedians are forty years ahead. Many of them are in the lower station and some higher up are vile actors and more illegitimate than colored performers. Any colored actor who can afford to excuse himself by doing as they do will hurt himself and retard the race he represents.[49]

In Russell's opinion, maintaining the fictional matrix of character was an important route to achieving bourgeois respectability for a still emergent professional black entertainment industry. Stepping out of a role received particular condemnation, because "talking to an audience or asking an audience questions belongs to vaudeville, burlesque and minstrelsy."[50] Russell branded those who broke character and spoke to the audience as "illegitimate novices" and "ignorant figureheads."[51] Breaking the fourth wall was, under all circumstances, verboten: "We have the unthankful pleasure of once more reading the laws of the 'legitimate standard' . . . by force of commandments. . . . : 'Thou shalt not talk across the footlights to the audience. Thou shalt not introduce thy songs at any time. . . . Thou shalt not make any speeches to an audience.' . . . Speeches are no good."[52]

Vaudeville and tent show stars such as Rainey and Smith—as well as lesser-known touring tent performers of variety, burlesque, and blues—were the unnamed foils to Walker's and Russell's "respectable" theater practitioners. Walker's and Russell's criticism placed blues performance and its larger context (tent shows in the South, cabarets in the North, vaudeville theaters everywhere) in a substandard category, one that stood in contradistinction to moral performances of uplift that linked realistic drama to moral legitimacy and artistic value. These performers were, as Walker suggested, always in the public eye, but they did not behave according to Walker's recommendations. In addition to violating the bourgeois theatrical conventions advocated by Russell and others, Rainey and Smith repeatedly appeared in spectacular scenes of scandal in the press, from public drunkenness at an elite New York event (Smith) to an interrupted orgy with several young women (Rainey). Located outside the regional and economic centers of uplift ideology and tactics, Rainey and Smith were seen as ambivalent representatives of black advancement. Rather than attempt to perform their way into a middle-class politics of respectability, they embraced the role of the "bad actress," not only asserting their own deviance in performance but also devising strategies for resisting the character and caricature of naturalized racism.

By wholeheartedly assuming the cultural role of "the actress," Rainey and Smith created a space for themselves that emphasized not realism, not the autobiographical *I* of their lyrics, but the show(wo)manship and protean possibility of a life always on the stage.[53] While Walker rejected the debauched associations of a life on the stage, as well as the spectacular titillation that accrued to the public reputation of many actresses, Rainey and Smith did not harbor the same concerns. Bucking Russell's prescriptions regarding dramatic character, Rainey and Smith fashioned themselves as stars, and, in doing so, refused the matrix of interiority and dramatic character. To perform not as a character but as an actress—as a star—is to refuse to disappear into a role. No matter what costume she wears, the star's celebrity supersedes the suspension of disbelief that realism requires. But to perform as an actress also means that one's interior life—the "true" self—is permanently unavailable. To always be playing a role confounds those audience members—and scholars—who would ascribe intention or psychological motivation.

Keeping in mind that the available roles for black Southern women were generally variations on Topsy and mammy figures—prevalent in the surfeit of Tom shows touring at any given time—Rainey's and Smith's embrace of the controversial strategy of breaking character operated as a strategic refusal of the roles they were expected to play. In a "successful" matrixed performance, when the performer subsumes himself or herself within alternate—that is, fictional—matrices of time, space, and character, the performer's self disappears completely: the performer *is* Topsy, one who can be beaten but never killed, a child who lives within a fictional world where slavery and black inferiority are the natural order of things.[54] Dramatic character and its maintenance consequently take on a complex double edge: the more accomplished the actress playing Topsy, the more the fictional circumstances of slavery become naturalized and sutured to the performer herself. In a world of Tom shows and *The Birth of a Nation*, then, a nonmatrixed performance was not necessarily a less sophisticated or legitimate theatrical choice, as Russell would have it, but a kind of escape hatch, an interruption of the matrix of naturalized racism that manifested as a literal stepping out, a stepping forward, a stepping downstage: all actions that Russell deplored.[55]

This breaking of matrixed character is most evident in the way that Rainey and Smith navigated the role of mammy. As large, dark-skinned women, neither could circumvent being cast as mammy figures, whether on the stage or in the press. The variety stage, however, offered an opportunity for these performances to register doubly, inhabiting the outlines of a familiar character while seizing upon the opportunities that live performance offered for play and multisignification.[56] Both performers used their stage acts and their stage personas to refigure black motherhood, calling some of the naturalized assumptions about black maternity into question, even while they performed as mammies.[57] To put it another way: there is nothing straightforward about the nomination of Rainey as "Ma." Rainey and Smith rarely, if ever, addressed themes of motherhood in their lyrics, but this does not mean that a discourse on motherhood was absent from their performances.[58] Rainey—who, in fact, preferred "Madame" to "Ma"—was repeatedly invoked as the "mother of the blues," particularly in the Paramount advertisements that appeared in the *Chicago Defender*. Just as the mammy figure nurtured and raised children who were not her biological offspring, Rainey nurtured her traveling company while mothering a formally and informally adopted brood; her son, Danny Rainey, was celebrated as an accomplished "juvenile stepper" on the tour.[59] Rainey's personal and professional performance as mother and mammy points to, but also revises, the model of white women's supervision of touring pickaninny choruses, explored elsewhere by Brown, whereby children were shepherded through on-stage singing and dancing, sometimes accompanied by their white wardens, who occasionally blacked up themselves. While white women who supervised the touring of pickaninny choruses in the early twentieth century emphasized the moral education of their charges and their own privileged position as "metonymic signifier[s] for the moral . . . well-being of the national body," Rainey's mothering of her adopted children anticipated the political possibilities of nonbiological kinship structures.[60]

Smith played a mammy figure in her act for a time, a performance that is documented in a rarely circulated 1924 photograph of the star clad in a kerchief and polka-dotted dress, surrounded by her niece Ruby Walker and several young men, a side band known as the Dancing Sheiks. How can we understand Smith's performance—itself nearly vaporized from historical record—which does not at all seem to square with the defiant woman who attacked a Klan member who attempted to disrupt her show and who sang "I've Been Mistreated and I Don't Like It"? To acknowledge the mammy as a vector of the disgraces of blackface minstrelsy is to complicate our understanding of Smith as a performer. Clearly there were moments when the demand to address the white audiences who sometimes filled the tents superseded the ability of a singular performer to launch a full-scale performance of resistance. But in the case of Smith as mammy, her status as a star actress worked to her advantage, as did the quick-change aesthetic of the variety show, which allowed for constant transformation, shifting, and multidirectional signification. When Smith played mammy, she used the role as an opportunity to assert her own status as a star. Walker reported that Smith used her broom to comically sweep the chorus line of young girls off the stage at the end of the act, leaving her alone on the stage. Smith actively staged herself as the center of attention, literally removing any and all who might compete with her for the audience's admiration, and she, like Rainey, signified on the white women who served as the mammies to the pickaninny choruses. Smith followed this playing at white women's imitations of black women with a lightning-fast costume change, reappearing as a regal queen, underscoring her ability to put on and take off roles at will. And, indeed, it was as queen that Rainey and Smith became most well known. By replacing the mammy with royalty, Smith and other blues queens located a new type that enabled them to at least momentarily sidestep an old one.

Foregrounding all their roles as protean performances that could be embodied or cast off by skillful manipulation of theatrical tools—especially the many costume changes that characterized their acts—Smith and Rainey destabilized the conflation of black womanhood with the nurturing, self-abnegating maternal figure of the mammy. Costume play was a key element of Rainey's and Smith's theatrical self-fashioning, a quick-change performance strategy that never let one role completely settle on the body of the performer and that, consequently, never let the star disappear completely from view. At the same time, however, the crossover between costume and everyday fashion—and between the performances on the stage and the spectacles in the street that Aida Overton Walker warned against—made the line between public and private life indistinct. For actresses of illusionistic theater and film, the distinctions between their onstage and offstage personas were more precise; Walker, with her first-person voice in the press, stood at quite a distance from her character of Salome in *Bandanna Land*. But the nonmatrixed performance styles of Rainey and Smith did not permit the same unambiguous distinction between their "real-life" personas and their stage personas. Their performed monarchy affirmed their birthright: a sense of worth and value that was inherited and entitled rather than earned. Their play with the performances of femininity signified on the idea(l) of white Southern womanhood, a typology that bolstered racial violence in the turn-of-the-century South, when lynchings skyrocketed, often on the presumed violation of a white woman's chastity. In sum, the tent show's retention of the variety format and Rainey's and Smith's rapid costume changes and transformations resulted in a sidestepping of the (dramatic and moral) character questions advanced by Russell and Walker. Dispensing with the coherency of character almost entirely, Rainey and Smith did not play matrixed roles; rather, they played the role of the shape-shifter—one who neither participated wholly in the illusionistic world she inhabited nor one to whom autobiographical intention was ascribable.

COSTUME, SELF-FASHIONING, AND PHOTOGRAPHY

Through onstage and photographic performances, Rainey and Smith inhabited personas of glamour, wealth, and extravagant costuming—the glitter of their gold, jewels, furs, and feathers blinded their audiences to what they may have expected to see. The musician Clyde Bernhardt provides the most descriptive account of Rainey's performance in a tent show; her Georgia Smart Set came to his North Carolina town in 1917. In his autobiography he recalls a pavilion, bandstand, and a "dancing space" that held a string band, chorus lines, comedians, and an enormous backdrop with "a large illustration of a cotton field."[61] This set dressing was not uncommon; minstrel shows and tent shows frequently used similar backdrops. Smith's 1923 tour, for example, featured a backdrop of silhouetted magnolia trees and the moon.[62] But these plantation musical aesthetics were disrupted by the appearance of the performer at the heart of the production, who did not resemble Topsy or mammy but bejeweled royalty. Rainey was the closing act of the show. Though she was not yet doing the Victrola routine for which she would later become famous, her entrance was no less spectacular. Out of sight, hiding in the wings, Rainey began to sing. She then made a grand entrance, showing off her "gold plated teeth and expensive gold necklace." Bernhardt remembers: "She wore a long, gold silk gown that swept along the floor, gold slippers, and carried a sparkling rhinestone walking cane. Her hat was high and wide with large feathers stuck in it, had gold earrings dangling and diamond rings on all her fingers. When she got to center stage under those amber spotlights, the audience just went wild. She was all of what show business was supposed to be. *She was show business.*"[63] Rainey's gold and diamonds clashed with the backdrop of the cotton field that enframed her. The incongruity of this glittering queen in a cotton field (which is how she must have appeared to audiences), worked against the familiar aesthetics of Tom shows and plantation musicals, showing them up as representations, primed for adjustment. And while a glittering queen must have seemed out of place in the cotton field, such cognitive dissonance was nothing short of the point. In these performances of bejeweled glitz, Rainey and Smith restaged black Southern womanhood as a performance of wealth and value, far from the Topsy or mammy figures that preceded them on the stage. They did so by embracing the glamour of costume and fashion, aided by fashion's theatrical partner, publicity photography.[64]

Rainey's and Smith's glamorous self-styling underscores the role of costume, presentation, and display in early classic blues performance; as Monica Miller concisely explains: "In the black entertainment industry some form of dandyism or play with costume has always been de rigueur."[65] Like the male dandy, whose practice of "dressing up" on stage and in the performances of everyday life shed "the degradation of work," according to Robin D. G. Kelley, the glamorously styled blues queen called attention to histories of chattel slavery by highlighting the property and wealth of those who were once claimed as property.[66] Famously listing the "Will to Adorn" second only to "Drama" in her "Characteristics of Negro Expression," Zora Neale Hurston puts it most succinctly: "The feeling back of such an act is that there can never be enough of beauty, let alone too much."[67]

Signifying on the history of black flesh as capitalist currency, Rainey's and Smith's play with another commodity—gold—functioned as a sly commentary on their own commodification as products of the emergent race-records industry. For female blues performers, costumes operated not only as a vector for sexual play and display but also an embodied critique— and technique—of concepts of value and valuation. Rainey bypassed coded representations of wealth in favor of its direct presentation. Bernhardt describes Rainey's famous necklace as "one-hundred-dollar gold coins all strung together with some fifty-dollar, twenty-dollar, and ten-dollar ones

1.3 *(above left)* Publicity photograph of Gertrude "Ma" Rainey, ca. 1923. Courtesy of the Frank Driggs Collection at Jazz at Lincoln Center, New York.
1.4 *(above right)* Photograph of Bessie Smith for Columbia Records, 1923. Courtesy of the Frank Driggs Collection at Jazz at Lincoln Center, New York.

stuck in between. The smallest was five-dollar pieces." Wearing currency as adornment, Rainey's necklace stood out against the poverty expressed in songs such as "Ma and Pa Poorhouse Blues," just as her spangled gowns stood out against the mise-en-scène of the cotton field that was her backdrop.[68] Further enhancing the aesthetic sense of disconnection, though, was the fact that Rainey shared a regional and class background with much of her audience. The disconnect between the poverty of Rainey's surroundings and her glamorous self-presentation on stage thus posed a question: to what extent could poverty and oppression be styled away? Were the trappings of theatricality just that—trappings—or were they the route out of a particular kind of experience and into a new life of economic opportunity?

Rainey's and Smith's self-fashioning and performed glamour is most evident today in their publicity photographs, which continue to circulate throughout biographies and across album covers as illustratively suggestive of the performers' true selves (see figures 1.3 and 1.4). Rather than provide unmediated access to the singers, however, these photographs point to their performances and theatrical self-fashioning at a historical moment when photography played a key role in the cultivation of the star persona. While publicity photographs had long been used by vaudeville performers and were on their way to becoming an enormously important component of the production of stars by the Hollywood studio system, they were only beginning to be used by the emergent race-records industry in the early 1920s. The process of taking and making these photographs—the scene of their creation—remains largely unknown and unstudied; what is clear is that the making of the early photographs was largely an ad hoc affair. Most important, early photographs were made by and for African American fans; in contrast, white employees of the new race-records industry made many of the racist caricatured hand-drawn advertisements that appeared in the *Chicago Defender*.[69] Dan Burley, a theater and music enthusiast in his early twenties who was a sports writer for the *Chicago Defender*, took some of the early photographs of the Paramount artists who recorded at the studio's Wisconsin location, including, possibly, those of Rainey.[70] After 1928 many of the recording artists had their photos taken at the Theatrical Arts Studio in Milwaukee. These photographs reached a large and geographically diverse black public, serving as cover art for records and sheet music, as well as elements in *Chicago Defender* advertisements in the late 1920s. While many witnessed Rainey's and Smith's live shows in the teens and twenties, even more were spectators to the singers' photographic performances. These photographs have not received much scholarly attention, perhaps because of the assumption that the performers did not have much agency over their self-presentation. But the improvised conditions of their production—particularly the stars' collaboration with inexperienced photographers in a new industry—suggest that the artists did retain a degree of control over their own self-presentation, accustomed as they were to producing their own tours, choosing their own costumes, and booking their own arrangements.

If we read these photos not simply as culture-industry come-ons (though they were often also that) but as opportunities for theatrical play by their subjects, the images emerge as sites of performance where the line between costume and fashion could be blurred and the proximity and distance between performer and role could be enjoyed and teased. The artists' costuming choices suggest that they took these moments of photographic composition as opportunities to align their photographic representations with their onstage personas. Significantly, these photographs do not closely resemble male country blues musicians' publicity shots, many of which were made in the thirties and are straightforward portraits where clothing and costume seems to be of little importance; the men's photographs are as "everyday" as the women's photographs are "theatrical." They are also comparatively more flamboyant than some publicity photographs of Northern black performers of the uplift stage, such as Sissieretta Jones, the opera singer, who often posed in everyday ladylike gowns rather than the excess of feathers, jewels, and headdresses taken up by Rainey, Smith, and their cohort. Adopting the medium of photography as fashion's theatrical partner in crime, these photographs share more in common with the publicity photos of vaudeville and Hollywood actresses than with those of other musicians. The blues actress anticipated a Hollywood trend of female film stars being photographed in costumes similar if not identical to those they wore on screen, presenting a persona of a protean actress, always somewhere between the artist and the role: whether costumed as Mata Hari or Queen Christina, Greta Garbo was always Greta Garbo. Moving from one role to another, without ever disappearing into any role, the photographed star lands somewhere between self and persona, calling the autobiographical *I* of the blues lyric—and the blues performer—into question. Highlighting the protean potential of the star-as-actress, as well as the self-fashioning possibilities available to black female performers in the era of the New Woman, these photographs of Rainey and Smith represent a theatrical extension of their nonmatrixed stage acts.

STAGING SALOME

Both on stage and in photographs, Rainey and Smith played at—and played with—the theatrical figure of Salome, the most popular female role of the period. In tent shows and black vaudeville acts, this Afro-Orientalist stage figure—and the craze of "Salomania"—staged a crossroads of Hollywood, French, Middle Eastern, and rural Southern imaginaries; Salome became a glittering site of glamour and desire, of imaginative identifications and ludic appropriations. Rainey's and Smith's Southern audiences may not have consciously understood the performers to be playing Salome—nor is there direct evidence that the stars thought themselves to be doing so. But through their fashion and costume choices, clearly legible within an Orientalist vogue that gripped early twentieth-century consumer culture, high art, and popular entertainment, they opened up new avenues for sexual expression. This role-playing, in turn, allowed the performers to simultaneously explore a variety of subject positions, from sapphic lover to New (white) Woman to Arab wanderer. The rage for Salome began with Oscar Wilde's 1896 *Salome*—whose lead role he originally wrote for Sarah Bernhardt—which tells the biblical tale of the young woman who, upon being offered a reward for dancing for Herod, demanded the head of John the Baptist. The character of Salome appeared in the concert dance of Ruth St.

Denis and Loie Fuller, and in the celebrated Richard Strauss opera, but she did not remain confined to the venues of high-art modernism. Hundreds of white female vaudeville performers staged their own interpretation of Salome's dance of the seven veils, so titillating audiences that, in the case of the Canadian dancer Maud Allan, a moral panic erupted. The anxiety generated by these proliferating vaudevillian Salomes responded to the threat of onstage nudity, to be sure, but it also signaled immense and rapid transformations in women's domestic and political lives in the United States and beyond during the period of the New Woman.

As Brooks and Brown have persuasively demonstrated, the Salome craze was not limited to white women: in 1908 Walker, who had so vigorously argued for the respectability of actresses, entered into the fray, performing the role of Salome in two celebrated New York City appearances, one that year (*Bandanna Land*) and another in 1912, at the Victoria Theater (see figure 1.5). Recalling Walker's uplift orientation and her demand that black actresses maintain a public image of moral respectability, the choice of Salome seems incongruous. But Walker's experiment with Salome precisely highlighted those strategies of (moral and dramatic) character that a black actress could employ. As Brooks emphasizes, Walker's deliberate, veiled negotiation of Salome's infamous striptease frustrated visual access to her body, not only refusing hypersexualization but also "confounding the discourse of [an] imperialist scenario" that imbued the nonwhite figure of Salome with a sensuous and submissive corporeality, one that mapped onto a feminized "Orient," vulnerable to colonial and imperial exploitation.[71]

Fed by an Orientalist vogue, Salomania's hold on the United States and Europe coincided with the zenith of tent show entertainment and the popularity of its theatrical blues-singing star actresses. The film scholar Gaylyn Studlar has identified the years 1916 to 1926 as the height of Orientalism in U.S. film and popular culture; these years were also the height of Rainey's and Smith's stage careers.[72] Orientalist themes, lenses, and figures constantly materialized and refigured themselves in film, fashion, popular theater, and music, often with reference to one of a few key touchstones: the 1916 U.S. tour of Sergei Diaghilev's Ballets Russes, known for their *Scheherazade*; the Garden of Allah novels, plays, and films; and the wildly popular 1921 *The Sheik*, featuring the seductive Italian Rudolph Valentino in the title role. Consumer culture, too, got in on the act, often combining department-store display, contemporary fashion, and theatrical spectacle to produce in-store runway shows organized around a Garden of Allah theme. The overlap of theatrical costume and contemporary fashion was in full effect when Marshall Fields, the Chicago department store, displayed the Bal-

1.5 Aida Overton Walker, costumed as Salome, 1912. Billy Rose Theatre Division, the New York Public Library for the Performing Arts, Astor, Lenox, and Tilden Foundations.

lets Russes designer Leon Bakst's costumes in its shop windows when the company performed in the city, noting in a promotional flyer that "it will be interesting to note the influence of these Costumes on women's clothes of the moment—the new Suits, Coats, Frocks, Skirts and Blouses revealing this Russo-Oriental influence in pleasing modification."[73] As Melani McAlister notes, the widespread use of Orientalist imagery in department stores and consumer culture from the turn of the century through the 1920s particularly appealed to women and laid the groundwork not only for the popularity of Orientalist-inspired fashions but also for new models through which to imagine feminine—and feminist—subjectivity. "Commodity Orientalism," she maintains, participated in the production of "a multilayered rhetoric of 'emancipation' linking the New Woman, companionate marriage, modernity and consumerism."[74] The adoption of Salome by black women makes McAlister's "emancipation" sing with possibility: what implications

1.6 One of Paul Poiret's iconic designs. Evening Tunic, ca. 1913. Courtesy of the FIDM Museum at the Fashion Institute of Design & Merchandising, Los Angeles. Accession 2008.25.4. Funds provided by Mrs. Tonian Hohberg. Photographed by Brian Sanderson.

for freedom and self-determination might Salome have held, not just for a New Woman but for a New Woman of the Jim Crow South?

Rainey's and Smith's sartorial choices located them squarely within the Orientalist vogue that characterized both everyday fashion and theatrical costume. Salomania was a glittering bridge between the world of theatrical costume design and high modernist fashion, and nobody traversed—indeed, actively linked—these two worlds more frequently or with greater ease than the designer Paul Poiret. Poiret, the most significant artist of Orientalist fashion, created both haute couture and theatrical costumes for Parisian works such as *Le Minaret* (1913) and *Aphrodite* (1914). Known for "bringing the world of performance (and the imaginary Orient) into the realm of the everyday," Poiret dispensed with the corset and embraced harem pants, feathers, tassels, jewels, and "lampshade" tunics (see figure 1.6).[75]

1.7 Bessie Smith in a Poiret-inspired gown, with dropped waist, 1923. Courtesy of the Frank Driggs Collection at Jazz at Lincoln Center, New York.

A man of the theater, Poiret reportedly taught himself design by sketching costumes during intermissions as a young man, and he made a name for himself by designing for French actresses, most notably Bernhardt.[76] Poiret's fashions, and the more homespun creations they inspired, were worn by stage performers in Orientalist roles, everyday ("New") women, and, significantly, black stage performers of popular music, such as Smith and Rainey (see figure 1.7). Poiret and black performers were part of a Möbius strip, each shaping the artistic work of the other in a feedback loop of influence and inspiration. While black stage performers embraced the designs of Poiret with enthusiasm, he developed his famous fashions in the midst of a Paris thoroughly enchanted by African and African American art, music, dance, and performance. Josephine Baker wore Poiret's dresses throughout Paris, and she acted not only as model and muse but also, according to her son Jean-Claude Baker, as Poiret's design assistant.[77]

The visual record makes evident the stylistic grammar common to early twentieth-century performances of Salome. The most significant element was the headdress, a tonsure-like strand of pearls encircling the skull, embellished with multiple loops of pearls that draped on either side of the head, over the ears; other trends in both theatrical costuming and everyday fashion included the dropped waist, the elimination of the corset, and the use of feathers and jewels, especially pearls. Allan and Wilde himself wore this costume on the stage; Theda Bara (her stage name an anagram for "Arab death") and Alla Nazimova wore it memorably in Hollywood films and publicity shots (see figures 1.8 and 1.9). Seizing on current trends, Rainey and Smith regularly wore Orientalist and Poiret-inspired fashions, especially enjoying the creative opportunity afforded by the headdress. Rainey posed in a headdress in an early publicity photograph, its many loops asking to be shaken with a toss of the head.[78] Inert in the photograph, the headdress offers marked choreographic stage potential. Smith, for her part, takes the fashion over the top. In a photograph signed "To Palamida, my gown designer," Smith wears a headdress to match her gown (see figure 1.10). Highly structured "wings" extend a few feet from the sides of Smith's head, each one dripping with fringe. Elaborately detailed and embroidered with baubles, Smith's gown and, especially, her headdress, take fashion in the direction of camp. Here is Salome camped out, her theatricality disrobed and re-dressed, her status as fantasy figure acknowledged with a wink. To play an Orientalist figure, this photograph suggests, is to always already be embedded in a matrix of theatricality, to be over the top, to complicate any notions of spectatorial access to an actress's interior life. Smith's campy homage to Salome's headdress suggests that the performers saw Salome not as a dramatic character to be faithfully enacted but as an available motif, a repository of pliant theatrical tools. It comes as little surprise that, as a figure of supposedly dubious (moral) character, Salome was luxuriantly appealing to those performers who, according to Sylvester Russell, had no truck with character, dramatic or moral. If Walker's Salome was characterized by her decorous and considered modesty—what Brooks calls a "spectacularly visible opacity"—in response to the hypersexualization of the black female body, then Rainey and Smith's Salomes brazenly flaunted a certain nonnormative sexuality.[79]

For performers who used theatrical techniques to regularly interrupt what masqueraded as a confessional *I*, the association of Salome with lesbianism offered an opportunity to play from the stage with rumors, gossip,

To Alameda
My Gown
Designer
from
Bessie Smith

and hearsay. Dissemblance and disclosure took place not from behind the veil but under the headdress, queering the confessional mode that their songs seemed to inhabit. If, as Emily Apter has noted of fin-de-siècle Paris, "Orientalist stereotypes were used as a means of partially or semi-covertly outing Sapphic love," then Rainey's and Smith's uses of Orientalist stage conventions play with the expectation *of* disclosure, where Orientalism operates as "a genre of theatricality in which acting 'Oriental' becomes a form of outing, and outing is revealed to be thoroughly consonant with putting on an act." This "acting/outing slippage" emerges most thoroughly in those songs in which Rainey and Smith *challenge* their audiences on matters of hearsay.[80] In "Prove It on Me Blues," Rainey sings the story of a woman who, while out with her friends, "had a great big fight." She continues:

To my surprise
The gal I was with was gone.
Where she went, I don't know
I mean to follow everywhere she goes.

In Rainey's performance of the song, the narrator traces her encounters with rumor and hearsay. "They said I do it" repeats throughout. The "it" refers doubly when sung by Rainey: "it" is a presumed act of violence done to the narrator's "gal." In the larger context of the song, though, "it" connotes lesbian sex. "Folks say I'm crooked," Rainey (or the narrator) sings. Yet all remains unstable. The supposition that the narrator is sexually involved with women is never verified; when she describes her friends, she avoids statements of fact, choosing only suggestion as she sings: "They *must've* been women, 'cause I don't like no men." And even though she sings, "It's true I wear a collar and a tie" and "talk to the gals just like any old man," the song's refrain and final line challenges audience members to do what Rainey knows they cannot: "Sure got to prove it on me!"

The Paramount records advertisement for the song also engages in some "is she or isn't she?"—a sales tactic, perhaps, but one that correlates with Rainey's subversion of the confessional mode from the stage. The ad, fittingly, shows *two* Raineys. Both Raineys are drawings: the first is a reproduction of a widely circulated Rainey head shot; the second is a scene of a large woman dressed in vest, jacket, and hat, seducing two femmes on a street corner, while a policeman watches from a distance (see figure 1.11).

1.8 *(opposite, above left)* Theda Bara costumed as Salome with pearl headdress, 1918.
1.9 *(opposite, above right)* Alla Nazimova costumed as Salome with pearl headdress, 1923.
1.10 *(opposite, below)* Bessie Smith wearing a headdress, 1924. Courtesy of the Frank Driggs Collection at Jazz at Lincoln Center, New York.

The copy asks, "What's all this? Scandal? Maybe so, but you wouldn't have thought it of 'Ma' Rainey—But look at that cop watching her! What does it all mean?" Like the song, the ad demands that spectators ask the question: which image is the one of the "real" Rainey? This is a question that is ultimately confounded by Rainey herself, the bad actress.

Smith's "'T'Ain't Nobody's Bizness If I Do" is also built around rhetorical practices of hearsay and gossip; like Rainey, Smith refuses to set the record "straight." A litany of self-destructive possibilities, "'T'Aint Nobody's Bizness If I Do" reads on the page as morose, particularly in its final lines, when the narrator suggests that she may remain with an abusive lover who beats her. In performance, though, Smith is upbeat and defiant, her narrator explaining,

> There ain't nothin' I can do or nothin' I can say
> That folks don't criticize me
> But I'm going to do just as I want to anyway
> And don't care if they all despise me.

It is tempting to map Smith's stormy relationships with her lovers onto the lyrics of this song. But, like Rainey, Smith couches her lyrics in the conditional. Refusing to confirm what has been said by others, she speaks only in the conditional: "*if* I do." Indeed, the proliferation of *ifs* in the song teases the audience, tantalizing them with rumor while simultaneously telling them to butt out: "'T'Ain't Nobody's Bizness."

Playing at Afro-Orientalism on the tent-show circuit provided Rainey, Smith, and the other classic blues performers an opportunity to undermine the confessional mode that their songs seemed to signal. Simultaneously, their role-playing of exoticized figures offered an alternative to the naturalized nostalgia of the plantation musical, staging the South as a site of sexual freedom, economic desire, and African American value. As a figure of ethnic and sexual difference and decadence, Salome is characterized by her unruly excess desire: a desire that is not exclusively sexual but more generally acquisitive. Naming themselves queens, empresses, and madames, tent-show actresses turned away from the mammies and Topsys of the postbellum stage and toward a re*vamp*ed decadent figure of the woman of appetites, their desires reflected in the unruly display of pearls and feathers. Seizing on artistic flamboyance that codes both sexual "deviance" and economic ambition, Rainey and Smith refashioned the image of the black woman on stage.[81]

But the question remains: in what ways was the figure of Salome specifically significant or attractive to *Southern* black female performers and

1.11 Paramount advertisement for "Prove It on Me Blues," 1928. Courtesy of Jas Obrecht.

audiences? As Brooks and Brown suggest, the Northern actress Aida Overton Walker can be understood to be alternately aligning herself with white modernist dancers of Salome and with a broader political project of black diasporic consciousness and pan-Africanist aesthetics. Then the Southern Salomes of the tent-show and vaudeville stages were, like the performers themselves, migrant travelers and itinerant laborers. Cleopatras, Salomes, sheiks, harems: these characters populated the last days of silent film, and also performances of black popular music in the South. Examples abound. Smith's touring band was named the Dancing Sheiks; the Mississippi Sheiks, who reportedly drew its name from the Valentino film, was one of the most prominent regional bands for decades. Papa Charlie Jackson, who spent his early career touring with tent and medicine shows and recorded with Rainey, recorded "The Sheik of Desplaines Street" in 1927 with banjo accompaniment. The theatrical entertainer Frank Stokes, forever linked to the Memphis blues style, recorded as part of the Beale Street Sheiks in the 1920s. While the proliferation of imagined Oriental figures in national popular culture certainly contributed to this naming practice, Southern touring shows may have had a closer relationship to actual Arab immigrants, many of whom shared the highways and byways of the rural South with these itinerant actresses, both before and after World War I.

Immigrant Arab peddlers were a small but significant element of the broad spectacle of migration and itinerant labor that characterized the rural South during the period of the Great Migration. Following many of the same routes as the traveling tent show, these peddlers, described as "indefatigable men and women of steely determination who trekked along, laden like beasts of burden," likely supplied the touring companies with necessities and notions.[82] The Mississippi Delta was—and continues to be—home to a significant number of Syrian Lebanese immigrants, who, like the region's Chinese, Greek, Italian, and Jewish populations, populate a Delta far more ethnically diverse than its historically black-white legal, social, and cultural codes would seem to indicate.[83] After fleeing religious persecution from the Mount Lebanon area, most of these Christian Syrians immigrated to the Mississippi Delta between 1878 and 1924, when the Immigration Act of 1924 placed severe restrictions on non-European immigration.[84] Peddling was not limited to the Delta; drawn by the mild climate and a large rural population, Syrian peddlers traveled throughout the Southern states, including Mississippi, Tennessee, Kentucky, Texas, and Louisiana. Most men, and some women, initially made their livings as roving peddlers, selling notions, fabric, housewares, combs, mirrors, and costume jewelry from rucksacks, horse-drawn carts, and, eventually, cars and trucks. Observing that few black sharecroppers had easy access to transportation that would allow them to come into town regularly, the peddlers brought the shop to the tenant farms, plantations, and living quarters of rural blacks and whites.[85] When nightfall came, the peddlers slept in barns, outdoors, or in the homes of whites and blacks—a practice nearly unheard of in the deeply segregated Jim Crow South.

In exchange for the hospitality, peddlers regaled their hosts with tales of Syria. Lu Ann Jones captures this reciprocal economy of hospitality and entertainment, which, for the hosts, also served as an opportunity to consume tales of the Levant: "After the dickering had ended, Coleman's grandmother offered to board the peddler for the night, her gesture of hospitality repaid with stories 'of his home country in the great world beyond our doors' and with a gift such as fine linen towels."[86] The regular encounters that Southern women had with Syrian immigrants revolved around travel and fashion, arguably the two most important themes offered up by Rainey, Smith, and other stars of tent and vaudeville shows. The star actress, known for playing roles that had strong, if vague, associations with the Arab world, and the Syrian peddler, a crystallized image of itinerant labor, stood as strange doubles to each other, an uncanny reflection of the malleability of race and the physical and psychic demands of economically mandated itinerancy.

THE DEATH OF BESSIE SMITH

Rainey achieved her greatest theatrical fame in her nightly materializations from the Victrola; in these resurrections without death, she thrilled her spectators with the life-affirming power of her blues. Rainey's actual death was, ultimately, a quiet one; in 1939, years after she had returned to her home state of Georgia to run some local theaters, she died of a heart attack. After her death, Rainey's brother Thomas Pridgett Jr. underscored Rainey's theatrical career in an obituary he wrote for *Jazz Information*. It is a curious piece, one that suggests Pridgett's awareness of the generic transformations that took place throughout Rainey's career.

> Gertrude Rainey, better known to the theatrical world as "Ma" Rainey, . . . [was the] "songbird of the South." . . . At a very early age her talent as a singer was very noticeable. Her first appearance on the stage was at the Springer Opera House, Columbus, Ga., with the "Bunch of Blackberries," a small show that was gotten up among the local talent of Columbus. . . . "Ma" Rainey operated two theaters in Rome, Ga., viz. "The Lyric" and

"The Airdrome." Her career as a recording artist did not interfere with her stage work. She was in the theatrical business for a little better than thirty-five years.[87]

As if he knew that Rainey would be remembered by and for her records, Pridgett emphasized Rainey's theatrical career as a hedge against forgetting. Pridgett was so careful to prioritize Rainey's onstage career ("Her career as a recording artist did not interfere with her stage work.") that one detects a hint of defensiveness. He was right to worry: as the next chapter will relate, antitheatricalism in blues discourse was ascendant in the 1930s, as scholars and folklorists enthusiastically recorded and collected songs by male blues singers such as Huddie Ledbetter and Blind Lemon Jefferson, producing their rural male authenticity in counterpoint to the theatrical women who had preceded them.

In contrast to Rainey's relatively unheralded death, the death of Smith in 1937 in an car accident near Clarksdale, Mississippi was a media spectacle. Just as Rainey's brother made sure to emphasize the star's career in the theater in his *Jazz Information* obituary, the black press memorialized Smith as a theatrical star. St. Clair Bourne, writing for the *New York Amsterdam News*, described Smith as "heralded as royalty among theatrical performers," claiming that "in the recent passing of Bessie Smith, 'Queen of the Blues,' a brilliant chapter in the history of the theater came to a close."[88] Harry Fiddler, of the *Chicago Defender*, echoed the praise of Smith as "the greatest trouper of them all," opening his article with a show-must-go-on anecdote: "She made a valiant fight against death and smilingly told friends at the bedside that she was certain she would be able to make the evening performance of the Winsted Broadway Rascal [*sic*] minstrels show in Memphis."[89] Bourne and other journalists relished the dramaturgies of melodrama in recounting Smith's life story, describing the love affair between Smith and her husband, Jack Gee, in theatrical terms: "Even before their first engagement, fate stepped into the spotlight and cast a dramatic shadow on the romance."[90] It was a relationship that rivaled "the gilt-studded fabrics of Hollywood."[91] Smith's biography was not entirely separable from her iconic status: her death straddled the blurry line between art and life, just as her stage performances had done. Multiple tributes were made to Smith just prior to and immediately after her death; these tributes, particularly the portrait photographs of Smith made by the New York impresario Carl Van Vechten, explored Smith's persona, attempting, and ultimately failing, to locate the bright line between the star's onstage and offstage life. Strikingly different from Smith's early publicity photographs, Van Vechten's photographs purported to reveal the real star behind the theatrical mask. The photographic production of Smith's afterimage, however, was embedded in and produced multiple theatrical frames.

Despite—or perhaps because of—the massive enthusiasm with which her image and her songs were and continue to be consumed, the private life of Smith remains somewhat unknown to the fans, scholars, and cultural critics who have explored her life and work. Even at the height of her career, she gave no interviews, unlike Walker; nor did Smith write an autobiography, as Ethel Waters did. As a result, many of the details of Smith's life are accessible only through hearsay and are laden with speculation, conjecture, and gossip. Chris Albertson, Smith's biographer, takes up these challenges in the opening pages of his book, where he sets out to remedy the misperception that Smith "seemed not to have had much of an offstage life."[92] But Albertson's task and mine are different. Surely Smith could have spoken as herself, separating herself as a working artist from the persona she projected on stage. Yet she maintained a deliberate opacity, refusing literary or spectatorial access to her interior life, a right of entry that is structurally promised by the format of the interview or the tell-all.[93] While such seemingly transparent genres must remain suspect for scholars—particularly scholars conscious of the performances of everyday life—Smith's refusal to speak publicly, her opting out of disclosure, must also be taken up as a tactic. I read Smith's declining to speak to the press not as an expression of desire to maintain a "private" life but as a move to make performance speak for itself. The first-person narration of Smith's lyrics—the *I* that seems to promise autobiographical disclosure—takes on even greater freight in the absence of any correlative "true" information. Rather than keeping her private life and her public life separate, Smith folded them into each other, creating an indistinct zone of stardom, where her onstage and offstage roles overlapped and merged.

Nowhere is this confounding of public and private, of the theatrical *I* and the autobiographical *I*, more apparent than in Van Vechten's photographs of Smith. These photographs are a counterpoint to the publicity photographs that defined her image at the height of her career—Van Vechten made his famous photographs of Smith toward the end of her dramatically shortened life, when swing and hot jazz had replaced blues, and Smith's star had dimmed a bit. Van Vechten's photographs of Smith were part of an extensive series of photographs of black Americans, many of them performers, that Van Vechten took over a period of decades. Many of these photographs made use of a backdrop, one that often transformed into a curtain quickly and easily. As Bruce Kellner has noted, Van Vechten's theatrical sensibility carried over into his photographs. While the photographer Dan Burley, who took some of the earliest publicity shots of blues singers, later became a theater critic, Van Vechten, an avid consumer of black cultural life in New York City, traveled in the opposite direction. Trained as a music and theater critic at the *New York Times* and *New York Press*, Van Vechten turned to fiction writing in the twenties and, finally, to photography in the 1930s. His lifelong interest in photography, however, had always been informed by a theatrical approach; in his first experiments with a camera in his hometown of Cedar Rapids, Iowa (a noteworthy location for vaudeville and touring acts, which frequently stopped there after stints in Chicago), Van Vechten posed his childhood friends in various theatrical scenes: one played an opera singer, another approximated Juliet, lying still as if in a tomb. Many of the thousands of photographs of black Americans that he took in the 1930s retained a similar theatrical sensibility, manifesting an obsession with role-playing and the enthusiastic use of costumes, props, and character.

Photography, for Van Vechten, was a vector for discovering Smith's "real personality," just as, he implied, other photographs had obscured it. Van Vechten claimed that, with his photographs of Smith, he came "closer to her real personality than [he] ever had before and these photographs, perhaps, are the only adequate record of her true appearance and manner that exist."[94] Van Vechten's photographs of Smith in the mid-1930s markedly differ from the publicity shots taken a decade earlier. In the Van Vechten photos, her hair is short, and she wears no hat. Gone, too, are the elaborate costumes, though traces of them remain, gesturing to the photos of the past, such as when Smith holds feathers as a prop. While the earlier photographs feature a posed Smith smiling at the camera, the Van Vechten photographs seem to catch Smith unaware, in moments of apparent repose, looking pensive and distant. The full-body shots of many of the publicity photos are, for the most part, replaced by the conventions of portrait photography. The tighter focus on Smith's face invites the spectator to decipher the star's enigmatic expressions, to search for evidence of psychic interiority. Van Vechten printed the photographs that appeared candid and spontaneous and that seemed to capture an unguarded moment; the elevation of the candid over the pose establishes a rhetoric of insight and truthfulness, as does the literal removal of Smith's theatrical costumes.[95] In a photograph that features feathers similar to those that adorned her famous headdresses, Smith holds the feathers in such a way as to cover what appears to be her naked torso (see figure 1.12). By removing the feath-

1.12 Bessie Smith, 1936. Photograph by Carl Van Vechten. Yale Collection of American Literature, Beinecke Rare Book and Manuscript Library, New Haven, CT. Permission granted by the Carl Van Vechten Trust.

ered costume and replacing it with a feathered prop, Van Vechten stages a pastoral melancholy of the fallen star; the feathers stand in as an Edenic fig leaf, producing a narrative of Bessie Smith, shamed.

Despite the fact that Van Vechten's photographs purport to reveal the real (naked) Smith, the theatricality of these supposedly transparent images is profoundly apparent; the photographs reassert Smith's role as an actress, a protean player of roles. Taken in sum, the series showcases nothing so much as Smith's tremendous dramatic skill. In a few shots in a white dress, her expression shifts from delight to pained regret, her eyes cast down, her brow pinched and furrowed (see figures 1.13 and 1.14). The photographs invite the spectator to screen the scene of the photograph's creation in his or her mind's eye: what events could have precipitated such distinct and varied emotions in such quick succession? Perhaps Van Vech-

1.13 *(above left)* Bessie Smith, 1936. Photograph by Carl Van Vechten. Yale Collection of American Literature, Beinecke Rare Book and Manuscript Library, New Haven, CT. Permission granted by the Carl Van Vechten Trust.

1.14 *(above right)* Bessie Smith, 1936. Photograph by Carl Van Vechten. Yale Collection of American Literature, Beinecke Rare Book and Manuscript Library, New Haven, CT. Permission granted by the Carl Van Vechten Trust.

ten walked Smith through a series of memories, capturing her authentic emotional responses as he went. Just as likely, though, is that Smith took an active role in staging this series, manipulating facial expressions with far greater speed and acuity than the actual experiencing of emotions would allow. The viewer is left with the question: who—or what—am I seeing? The emotionally volatile and vulnerable true self of Smith? Or the technically nuanced performance of an extremely accomplished actress? Van Vechten was clear in his answer; in a 1947 column in *Jazz Record*, he described Smith's appearance at one of his parties in the late 1920s: "I am quite certain that anybody who was present that night will never forget it. This was no actress; no imitator of a woman's woes; there was no pretence. It was the real thing: a woman cutting her heart open with a knife until it was exposed for us all to see." Van Vechten seems largely unaware of the paradox at the heart of his claim: that the most accomplished actress would hide her labor, making her craft invisible to those spectators who hoped to gain access to the "real thing" of black suffering.[96]

As if acknowledging the inscrutable doubleness produced by these portraits of Smith, Van Vechten's photographs are filled with playful treatments of theatrical iconography. Working with masks and busts, particularly African and pseudo-African masks, was one of Van Vechten's habitual

1.15 Bessie Smith, 1936. Photograph by Carl Van Vechten. Yale Collection of American Literature, Beinecke Rare Book and Manuscript Library, New Haven, CT. Permission granted by the Carl Van Vechten Trust.

strategies. His photographs of Smith, like some of his other works, traffic in fairly unsurprising tropes of modernist primitivism, aligning his subject's racial difference with undifferentiated Africanness. Like so many other modernists, Van Vechten's use of tropes of minstrelsy and masquerade stages a rejection of bourgeois values and normative middlebrow cultural expression.[97] The photographs of Smith with these objects, however, reveal the star's inability—or refusal—to play along. In one, a classical marble bust appears to be pinned to the backdrop far above Smith's head; as she gazes upward at the bust's blinding whiteness, her smile of delight betrays a hint of disbelief; she raises her eyebrows in quizzical skepticism (see figure 1.15). The barely perceptible raise of an incredulous eyebrow punctures the continuity of Van Vechten's series; the conflict over the production of

1.16 Bessie Smith, 1936. Photograph by Carl Van Vechten. Yale Collection of American Literature, Beinecke Rare Book and Manuscript Library, New Haven, CT. Permission granted by the Carl Van Vechten Trust.

meaning between artist and subject plays out before our eyes. Van Vechten also introduced a caricatured sculpture of a black boy; in this photograph Smith gazes up at the black bust, her expression one of wary resignation (see figure 1.16). In one image, Van Vechten stages the photograph so that Smith's gaze in the direction of stage right mimics the eyes of the sculptured head that sits on her shoulder, its eyes parallel with hers; in another, the marble bust remains in the frame, its frontal gaze and white sheen more unrelenting than ever, caught in the overexposure. These photographs follow the opposite trajectory of what they seem to. The images, initially appearing to reveal the "real" Smith, as Van Vechten claimed, were staged by a photographer with a penchant for the tools and techniques of the theater and were littered with theatrical trappings and masks. What's more, the actress-subject of these images was anything but passive; she, too, took part, at times pushing back against a photographer who wanted more than she was willing to provide.

In this analysis of Smith's confounding of the "real personality" that Van Vechten reportedly aimed to access, the curtain emerges as a central image, a theatrical tool manipulated by both photographer and subject to produce Smith as both a real personality and as a star. Several of the photographs of Smith highlight her relationship to the curtain: she poses before it, echoing a striking 1936 Gilles Petard photograph in which she was captured as she emerged from backstage to on stage, a smile pasted on her face that is familiar from the early publicity photographs. If in the illusionistic theater, as Bert O. States eloquently argues, the curtain call operates as a "seam" between the role-playing of artistic illusion and the role-playing of polite gratitude, it is also the seam between the matrix of dramatic character and the demonstration of mannered character. But for Smith the curtain was more of a Du Boisian veil; the maintenance of a persona was, for her, dependent on the obfuscation of the public-private binary. As States puts it: "There is no moment in which the actor is more ambiguously real than when he emerges from the play and bows to us at this unstable border between two contradictory realms."[98] But as Smith emerges from the curtain in a photograph, she is both entering the stage for the beginning of an act and returning to her audience for a curtain call at its end. This instability produces a Smith who is both moving in and out of character, in and out of the theatrical world, an actress whose relationship to her role is decidedly, and pointedly, unstable.

Smith's 1936 entrance through the curtain eerily foreshadows what the press dubbed her "final curtain call." The press recognized the significance of the curtain in its discursive construction of "Bessie," a task that largely took place after her sudden death. The analogies were worked over to the point of excess, to the point that death could not discretely belong to either life or the stage. Numerous articles suggested that death was Smith's final performance; her funeral proceedings were described as "dramatic," complete with professional pallbearers cast for the occasion, their attire of "morning coats, white vests, striped ties, black shoes and white spats" as carefully described as Smith's peach-colored dress.[99] The props—and their expense—were also chronicled, an implicit celebration of Smith's status as the highest-paid black entertainer of her time. The cost of the funeral was estimated at $1,000: "The metallic casket, done in floral gold-tone, cost $800 alone." The mourners, too, were tallied, and the clogging of the city streets with thousands of spectators who spilled off the sidewalks, stopping traffic, remapped the racial and spatial geography of Philadelphia, if only for a few hours.

The chronicling of every detail of the funeral-as-spectacle on South Philadelphia streets stood in marked contrast to the unknowable and obscured circumstances of Smith's death. Smith's final journey through the streets of Philadelphia was juxtaposed with her fateful final journey down a "country road"—Highway 61, one of the key routes of both black migrants and touring entertainers. Highway 61's significance in early twentieth-century black travel eluded some journalists, who repeatedly described its "darkness." The location of Smith's death was often mistakenly said to be "Clarksville," rather than Clarksdale, the epicenter of the traveling tent show that had jump-started both Rainey's and Smith's careers. Even in death, the roads of both Clarksdale and South Philadelphia, migratory and processional, framed Smith's theatrical persona. Theodore Stanford opened his September 30 *Philadelphia Tribune* tribute with an evocation of "a long trail and a hard trail" that characterized Smith's early life travels and chronicled her early performance career with Rabbit's Foot, attributing Smith's drive—and her success—to "the call of the long road." Surveying Smith's career, and her astonishing financial success, Stanford closed the article by linking the decline of Smith's career in the mid-1930s to the accident that claimed her life: "The automobile accident at Memphis, Tennessee [*sic*], Monday, brought swift death to the 'Empress of the Blues.' It eased, perhaps, her sorrow, as she watched the lights that framed her name grow smaller and dimmer as the years sped by."[100] Stanford transformed Smith into a spectator of her own gathering darkness, the sole participant in a melodramatic denouement that was not as swift as it appeared. The murky darkness of Smith's death scene was only further emphasized by the producer John Hammond's claim a few months later that the circumstances surrounding Smith's death were even more troubling than initially recognized.

In an article published in the December 1937 issue of *Down Beat*, Hammond spread the powerfully persuasive rumor that Smith had been denied medical care by a white hospital following her accident and had bled to death while waiting for assistance. A later investigation clarified that Smith was never taken to a white hospital, but to the black hospital in Clarksdale, where she later died. Now the Riverside Hotel, a historic haven for traveling musicians and blues tourists, the site of the former hospital is a tourist attraction in its own right and stands for what is true about Hammond's now-debunked story—that it *could* have happened the way he described. Just as Smith's maintenance of her star persona refused bourgeois notions of black women's private life, the preservation of a fictional story keeps the dangers—and not the romance—of the road front and center. Soon after Smith's death, articles in Baltimore's *Afro-American* chronicled what many already knew intimately—that black entertainers met not only inconvenience but danger as they traveled the Jim Crow South.[101] The dangers of "the road" were not just automotive ones; there was also the threat of racist violence. These were two dangers that intersected in the rumors that swirled (and continue to swirl, to this day) around the circumstances of Smith's death, rumors so persuasive that they live(d) on in Edward Albee's play *The Death of Bessie Smith* (1959), a play in which Smith herself, tellingly, does not appear.[102] That Rainey and Smith both inspired famous plays—Albee's *The Death of Bessie Smith* and August Wilson's *Ma Rainey's Black Bottom*—is no surprise when one considers their theatrical innovations and their use of theatrical song to craft a model of protean Southern black womanhood.[103] In the end, Smith's refusal to draw a bright line between public and private, between interior truth and exterior spectacle, destabilized the theatrical-authentic binary that retrospectively governs many assessments of these early blues.

In blues historiography, Rainey and Smith—and their influence—disappear after their deaths. Largely forgotten or marginalized by many blues aficionados and critics, they are often displaced from their position as "mother" by the critical celebration of several "founding fathers" of blues performance, such as Lead Belly, Blind Lemon Jefferson, John Lee Hooker, and Son House. While scholarly accounts of Rainey, Smith, and their largely female cohort frequently emphasize—and often demean—the popular, theatrical qualities of their work, these same accounts celebrate the founding fathers as the torchbearers of blues authenticity. But this division into "theatrical" and "authentic" blues performers is a false one. Both the mothers *and* fathers of the blues exploited theatrical tropes and practices—at some times, as we have seen, in an attempt to recuperate broader possibilities for black subjectivity, and at other times, as we shall see, as a strategy for highlighting the fictional frames of authenticity that accrued to them. These founding fathers preserved the legacy of theatrical performance begun by these women, even as the political economy and racial ideology changed around them. One of these men was Huddie Ledbetter, better known as Lead Belly, whose career is the subject of the following chapter. Through dance, monologue, and costume, Ledbetter sustained a vaudevillian theatrical tradition, even while audiences and producers actively worked to suppress it—all in the name of racial authenticity, a paradigm that Rainey, Smith, and their cohort consistently undermined from the tent-show stage.

Writing for *Harper's* magazine in 1928, James Weldon Johnson reflected with optimism on "the art approach to the Negro problem" recently taken by "the conscious artist." Johnson praised the Harlem Renaissance–era poets, playwrights, and performers who had garnered widespread "admiration for the creative genius of the race," persuading white Americans to recognize the humanity and achievements of black Americans. As Johnson saw it, these artists were harbingers of a new era of racial self-confidence and uplift; bolstering the self-assurance of black citizens, they helped break down "the inner walls of race prejudice." Amid all this optimism, however, Johnson noted a closing door. "The ending of the creative period of the Blues," he observed, seemed "to be at hand." With its demise, "the whole folk creative effort of the Negro in the United States will come to a close." Before Muddy Waters, before Robert Johnson, before Lead Belly, the blues were (already) over. So it comes as something of a surprise that, more than six years after Johnson's eulogy, Huddie Ledbetter—a man who would later be identified as the "original vision"— would capture the attention of New York audiences.[1]

Though his performance career spanned nearly five decades, Ledbetter's emergence on the national stage came both too late and too early—after the period of what is now called classic blues had given way to jazz and swing and before the full flowering of blues' "revival," a movement that he arguably helped inaugurate. He was too late for commercial success, and commercial success came too late for him: one year after his death in 1949, the Weavers released their recording of "Goodnight, Irene," which went to number 1. Like "Goodnight, Irene," many of Ledbetter's recorded songs achieved broad recognition when they were covered by other artists, such as Kurt Cobain, who recorded "Where Did You Sleep Last Night," and Led Zeppelin, whose "Gallows Pole" became a staple of its live shows. As a singer of blues, ballads, ragtime, and country and western, Ledbetter's extraordinary reach and influence on twentieth-century popular music can scarcely be overestimated. Though Ledbetter was well known in his lifetime, widespread recognition of his impact on popular music has mostly come posthumously. As Janis Joplin reportedly put it: "It was Lead Belly first." In 1988, one hundred years after his birth, he was inducted into the Rock and Roll Hall of Fame, as was his contemporary and friend Woody Guthrie.

Better known as Lead Belly, Huddie Ledbetter's story has been told dozens of times, by turns sensationalist, triumphant, indignant, and hagiographic. Many of these accounts center on his working relationships with John and Alan Lomax, relationships that have long raised questions about what happens when folklorists and "the folk" meet. Why revisit this scene of encounter yet again, especially when the paradoxes around Ledbetter's so-called authenticity have already been explored widely? Taking into account Ledbetter's early years in the black entertainment industry, as well as the theatrical thinking employed by the Lomaxes and their contemporaries, sheds new light on Ledbetter's position within a history of theatrical blues in the twentieth century. An attention to the long arc of Ledbetter's career provides a more complete understanding of the singer not exclusively as a representative of the folk, nor as a hapless victim of his handlers, but as a "conscious artist," albeit one caught in the crosshairs of market and academic exploitation. Johnson characterized the conscious artist as "a creator as well as a creature"; indeed, Ledbetter struggled to assert his creative agency among those who were determined to paint him as an untutored simpleton.[2] Ledbetter, who absorbed the influences of classic blueswomen, migrated north to work in an environment of professional folklorists and record producers, and finally became part of the musical mobilization of the cultural front, serves as a hinge between the theatrical blues of the Southern tent show and a new political economy of blues' revival in the postwar years. His career encapsulates a transition from majority-black audiences to majority-white ones, as well as a shifting understanding of the blues from a self-consciously theatrical form to one supposedly vested with folk authenticity. And yet, as shall become clear, theatrical energy and repertoire remained present in Ledbetter's performances, albeit in a more submerged way.

The previous chapter explored the emergence of blues in the popular theater and its dissemination by female blues artists on the tent show and Theater Owners Booking Association (TOBA) circuits; this chapter asks: Where do blues' theatrical traditions and practices—so prevalent in the teens and twenties—*go* in the 1930s and 1940s? How did the changing industry of popular music impact live performance? What happens when collectors and folklorists get in on the act—when emphasis shifts from blues *on stage* to a self-conscious *staging* of the blues? While not the focus of my analysis here, theatrical blues continued to be performed in urban settings, particularly in the cabaret blues of Ethel Waters, Alberta Hunter, and Gladys Bentley, and in the lyrical works of Langston Hughes. While it may seem counterintuitive to turn this study away from this apparently obvious connection to the Southern tent show, I am interested in exploring the unexpected link between Southern variety and the postwar blues revival: that link is Ledbetter, someone not typically thought of as carrying the theatrical energy of a Waters or a Bentley. As a hinge between the theatrical classic blues of the early twentieth century and the revivalist folk strain of the post–World War II era, Ledbetter's career, which can be understood as a series of musical encounters with the popular theater, is an instructive lens through which to examine wide-ranging cultural and artistic transformations.

In the 1930s and 1940s, recordings and radio asserted their primacy over live performance, folklorists extended their influence, and the aesthetic and cultural valuation of authenticity became more fully entrenched.[3] In spite of these transformations, theatrical practice—and theatrical thinking—remained part and parcel of blues performance. At the same time, though, this period also witnessed the gradual abjection of the theatrical elements that were previously inherent to blues on the stage. This abjection resulted in the performance imperatives imposed by authenticity-obsessed revivalists and a determined and persistent forgetting of blues' theatricality by fans and historians alike. Still, the theatrical heritage of blues performance was plain at times, such as when Ledbetter incorporated a cakewalk into his live shows. An examination of the career of Ledbetter shows these forces at work and how he ultimately preserved not only the folk songs of the South but also the theatricality of the tent-show and vaudeville era. This examination is difficult but not impossible: on the one hand, Ledbetter left little conventional material, such as a traditional autobiography, for the performance historian to interpret. Yet if, in addition to the wide range of reviews, firsthand accounts, and liner notes, we consider Ledbetter's performance oeuvre, we find that he left a very large body of historical material indeed. Furthermore, to tell this story requires an examination of the performance careers of others, particularly John and Alan Lomax, performers in their own right, whose theatrical thinking shaped their stagings of Lead Belly. Theatrical thinking shaped the performances of all three men in unacknowledged, and often unobserved, ways.

While none of these men identified as theater artists, they were part of a loosely affiliated group of "theater folk": black and white intellectuals and artists of the 1930s and 1940s who married theatrical approaches to the collection and dissemination of folk music.[4] Among this group, many black artists and critics, such as Sterling A. Brown, Langston Hughes, and Zora Neale Hurston, saw folk music and theatrical performance as mutually enriching, if not coterminous. But as white folklorists began to take a greater role in shaping performances of black music for white audiences, a shift away from explicitly theatrical presentations of folk blues began to become apparent. As Michael Ann Williams notes, many midcentury theater folk eventually took "full flight" from "the inescapably theatrical nature" of early folkloric presentation.[5] While the previous chapter explored the live performances of blues within the popular theater, this chapter observes a shift to blues' collection, preservation, and dissemination by means of theatrical strategies. By sustaining a theatrical tradition while encountering new technologies of mass media and transformations in the political economy of musical production, Ledbetter crystallized the stakes of theatrical blues in the interwar period—from the threat of a resurgent minstrelsy to the thrilling possibility of global celebrity. In this chapter, I map the collision course between Ledbetter's employment of a performance repertoire derived from vaudeville and other forms of black entertainment and the Lomaxes' more ambivalent relationship to theatricality, something that they alternately embraced and disavowed. This struggle over Ledbetter's representation—a decades-long contest that played out both onstage and in the press—highlights the shifting role of theater in the presentation of blues and folk music, especially as folklorists, producers, and academics attempted to shape these performances, both onstage and on record(s). By examining Ledbetter's career, a number of larger trends in blues staging are illuminated: the privileging of the male bluesman, the rising significance of the site of the prison, a growing antitheatrical theatricalism, and the mobilization of blues for political and cultural movements.

THE FIRST FORTY-FIVE YEARS

The story of Lead Belly often begins with his "discovery" by John and Alan Lomax at Louisiana State Penitentiary (better known as Angola) in 1933 and often ends when the singer broke from these two in 1936.[6] Much less has been written about the decades of Ledbetter's life and career prior to his encounter with the Lomaxes, but an examination of these first forty-five years shows how Ledbetter gathered the resources and techniques that he later deployed in the deep struggle over the public presentation of "Lead Belly." Time and again Ledbetter attempted to make use of the elasticity and impermanence of live performance to make visible what James C. Scott calls the "hidden transcript," "those offstage speeches, gestures, and practices that confirm, contradict, or inflect what appears in the public transcript."[7] While Scott refers to the hidden transcript as that which occurs "offstage," Ledbetter, through code-switching and subterranean parody, occasionally found ways to play out a hidden transcript in full view of cultural power. His alteration of lyrics, his self-designed stationery, his play with tempo, and his dogged insistence on dancing: these evidentiary traces show us a Ledbetter determined to shape his public persona through tactical—if at times ambivalent—means.

Prior to his encounter with the folk-song hunters at the age of forty-five, Ledbetter's career directly maps onto the histories of theatrical blues explored in the previous chapter. Closely looking at and listening to Ledbetter's performances both before audiences and in recording studios reveal an artist deeply indebted to theatrical traditions of dance, vaudevillian comedy, and dramatic monologues, as well as to ragtime and Tin Pan Alley composers. Raised on the traveling tent shows and TOBA acts that integrated blues singing with recitation, comic skits, dancing, and acrobatics, Ledbetter regularly incorporated these elements—especially dance—into his live performances, retaining the variety format of the tent shows, even while the backdrops and elaborate costume changes, for the most part, disappeared. Though the techno-economic conditions of popular music's performance, distribution, and collection radically changed throughout his lifetime, Ledbetter, in his performances, preserved and reinvigorated not only nineteenth- and early twentieth-century African American folk traditions but also the theatrical elements, many of them innovated by women, that characterized tent-show blues.

A contemporary of Gertrude "Ma" Rainey's, Ledbetter was born in 1888 and grew up in Caddo Lake Parish, Louisiana. The region was primarily rural, but densely populated—Ledbetter later observed that "there were no white people for twenty miles around"—and provided a large and enthusiastic audience for touring entertainments.[8] Traveling musicians, vaudevillians, tent shows, and string bands consistently passed through the region, and local musicians, including Ledbetter, absorbed and reinvented the musical catalogs and choreographic innovations of their visitors. Ledbetter learned "Goodnight, Irene" from an uncle who most likely learned it from Haverly's American-European Mastodon Minstrels, who toured the region in the late 1880s.[9] Ledbetter picked up songs by ear, mostly "by listening to other singers," and only "once in a while off phonograph records," and quickly built his reputation as an entertainer, playing on a windjammer (a button accordion popularized in the nineteenth-century minstrel show), at sukey jumps (dances), and house parties.[10] Upon leaving Caddo Lake, Ledbetter immersed himself in the world of touring theatrical entertainments, particularly those headlined by blueswomen. He memorialized the barrelhouse world of Shreveport, Louisiana, in his "Fannin Street"; in New Orleans he took in the touring TOBA shows, including one starring Sissieretta Jones, the "Black Patti" of the Black Patti Troubadours. In Texas, sometime around 1912, he befriended Blind Lemon Jefferson; the two toured and performed throughout the South, with Ledbetter sometimes accompanying Jefferson's guitar with a tap dance.[11] In 1915 the pair arrived in Clarksdale, Mississippi, where Bessie Smith was in town, performing with the Florida Cotton Blossoms. Esther Mae "Mother" Scott, herself a renowned tent-show performer, introduced Ledbetter and Smith on that day.[12] In the mid-1920s, after his release from Texas's notorious Imperial State Prison Farm—better known by its location, Sugar Land—Ledbetter went to Houston, where he frequented the vaudeville theaters and saw performances by Ethel Waters, Ida Cox, Smith, whom he remembered singing "Ground Hog Blues," and Clara Smith, who sang "Death Letter Blues," a song that he eventually recorded. Ledbetter then joined the vaudeville circuit himself, though the specifics of his act remain largely unknown.[13] A studio photograph rarely circulated by folklore scholars or record producers but widely distributed by Ledbetter himself provides suggestive evidence of his stage persona during this period. In the photograph, likely taken in the 1920s, Ledbetter poses in full costume, wearing a tuxedo with tails, a bowler hat, and shiny black shoes. It is one of the few publicity shots in which he is smiling. Standing before a painted stock backdrop of a theatrical curtain and holding a cane, Ledbetter carries himself with a dancer's lightness, his right foot cocked, about to burst into movement. Captioned "only act featuring gun tap dancing," the photograph was prized by Ledbetter and played an important role in the artist's self-fashioning as theatrical and folk, urbane and rural, popular and vernacular.

In later years, Ledbetter used this vaudeville portrait to signify on the role played by photography in the construction of his public image as a supposedly premodern folk subject. When he designed his personal stationery in the mid-1930s, Ledbetter adorned it with this portrait—as well as with the more widely circulated photograph that had served as a frontispiece to the Lomaxes' *Negro Folk Songs as Sung by Leadbelly*.[14] In this photograph, which conformed with widespread photographic documentation of the rural poor in the Great Depression, the singer appears barefoot, clad in denim overalls, with a red bandana around his neck; perched atop some cotton sacks and oak barrels, he sings with his mouth open wide, a missing tooth clearly visible.[15] The copresence of these two very different photographs of the same performer underscored Ledbetter's ability to put on and take off stage personae at will—or under coercion. The banner headline, "Sweet Singer of the Swamplands"—a description bestowed by the press when Ledbetter first arrived in New York—did double duty, bridging the swamplands of the barefoot yodeler with the sweetness of the smiling young man in a tuxedo. These two distinct portraits of the same man destabilized the supposedly folksy realism of the barefoot singer unaware of the camera's presence, while also signifying on the medium of photography and its role in the production of truth claims and authenticities in the 1930s. Ledbetter could not have known in the 1920s how he would be portrayed in later years. But when faced with his representation in the white press and academic circles, he reached back into his own personal archive to offer up a persona that was not *more real* but *equally false*. Marketing himself as a protean performer on his business stationery, Ledbetter suggested that he could be anything producers or bookers wanted him to be—smiling vaudevillian or hapless rube—provided they were willing to pay.

Ledbetter's play with studio photography recalls Bessie Smith's disruption of Carl Van Vechten's portraits of the singer. Unlike Smith, however, Ledbetter made sharp distinctions between his public and private personae—a distinction he cemented through his very name. Ledbetter used naming to oscillate between his onstage and offstage identities, and, at times, to distance himself from the way "Lead Belly" was so often presented to the public. Ledbetter acquired the nickname "Lead Belly" in prison; the Lomaxes seized on the name, tying Ledbetter to his years of forced labor and presenting him as a carceral subject first and foremost. But Ledbetter stood apart from his star persona—and his years of incarceration—in his private communications. Preferring to be addressed by his given name and signing his letters "Huddie Ledbetter" or "H. Ledbetter," he marginalized his stage name in his offstage life.[16] On his stationery, too, he emphasized his given name. Though the two photographs of Ledbetter as theatrical vaudevillian and as rural folk received equal billing, "Huddie Ledbetter" appeared in a larger and more prominent typeface above the more familiar "Lead Belly." In his songs Ledbetter also made sure that everyone knew his given name. On several recordings of "Boll Weevil Blues," "Fannin Street," and "I'm On My Last Go Round"—and, we might imagine, in live performances—the singer inserted a coda: "If anyone should ask you people, who composed this song/Tell them it was Huddie Ledbetter, done been here, and gone!" As an assertive claim of authorship and ownership, Ledbetter's coda reminded listeners that, while Lead Belly may have been the singer, Ledbetter—the artist—was the composer. Frequently disrupting the ever-escalating meter of the song, the five syllables of *Huddie Ledbetter* nudge the listener into a new rhythm, one that produces attention. Ledbetter's sung coda attempted to close the book on his artistry and authorship by addressing the gap between his stage persona and his artistic contribution, as well as the Lomaxes' consistent assertion of copyright for his songs.[17]

Ledbetter was also musically indebted to the blueswomen of the teens and twenties. Though he was often shoehorned into singing folk songs, prison blues, and field hollers, Ledbetter's recordings are littered with popular songs, such as "Hesitation Blues," that he likely learned on the vaudeville circuit.[18] Ledbetter also carried forward a tradition of ribald double entendres, in songs such as "I'm Gonna Hold It in Her" and "What You Gonna Do with Your Long Tall Daddy." As Karl Hagstrom Miller and Elijah Wald astutely demonstrate—and Ledbetter's own repertoire made clear—the musical catalogs of Southern musicians were neither as racially segregated nor as musically homogeneous as record producers and folklore collectors wished them to be.[19] Ledbetter's musical fluency in blues, folk songs, and children's music, as well as ragtime and popular song, disregarded the "musical color line" that attempted to break apart white (country-and-western, hillbilly) vernacular genres from black (blues, work songs), while often shelving Tin Pan Alley tunes altogether. Ledbetter reported learning "Aggravatin' Papa" before World War I; though not published or recorded until the 1920s, this song circulated in the TOBA repertoire well before that. The melismatic style employed by Bessie Smith, Alberta Hunter, and Lucille Hegamin (as opposed to the more syllabic recording of Sophie Tucker) recurs throughout Ledbetter's oeuvre and is particularly pronounced in his a capella recordings. Likewise, his "Hawaiian Song," later made famous as "Hula Hula Love" by Buddy Knox in the 1950s, was a Tin Pan Alley composition that seized on the craze for Hawaiian music in the teens and was popularized by white female vaudeville stars. The song was recorded several times in the early teens, and then it disappeared from recordings for decades, until it reemerged on Ledbetter's *Last Sessions* in 1948.

Blues "are meant to be danced to," Ledbetter once remarked, an observation echoed by Hurston when she described her rationale for her theatrical revue *The Great Day*: "I explained . . . that music without motion was unnatural with Negroes."[20] For Ledbetter and many others who honed their craft on stages long before entering recording studios, music and dancing were coextensive. Until he was hobbled late in life by amyotrophic lateral sclerosis (ALS), Ledbetter, an expert in the buck-and-wing, soft-shoe, and tap, danced—and made music for dancing.[21] Yet dance is an aspect of Ledbetter's performance repertoire that has been underdiscussed, and it was the talent that was least encouraged when he began performing with and for the Lomaxes. Not all folklorists of this period rejected dance. Katherine Dunham and Hurston approached folk dance from an anthropological perspective and were dancers themselves; in the 1960s Alan Lomax committed himself to the study of dance, augmenting the notation system of Labanotation with his own system that he named Choreometrics.[22] But in the 1930s, John Lomax demonstrated little interest in dance, which had no place within the folk-literary tradition in which he was trained. Strategically selective in his accounts, he rarely discussed Ledbetter's dancing, except for some dismaying comments about the singer's tendency to "show off."[23]

Traces of Ledbetter's singing and dancing in performance do persist, however paradoxically, in his recordings, most notably in musical interludes. On vocalists' records these instrumental breaks or solos often functioned as opportunities for the band to take center stage; in performance these musical interludes more often functioned as dance breaks. Blind Lemon Jefferson's 1927 recording of "Hot Dogs," for example, sonically marks Ledbetter's danced accompaniment to Jefferson's song. "Hot Dogs" is a strange recording, in part because the song's raison d'être—it is a song about social dance and is accompanied by dancing—is unable to be fully communicated through the medium. The verses of the song, spoke-sung by Jefferson, stage the scene of a party being broken up by the law and are accompanied by a rhythmic tapping of the feet. Though Jefferson recorded the song as a solo in 1927, he had performed it years earlier as a duet with Ledbetter, who tapped between verses. "Hot Dogs," a record of a singing and dancing act, describes the dance in its very first line:

Feets all right, just now from the doctor
Give me my box, and let me try 'em again
Told you my feets gonna dance
These are hot dogs.

As the song continues, Jefferson's guitar resolutely accelerates, a musical signature that Ledbetter often employed in his own recordings, egging on the dancer. The lyrics outline the dancer's ability to evade pursuit, even while he continues to entertain: "Now on my feet's the Gypsy Hound/You oughta see me do the Black Bottom now." Whether or not Ledbetter actually danced the Black Bottom remains unknown, but "Hot Dogs" provides a tantalizing piece of sonic evidence of Ledbetter's career as a tapper.[24]

Ledbetter's biographers Charles Wolfe and Kip Lornell describe his sig-nature dances as percussive and humorous, illustrative of and heightening the situations of everyday life. Speaking from the stage—"My mama used to make flapjacks and here's the way she'd make 'em up"—Ledbetter il-lustrated the flapjack routine, slapping and tapping his hands and feet, percussively patting the body in a style reminiscent of nineteenth-century juba dances. In the "gun tap dance," Ledbetter mimed a duck hunt, using a cane or a broomstick to "shoot" in the air over the heads of the audience. While ostensibly innocuous, the dance played on Ledbetter's public reputa-tion as a hardened criminal. For the white audience members attending his concerts, the potential for the singer to violently erupt proved an irresist-ible draw; indeed, this expectation was seeded by the press, and by John Lomax himself, whose numerous references to "Lead Belly's knife" in his letters to his wife Ruby Terrill betrayed not only the folklorist's unrelent-ing discomfort but also his promotional savvy.[25] The "gun" in Ledbetter's hands, then, became a potent prop for the acting out of a scene widely imagined, both privately by individuals and publicly in the press. Osten-sibly used for hunting ducks, Ledbetter's cane teetered between weapon and prop, highlighting the unstable relationship between theatrical and actual violence—an instability that both Ledbetter and the Lomaxes would attempt to exploit for their own advantage as their relationship worsened.

Finally, though he may not have been, as his friend and photographer Abe Greiss described, "a man to make jokes," Ledbetter used dance to cre-ate bits of physical comedy, just as Rainey and other tent-show performers had done.[26] While Ledbetter playfully terrorized his audience with the gun dance, signifying on the rhetoric of criminality that seemed to follow him everywhere he went, his performance of a cakewalk-inspired dance com-mented on his own geographic command and linked him to a long tradition, peaking in the 1910s, of cakewalk performances in tent shows, vaudeville, and black musical comedy.[27] He introduced the dance by proclaiming: "I used to walk down to the levee with my gal and here's the way she'd walk." Led-better used the cakewalk to comically imitate men and women, black and white, and Northerners and Southerners of various classes from widely disparate regions, such as New Orleans, Shreveport, Los Angeles, and New York City. These riffs on the cakewalk highlighted the embodied differences of the imagined community of the nation, but they also showcased Ledbet-ter as well traveled and worldly, an astute observer of regional differences. Marking the collision of his own rural upbringing with the urban variety stage, and the elaborate cakewalk finales of the variety shows, Ledbetter's dance spoke to his own reinvention as an urban subject in the midst of migration. If black vernacular dance is, as Jayna Brown argues, "a collective dialogue of cultural and social self-formation under conditions of migration," then Ledbetter's geographically flexible cakewalk offered its audience a localized, embodied experience of migration and travel.[28] By showing how geographic, class, gender, and racial differences were not inherent but a matter of performance, Ledbetter's cakewalk showcased his virtuosity while cloaking him in a protective shield of imitative play.

If Ledbetter was so virtuosic, why did John Lomax discourage him from dancing? The fact that dance had little importance in the academic folk-literary tradition is one possible explanation. Twentieth-century dance's association with femininity is another: Lomax's stagings of Lead Belly's hypermasculine virility may have been threatened by the performer's aptitude for such a feminized skill. Additionally, black dance's close association with the theater threatened to undermine the integrity of the folklorists' project. Finally, and most significantly, choreography discloses craftsmanship. Far from an instinctual expression, dancerly aptitude betrays a studied cultivation of the body's abilities and the years of practice required of the performer: one may be "naturally" graceful, but it is difficult to argue the artlessness or the spontaneity of the time step. To watch an accomplished dancer, then, is to bear witness to physical labor, to acknowledge the process of considered creation, as well as the evidence of disciplined rehearsal. Ledbetter's expertise as a dancer belied the myth on which John Lomax depended—that of the instinctive, untutored Lead Belly, whose musical gifts were a supposedly natural outgrowth of his blackness, of incarceration and forced labor. On stage Ledbetter the dancer imperiled Lomax's attempts to promote him as an unskilled talent with no exposure to urban (or theatrical) performance training. Instead, bringing his full complement of skills to the stage and the studio, Ledbetter revealed himself to be everything Lomax did not want: learned, professional, and sophisticated.

Through their virtuosic play with speed and tempo, Ledbetter's dances signified on the choreographies of labor and the labor of choreography, offering his audiences a critique of performance as supposedly natural labor. Ledbetter developed a dance repertoire that signified on various levels and was legible to audiences with differing investments in his physically powerful and choreographically nimble body. Playing with modes of choreographic and rhythmic excess, Ledbetter's dances reproduced antebellum and prison plantation "scenes of subjection" while condemning those who demanded such spectacles of compulsory black entertainment. James Weldon Johnson, observing the long history of performance's multivocality, noted "in countless and diverse situations, song and dance have been both a sword and a shield for the Negro."[29] Nowhere was this more evident than in the Sugar Land Shuffle, a dance Ledbetter first performed before a small and influential audience, and for decades after at colleges, social clubs, and private parties. The governor of Texas, Pat Neff, who later took credit for Ledbetter's release from prison, famously enjoyed Ledbetter's singing and dancing at Sugar Land. In 1948 Ledbetter recalled Neff's visit to Sugar Land in 1924, accompanied by four cars full of white women, each of whom "would have these little automatics in their pocketbooks; they didn't take no chances."[30] Under the disciplinary gaze of the prison warden and guards, it is doubtful that the women would have had needed to use them. Coercive weapons that masqueraded as agents of self-defense, the pistols were the props of those who entered the scene determined to see it not as one of artistry but as one of titillating proximity to black men, always already established as a violent sexual threat to the virtue of white women. A seemingly innocuous bit of chitchat took on overtones of sexual violence and the threat of reprisal: in response to the governor's question, "How you feeling? Still dancing?" Ledbetter answered boldly, "I can dance all night." Responding to the impertinence, Neff shot back, "You are some nigger!"[31] Clad in a white suit, Ledbetter played several songs for the governor, including the direct address "Governor Pat Neff." In the song Ledbetter sings about "Sweet Mary," the narrator's wife, and the sadness they experience at their parting. Ledbetter played up the sentimental angle of incarceration, drawing on the trope of family separation that nineteenth-century abolitionists persuasively employed in their arguments against slavery: "I was watching him, but I was watching the women, too." "Goodbye, Mary, woo-hoo," he sighed. Staging a scene of counterfactual history, Ledbetter lyrically imagined a nearly unfathomable reversal of roles: "If I had you Governor Neff, like you got me/I'd wake up in the morning and I'd set you free." Making his empathic appeal, Ledbetter daringly encouraged Neff, and his female companions, to imagine the inversion of the racialized dynamics of power—and to imagine themselves as "got" by Ledbetter himself.

Ledbetter's Sugar Land Shuffle embodied the coextensivity of coerced labor and coerced entertainment. The dance imitated the one single activity that occupied the majority of Ledbetter's waking hours: picking cotton. Like in the companion song "Pick a Bale of Cotton," the tempo of the Sugar Land Shuffle relentlessly gathered steam; some described the dance as "frantic" and "demented," suggesting that both the guitar and Ledbetter's body had transformed into unregulated machines.[32] While both making light of and showcasing the physical demands of cotton picking, the Sugar Land Shuffle presented a crazed laborer, on the verge of losing control of his body, but working at the edge of his abilities at all times. That is to say: the song presented Ledbetter the laborer as the ideal profit generator, providing corporeal evidence not only of Ledbetter's fluency as a performer but also of his real economic value. His dance transformed the prisoner into a machineman; his performance, which charged ahead with music and movement beyond a speed that seemed humanly possible, made a case for his value to a penal system, itself a replacement, and a scant reinvention, of plantation labor. Ledbetter's demonstration of musical and agricultural mastery operated as a gesture of deference to Neff and his entourage, and doubly signified on black value. The Sugar Land Shuffle always provoked laughter, particularly as the music cooperated in the comedy, metronomically ramping up the speed of the "picking." The Sugar Land Shuffle allowed for the masking of criticism with comedy, communicating the physical demand of forced labor, be it picking or dancing. "Discursively reelaborat[ing] the conditions of subjection and repression" that organized the plantation-prison system, Ledbetter made dancing visible *as* compulsory labor.[33] Signifying on the injunction to "keep moving"—the primary demand placed on convict laborers—the Sugar Land Shuffle "kept moving" to the point of comic excess.[34] In a show of paternalism, Neff told Ledbetter that he would indeed release him, but only "after a while"; Neff wanted Ledbetter to remain in prison for a reason: "So you can pick and dance for me when I come down."[35] And Neff did come back—several times, including one time when he threw a party at Sugar Land, with Ledbetter serving as the entertainment.

DOCUMENTARY MOTIVES AND THEATRICAL THINKING: ZORA NEALE HURSTON

The zeal for the collection, documentation, and presentation of the folk in the 1930s was informed by multiple—and sometimes contradictory—economic, cultural, and political priorities. Nostalgic longings for a premodern, precapitalist past; anxiety about increasingly homogeneous consumer culture and mass media; nationalist desires to reconstitute the body politic in the midst of the Great Depression; and strengthening political and affective ties of the Popular Front formed the backdrop to the many projects of constituting "the folk," as undertaken by scholars, artists, entrepreneurs, and federal agencies. During the 1930s, scores of collectors, both amateur and professional, took up the task of documenting the supposedly disappearing vernacular cultures of American rural life. Well-known collectors such as John and Alan Lomax, Sterling A. Brown, Zora Neale Hurston, and

Katherine Dunham approached their subjects from varied intellectual and artistic perspectives; Brown and John Lomax came from folklore and literary studies and approached ballads as poetry, while Hurston and Dunham trained as anthropologists and translated their findings into choreography. What they shared—and what distinguished them, at least somewhat, from the executives of the booming race-records industry—was an abiding interest in live performance as both object and method. In addition to being collectors, they were themselves performer-interpreters of the work that they amassed; their fieldwork expeditions and collecting projects were mediated by and communicated through their own performances of poetry, song, theater, and dance.

The Lomaxes, who were deeply influenced by Hurston, married the Depression-era "documentary motive" to "theatrical thinking," an approach that manifested in their habits of spectatorship and in the hypothetical and realized performance projects they created in order to communicate their findings.[36] That is to say: in addition to collecting, they also identified the people they encountered as raw material for artistic—often theatrical—spectacle. The growing institutional power of academic folklore studies, often housed in departments of English, anthropology, and music, when combined with employment by Works Progress Administration programs, provided these collector-performers with material and institutional support for their investigations and stagings of black diasporic life.[37] Hurston's and the Lomaxes' involvement in the federal folk project was far from exceptional: the Works Progress Administration sent thousands of volunteers into the field in the 1930s; under the auspices of the Federal Writers' Project, the Federal Theatre Project, and the Federal Music Project, they completed the American Guide series, recorded thousands of interviews, created pageants for casts of hundreds, and photographically documented urban and rural life throughout the country. Into this frenzied milieu of accumulation stepped Ledbetter, whose "discovery" and promotion by the Lomaxes has been widely recounted. The ongoing debates about what happened between these three men have, in turn, exemplified the ethical and intellectual stakes and debates of folklore studies, including the principles of documentation, the risk of commercial exploitation, and the role of the scholar-entrepreneur in the constitution of folk authenticity. Though returning to the story of Ledbetter and the Lomaxes revisits well-trod territory, my aim here is to contextualize their encounter as one that took place in an environment where *theatricality* and *theatrical thinking* played a key role in the conceptualization and presentation of vernacular culture. Building on performance templates laid down by Hurston—a figure often marginalized in this history—the Lomaxes' methods of collecting and disseminating Ledbetter's songs were deeply informed by the frames and practices of theatrical spectacle.

Harlem Renaissance–era black intellectuals and artists often disagreed about the stakes of valorizing the vernacular culture of the black South; these arguments were exacerbated by growing class conflict in Harlem, where most intellectuals were based, and where many poor and uneducated Southern migrants were settling. Even for those who celebrated "the folk," theatrical representation of folkways remained suspect, as the specter of minstrelsy continued to vex artistic folk production. Transforming Southern folkways into urban artistic spectacles risked playing into forms of racial and racist spectatorship that painted poor Southern blacks as primitive and childlike, allowing spectators to romanticize a rural past that never was, even as they remained blind to the urbanization that was happening at that very moment. Others, such as Brown, whose poetry integrated the lyrics and formal qualities of folk blues with modernist literary style, felt that this material represented the great cultural store of black life and could and should be recognized as such. And even Johnson, who wrote the preface for Brown's 1931 *Southern Road*, later acknowledged that the issue was more complex than he had realized.[38]

But for some artists—particularly Brown, Hughes, and Hurston—who sought to ground discussions of black life in the arts and ways of "the folk," the link between theatrical and folk expression was an obvious, indeed, central, tenet. Brown, whose attendance at Missouri tent shows inspired him to write "Ma Rainey," employed what he called a "socio-historical approach." His poem serves as lyrical reflection as well as theatrical criticism, replete with sociological analysis of the migration of both performer and audience.[39] In Brown's opinion, drama and blues music were best considered jointly, under the category of lyrical and vernacular folk poetry; his 1937 book, *Negro Poetry and Negro Drama*, brought poetry and drama together under a common literary critical umbrella (notably, he reserved fiction for a separate investigation).[40] Examining poetry, ballads, and spirituals alongside the contemporaneous folk drama, Brown invited his readers to think about blues alongside his beloved *The Green Pastures* or—with more tempered enthusiasm—the "Negro theatrical tradition" of "the song and dance show."[41]

The Green Pastures, one of the most significant black theater events of the 1930s, brought to the surface complicated relations between the form and politics of the pastoral and the theatrical and economic relations between Broadway and black vernacular forms. In the black-cast musical, which James Weldon Johnson described as "a play in which the line between the sublime and the ridiculous is so tenuous that the slightest strain upon it could bring the whole play tumbling down," the white playwright Marc Connelly dramatized well-known biblical scenes set in an imagined South, including the expulsion from the Garden of Eden, the flood, and the exodus of the Jews from Egypt—a scene that drew comparisons to the Middle Passage in some of the show's reviews.[42] The renowned Hall Johnson Choir punctuated the action with spirituals. A crowd-pleasing hit, *The Green Pastures* ran for 640 performances, won the Pulitzer Prize for Drama in 1930, was revived twice (in 1935 and 1951), and was released as a hugely popular film in 1936. White audiences were rapturous while many black critics and audiences were divided; some rebuked the representation of black spirituality as naive and childlike, but others saw the musical as an astounding theatrical achievement.[43] Beloved by Brown and Johnson (and by John Lomax and his wife), derided by Hughes, and treated skeptically by Hurston, *The Green Pastures* operated as something of a litmus test for those engaged in debates about the theatrical presentation of black folk. Brown revered the musical, calling it "a miracle in the medieval sense of a biblical story presented upon the stage, and in several more important ways," which included "the length of its run," its "tenderness and reverence," the "beautifully compelling acting," and the "perfect appropriateness of the sonorous Hall Johnson spirituals to the narrative.[44] While noting the potential for the production to tip over into stereotype in the hands of less accomplished performers, Johnson called it the "high mark of the Negro in the theatre."[45] And Ledbetter himself was well aware of the musical's hold on the public imagination: it was allegedly his desire to play the part of "De Lawd" in a remake of the 1936 film that drew him to Hollywood in 1944.[46]

Though Hughes and Hurston, like Brown, saw the theater as an ideal place to represent black vernacular forms (a project they would attempt together, in their ill-fated play *Mule Bone*), they objected to *The Green Pastures*, even as they were motivated by its financial successes. Their objections, especially seen in light of their own attempts to stage the folk, shine a light on aesthetic and political stakes of collecting and staging vernacular forms in the 1930s. In his essay "Trouble with the Angels" (1935), Hughes acerbically describes a thwarted strike attempted by black "angels" of *The Green Pastures* to protest segregated theaters in Washington, DC. Describing *The Green Pastures* as a play "about the charming darkies who drink eggnog and fry fish in heaven, and sing almost all the time," Hughes reserves his greatest criticism for the actor playing De Lawd, who sided with the white producers in discouraging the strike; Hughes proclaimed him "Uncle Tom come back as God." Alert to the commoditization of the folk for the profit of white playwrights and producers, Hughes reluctantly concludes that larger economic forces trump all: "Nobody really wanted to sacrifice anything for race pride, or decency, or elementary human rights. No, they only wanted to keep on appearing in a naïve dialect play about a quaint funny heaven full of niggers."[47] For Hughes, and for Hurston too, *The Green Pastures* was not a miracle but a cautionary tale, one that demonstrated a white audience's hunger for nostalgic representations of black contentment. Though she praised Richard Harrison's performance as De Lawd, Hurston criticized the musical's reductive representation of black spirituality: "The Negro's idea of heaven . . . is certainly not dusting out a plantation boss's office with aprons on their wings. Nothing like work and bossy white folks in our heavenly concept."[48] It was perhaps *The Green Pastures* that Hurston had in mind when she distinguished *The Great Day* by explaining in *Dust Tracks on a Road*: "I aimed to show what beauty and appeal there was in genuine Negro material, as against the Broadway concept, and it went over."[49]

Though widely remembered for her literary and anthropological work, including novels, stories, and collected folktales, Hurston seemed destined, for a time, for a theatrical career.[50] Recent studies of Hurston by Anthea Kraut and Daphne A. Brooks have emphasized the anthropologist and author's commitment to and pleasure in singing and dancing. Additionally, the discovery in 1997 of ten previously unpublished plays written by Hurston underscores the extent to which she was—and quite likely considered herself—a "theater person," particularly in the early days of her career, before she achieved widespread literary recognition. Like Bessie Smith and countless other young black Southern women, Hurston's route out of the South was through the traveling theater. In 1915 Hurston was in her early twenties (but, in a theatrical twist of her own, pretended to be much younger) when she left Florida to serve as a ladies' maid in an all-white Gilbert and Sullivan touring company, traveling with them for eighteen months. In *Dust Tracks on a Road*, she reflects on the practical jokes she endured and the camaraderie of theater people on the road. Her affective and sensorial ties to the theater are evident: "My feet mounted up the golden stairs as I entered the stage door of that theater. The sounds, the smells, the back-stage jumble of things were all things to bear me up into a sweeter atmosphere. I felt like dancing towards the dressing room when it was pointed out to me. But my friend was walking with me, coaching me *how to act*, and I had to be as quiet and sober as could be."[51] Feigning youth, acting unmoved by the thrill of the greasepaint: though she worked backstage, Hurston was immediately aware that she too was an actress. In later years, Hurston's theatrical concerts and plays garnered such interest that, in 1934, she faced a crossroads in the form of two compelling professional opportunities. The president of Fisk University, Thomas Jones, invited Hurston to apply for a faculty position in drama, where she would teach her own methods of staging black folklore; Jones offered to augment Hurston's training by paying for her to study at Yale for a year. The next month the Julius Rosenwald Fund invited Hurston to apply for a fellowship to study for a PhD in anthropology at Columbia University. As communications with Fisk faltered, Hurston chose Columbia.

Though she wrote fewer plays and staged fewer concerts and revues after 1935, Hurston's conviction that "the Negro material is eminently suited to drama and music," that "it *is* drama and music," meant that her theatrical concerns and anthropological concerns were never far apart, an interdependence demonstrated by her theatrical thinking and creative approach to the dissemination of her collected materials.[52] In Hurston's recollections of her earliest days, she thinks of herself as a performer. Her account of joining the Gilbert and Sullivan troupe demonstrates her savvy awareness of a constant oscillation between performer and audience: eager to serve the company's lead actress, Hurston becomes one herself. In both "How It Feels to Be Colored Me" and *Dust Tracks on a Road*, Hurston describes watching white Northerners drive through her Florida town on their way to Orlando: "The front porch might seem a daring place for the rest of the town, but it was a gallery seat to me. My favorite place was atop the gate-post. Proscenium box for a born first-nighter. Not only did I enjoy the show, but I didn't mind the actors knowing that I liked it." Calling out to the passing cars, though, Hurston herself became the spectacle: "They liked to hear me 'speak pieces' and sing and wanted to see me dance," she writes. For Hurston, then, the front porch was both box and stage, and the interpenetrating gaze of two mutually curious parties—what Hurston would later memorialize in her famous phrase "the spy glass of anthropology"—generated a necessarily theatrical situation, a "show" that regularly called into question who was on stage and who was in the audience.[53] This deft reversal and inversion of her role—as insider, as outsider, as anthropologist, as performer—became a signature of Hurston's public and intellectual life.

Hurston's 1932 *The Great Day* arguably wrote the playbook for the theatricalization of vernacular music and dance in the 1930s.[54] Performed to great acclaim and described by Hurston as "a dramatization of a working day on a Florida railroad camp with the [Bahamian] Fire Dance for a climax," *The Great Day* was a discrete performance that enclosed numerous other performances and incorporated both Southern and Afro-Caribbean vernacular music and dance in a variety format that offered its audiences spirituals, work songs, and a performance of "East Coast Blues" by a character named Maimie, a reference, perhaps, to the popular blues singer Mamie Smith, or to Bessie Smith, whom Hurston and Hughes had seen perform in a vaudeville show in Macon, Georgia, in 1927.[55] Hurston prioritized the social and economic conditions of musicking and strove to re-create those environments—the work camp, the juke joint—where music was made, and she presented vernacular music and dance in a form that resembled a black musical revue. As Anthea Kraut chronicles, Hurston's production was widely influential, and bits and pieces of her choreographic and directorial work popped up in numerous theater and dance spectacles throughout the 1930s.[56]

The Great Day was a touchstone for John and Alan Lomax who, like Hurston, brought conceptual architectures of the theater to bear on their understanding of black vernacular culture.[57] Hurston's role in shaping the Lomaxes' modes of presentation has gone largely undiscussed—a casualty, perhaps, of an attempt to establish the Lomaxes as the father figures of modern ethnomusicology and ethnographic practice. But in the early years of the Lomaxes' collecting—a time when theatrical presentation was understood as broadly compatible with the collection of vernacular music—Hurston's work, as a collector, a director, and a choreographer of theatrical spectacles, reverberated throughout New York and the ethnographic community. She and John Lomax exchanged letters; no doubt well aware of her skill and influence, he requested that they work together, though there is no evidence that they ever did.[58] Alan Lomax himself worked directly with Hurston, traveling on a fieldwork expedition with her to Georgia and Florida; though he did not often directly speak of her influence on him, he memorialized Hurston after her death in *Sing Out!* magazine, describing her theatrical productions as "brilliant." To Lomax, Hurston was first and foremost a performer: "Anyone who ever had the pleasure, as I did, of spending time with Zora, can testify that she was no reserved scientist, but a racconteur [sic], a singer and a dancer who could bring the culture of her people vividly to life."[59] Like Hurston, John Lomax sought to turn his collected music into theatrical spectacle, a desire that is evident in the letters he exchanged with his wife, Ruby Terrill. It was this theatrical approach—with Lomax as both performer and producer—that decisively informed his encounter with Ledbetter in 1934.

Like Hurston, John Lomax played a central role in shaping the evolving relationship between theatrical practice and blues performance; throughout
his career, he shared Hurston's search for "a variety of formal possibilities
for the representation of black rural folk culture."[60] Live performance was
paramount among these formal possibilities. For three decades Lomax, a
man who referred to himself as a "ballad hunter," performed the songs he
collected—both the trail songs of cowboys and the work songs of prisoners.[61] Initially improvisatory, and then scripted and honed through years of
repetition, Lomax's touring lecture-performances both supplemented his
income and promoted folk-song appreciation, collection, and preservation.
Lomax's legacy has paled in comparison to that of his son, whose accumulated recordings of the world's vernacular music composed a massive portion of the Archive of American Folk Song at the Library of Congress. The
reproducibility of Alan Lomax's records, many of which have since been released as commercial recordings, stands in sharp contrast to the ephemeral,
nonreproducible performances of his father. Like Hurston, the elder Lomax
began his collecting work before recording technologies became portable,
affordable, and reliable enough to regularly take into the field. Late in his
career, he did take these recording machines into the field, but it was Alan
Lomax's career that was thoroughly defined by the possibilities offered by
recording and mass media. I draw attention to John Lomax's career here
not to offer it as merely a foil to the work of his son but to emphasize the
performance practices at the heart of folklore studies and to suggest these
practices' long-lasting influence on the staging and presentation of musicians, particularly Ledbetter.

Though trained at Harvard by George Lyman Kittredge and Barrett
Wendell, themselves largely responsible for incorporating the study of
ballads and folk poetry into the curriculum of the English department,
John Lomax declined to pursue a traditional academic path in favor of a
freelance career as a singing lecturer. When Lomax began his studies in
the first decade of the twentieth century, studying folk music meant ob-
taining or creating sheet music: music was collected and archived—made
material—by textual notation. Yet this model of collection dissatisfied Lomax; instead, he sought the wealth of "made-up" songs not written down
anywhere, songs subject to repetition and revision over time. Fieldwork
and performance, then, became Lomax's method for the collection and
circulation of these made-up songs. Once he had learned the songs while

out in the field, Lomax traveled widely, staging lecture-performances for curious audiences at universities, prep schools, and social clubs. Lomax alternately referred to these events as "lectures," "recitals," "shows," and "performances"; at almost all of his public appearances, Lomax sang his collected material.[62] Just as Hurston had interrupted the action of *The Great Day* with an improvised explanatory lecture, Lomax balanced showmanship with rhetorical explanation. Academic audiences offered him his greatest successes: in the 1920s Lomax made a name for himself among folklorists as a star of the Modern Language Association's annual meeting, where he not only reported on his cowboy ballad findings but regularly performed them in full yodel, much to the delight of his audience. During the 1920s and 1930s, Lomax emerged as a preeminent touring performer of folk music in the United States. According to his own records, he had an aggregate audience of thousands, perhaps even tens of thousands, during his years on his lecture-performance circuit. Lomax, who was more widely traveled than many in his audiences, often students, transformed the scenes he witnessed on his travels into a drama of national mobility in which he was both surrogate and star; inviting his audiences to experience a bit of armchair tourism, he solicited their identification with *him*, even as he sang the songs of others, including Mexican cowboys and black prisoners.

John Lomax's lecture-performances were informed by an embrace of the power of performance *and* by antitheatrical prejudices—a conflicted and sometimes contradictory stance that would have lasting impact on the conventions that governed the staging of black vernacular music. On the one hand, Lomax demonstrated an attitude and an aptitude for performance, and he was clearly invested in the body-to-body transmission of folk material that performance allowed. In addition to the performances he staged, his letters are filled with many other theatrical events that he imagined. But even though he embraced performance, Lomax, at least rhetorically, abjured theatricality, both in his own performances and in those of Ledbetter. Like Hurston, Lomax embraced the paradox of performativity as constitutive of authenticity but, unlike Hurston, he felt the need to expel theatricality from the equation. There is a disquieting sense that Lomax's performance career undoes the significance of his archival project, an attitude captured by Roger D. Abrahams, who observes contemporary folklorists' and ethnomusicologists' discomfort with Lomax's "slippery way of reporting texts" that "didn't seem to cleave to the standards of authenticity thought to record more accurately the waifs and strays of old-time Singing America."[63] Abrahams's comment suggests that, for scholars of folklore, "standards of authenticity" can be—and often are—undone by theatricality's proximity to fiction and fakery. Rarely acknowledged, however, is the extent to which folklore's objects have been theatrically produced, something both Hurston and the Lomaxes took on with gusto. In doing so, they undid the binaries at the heart of the documentary enterprise—authentic and faux, folk and commercial, rural and urban—and revealed the radical instability that theatrical practices of inversion, parody, and excess contributed to the supposed objectivity of documentary.

Even though Lomax used performance as a strategy for the transmission of folk music, he tempered his performances with antitheatrical choices, embodying what Charlotte Canning calls the "seemingly insoluble paradox" between a desire for a highly theatrical event and the simultaneous reluctance to acknowledge the theatricality that pervades that work. This "antitheatrical theater," she suggests, was at the heart of the Chautauqua circuit performances of the early twentieth century, performances that both influenced John Lomax as a young man and in which he took part as an older man.[64] Wary of becoming "a cheap theatrical hustler," Lomax always attempted to redeem the theatrical with utilitarian value. Taking care to balance entertainment with education, Lomax frequently included Professor William Lyon Phelps's assessment of his lecture-performances on his promotional circular: "He succeeds to a high degree in combining definite instruction with continuous entertainment."[65] These promotional materials emphasized Lomax's ability to transmit not only information but also what T. A. Armstrong, president of the Waco Press Club, describes in the circular as "the reality, the truth to life[,] . . . [the cowboys'] stride and stridency, and their rough tang"—that is to say, the embodied, gestural life of his folk-song subjects. In short, Lomax's lecture-recitals embodied an antitheatrical theatricality that disavowed the practices of the theater even while they were invoked.

In spite of all of his expert imitation, clothes and costume were flashpoints for Lomax's anxieties about theatrical "hustling." In the circular Armstrong further described Lomax's performance as follows: "Hard-riding centaurs, herding migrating cattle among the cacti, gallop across imagination's stage so plainly that it becomes unbelievable that they are conjured up by the professorial gentleman who stands talking alone behind the lecture table in wing collar and drawing-room clothes." Championing Lomax for the theatrical "truth" of his performance, even though he spurned the masking effect of costuming, Armstrong elevated "imagination's stage" above any kind of sartorial transformation that Lomax himself might have enacted. Lomax's "conjuring," the testimonial implies, was achieved not by the illusory strategies of theatricality but by the affectively communicative power of speech and song. It was the spirit of the cowboy or convict laborer that mattered, not full-blown resemblance. Just as in the Chautauqua entertainments, the dispensation of the visual, feminized properties of illusion—especially costume and makeup—allowed Lomax to retain both his masculinity and his scholarly authority.[66] A white man, Lomax presented himself as a corporeal linchpin—a transitive figure who invited mostly white university and prep-school audiences to identify across space and time with the black, Mexican, and Native migrant laborers whose songs he sang. This identification was unidirectional, however, and founded upon Lomax's rejection of absolute mimesis. By refusing to costume himself as a cowboy, he avoided a complete performance of minstrelsy, but he did not circumvent it altogether. Ultimately, he enabled audiences to identify not with the cowboy but with the journeys of both the cowboy and Lomax, journeys that Lomax superimposed through a strategy of antitheatrical theatricalism.

He came by it honestly: a similar tug-of-war between the avowal and renunciation of theater had already taken place among the senior faculty during Lomax's years at Harvard. The adjacency of theater studies and folklore studies at Harvard in the early twentieth-century academy draws attention to the absent presence of theater and theatricality at the heart of early folklore studies, even though theatricality later became the very quality against which folklore studies defined itself. Though theater studies and folklore studies appear to be held at a distance by their objects of study, their methods, and their aesthetic orientations, they simultaneously emerged from English departments in the early decades of the twentieth century. That is to say, theater studies and folklore studies are, in the words of Shannon Jackson, "now-different fields [that] were once-the-same."[67] While contemporary folklore studies and theater studies have relatively little to do with each other (and never were, of course, exactly the same), they share a common intellectual and institutional genealogy. As the Harvard English department struggled through a "shift . . . from a classical to a vernacular curriculum," theater and folklore studies, bound together by their intellectual roots in philology and rhetoric, emerged as fields that, in different ways, approached literature as both a written and an oral form.[68] This shared interest in the oral dimension of literary study accounts for the proximity of dramatic interpretation and folkloric performance and helps explain the amalgamation of theatrical thinking and folk-song collection that Lomax brought to his work. Still, the determined rejection of theater by both Lomax and his mentors indicates nothing so much as the dangerous contiguity shared by folklore studies and theater studies.

Lomax's time at Harvard is also significant because of the way folklore scholars at Harvard mapped their relationship to theater along gendered lines. Under the supervision of Kittredge and Wendell, literary folklore studies at Harvard formulated itself as masculine, rigorous, and scientific, in opposition to the fey, feminized "pretty talking" of theater studies and speech elocution. Jackson underscores the gendered dimensions of field formation: "Emerging literature professors worked to define their object of knowledge with clear rules to replace nebulous belletrism and to fend off their association with the feminine. German philology entered and/or was imported precisely to lend the study of literature this necessary positivism."[69] The positivist methods that Kittredge and his student Lomax adopted implicitly gendered folk-song collection and performance as masculine. Throughout the long arc of his career, Lomax emphasized the virility of the folk-song project—and, eventually, that of Ledbetter, Lomax's most famous collaborator. This gendering of folklore studies as masculine resulted in a dismissal of feminized theatrical forms and, ultimately, contributed to the severe undervaluing of women's theatrical blues. When Ledbetter was "showing off," he was not just upstaging the Lomaxes; in dancing and preserving female-authored vaudevillian traditions, he was undermining the virility of the folk-song project. Ledbetter, therefore, is staged as the apex of blues' masculinity and virility, *replacing* women as "original" blues singers by means of a concerted antitheatrical theatricalism.

Lomax transformed his collected material into lecture-performances, and he also imposed his theatrical thinking on his folk-song subjects. Theatrical thinking, as I have begun to suggest, is a perceptual act imposed on the quotidian events of the everyday: it is the act of perceiving another *as* theatrical. Josette Féral sums up this "process," which she calls theatricality, as "a 'gaze' that postulates and creates a distinct, virtual space belonging to the other. . . . Such actions create a cleft that divides space into the 'outside' and the 'inside' of theatricality. This space is the space of the 'other'; it is the space that defines both alterity and theatricality." Féral suggests that anyone or anything can be constituted as theatrical; the spectator determines the Other as such and takes up a theatrical point of view. And yet certain subjects, spaces, and places are more prone to this imposition of the theatrical gaze than others. Like Mary Louise Pratt's analysis of the colonial logic of travel and touristic perception, Féral's corroboration of theatricality and alterity invites us to consider how the Eurocentric encounters with (racial, ethnic, national) Others encourage habits of perception that instill theatrical frames.[70]

Theatrical thinking and looking framed Lomax's encounters with racial and spatial Others, allowing him to position them as particularly given to performance. In their letters, he and Ruby Terrill constantly transformed his encounters with his Southern musicians into hypothetical artistic spectacles. Writing to Terrill in August of 1933, when he made his first visit to the notorious Mississippi State Penitentiary (Parchman Farm), Lomax described a singer nicknamed "Lifetime," who sang of the "midnight special": "The simple directness and power of this primitive music, coupled with descriptions of a life where force and other elemental influences are demonstrating impresses me more deeply every time I hear it. A play built around the theme of the imprisoned Black and the songs he has made about his life and work would probably have more appeal than did 'Green Pastures.'"[71] Lomax and Terrill's affective connection to *The Green Pastures* is evident in their letters. Corresponding about the musical was an important part of their early courtship: he expressed his wish to escort her to the touring production in Austin, while she took his youngest daughter, Bess, to a return engagement while he was away.[72] A frequent touchstone that was both personal and emotional, *The Green Pastures* was also a dramaturgical structure that helped Lomax make sense of the musical performances he witnessed in the Louisiana and Mississippi prisons.

Lomax, who was careful to set the stage and describe the characters and scenarios of both the formal performances and the everyday events he observed, constantly transformed the "scenes" he witnessed in prison into hypothetical performance events, anticipating both his lecture-performances and his staging of Ledbetter. Though *The Green Pastures* is the only play he mentions in his letters to Terrill, Lomax repeatedly presented the black prisoners he met as always already aestheticized and as possible participants in his entrepreneurial ventures. In a letter from Clemens Unit prison in Brazoria, Texas, that echoes the letter written from Parchman a few months earlier, he wrote: "Yesterday morning I read about 75 outgoing letters from the convicts to their wives, sweethearts, women, mothers and sisters—revealing, pathetic, saddening because of their immaturity—a book based on such correspondence would be of great human interest."[73] Terrill also got in on the act; after attending an evening dance performance by Ted Shawn and His Male Dancers in Austin, she suggested to Lomax: "I should like to see him portray some of your negro work songs. He gave a group of play and labor songs . . . in dance movements, of course. 'Great God Almighty' would be a good one for him. He did one last night called 'Cutting Cane.'"[74] Likely inspired by Hurston and her success, Lomax and Terrill long wanted to transform the material he collected into *something*: a black-cast musical, a book, or a dance concert.[75]

In his collecting expeditions and in his lecture-performances, Lomax became the site, sight, and sound of spatial—and racial—difference, privileged as one who could move with ease between men of letters and men of the land. Forgoing the blueswoman's train for the collector's automobile, with "the little roll of cowboy songs that [he] carried in his trunk," he shuttled between prep schools and prisons, proudly recording the tens of thousands of miles accumulated by his "brave little Ford." Lomax's lecture-performances remapped the imagined community of the nation, producing what he would later call *Our Singing Country*.[76] But as Lomax transferred his interest from trail cowboys to prisoners—and one prisoner in particular—his idealization of mobility shifted too. Bringing theatrical thinking to bear on his travels and on his collecting, Lomax longed to stage a musical drama built around the musicians that he met on the road; when he met Ledbetter, he found in the Louisiana singer a collaborator who could star in that drama of circulation.

BRIDGE: LEDBETTER MEETS LOMAX

The theatrical thinking that John Lomax had long employed in his collection and performances of vernacular music came to fruition in his staging of Lead Belly. Still, when Ledbetter replaced Lomax as the featured performer in his shows, the drama of circulation in which Lomax was so invested had to be adjusted. The romance of the road now stood in sharp contrast to the fact of black imprisonment.[77] The Lomaxes changed tactics. No longer highlighting the thrill of traveling the open road by automobile, they—with the cooperation of the press—identified song, and prison blues in particular, as a means to "freedom."[78] In a 1934 report to the Library of Congress, they justified their attention to prison populations: "Folk songs and folk literature flourish, grow—are created, propagated, transformed—in the eddies of human society, particularly where there is isolation and homogeneity of thought and experience. These communities of Negro men and women, shut out from the clamor of the world, thrown back almost entirely on their own resources for entertainment, lonely, few with any background of reading, naturally resort to song."[79] Like many collectors, the Lomaxes reasoned that prison populations were "protected" from the corrupting influence of radio and rapidly transforming popular culture; what's more, work songs flourished in the forced labor of Southern prisons. Ledbetter thus found himself implicated in a dramaturgy that required imprisonment in order to represent and romanticize mobility.

John Lomax announced his coup de théâtre in a 1934 letter to Oliver Strunk at the Library of Congress: "When I come to Washington in January I'll bring [Lead Belly] along and give you . . . a specimen of Negro music as interpreted by a real Negro."[80] After his August 1934 release from Angola prison, Ledbetter traveled to Marshall, Texas, where he renewed his acquaintance with Lomax and became his personal servant, serving as both driver and body man. Though "free" from the compulsory agricultural labor of Angola, Ledbetter's dubious employment by Lomax underscores the muddled line between slavery and emancipation, as the singer passed from one mode of servitude and economic exploitation to another.[81] The two traveled throughout the South that autumn, and Ledbetter aided in the song-collecting process. Ledbetter, who served as an ambassador to the African American communities they visited, both in and out of prisons, was regularly enlisted to perform a few songs in order to show the informants what kind of music Lomax was seeking. That December Lomax and Ledbetter traveled to Philadelphia, where Ledbetter replaced Lomax as the featured performer at the Modern Language Association's annual meeting, illustrating the academic talks given by the Lomaxes. The line between scholarly inquiry and racialized entertainment was thin: Ledbetter performed at the meeting's smoker, an evening entertainment for the academics in attendance, as well as during John Lomax's paper presentation the following day. At these "shows," as Lomax called them, "Leadbelly passed his hat both times, even among the lofty audience of Comp. Lit. academics."[82] For Lomax, academic stardom was his long-awaited triumph; for Ledbetter, it was the price of "the boss's" success. The Lomaxes then brought Ledbetter to New York, where the white press enthusiastically received him. The black press was more circumspect, questioning whether Ledbetter was a fit representative of black uplift. In response to James Weldon Johnson's favorable review of the book *Negro Folk Songs, as Sung by Lead Belly*, Floyd J. Calvin, a columnist for the *New York Amsterdam News*, opined: "We might humbly inquire, what might Professor Johnson's students of creative literature at Fisk think when they note that our No. 1 critic glorifies an avowed murderer and convict and leaves unsung those who really try to raise the status of the group."[83]

With the cooperation of the press, the Lomaxes crafted a Lead Belly narrative that framed the remaining years of the singer's career, as well as his legacy. The parameters of this legend are familiar: with John Lomax's assistance, the convict Lead Belly's recordings found their way to Governor O. K. Allen of Texas, who released him from prison due to his talent. A headline in the *Philadelphia Independent* summed up this new point of view: "Two Time Dixie Murderer Sings Way to Freedom! The Magic of Song!"[84] Often overlooking the compromised conditions of Ledbetter's employment, the rhetoric of freedom advanced the power of song to liberate the body, as well as rehabilitate the soul.[85] Music assumed a presumed power—a "magic"—that released the wandering minstrel to the road and, eventually, led him to the freedom, and the stardom, of the stage. This Lead Belly legend, a simplistic rendering of a complicated artist, has been assiduously dismantled, an undertaking that I shall not repeat here.[86] Rather, I would like to examine the significance of the Lead Belly legend for Ledbetter's post-Lomax performance persona and to think about the ways the myth itself traveled from the convention halls of the Modern Language Association's annual meeting to the stage of the Apollo Theater. Pursuing these enactments of the Lead Belly myth allows for a glimpse not only at the way folklorists framed the blues during this period but also at the dilemma faced by a performer attempting to slip the yoke of a character too successfully created.

In all iterations of the Lead Belly legend, musical virtuosity—and the affective power of music—trumped the juridical power of the state. A quarter century after Ledbetter left Angola, Alan Lomax was still describing him as "a man whose music melted prison bars."[87] Writing to the Library of Congress in 1934, John Lomax established the story he would publicly maintain for the rest of his life: "My driver and assistant . . . is a Negro ex-convict, Lead Belly by name, who two months ago sang a petition for pardon on a record, addressed to Governor O. K. Allen. I carried that record to Baton Rouge, a hundred miles away. The Governor listened to it, and then pardoned Lead Belly."[88] But the evidence does not corroborate Lomax's account; both Benjamin Filene and Nolan Porterfield have persuasively demonstrated that Ledbetter's release was scheduled due to good behavior and time served, and that his recording had little or no impact on Allen.[89] Lomax never backed down from his tale, even though he knew that his assertion was false. In a footnote in *Negro Folk Songs as Sung by Lead Belly*, Lomax acknowledged that Ledbetter was pardoned for "good time," and in a 1934 letter to Terrill, he confessed: "He thinks I freed him. He will probably be of much help."[90] Lomax's story was propagated by the press, which described Ledbetter as a "swamp singer whose voice and guitar opened for him the gates of the Louisiana state penitentiary"; over time, the story congealed into an uncontested truth.[91] Even the frequently skeptical Lawrence Gellert accepted Lomax's account at face value when, in *New Masses*, Gellert criticized the "Southern landlord" tradition of "getting 'our niggers' out of difficulties with the Law when we need them to work or to entertain."[92] Effectively erasing Ledbetter's participation in a Southern black entertainment industry prior to his period of imprisonment, the press's dissemination of the story of Ledbetter's release from prison—as well as Lomax's insistence that Ledbetter wear his prison clothes while performing—had the effect of fixing incarceration and forced labor as the singular site of the birth of blues.[93]

Performance, as both object and method, was an organizing logic of the Lomaxes' collecting project. Models of both preenactment and reenactment, in particular, structured the Lomaxes' collection and dissemination of folk music. Often the collectors coerced prisoners into reenacting their compulsory labor in order to re-create work-song conditions—a funhouse doubling of Hurston's "Working on the Railroad" scene in *The Great Day*. The Lomaxes' strategy may have been born of the stonewalling of their informants: young Alan Lomax was surprised and frustrated by his frequent encounters with people who, though they sang as they worked, politely refused to perform for him, embodying the "feather-bed resistance" described by Hurston in her introduction to *Mules and Men*: "We smile and tell him or her something that satisfies the white person because, knowing so little about us, he doesn't know what he is missing."[94] Upon arriving at Parchman Farm in August of 1933, the Lomaxes faced resistance from the singers, whose time for rest was scarce, and from the wardens, who would not permit the Lomaxes to record in the fields. In response, the two men (re)doubled the day's work, piling logs, handing out axes, and "stag[ing] work-gang songs."[95] This constant restaging of the daily life of the Southern prisoner would haunt Ledbetter's later performances with and for the Lomaxes. What's more, the legendary tales that sprang up around these collecting excursions propagated a convincing origin story for black vernacular music; this myth of blues' *terroir*—its inexorable tie to agricultural labor—marginalized or excluded the theatrical performances by women in favor of prison blues or work songs sung by men.

In addition to staging reenactments of labor, John Lomax pre-scripted elements of the Lead Belly legend in his letters to the Library of Congress and to his wife. Examined in retrospect, these letters predict the plot points of the Lead Belly myth. In one letter, Lomax described meeting Ledbetter in Marshall, Texas, after the singer had been released from Angola. But rather than narratively describe these events, Lomax took the unusual step of scripting them in full dialogue, complete with his own approximations of black vernacular speech:

> I asked him what weapons he was carrying along. "Only this knife, Boss," and he showed me a dangerous looking one. . . . I held it in my hand and said, "Leadbelly, whenever you decide that you are going to take my money and car, you won't have to use this knife on me. Just tell me what

you want and I'll give it to you without a struggle." "Boss," he almost cries as he talks—"please suh, don't talk that way. You got me out of the pen. Ise yo man. You won't ever have to tie yo shoes again if you don't want to. I'll step in front of you if ever anybody tries to shoot you. I'm ready to die for you, Boss."[96]

These scenes of dialogue pepper Lomax's letters about Ledbetter; significantly, dialogue scenes do not appear in any of his other letters from this period. Well before introducing Ledbetter to the press, Lomax was scripting the Lead Belly myth. Strikingly, these scenes reappeared, often verbatim, in press accounts written by others for years to come. Ultimately, the scripted letters reached fruition in a proper script, for a *March of Time* newsreel coauthored by the Lomaxes in 1935. In it a scene between Lead Belly and Lomax—performed by Ledbetter and Lomax, playing themselves—replicated the lines of the letter almost exactly.

Initially a highly successful radio show supported by *Time* magazine, *The March of Time* made the leap to film on March 8, 1935, inaugurating "a style which the film's producers called 'pictorial journalism.'"[97] While the radio program had exclusively relied on professional actors, the motion-picture iteration often incorporated actual news footage and participants into its staged (re)enactments of current events. Though the producers of the radio program made an effort to use actual transcripts when possible, they made no claims of journalistic or documentary accuracy. Instead, they encouraged the actors to focus on the precision of impersonation, re-creating dialects and speech patterns as exactly as possible: mimetic perfection.[98] In contrast, the motion-picture version more completely merged the formal elements of documentary (actual news footage, original participants) with the theatrical reenactment framework of the radio version. Cloaked in a formal rhetoric of documentary authenticity, *The March of Time* blurred the line between theatrical enactment and journalistic reportage. Not unlike John Lomax's lecture-performances, *The March of Time* employed an antitheatrical theatricalism, its use of theatrical elements concealed and disavowed by its documentary truth claims. Mixing professional actors, actual participants, documentary footage, and staged reenactments for a public naive to its strategies, *The March of Time* saw itself, as Henry Luce privately described it, as "fakery in allegiance to the truth"—though it is not at all clear that audiences understood the reels in this way.[99]

In its account of the Lead Belly legend, *The March of Time* attempted, by documentary means, to elevate myth into history in four short scenes. In the first, Lomax, the protagonist, "discovers" Lead Belly at Angola and agrees to take his record to the governor. The second scene finds Lead Belly seeking Lomax at a Texas hotel; the lines in this scene closely correspond to those written by Lomax in his scriptive letter to Terrill some months earlier. Newly released from prison, Lead Belly subserviently pleads for Lomax to take him on as his "man." The third scene shows Lead Belly's wedding to Martha Promise in 1935 at the Connecticut home where they lived with the Lomaxes; filming this segment required the participants to reenact the ceremony and celebration that had taken place only a few weeks before. In the final scene, Lead Belly's songs are triumphantly deposited at the "great national institution," the Music Division of the Library of Congress. A close-up on the Declaration of Independence is the final, and unintentionally ironic, shot. The scene fades out as "Goodnight Irene" swells, securing Lead Belly's citizenship by song, if not his birthright. One of *The March of Time*'s many ironies is that it is the only extant footage of Ledbetter and John Lomax working *as actors*, albeit actors playing versions of themselves. Their differing skill levels were evident to those on the set: Lomax was stiff and self-conscious; he flubbed his lines repeatedly, resulting in a grueling process of multiple takes for every scene. Ledbetter, on the other hand, was reportedly at ease during the filming and "seemed to have little trouble with his lines, or with his singing."[100] But Ledbetter's ease and professionalism were perhaps too adept. Recalling the politics of racial authenticity inherent to realistic forms in the variety theater, we can see how Ledbetter's seamless performance ultimately undermined appreciation for his theatrical abilities or professional training. Ironically, Ledbetter's expert performance as Lead Belly, crafted as it may have been, helped to shore up the myth as fact.

The continuous propagation of the Lead Belly myth provoked a crisis just a few weeks after the release of the *March of Time* reel. After just a few months in the Northeast, Ledbetter began to refuse to occupy the stage the Lomaxes had so carefully constructed and chafed against the demands of the man he called "Boss." The most controversial point of contention is well known: Ledbetter did not want to wear his prison clothes on stage. Nor did he want to stop dancing on stage, or restrict his repertoire to blues, work songs, and field hollers. More and more frequently, Ledbetter "got lost," slipping away for days at a time, a one-man work stoppage in the golden age of strike tactics. Through this series of flights and escapes from the Lomaxes' control, Ledbetter rehearsed his final departure. What happened next is unclear, but John Lomax later represented the scene as self-fulfilling prophecy, nearly identical in detail to the horrors he had imagined in advance. As Lomax had told it, Lead Belly threatened the folklorist with a knife in a Buffalo library, demanding the money that he was owed.[101] Though he would return to Louisiana for a time, Ledbetter was not through with the Lead Belly myth and would restage it at least once more with a subversive, even satirical, energy, live at the Apollo Theater.

LIVE AT THE APOLLO

After a short visit to the South, Ledbetter returned to New York in 1936. Though accounts of Ledbetter's career during this time often frame this period as one of misguided attempts at stardom, Ledbetter himself did not seem at all uncertain about where he wanted to go: Harlem. In the context of the broad sweep of Ledbetter's career—a career spent primarily performing before black audiences—the choice of Harlem made perfect sense. Even during his six tightly controlled months with John Lomax, Ledbetter regularly found opportunities to perform before black audiences in Harlem and in black neighborhoods in other cities they visited, such as Rochester, New York. And so when the time came to book engagements in the spring of 1936, Ledbetter, advertising an act called Southern Melodies, headed straight for the Lafayette and the Apollo, where he sang and performed short sketches that reimagined the first scene of the *March of Time* reel, a script that now inevitably preceded him. Much of what happened during Ledbetter's performance engagement at the Apollo remains unknown: only one review of his performance survives, and just a few first-person accounts. The review was largely negative, and Ledbetter did not book any repeat engagements. The fragmentary accounts of this performance that do remain, however, shed light not only on the singer's attempt to remake the Lead Belly legend but also on the shifting production and consumption of blues on stage in the late 1930s.

The 125th Street Apollo Theater, a former burlesque house reopened under the management of Frank Schiffman and Leo Brecher in 1934, quickly established itself as the cultural and entertainment center of Harlem life. What's more, the Apollo almost immediately became the most important springboard to success in the black entertainment industry; along with the race-records business, it played a signal role in the consolidation and centralization of black mass culture. While other Harlem performance venues, such as the Cotton Club and Connie's Inn, produced spectacles designed to appeal to white audiences, the Apollo, which employed black workers on stage and off, addressed itself to a black Harlem public, many of whom were recently arrived Southern migrants and their descendants.[102] In terms of its offerings, the Apollo came as close as any urban theater did to replicating the all-black tent and variety environments of the rural South that many migrants had left behind. The biggest stars of the early days at the Apollo were many of the same performers—especially the comedians—who had started out with the tents or made their names on the TOBA circuit, among them the team of Butterbeans and Susie, Jackie "Moms" Mabley, and Dewey Pigmeat Markham, who toured with Bessie Smith and recorded Gertrude "Ma" Rainey's "See See Rider." Markham's career and long tenure at the Apollo is particularly instructive, as it microcosmically narrates the migration and trajectory of black vernacular entertainment from the rural tents to the urban stages of Harlem. Born in North Carolina in 1904, Markham left home as a teenager with a "gilly carnival," which he described as "a little carnival on trucks. . . . We had a little minstrel show, a ferris wheel, a merry-go-round, and a whip. . . . In those days we didn't have no band." With the gilly carnival he became known for singing "I Like You 'Cause You Got Such Lovin' Ways," a blues song later recorded by Lucille Hegamin. Markham graduated to a bigger carnival, and then in 1921 to the Florida Blossom Minstrel Show, where Rainey had also appeared. From there Markham moved to the TOBA circuit, and then to Harlem in 1928. In Harlem he performed at the Lafayette, the Alhambra, and the Apollo, where he played continuously from 1934 to 1938.[103] Markham performed with Ledbetter in 1936, anchoring the singer's performance in a tradition of black vaudevillian entertainment.

Ledbetter's appearance at the Apollo, far from a career anomaly, was a return to what he knew best: the variety stage that had been the key site of his professional development in the years before his encounter with the Lomaxes. Many performance elements from the tent and TOBA circuits remained in place at the Apollo; foremost among these was the variety format, which structured performances at the theater until the late 1940s. A typical show at the Apollo during this period, according to Tuliza Fleming, "would usually start with a short film, a newsreel, or a feature film, followed by a revue. These revues would consist of six or seven separate live performances surrounding a headliner act, which during the '30s was generally a big swing or jazz band. Secondary forms of entertainment featured in these Apollo revues included singers and musicians, dancers, female impersonators, animal acts, one-act plays or scenes from plays, athletes, chorus line dancers, acrobatic acts, and comedians who would often joke with the hosts, Ralph Cooper and Willie Bryant, throughout the show." Nearly insatiable demand supported up to five shows per day.[104] The retentions of the tent shows ranged from the structural to the specific: scenic backdrops common to the tents adorned the stage and formed the background for the sketches, skits, and songs of the revue, while the stagehand Norman Miller's notorious adjudication of the theater's famed Amateur Night recalled Bessie Smith's use of the broom to sweep her chorus line off the stage. As in the tents, performers with skills in comedy and tap dance were especially in demand.

If the Lomaxes—and, later, the musical leaders of the folk Left—pushed for consistency in Ledbetter's musical oeuvre, the Apollo, with its variety format and embrace of heterogeneous styles and genres, seemed an ideal home for the diversity of the performer's repertoire. The fluidity of the variety format—and the sheer number of performers required for a single show—also meant for a lively backstage atmosphere, where comedians, dancers, and musicians rehearsed, relaxed, and cocreated during fifteen-hour days. As Lonnie Bunch has put it, the Apollo in the thirties was a "place of possibility," where "singers would learn comic timing from Redd Foxx or Pigmeat Markham, and comedians would learn from Ella Fitzgerald and Sammy Davis Jr. how to command and control the stage."[105] "Country" and "classic" blues artists worked and played together at the Apollo, its very structure countering the sharp distinctions made by folklorists and record producers. In addition to being a major venue for Bessie Smith, Billie Holiday, and Ella Fitzgerald, the Apollo also hosted Ledbetter, Howlin' Wolf, and Muddy Waters, as well as the gospel stars Thomas Dorsey and Sister Rosetta Tharpe. With more money, more institutional support, and a concentrated audience base, tent-show blues "moved up" at the Apollo—but they underwent several transformations during their transplantation from their Southern environs to the New York stage.

The variety evenings at the Apollo, which attracted an audience invested in markers of urban sophistication, carefully, and subtly, revised aspects of the tent show for Harlem's consumption. While the Apollo retained many structural features of the Southern tent show, and performed before an audience deeply conversant in these conventions, it only indulged selected aspects of its working-class heritage. Instead, the Apollo promoted an aspirational middle-class aesthetic. As Ted Fox puts it, the Apollo "was a legitimizer—[it] was the establishment."[106] That is, in spite of its retention of Southern theater ways, the Apollo, both on stage and off, established "an acceptable middle-class cultural ethos that was firmly grounded in African American culture but that also softened the roughest edges of cultural expression."[107] The management of the Apollo—a place that the *New York Telegram* described as "an uptown Met"—was conscious of the venue's role as a place of aspirational fantasy and went to great lengths to produce theatrical spectacle that reflected not only the economic aspirations of its audiences but also the consolidated consumer culture of the age.[108] As Bobby

Schiffman, son of the founder Frank Schiffman, observed, "We knew that people would come to the Apollo to escape from reality. For the couple of hours they were there, they could fantasize that they were part of the elegant living they were seeing portrayed on the stage. The six-hundred-dollar mohair suits, the fancy shoes, fancy cars, and the beautiful women, all the other things that were part of the glamour of show business—we used to try to capitalize on that. We would spend hours and hours planning on a weekly basis how to glamorize the stage. We used to change scenery every week."[109] The staging of glamour was just as important offstage as on, and audiences dressed to the nines for a night at Apollo—their best clothes serving as markers for just how far they'd come, both economically and geographically. Still, some were not satisfied, and the New York Age sharply criticized the "vulgarity, suggestive dancing and black-face comedy" of the Apollo, advocating instead for "wholesome" "family" entertainment.[110]

Elements reminiscent of the tent show and the TOBA circuit underwent significant transformations at the Apollo, reflecting the shifting class politics of Harlem in the thirties. The single biggest change was musical, as swing and big bands replaced solo blues performers as headliners. Jazz, swing, and big band were the staples of the Apollo: the Count Basie Orchestra, Ella Fitzgerald, Lena Horne, Billie Holiday, and Cab Calloway were among the most visible and audible players of the new, urban, microphoned modernist sound in Harlem's theaters.[111] By and large, blues did not do well; even those theatrical blues stars that did appear at the Apollo, such as Bessie Smith and Ethel Waters, were backed by a big band. Middle-class resistance to blues remained strong; in his 1965 Music on My Mind, Willie "the Lion" Smith observes: "The average Negro family did not allow the blues, or even raggedy music, played in their homes."[112] Blues' challenge to normative standards of sexual behavior no doubt played a role in their absence from the Apollo stage. For others, blues were a reminder of a past better left in the past. Ever since folklorists and record producers began to market blues as a product of black misery, rather than as an exuberant expression of survival and endurance, blues seemed too demoralized, too limiting, to be embraced, especially as American popular culture thrived on glamour, optimism, and displays of opulence in the midst of the Depression.

As a result of a talent surplus, as well as market demands for professionalization, former "triple-threat" artists began to focus on one exclusive offering for their few moments on stage. While Rainey was known as monologist, comedienne, singer, and dancer, the stars of the next generation more precisely segmented and demarcated their areas of expertise, becoming primarily known for one particular stage contribution: tapping, or comedy, or singing. Rarely were all three interwoven as they once had been. Comedy and music, especially, began to diverge. While both Mabley and the duo Butterbeans and Susie had long incorporated singing and dancing into their acts, they began to emphasize comedy more and more, gradually leaving the music to the big bands and dancing to tappers like Bill "Bojangles" Robinson. In the performances of self-consciously "down-home" stars such as Markham and Mabley, comedy at the Apollo was allowed, even encouraged, to reference a black Southern past, to indulge in racy sexual content, and to resurrect the material of the tent show, from minstrel routines to vaudevillian duos. But while comedy retained its old ways, the Apollo aimed to establish itself as musically modern, exchanging blues for jazz and swing. Comedy and music increasingly occupied two different conceptual, temporal, and ideological worlds in the Apollo variety shows, one laughing at the poor, rural past, and the other looking toward a bourgeois, urbane future.

Ledbetter's Apollo performance of *The March of Time* shows the performer comically manipulating the Lead Belly legend. Instead of simply restaging the first scene of the reel, Ledbetter's reenactment of Lead Belly's freedom-making performance added a dimension of satirical comedy to a form that had initially been understood as sober documentary. In the skit Ledbetter's most significant revision was the total elimination of *The March of Time*'s protagonist, John Lomax. Instead of Lead Belly playing for Lomax, as he had done in the newsreel, he played before the governor himself, a change that cast Ledbetter as the agent of his own freedom making. But Ledbetter's redo of *The March of Time* had another comic ace up its sleeve: by casting Monte Hawley as the governor, the reenactment bent the documentary to the satirical.[113] Jack Schiffman suggests that Hawley's casting was motivated by the fact that he was very light skinned and could pass as a white character.[114] But by 1936 Hawley was already widely known among Harlem's black theater audiences as a performer in vaudeville and musical revues. Had passing been the only goal, a noncelebrity actor would likely have been cast in the role. Instead, casting the recognizable—and recognizably black—Hawley exploited the comedy of the scene and inverted blackface minstrelsy's politics of theatrical authenticity. Ledbetter's redo of *The March of Time* at the Apollo put a satirical frame around a scene that had been used to portray Lead Belly as an untutored genius and presented the audience with the figure of a powerful black Southern governor—one who, by the power of his office, could intervene in the widespread juridical and economic system of convict labor. While *The March of Time* had trafficked in "fakery in allegiance to the truth," Ledbetter's restaging of the newsreel signified on both the formal structures of documentary and *The March of Time*'s intersection with the illusory practices of the theater. Ledbetter replayed the story of his "discovery," but with a difference, exchanging a white folklorist for a black governor. This repetition with revision challenges the primacy of the Lomaxes in Ledbetter's professional history, reclaiming his career as one closely connected to the sketches and comic scenes of the Southern variety stage.

The transformations of variety conventions enacted on the Apollo stage—the increasing specialization of artists, the shifting class politics, and the preference for jazz and swing over blues—likely contributed to the lackluster response to Ledbetter's act. What's more, Ledbetter appeared on Easter weekend, a notoriously difficult one for theaters. Ledbetter's attempts to reframe his narrative, which was too closely tied in the public eye to discourses of criminality and black suffering, were challenged by public representations of him as an unfit representative of the aspirational black bourgeoisie. A poster advertising his appearance at the Apollo, for example, reduced Ledbetter's career to a visual metonym of imprisonment: a drawing in the style of Prentiss Taylor featured two shackled wrists (see figure 2.1). A critic from the *New York Age* observed: "The advance publicity stated that this man had been in two jails under murder charges and that the wardens, on hearing him work out on the guitar and vocally, set him free. Maybe they did, but after hearing the man myself, I'm not so sure."[115] Ledbetter was nearing fifty at a time when young new stars were discovered weekly, and he was playing music that many New Yorkers associated with the past. Indeed, it is the ultimate irony that had Ledbetter never gone to prison or met the Lomaxes, he might have become a Markham, or a Robinson; because he spent much of the 1920s in prison, though, the pipeline from rural carnival to TOBA to New York stardom that Markham traveled was unavailable to Ledbetter.

Ledbetter's "failure" at the Apollo might be best understood as a performance out of time. Appearing on the scene years after James Weldon Johnson had proclaimed the death of blues, Ledbetter arrived too late for commercial success among Harlem audiences. His career was interrupted by years of imprisonment, and so he arrived in Harlem dragging a musical form and a public image that were too retrograde for many Harlem moderns to accept. In spite of this belated arrival, he used his performance opportunities at the Apollo and elsewhere to play with time, using music, meter, and reenactment to explore the rewriting of history and the rescripting of his legend. Years later Ross Russell criticized Ledbetter's temporal insurrections in *Down Beat* magazine: "Leadbelly's main fault, one that would have been fatal in a jazz musician, was his chronic inability to maintain the selected meter. His performances invariably accelerated."[116]

2.1 Advertisement for Lead Belly's appearance at the Apollo, 1936. From Jack Schiffman, *Harlem Heyday* (Amherst, NY: Prometheus Books, 1984), 53. Copyright © 1984 by Jack Schiffman. All rights reserved. Used with permission of the publisher; www.prometheusbooks.com.

What Russell hears as a fundamental *error*—Ledbetter's "inability to maintain"—can also be read as a refusal to "keep time," the central directive for laboring lines of penitentiary convicts. As Ledbetter resolutely sped up "Pick a Bale of Cotton," his accelerating rhythm highlighted his virtuosic skill and speed, both on the guitar and in the fields, and critiqued the disciplinary temporal logics of convict labor. In a draft of a review of *Negro Folk Songs as Sung by Lead Belly*, Johnson observes these temporal disruptions as Ledbetter's fundamental black aesthetic contribution: "In listening to Negroes sing their own music it is often tantalizing and even exciting to watch a minute fraction of a beat balancing for a slight instant on the bar between two measures, and, *when it seems almost too late*, drop back into its own proper compartment. We have not yet derived an exact notation for this sort of 'time,' and perhaps we never can, for the 'time' is itself inexact."[117] Seizing on the deformation of strict metronomic time, Johnson here offers a kind of poetic shorthand for Ledbetter himself: both too early and too late, his belated success enabled him to bridge the theatrical environment of the popular theater—a "dying" form—with the first of blues' resurrections: its first "revival."

THE "CONSCIOUS ARTIST" AND THE CULTURAL FRONT:
BOURGEOIS BLUES ON TOBACCO ROAD

After being rejected by Harlemites in the late thirties and early forties, blues segmented from the uptown black entertainment industry and took up residence in a downtown world of interracial "theater folk," a transition crystallized by the late career moves of Ledbetter, as well as those of fellow blues artists Josh White, Brownie McGhee, and Sonny Terry. Ledbetter was a frequent performer for organizations of what Michael Denning terms the "cultural front": the "extraordinary flowering of arts, entertainment, and thought based on the broad social movement that came to be known as the Popular Front."[118] The cultural front was a hospitably hybrid musical environment that was perfectly in line with Ledbetter's own songster ethos and repertoire. As Denning observes, "the lines separating folk, gospel, blues, jazz, rhythm and blues, and Broadway musicals were not as absolute for musicians of the cultural front as they have become for critics and historians."[119] This period in Ledbetter's career has been recounted as a geographic reorientation (from Harlem to downtown), a racial reversal (from black audiences to white), and a musical reinvention (from blues to folk). But to present Ledbetter's new career direction as a 180-degree turn away from Harlem is to misunderstand the Left as exclusively white and marginalizes Ledbetter's personal and artistic connections with many black artists who were explicitly identified with the cultural front, among them Richard Wright, Josh White, Sonny Terry, and Brownie McGhee. Observing the *continuities* between Ledbetter's uptown and downtown careers proves critical, not only for our understanding of the cultural front as a hotbed of activity for both black and white artists but also for Ledbetter as a key figure in cultural-front activism and politics.

The formal aesthetics of cultural-front performances demonstrate continuity between uptown and downtown, between the Apollo and the Labor Stage Theatre. Many cultural-front events, from the benefit to the cabaret, were characterized by an episodic feel; different artists cocreated together, producing a varied mix of comedy, dance, and song. The *songspiel*, a loosely held together song cycle, advanced by Bertolt Brecht and Kurt Weill, was stylistically influential in the late 1930s and early 1940s, and informed everything from the Theater Arts Committee (TAC) cabarets to pageants of black history. Rejecting narratives of continuity and dramaturgical inevitability in favor of an aesthetic of interruption, discontinuity, and nonmatrixed performance, the proletarian variety aesthetics of these cultural-front events shared as much in common with black vaudeville, the black minstrel show, and the Apollo extravaganzas as they did with the European Brechtian cabarets. Writing in a 1939 issue of *TAC*, the magazine published by the TAC, Alfred Brennan explained why the "blackout" form was so suited to political intervention: "You don't have to prove anything in a blackout." Furthermore, "the rising tide of [social] criticism finds an outlet more easily though the brief episodes of songs and sketches than in the more stringent and demanding medium of the full-length play."[120]

Like Paul Robeson, Marian Anderson, Josh White, and other black cultural-front artists of the thirties and forties, Ledbetter powerfully critiqued racism, fascism, and labor exploitation through song. Ledbetter sang at benefit concerts that raised funds for the Spanish Civil War, the mothers of the Scottsboro Nine, the Highlander Folk School, the Young Communist League, dust-bowl relief organizations, the National Negro Congress, and striking Kentucky miners.[121] It is somewhat surprising, then, that Ledbetter—a man who read the *Daily Worker* every day—has been cast by his biographers, and by some of his peers, as either apolitical or only "mildly sympathetic" with the Popular Front, a political actor playing a role in a drama in which he had little investment. In their detailed account of this period of Ledbetter's career, the biographers Wolfe and Lornell rely on statements made by Pete Seeger, Frederick Ramsey, and others to suggest that, for Ledbetter, "the protest rallies and labor meetings were simply new venues to replace his traditional black audiences that had turned their backs on him at the Apollo," and that he "seldom revealed any strong political feelings on his own."[122] And yet Ledbetter's life, as well as his music, gives lie to this supposed lack of political consciousness. Though he made few public statements (a quality that distinguished him from his peer Robeson) and never joined the Communist Party (a fact Denning warns scholars not to "fetishize" when analyzing artists of the Popular Front), even a glancing look at Ledbetter's musical repertoire during this time reveals his sophisticated advancement of an antifascist *and* antiracist cultural agenda in song.[123] Ledbetter's coding of his political statements in song seems more than sensible when one considers the environment of racial terror and communist baiting in Dixie where many of his and Promise's loved ones still lived, not to mention the FBI surveillance that Ledbetter was already experiencing by dint of his association with Robeson. Ledbetter himself acknowledged these risks when he once jokingly remarked to a friend: "All us niggers is communists, you know."[124]

Like many of his peers, Ledbetter was a vocal advocate for the Scottsboro Nine, and he composed at least two songs decrying the injustices of the case, one of which was transcribed by Richard Wright in his 1937 profile of the singer in the *Daily Worker*.[125] Ledbetter's cry of protest is upbeat and rhythmically contagious; while Ledbetter narrated the story of Scottsboro in the verses of the song, its jaunty, swinging refrain invited audiences to sing along, repeating the line "Why? 'Cause it's Jim Crow and I know it's so!" The conclusion makes a strong case for Ledbetter's own particular brand of musical education and activism. After repeating the dangers of the (Southern) "landlord" who will "get ya" in Alabama, Ledbetter addresses his audience with a directive:

I'm gonna tell all the colored people
Living in Harlem swing
Don't you ever go to Alabama
Just try to sing!

At a private party held in Minneapolis in 1948, Ledbetter opened with three songs that, taken together, launched a withering assault against Jim Crow lynching and the failure of the government to protect its black Southern citizens, even while relying on them as a fighting force. Performing before a majority-white audience, one of whom recorded the evening, Ledbetter opened his set with "Nobody in This World Is Better Than Us," a song also known as "Equality for Negroes." Articulating the indignities experienced by black soldiers who returned home from the world wars only to face racial violence and segregation, Ledbetter inquires: "If the Negro was good enough to fight/Why can't we get a little equal rights?" He continues:

In my own opinion
It's a rotten shame
Like they want to bring back slavery again
But God made us all and him we trust:
Nobody in this world is better than us.

The song is upbeat and singable, its direct lyrics tempered by its jolly rhythm and Ledbetter's straightforward and somewhat emotionally distanced singing. But who is the "us" in the lyric? It is a song that invites its (white) listener to sing along, and the lyric seems to send the message that nobody is superior to anybody else. But especially when the title "Equality for Negroes" is attached to the song, the "us" loses its universal quality; couched within a song that grammatically interpellates its listener into a childlike logic of equality (indeed, Ledbetter frequently performed this song for children) is a coded expression of black superiority. Ledbetter followed this song with a story about meeting the president and a leafleting campaign targeted at restaurants that refused to serve black customers. Ledbetter then sang "Jim Crow" and concluded his set with "Gallis Pole," a song with deep roots in the folk tradition that, when sung by Ledbetter, registered as a cry of protest against the economics of lynching in the Jim Crow South. He introduced the song to his audience by saying, "I gotta tell you about Mississippi." The song tells of a condemned man, whose father, mother, and wife bring the hangman quantities of silver and gold as payment for his life. And yet the song's conclusion suggests that the financial extortion was not successful; ending on an interrogative, "what did you bring me, to keep me from the gallis pole?" Ledbetter fingerpicks furiously, as if for his life.[126]

Injecting civil rights discourse into antifascist and labor advocacy, Ledbetter emerges as an adherent to a Southern radical tradition that jointly pursued racial and economic justice.[127] Ledbetter observed the paradoxes of racial capitalism as early as 1912, when he wrote a ballad in response to the sinking of the *Titanic*, a disaster that, surprisingly to many, seemed to claim no black lives. Ledbetter wittily reflected on the absence of blacks from the luxury liner in a lyric that imagines the world champion boxer Jack Johnson attempting to board, only to be told that he would have to shovel coal.[128] While the lyrics of the song mourn the tragedy of the ship's sinking, the Johnson lyric observes with irony the limits of a black champion's economic success as well as the comeuppance visited on those captains of industry whose prosperity depended on the racialized exploitation of labor. Ledbetter's most forceful—and humorous—critique of racial capitalism emerges in "Bourgeois Blues," a song he wrote and recorded after a dispiriting 1938 trip to Washington, DC, where he was refused service at local restaurants and drew the ire of the neighbors of Alan Lomax, with whom he was staying. He sings,

Home of the brave
Land of the free
I don't want to be mistreated by no bourgeoisie.

Here Ledbetter invokes the language of "mistreatment" commonly used in blues lyrics to reference the abuses of sharecropping. Recounting numerous instances of discrimination seemingly based on race rather than class ("We heard the white man sayin', I don't want no niggers up there"), Ledbetter seems to be misusing the accusation of "bourgeois," an assumption reinforced by Alan Lomax's widely circulated account that Ledbetter did not know the meaning of the word. But by using *bourgeoisie* as a code for *racist*, Ledbetter invites the listener to think about the relationship between exploitative class politics, Jim Crow segregation, and racially motivated economic injustices. Finally, Ledbetter indicts a racialized performance culture:

> Them white folks in Washington
> They know how
> To throw a colored man a nickel
> Just to see him bow.

Just months before Marian Anderson was denied permission to sing before an integrated audience at Constitution Hall, Ledbetter interrogated the meaning of *bourgeois*, observing the confluence of racial and class discrimination at the heart of the nation's capital.

Though many of his audiences during this period were largely white, black artists of the cultural front embraced Ledbetter and recognized him as a kindred spirit. Richard Wright, a fellow Southerner and a good friend, promoted the singer in a *Daily Worker* profile that positioned itself as a corrective to prior representations of the artist "as a half sex-mad, knife-toting, black buck from Texas."[129] Ledbetter's musical activism on behalf of the Scottsboro Nine appealed to Wright, who noted: "It seems that the entire folk culture of the American Negro has found its embodiment in him." The cultural wing of the National Negro Congress, for whom Ledbetter sang with Robeson at a 1946 benefit, also found Ledbetter to be a fitting representative of its Marxist-inspired approach to histories of racial and class struggle and its advocacy for multiracial alliances, a position perhaps best expressed by Ledbetter in his rollicking sing-along "We're in the Same Boat Brother." In 1943 the artist Charles White painted Lead Belly into *The Contribution of the Negro to American Democracy*, a mural installed at the Hampton Institute (see figure 2.2).[130] While the title of the piece implies a rosy, tranquil view of history, White's mural is filled with scenes of suffering and struggle, a mood enhanced by a dark and stormy palette of deep reds, dark blues, and, above all, the various shades of brown skin of the figures that crowd its frame. In the mural Ledbetter's image sits in a "heroic continuum" with fellow black freedom fighters, among them Denmark Vesey, Harriet Tubman, Nat Turner, and Max Yergan, the president of the National Negro Congress. White shows a nonlinear version of black history, one that, in Celeste Bernier's words "dramatises the ways in which forms of political, social, and cultural resistance were intertwined."[131] Ledbetter anchors the bottom right corner of the mural; adjacent to him are Anderson and Robeson, two figures more widely recognized as leaders in black freedom struggles (see figure 2.3).

In addition to serving as a symbol of resistance, Ledbetter participated in events that theatrically narrated histories of black struggle. In 1939 Ledbetter was a featured performer in "a pageant of Negro music," an event that drew on the popular musical-historical pageants of black history such as W. E. B. Du Bois's 1913 *The Star of Ethiopia* and Langston Hughes's 1938 *Don't You Want to Be Free?* The 1939 pageant was structured as a linear history of black musical evolution, from the "tom-toms" of Africa to contemporary boogie-woogie and jazz, and included the artists Albert Ammons, Meade Lux Lewis, Ruby Smith, Walter P. Johnson, Asadata Dafora, and the Archie Savage dancers. While the similar, and more well-known, "From Spirituals to Swing" event produced by the jazz aficionado John Hammond was performed at Carnegie Hall in 1938, the 1939 musical drama was sponsored by an offshoot of the American Labor Party and was performed at the Labor Stage, which was concurrently running the International Ladies' Garment Workers' Union's musical *Pins and Needles*. The structure of the evening closely hewed to the variety format of both the Apollo and the proletarian "blackout" sketch, including multiple dance acts in its evening program. Staff from *Pins and Needles*, including the set designer, S. Syrjala, and the choral director, Simon Rady, assisted with the production. Robert H. Gordon, who had directed the "Negro TAC" in Harlem some months earlier, directed the piece. Indeed, the labor of the artists themselves was made visible in an article for the *Christian Science Monitor*, where it was reported that the black artists rehearsed from midnight until six in the morning, the only time that the theater was not being used by the largely white *Pins and Needles* cast and crew.[132] In short, like White's mural, Ledbetter's 1939 concert linked black musical history and the black freedom struggle with labor activism, advancing an argument for interracial alliances of workers—including cultural workers—everywhere.

2.2 *(opposite, above)* Charles White, *The Contribution of the Negro to American Democracy*, 1943. Courtesy of Hampton University Archives, Hampton, VA.

2.3 *(opposite, below)* Detail of Charles White, *The Contribution of the Negro to American Democracy*, 1943. Courtesy of Hampton University Archives, Hampton, VA.

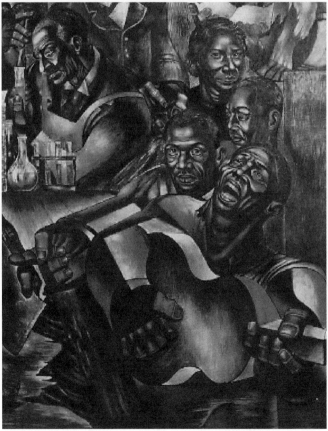

2.4 Stage set for *Tobacco Road*, 1933. Billy Rose Theatre Division, the New York Public Library for the Performing Arts, Astor, Lenox and Tilden Foundations.

One relief concert in particular gestured back in time to Ledbetter's early days with the theatrically inclined John Lomax and looked ahead to the stagings of American blues abroad. On March 3, 1940, the TAC and the John Steinbeck Committee to Aid Agricultural Organization sponsored what the *New York Times* called a "Program to Aid 'Okies.'"[133] Capitalizing on the recent release of the Darrell Zanuck film, the event billed itself as a "*Grapes of Wrath* evening." Organized by the actor Will Geer, who had recently appeared in Marc Blitzstein's labor opera *The Cradle Will Rock*, the benefit, held at the off-hour of midnight at the Forrest Theater, included performances by Ledbetter, Pete Seeger, Aunt Molly Jackson, and Woody Guthrie. The event was later described as "a watershed," "a turning point in American music," and "the real beginning of the folk song revival."[134] The set, designed by Robert Redington Sharpe and shown here in a 1933 photograph, changed little over the eight years of the play's Broadway run. At the time Geer was playing the role of Jeeter Lester, and the *New York Times* reported that several members of the cast planned to appear at the benefit and perform scenes from the play.[135] This significant detail is often only noted as an aside: the benefit concert took place on the stage set of *Tobacco Road*, the wildly popular theatrical adaptation of Erskine Caldwell's novel (see figure 2.4).

The "scene" of the "*Grapes of Wrath* evening," then, used theatrical frames, architectural and conceptual, to enclose and represent "the folk," renewing, on somewhat altered terms, the theatrical thinking that had characterized John Lomax's collecting enterprises several decades prior. For his part, Ledbetter sang, performed his "duck hunting" dance, and spent a portion of the evening seated on a part of the set that served as the front porch of the fictional Lester home. Guthrie also "seemed to fit in perfectly with Jeeter Lester's tarpaper shack on the *Tobacco Road* set behind him."[136] This "watershed" event, then, advanced one of the key tropes of black vernacular music production, reception, and representation that governed stagings of the blues in Europe in the 1950s and 1960s: the front-porch stage. Recalling Zora Neale Hurston's description of her front porch as a "gallery seat" and a "proscenium box for a born first-nighter," we see in the "Program to Aid 'Okies'" the emergence of the architecture of the front porch as a signal design that enframed the production and reception of the blues. Its use as scenic design would only grow in the decades to come. Once a representative of prison labor, Ledbetter was now cast as a representative migrant laborer, in solidarity with "Okies."[137] While his earlier performances provided audiences with an opportunity to reflect on the new presence of black Southerners in Northern cities, Ledbetter now performed as a surrogate for another class of travelers: the agricultural laborers, many (though not all) of them white, who were displaced by the farm policies and the meteorological chaos of the dust bowl. In the last decade of his life, Ledbetter was called on to both explicitly and subtly stage this scene of migration. All the while, he traveled constantly, touring to colleges and clubs throughout the United States, and, finally, to Paris in 1949, where he played one of his last concerts.

Three

Weakened by amyotrophic lateral sclerosis (ALS), Huddie Ledbetter played his final concert in Austin, Texas, in the spring of 1949. Singing from a wheelchair, he charmed his audience with "C'est Bon, Les Oeufs (Scrambled Egg Song)." Having just returned from a month in Paris, Ledbetter explained to laughter why he was served scrambled eggs every day: to change one's breakfast order, "you got to tell 'em in French. And I didn't know no French, so I couldn't tell 'em nothing. So they just kept on bringing scrambled eggs." After a few weeks, Ledbetter learned enough French to write "Les Oeufs," and he sang it to and with his Parisian audiences. Ledbetter was received in France as a cultural ambassador and representative of African American life, and his public return to the United States was marked by his translation of French language, foodways, and customs for his American audiences. Sung in both Paris and Texas, the song, which married French lyrics to blues and swing rhythms, is a tale of a traveler's education, and of translation's hazards and possibilities. Sung as a simple round, Ledbetter's 1949 live performance of the song recalled the many children's songs that he performed throughout his career. Opening with the story of his Parisian breakfasts, Ledbetter then coached his audience—who soon joined in as coperformers—by translating the lyrics. "C'est bon," he explained, means "it's good." Ledbetter humorously adjusted some of these translations for the Texans: "ne pas c'est bon brûlés," he claimed, translates as "don't scorch 'em." A patient teacher, Ledbetter led the audience as they tentatively stumbled through the French lyrics, encouraging them with a warmly paternal "that's good" as the sing-along grew louder and more confident. As a final step, Ledbetter informed the audience that he was "gonna swing it a little bit" and introduced the characteristic acceleration of his twelve-string guitar accompaniment. As the round sped up, its canon structure became more pronounced, and the guitar chugged along like so many trains, conjuring a sonic image of the song's precondition: the pleasures and perils of long-distance travel.

Ledbetter's 1949 trip to the International Jazz Festival in Paris paved the way for dozens of blues performers who were to follow in his footsteps. Ledbetter, the first "country blues" singer to travel to Europe, inaugurated several decades of European tours that both economically sustained American musicians and introduced European audiences to music that would prove foundational to British rhythm and blues and rock and roll. With a career spanning the entire first half of the twentieth century, Ledbetter bridged the generations marked by the classic blues and the blues revival. At the end of his life, he served as a mentor to a young cohort of musicians who made transatlantic tours a central part of their livelihoods. What transformations were effected by these new conditions of blues performance? How did the theatrical practices that so entertainingly structured the staging of blues under the tents and at the Apollo Theater transform as blues began to be widely performed for white audiences, many of whom had deep investments in concepts of racial authenticity? How were blues transmitted to foreign audiences, whose cultural worlds and life experiences were so different from those of the singers who appeared before them? Addressing these questions, this chapter explores the transmission, reinvention, and translation of blues performance in a transatlantic context in the postwar decades, looking closely at performers with major European careers, including Brownie McGhee and Sonny Terry, Sister Rosetta Tharpe, and Pleasant "Cousin Joe" Joseph. Following the examination of some broader conditions of transatlantic blues performance—the rise of the festival tour, the significance of television, and the revival's investment in representations of racial authenticity—the chapter focuses on one particular performance event, *The Blues and Gospel Train*, in order to explore and underscore the locally specific dimensions of the blues tour.

Performed before a live audience and taped for television on May 7, 1964, *The Blues and Gospel Train*, which the music historian C. P. Lee describes as "one of the most influential concerts held in Britain," was broadcast to British audiences on August 19, 1964; an estimated twelve to fourteen million viewers tuned in to watch Muddy Waters, Sister Rosetta Tharpe, Sonny Terry, Brownie McGhee, and Cousin Joe, among others, perform at an abandoned train station outside Manchester.[1] The venue of *The Blues and Gospel Train*, an outdoor, site-specific concert, was a rarity at a time when television production was still largely confined to in-studio presentations. The white British production team transformed the train platform into a whimsical stage that combined elements of a derelict Southern depot with those of a rural front porch, creating an elaborate and unique stage set for the featured performers. The program was essentially a double event, taking place "live" in May and when it aired in August, with each iteration shaped by different representational media and witnessed by different audiences. My analysis occasionally focuses on aspects particular to the live (such as the weather) or the taped (such as the camerawork), all the while acknowledging, as Philip Auslander has demonstrated, that "live" and "mediated" performances exist not in binary opposition but as intertwined practices that mutually produce and shape each other.[2] While the theatrical elaboration of *The Blues and Gospel Train* makes it seem anomalous among the broad panorama of transatlantic blues performance, I have chosen to explore it here for two signal reasons. First, the program's explicit references to the stage sets of American minstrel shows, tent shows, and Harlem clubs are not a deviation from the norm but rather an unambiguous expression of a theatrical practice that often more subtly pervaded the European tours. Second, *The Blues and Gospel Train* invites a focused consideration of the local reception of the musicians in Manchester. In advocating for sustained attention to local specificity in the midst of a supposedly homogeneous tour, this analysis offers ways to listen more closely and more precisely for the manifold resonances of blues "in translation."

In the early years of the postwar transatlantic tours, producers of blues in Europe were faced with a problem: how to make blues legible to a foreign audience for which it was never intended and for whom the form's aesthetics and cultural references were obscure at best? In the 1950s blues was familiar to just a few connoisseurs in Britain, most of whom had only encountered the music on records and on the radio. The live and televisual performances, then, bore the double burden of producing an entertaining spectacle and contextualizing and explaining the material sufficiently so that audiences could understand and appreciate what they were witnessing. I use the framework of *translation* to describe this contextualization, which was frequently realized by manipulating the performance elements around and between the songs: costume, mise-en-scène, and the banter of the musicians among themselves and with the audience. Accordingly, I use the term *translation* in its broadest sense, referring not to a strictly linguistic project but to an explanatory process by which blues were made sensible—audible—for audiences encountering them for the first time. Indeed, blues were almost always sung in English, even in non-English speaking countries, a characteristic that made the lucidity of the live event even more important.

As white European audiences replaced black audiences as the primary consumers of blues in the 1950s and 1960s, the theatricality of blues performance—particularly the aesthetics of the minstrel stage—became a tool of translation, a white-controlled frame designed to enable the comprehension and consumption of American blackness. "Translation is a mode," Walter Benjamin notes in his influential essay "The Task of the Translator."[3] By detaching translation from its objecthood or thingness, Benjamin emphasizes the "being in relation" that characterizes translation. To perform "in translation," then, is to steep in this amalgam of relations, to come face-to-face with the impossibility of the project that one undertakes.[4] Though Benjamin's essay explores literary translation, his insights are applicable to the cultural work performed by European blues events as well. "To comprehend [translation] as mode one must go back to the original," he argues.[5] But one must ask: what is "the original" for the European blues-revival performances? The tent shows of the teens and twenties? The ethnographic folklore festivals of the thirties and forties? The spectacles of the Cotton Club or the Apollo? The European translations of blues performance, rather than faithfully "incorporat[ing] the original's mode of signification" (the "task" that Benjamin sets out for his translator), picked and chose from a panoply of signifiers that historically accrued to both black performance and white performances of blackness: scenic tropes from the plantation musical, structural elements from the minstrel stage, and sartorial elements designed to denote authenticity.[6] What resulted from this selective, associative strategy was a translation of blues that, rather than "expressing the central reciprocal relationship between languages," *produced* an original: a theatrical image of an African American past.[7] If, for Benjamin, the task of the translator "consists in finding that intended effect [*Intention*] upon the language into which he is translating which produces in it the echo of the original," *The Blues and Gospel Train* and other European blues performance did not echo the historical conditions of tent shows and Jim Crow; rather, these performances echoed, by and large, the nostalgic desires for a black pastoral.[8] As a result, these European productions often resembled other scenarios of translation that played out across unequal relations of power. As Tejaswini Nirañjana points out in *Siting Translation*, "translation participates . . . in the *fixing* of colonized cultures, making them seem static and unchanging rather than historically constructed." This "fixing" produces colonized subjects as inhabiting an asynchronous temporality, not unlike the one assigned to the performers of *The Blues and Gospel Train*, who were called on to represent the nineteenth century in the midst of the twentieth.[9]

Though often stymied by producers who deployed tools of theatrical translation within a landscape of unequal power, performers also recognized the social and political utility of translating black music for non-American audiences during the years of the civil rights movement. It was during this time that some performers began to insist—in public, at least—that blues was *not* particular to a Southern black experience but rather could be shared by those of different backgrounds. For many black artists, including Paul Robeson, Langston Hughes, and Ledbetter, performing before European audiences underscored the essential mobility of black music and provided an opportunity to build affective bonds that would strengthen the global struggle for black freedom. For both political and economic reasons, it became increasingly beneficial for musicians who financially depended on the European tours and wished to build transnational alliances to emphasize that black music was music for everyone. In a transatlantic wire from the Middle East to President Eisenhower, Dizzy Gillespie cannily articulated both black ownership and worldwide legibility: "Jazz is our own American folk music that communicates with all peoples regardless of language or social barriers."[10]

Just as Benjamin's own theory of translation was closely tied to his historiographical approach, the translation of the blues enacted by *The Blues and Gospel Train* was also a historiographic operation, one that shored up collective memories that were central to Manchester's civic identity. In looking back to a nineteenth-century moment when Manchester's industrial progress was held up as the measure of all things, *The Blues and Gospel Train* recalled historic economic alliances between the British North and the African American South. But the histories and memories staged by the program were shot through with the concerns of the present; indeed, the program's staging of the blues looked to histories of African American migration in order to communicate the economically forced migration that Mancunian youths faced in their own immediate futures. Finally, the backdrop of U.S. civil rights conflicts informed the experiences of both audiences and performers alike. The program's "look back"—to cotton famines, abolitionism, and minstrelsy—generated numerous historical slippages, as well as a dizzying array of cross-racial, cross-temporal, and transnational identifications and misidentifications.

TRANSATLANTIC BLUES

Privately and federally sponsored music tours originating in the United States, long a staple of transnational cultural exchange, intensified during the Cold War. The transatlantic blues tours explored in this chapter, including the American Folk Blues Festival and the American Folk, Blues, and Gospel Caravan, joined the U.S. State Department jazz tours of the 1950s and 1960s in bringing African American music to the world. As chronicled by Penny von Eschen, these tours brought Gillespie, Duke Ellington, Dave Brubeck, and other jazz greats to emergent postcolonial nations, such as Ghana, Pakistan, and Burma.[11] The official script of the tours drew attention to jazz as a metonym for American democracy; still, the tours labored under an often unspoken contradiction: the performers employed to represent American values to the world lived under the banner of separate but equal while at home. But the federally organized jazz tours and privately organized blues tours were not mirror images of each other, as they traveled to different locations and played before different audiences. Western Europe, the primary arena for the blues tours, was deemed an inappropriate destination for the State Department tours, both because "jazz was considered already established, popular, and commercially viable" in Western Europe and because other nations, it was assumed, required more urgent politico-cultural interventions.[12] But there were significant points of overlap between the tours, particularly in the figure of George Wein. The founder of the Newport Jazz Festival and a cofounder of the Newport Folk Festival, Wein organized the American Folk, Blues, and Gospel Caravan, the Newport International Youth Band (which performed abroad with State Department sponsorship), and Festival Productions, a company that partnered with the State Department throughout the 1960s and 1970s.[13] Wein's diversified involvement in different types of transatlantic tours unsettles any sharp distinctions between the blues and jazz tours, no matter how different their political aims. While the State Department exported jazz to Africa, Latin America, and Eastern Europe as a soft power advertisement for American democracy, the American Folk Blues Festivals and the American Folk, Blues, and Gospel Caravan stayed away from politics. But just as the jazz tours sometimes staged the glaring contradiction between the rhetoric of American freedom and the social and political realities of Jim Crow, the blues tours ended up staging certain paradoxes of American capitalism. The stars of blues tours may have found themselves making more money than they ever had, and were celebrated as exporters of American culture, but their success often depended on being (literally) framed within a scene that recalled chattel slavery and sharecropping, systems that relied on black bodies as capital.

When Tharpe, Ledbetter, and Terry stepped onto European stages, they conjured deep memories of the minstrel shows, jubilee singers, and music-hall entertainers who flooded Britain and Western Europe in the nineteenth century.[14] In the early twentieth century, jazz and swing were wildly popular in both the United Kingdom and on the Continent; both Duke Ellington and Louis Armstrong, among others, played on celebrated tours in the early 1930s. The fervor for jazz in Paris, which vaulted Josephine Baker from chorine to star, was the most widely known, but by no means the only, craze for black music on a continent that saw in its performers a potent combination of the primitive and the modern, of essential authenticity and erotic spectacularity. The one exception to the persistent presence of black music on European stages was in the United Kingdom, where British fears about American musical domination, particularly during an economic crisis, resulted in stringent visa restrictions for American musicians wishing to perform there. As Roberta Freund Schwartz reports, these restrictions amounted to "a virtual ban on live American jazz" from 1935 to 1957.[15] In response, British audiences transferred their attention to recordings, many of them obscure and difficult to locate, as well as to the burgeoning blues scholarship being written by Paul Oliver and Samuel Charters.[16] The older generation continued to prize Gillespie, Charles Mingus, and other jazz greats, but in the late 1950s, spurred on by record releases, transatlantic radio broadcasts, festival circuits, and international tours, young Europeans began to shift their attention from jazz to blues and folk artists, embracing Waters, Big Bill Broonzy, and Tharpe.[17]

While Alan Lomax, Moe Asch, and other cultural brokers in their sphere planted the seeds for the American and European blues revivals in the prewar years, the postwar climate was the definitive period in which, as Ulrich Adelt concisely puts it, "the blues was reconfigured from black to white in its production and reception."[18] During the British and European blues revival in the 1950s and 1960s, young white audiences discovered—under the banner of "rediscovery"—folk and blues artists for the first time. A great deal of popular music emerging from the United Kingdom during the 1950s and 1960s drew heavily on twelve-bar blues; white English musicians began listening to and playing older British folk songs, as well as American folk blues, melding the forms together into skiffle, a style organized around guitar or banjo and enhanced by improvised homemade instruments, such as washboards and kazoos.[19] By the mid-1960s, informed by Tharpe and her rock-and-roll treatment of gospel standards, young English blues fans such as Eric Clapton, Mick Jagger, and Keith Richards were trying out the blues licks and hooks on the electric guitar, exploring sounds and writing songs that would soon reintroduce a mainstream American audience to a significant element of its musical heritage.

New avenues of distribution and circulation beyond the record enabled certain transformations in the transmission and reception of the blues. With the inauguration of the Newport Folk Festival, the American Folk

Blues Festival, and the American Folk, Blues, and Gospel Caravan, audiences could now attend live performances that, in their assortment of acts, resembled the variety shows of the early twentieth century. Collections of stars, traveling together, allowed audiences to hear their favorite musicians while also encountering less well-known singers. For the producers, the festival format offered an opportunity to curate or translate an unfamiliar musical form, much as John Hammond had done in his 1938 "From Spirituals to Swing" concert at Carnegie Hall. The musicians on the tour were often enlisted in this educational effort, framing their performances with references to other singers or offering a new interpretation of a familiar song. And while conversations about musical circulation generally focus on the production, distribution, and sale of records, live performance was central to the dissemination of blues music in Britain, especially after 1957, in part because the possibilities for radio and record distribution were limited. This centrality of live performance was matched—and bolstered—by one additional factor: the popularity of blues on television, which played a key role in stimulating British interest in new music.

Television crucially facilitated the introduction of blues performance to mass audiences in both Britain and Europe, and it was on television that the tools of blues' theatricality were often most enthusiastically employed. British television executives who had initially made their livings in the theater industry imported their training to their new medium, adorning the televisual blues of the early 1960s with stage sets and costumes. Granada Television, which broadcast *The Blues and Gospel Train*, was originally a theater-management company; Johnnie Hamp, the producer of the program, had as a young man worked in comedy at Granada-managed theaters, which generally offered an hour of live variety performance followed by two films. In the early 1950s he became a producer for Granada Theaters, managing both stage and cinema events.[20] Though he eventually worked exclusively in television, he retained a knack for the theatrical event, exemplified by *The Blues and Gospel Train*. Live blues performance thus found an ideal stage set in the television studio, which played a central role in translating blues to a foreign audience.

In spite of its proximity to the popular theater and music hall entertainment of both the United States and the United Kingdom, the transatlantic blues of the postwar period, particularly in England, was governed by a powerful strain of antitheatricalism. This (largely white) antitheatricalism manifested in several aspects of the blues tour, from the staging decisions, encouragements, and dissuasions of producers and promoters to the burgeoning industries of blues journalism, scholarship, and criticism. The negative association of the theatrical with the popular (and with the inauthentic) that was nascent in the 1930s and 1940s flourished among a broad listening public in the blues revival of the 1950s and 1960s. Many listeners preferred older performers, in part because they allowed for a certain nostalgic imagining of a distant African American past; indeed, some artists were aged beyond their years by audience members of *The Blues and Gospel Train*, who expressed surprise that Waters, Tharpe, and their colleagues were still living, let alone vibrant and energetic performers. This nostalgic look to an idealized past allowed young British whites to imagine themselves as modern and simultaneously bemoan what they saw as a decline in contemporary social and cultural life, due to mass culture and consumption. On the blues tours, theatrical elements were understood to be at odds with concepts of the natural and the authentic that governed audiences' encounters with black musicians. Singled out for particular scorn were those performers who paid too much heed to their personal appearances, a prejudice made particularly plain by Paul Oliver's review of the American Negro Blues Festival's concert at Croydon in 1964. Of Sonny Boy Williamson, the opening act, he complained: "He is now, I think, 'over-exposed' and a rest wouldn't do any harm at all. Something slightly irritating in his assumption of the lead role—'prima-donna-ish' was one comment made to me with not a little justification—put up a certain barrier to appreciation. He now affects a Harlequin suit of grey and black alternating and his gloves, umbrella, and a derby hat. It is an ensemble that doesn't really add anything to the performance."[21] Williamson's onstage persona was of great interest and occasional concern to those who saw him perform in 1964; though Oliver does not mention it, Williamson was also known to speak with a British accent.[22] As an American who lived off and on in London throughout the early 1960s until his death in 1965, Williamson navigated an idea of dual citizenship through his stage costume, but its status *as* costume was deeply troubling to Oliver and others, who suspected that Williamson may have been mocking his British audiences, even though he very well may have been aligning himself with them.

Emboldened by the barely veiled antitheatricalism of music journalism, audiences, producers, and promoters made a slew of demands on touring performers, requiring many of them to shelve pieces of their acts and encouraging them to strip their shows of anything that smacked as entertainment, showmanship, or conscious creativity. Horst Lippmann, of the American Folk Blues Festival, recalled his instructions to the musicians: "Before we started the tour, I held a meeting. I told the blues people, 'You are now here in a different area. You're not back in America anymore, where you have to use gimmicks to entertain the people. What we want to do is just bring your message as a blues singer, as a blues artist. You don't have to play the guitar backwards, or with your feet, or with your tongue. Just play the blues.' For some, it was very difficult to understand."[23] In opposing "gimmicks" to artistry, Lippmann established a high-low hierarchy of blues performance, one in which unembellished singing trumped costume, choreography, and comedy, which were viewed as lowbrow American stunts. Dancing, long a staple skill and frequent companion of blues, was nearly eradicated during this period; neither performers nor audiences did much dancing on most of the European tours, or at American festivals, such as the Newport Folk Festival.[24] Later in his Croydon review, Oliver bemoaned Howlin' Wolf's choreography: "Howlin' Wolf concluded the show and was an immense disappointment. . . . Howlin' Wolf is an actor, and just about the biggest ham actor on the stage. He clutched his heart for 'love,' pointed at his head for 'I see,' threw open his arms like a puppet for 'darlin'.' He also danced, a galumphing gorilla-like dance which was laughable if it hadn't gone on for so long. All this was extremely regrettable."[25] For the most part, the performers obeyed, though some musicians refused to leave their "gimmicks" behind. There were not a few occasions of the artists donning flashy costumes, experimenting with choreography, and playing outside the approved genre of the tour; all of this clowning around was strongly frowned upon, by audiences and critics alike. In an interview he granted some years later, Brownie McGhee made a sharp distinction between "musicians" and "entertainers," identifying entertainment with agency and musicianship with a work-for-hire arrangement: "I'm an *entertainer*, not a musician. . . . [A] musician plays for anything, for anybody. I play for myself. . . . An entertainer is a man who plays what he feels and feels what he plays. He don't give a damn and he don't play it the same way twice." Resistant to rehearsal and scripted spontaneity, McGhee noted that he occasionally put his guitar behind his head: "Because I feel like I wanna do that."[26]

As white authenticators stripped away the elements that had previously defined popular blues, they offered the resultant minimalist performances to European audiences as authentic representations of Southern blackness. In addition, an urban-rural binary began to take hold: city blues were determined to be "tainted" by popular music and the stain of entertainment, and Mississippi blues were hailed as the most significant.[27] Correlatively, female performers were largely marginalized. The myth of the Rural bluesman resulted in a full-scale masculinization of the form, both on- and offstage, with men making up the majority of performers, scholars, critics, producers, and promoters, in spite of the fact that British women listened to and enjoyed the classic blues artists, and that, as Sherrie Tucker aptly demonstrates, "all girl" bands flourished in the pre- and postwar eras.[28]

In spite of the widespread condemnation of theatrical elements, transatlantic blues-revival performance thrived on the exploitation of those elements. This paradox—disavowing theatrical traditions while simultaneously making extensive use of them—both produced and maintained authenticity's authority. Just as with John Lomax's staging of Lead Belly, authenticity—as grounded in a performer's appearance, repertoire, mythos, and stage conduct—was theatrically produced, a practice that is apparent in both *The Blues and Gospel Train* and the footage of the live concerts and the American Folk Blues Festival television specials from the early 1960s. While blues fans, especially during the revival, rhetorically rejected theatrical elements, most seemed blind to the role these elements played in producing the authenticity they consumed. Intriguingly, those who were aware of such manipulated concepts of authenticity came from the world of jazz criticism. In a piece in the April 1964 issue of *Jazz Journal*, John Postgate responded to readers' dissatisfaction with Hamp's 1963 blues television special, *I Hear the Blues*: "Why, then, this moan of discontent? The answer, of course, is that it was too authentic for most of us. The blues is still a living entertainment in the U.S.A., and a highly unsophisticated form of entertainment. This is what our visitors tried to provide. Gimmicks, novelty numbers, simple humorous and vibrant guitars are what the customers pay for in Nashville and points South. In a country where physical peculiarity is still a source of humour, Willie Dixon's *Nervous Blues* probably brings the house down, but to well-fed and educated Britons it was just poor jazz in bad taste."[29] Though Postgate, who preferred the (high-art) "taste" of jazz, didn't necessarily have a higher opinion of the "gimmicks" or "novelty numbers" than blues critics like Oliver or producers like Lippmann, he identified these qualities as being *integral* to the "authenticity" of the performance, rather than as an impediment to it.

FROM BROADWAY TO BRUSSELS

The stars of the transatlantic tours were thrown headlong into a new performance environment. Told that their gimmicks wouldn't translate to their new audiences, they most often performed not in nightclubs or under tents but in television studios and concert halls, before groups that sat stock-still, confirming their appreciation with polite attention and muted applause instead of dancing or shouting. All professionals, these performers quickly adapted, but one wonders what kinds of shows Terry, McGhee,

Tharpe, and Cousin Joe might have staged if they had been able to choose venues in addition to set lists. These artists, all of whom appeared on *The Blues and Gospel Train*, had extensive backgrounds in theatrical performance, from popular and political theater to cabaret and revue acts, from New York City's Broadway to New Orleans's Famous Door. A closer look at their careers reveals their fluency with theatrical media and the broad skill sets and performance traditions that white European authenticators had to either work with or attempt to stamp out.

Sonny Terry and Brownie McGhee, both from the Piedmont, formed a partnership in New York City in the early 1940s and performed together for the better part of five decades, with Terry on the harmonica and McGhee on the guitar. Closely associated with the Popular Front, McGhee and Terry lived with Ledbetter and Martha Promise in their East Village apartment for a year, during which time the elder singer mentored the younger pair in matters of music and self-presentation, constantly urging them to carry their instruments in proper cases, and to wear coats, ties, and polished shoes.[30] A full generation younger than Ledbetter, McGhee and Terry followed in their mentor's footsteps and extended the transatlantic touring he had begun to explore before being felled by illness; from the 1950s until their deaths, they routinely toured Europe and were central figures in the performance and dissemination of blues abroad during the 1950s and 1960s. Like Ledbetter, with whom they recorded, Terry (born Saunders Terrell) and McGhee (born Walter McGhee) were songsters who moved seamlessly among folk, blues, and rhythm and blues, performing for black and white audiences at hootenannies, political rallies, and benefit concerts, as well as in theatrical spectacles.[31] McGhee explained his repertoire of country, hillbilly, and blues music that he played before black and white coal miners in the 1930s: "Every music was mine; I liked it all."[32] Both performed with medicine shows in their youth; in an interview McGhee described his "longing for the road" that led him to join the traveling shows, where he sang blues and specialized in "flat foot buck dancing."[33] In New York they performed on the cabaret blues circuit, bringing the "radicalism of Harlem and the Carolina Piedmont" to Popular Front theatrical events.[34] Performing in the cabarets staged by the radical Theater Arts Committee, Terry, McGhee, Josh White, and others linked popular jazz, blues, Brechtian theater, and Popular Front politics. McGhee and Terry extended their political involvement in the Theater Arts Committee and continued to lend their performances to antilynching campaigns, combining black Piedmont labor activism with the political and artistic priorities of the cultural front.

In 1944 McGhee and Terry had singing and speaking parts in Hughes's radio play *The Man Who Went to War*, an early and significant attempt to translate blues to and for a British audience that also featured Josh White, Ethel Waters, Paul Robeson, Canada Lee, and the Hall Johnson Choir.[35] Recorded in New York City for broadcast on the BBC with the assistance of Alan and Elizabeth Lomax, the ballad opera was reportedly "conceived" by the BBC producer Geoffrey Bridson "in the eighteenth-century tradition of John Gay." As John Szwed points out, however, "Lomax and Hughes may have thought of it as being more along the lines of Zora Neale Hurston's folk-song-based *The Great Day*."[36] *The Man Who Went to War* tells the story of a soldier, Johnny (played by Lee), who must leave his wife (Waters) and children to fight at the front during World War II. Facing bombings, boredom, and heavy labor, he perseveres until he is seriously wounded. Following an otherworldly near-death experience, he returns home to his family. After a joyous reunion, the radio play concludes with Johnny's decision to go back to the front; he explains to his family: "I'm fighting so everybody can enjoy life like us."[37] Spirituals, sung by the Hall Johnson Choir, and blues, sung by McGhee, Terry, and White, pepper the script. Hughes grounded the action of the play in well-known songs, with McGhee and Terry singing "John Henry" at the front and "I Don't Feel No Ways Tired"—a spiritual that would become a civil rights anthem— as a rousing conclusion. Johnny hints at the freedom struggles to come when he explains that the spirituals heard throughout will someday be sung "by all the folks who long for peace—but who long most of all—for freedom."[38]

The Man Who Went to War translates black American music for a British audience by theatrically layering black vernacular America and war-torn London. The conceit of the opera amalgamates American music with a British setting, the first indication of which is that the front is close to home rather than across the sea, and the characters who sing blues and spirituals at the British front are all played by black American actors. Robeson, by this point widely known for his international performance career and political activism, introduced the radio play with a prologue that addressed the British people; though set in England, the story, he explains, "might be set anywhere that the war has been fought. . . . But . . . we are giving you a picture that you yourselves have lived through, Britain—only the words and the songs are our own, for these are the words and the songs that Negroes sing."[39] In these introductory remarks, Hughes, through Robeson, goes to some length to underscore the commutability of spirituals and blues, suggesting that their performance can enrich a representation of British life just as it can illuminate shared struggles across national, racial, and cultural boundaries.

The Man Who Went to War made blues legible to a European audience through the matrix of war against Germany. The experience of war became a filter through which blues was translated for British and European consumption for decades, a practice explained by Big Bill Broonzy in a 1957 interview: "It's no country I've been in my life that people don't have the blues. 'Course, they have it a different way. They have it through wars, and through the different destructions and things that we don't have here."[40] After acknowledging that the blues can be felt—and can be understood—by everyone, Broonzy took pains to acknowledge national and cultural differences around these blues. The artist, he notes, must "explain what you gonna play," so that audiences have the necessary background required to appreciate the subsequent song. *The Man Who Went to War* translated blues for a European audience by casting the music and the musicians in geopolitical terms, and then transcending those terms in favor of international solidarity. In the prologue Robeson, by means of his own star power and political reputation, sutures an antifascist European struggle to an antiracist American one; the black cast members, Robeson explains, are "just a few of your thirteen million Negro allies in the United States. We, too, are a part of this great global war against fascism. Like your own, they are the songs of one more freedom-loving people." At the same time, the play also pointedly suggests the injustices of Jim Crow and the ironies of black soldiers fighting for European freedom abroad while they are denied freedom at home.

In the later 1940s and the 1950s, Terry and McGhee garnered significant experience on Broadway, which staged a spate of plays and musicals that incorporated blues into their mise-en-scènes. In contrast to the black-cast revues that had been so popular in earlier decades, these productions featured mixed-race casts and often contained racially progressive messages. In 1947 Terry was cast as Sunny in *Finian's Rainbow*, a musical satire of racism and American capitalism. Writing for the *New York Times*, Brooks Atkinson praised the show's "social significance," a winking reference to the Theater Arts Committee's Popular Front cabarets, as well as the 1937 musical *Pins and Needles*, created with the International Ladies' Garment Workers' Union and whose "Sing Me a Song of Social Significance" quickly became shorthand for cultural-front theatrical experiments.[41] A transatlantic comedy in which hypocritical American values are revealed through the eyes of a foreigner, *Finian's Rainbow* tells the tale of an Irishman, Finian, who has stolen gold from a leprechaun. Together with his daughter, Sharon, he travels to Rainbow Valley, a utopian community of black and white sharecroppers living in the fictional U.S. state of Missitucky, and he attempts to bury the treasure in the ground. The sheriff and the bigoted senator Billboard Rawkins (a pointed nod to Mississippi's segregationist senator Theodore Bilbo and congressional representative John Rankin) threaten the happiness of the peacefully integrated town, unofficially led by the folksinger and union organizer Woody Mahoney (a clear reference to Woody Guthrie, played in the premiere by the actor and activist Will Geer, of *Tobacco Road* fame). In an unusual twist, *Finian's Rainbow* is a musical firmly on the side of desegregation, but accomplishes its point—and its comedy—through the use of blackface. The musical's turning point occurs when Rawkins, by dint of a bit of Irish magic and a bit of burned cork, is transformed into a black man and must live under the segregationist policies that he himself has put into place. In the end there are marriages and happy endings for all, including the senator, who is transformed once more, this time into a white man cured of his bigotry. All of these transformations are brought about by the central plot device: a pot of gold that allows for the casting of spells and the granting of wishes.

As Sunny, Terry played a small but crucial role in *Finian's Rainbow*. His harmonica was the first sound heard by the audience, an unexpected way to open a Broadway musical. For the first two minutes, Terry played a harmonica piece of his own composition—a piece that, regrettably, does not appear on the original cast album. This opening number, referred to by the *Boston Globe* as "Hooping the Blues," was a variation of the most famous number Terry played throughout his career: the alternately haunting and raucous "Hootin' Blues" (sometimes called "Whoopin' the Blues"), which opened *The Blues and Gospel Train* television special seventeen years later. In the second act he played another harmonica blues, this time from offstage, which accompanied the character Susan's "Dance of the Golden Crock"—also, lamentably, unrecorded. More than just accompaniment, the stage directions indicate that Terry's harmonica functions as a character of its own in *Finian's Rainbow*, explaining that the sound of "a lazy harmonica" is punctuated by "a note of urgency and alarm" when the musician "sees or senses something off-scene." Like an Irish flute, the harmonica summons the entrance of characters and is referred to by Finian as "the same skylark music we have back in Ireland!"[42] Terry performed with *Finian's Rainbow* on Broadway for many months, and then for almost an additional year on its national tour; he was one of the longest-serving members of the company. While the role of Sunny is quite small in the script, it's clear from reading reviews of the production that Terry was a much more central player in *Finian's Rainbow* than the script or score indicates.

Dramaturgically and musically, Terry acted as the authenticating agent of *Finian's Rainbow*'s satire of minstrelsy—itself a theatrical gamble that risked reinstating blackface's racist norms. For the most part, members of the black press were enthusiastic about the production; the *Pittsburgh Courier* approvingly described the way *Finian's Rainbow* "makes a huge joke of racial stereotypes" and "lightly caricatures some of the more stalwart defenders of white supremacy without ever dwelling too long on a sore subject."[43] Structurally, Terry and his harmonica acted as a bridge between the offstage world of the audience and the onstage world of Missitucky. By virtue of this dramaturgical arrangement, and the fact that Terry himself had biographical roots in the sharecropping South—a fact repeatedly emphasized in the press and in the production's playbill—Terry emerged as a "real" black Southerner dropped into the satirical fantasy world of *Finian's Rainbow*.[44] More than any of the other black characters, then, it was Terry whose presence authorized the use of blackface in the musical: by juxtaposing Rawkins, the white senator in blackface, with Terry, the "authentic" black man, *Finian's Rainbow* reveals blackface minstrelsy as an act, a "huge joke."

Terry and McGhee often worked together as actors, and Broadway roles followed for both men. They performed together in the premiere of Tennessee Williams's *Cat on a Hot Tin Roof*, appearing with the production from 1955 to 1957, and McGhee played the role of Gitfiddle in Hughes's 1958 *Simply Heavenly*, a character described as "a folk artist going to seed, unable to compete with the juke box, TV, and the radio, having only his guitar and his undisciplined talents."[45] Along with "the Barfly pianist," Gitfiddle played all the music in the show. These interludes remain unpublished by virtue of McGhee's skill; as Hughes notes in the published version of the play, "if the guitarist is a good folk musician, he can easily improvise" the blues chords and variations played during scene changes.[46] In both *Cat on a Hot Tin Roof* and *Simply Heavenly*, as in *Finian's Rainbow*, the actor-musicians were loosely integrated into the narrative of the play, serving as characters who provided diegetic musical accompaniment. While apocryphal stories circulate about the pair's theatrical naïveté, their long runs on Broadway and on tour suggest a level of preparation and professionalism beyond what many were willing to acknowledge.[47]

Both Terry and McGhee, who were frequently cast by white directors as representatives of African American culture and music, had a degree of autonomy when it came to choosing the songs they played on stage; these choices shaped the theatrical world of the production and occasionally provided a counterpoint to its dominant narrative. The 1955 premiere of *Cat on a Hot Tin Roof*, directed by Elia Kazan, featured five black actor-musicians:

Maxwell Glanville, an actor with the American Negro Theatre, played Lacey; Musa Williams, who had performed in the operas *John Henry* and *Porgy and Bess*, played Sookey; Eva Vaughn Smith, who had performed in *Four Saints in Three Acts* two decades earlier, played Daisy; McGhee played Brightie; and Terry played Small. Many reviewers did not see the black characters as anything other than supernumeraries: Brooks Atkinson does not mention them in his *New York Times* review, nor does Eric Bentley in his piece for *The New Republic*.[48] The black press, on the other hand, celebrated Williams, Glanville, Smith, McGhee, and Terry, all of whom were widely known in black theatrical and musical circles. The *Chicago Defender* marked the production's arrival in Chicago in 1957 with a lengthy feature that described the musicians' full collaboration in the rehearsal process, and the creative free rein given to them by Kazan. Terry, McGhee, Williams, Glanville, and Smith auditioned with much of the same material that was later incorporated into the show; though unknown to Northern audiences, the *Chicago Defender* noted, the seven songs of *Cat on a Hot Tin Roof* are "known in the Mississippi Delta where the action occurs."[49] In the context of the play, the songs, such as "John Henry" and "Pick a Bale of Cotton," both old Lead Belly favorites, do not serve Williams's injunction to create a "gently and poetically haunted" Mississippi Delta plantation on stage, but rather emphasize black labor in contrast to the white leisure of the play and reveal the underlying structures of white supremacy that bolster the play's action.[50] Using song as dramaturgical counterpoint to mise-en-scène, McGhee, Terry, and their collaborators developed a strategy for complying with the demands of the designers and director while, however obliquely, allowing for a registration of dissent.

The "preeminent heroine of the blues revival and its leading gospel protagonist," Tharpe was one of the biggest stars of the transatlantic blues scene, one whose outsized influence on rock and roll had been largely forgotten until the recent work of the historian and critic Gayle Wald brought renewed attention to Tharpe's life and career.[51] A pre- and postwar fixture at New York cabarets and Café Society, Tharpe came not from the world of the touring medicine or minstrel show but from the equally theatrical world of the touring gospel-music circuit. Though often rhetorically held at a distance from the world of secular music, sacred singing could be a direct pipeline to secular success; Cousin Joe put it some years later: "Most everything they sang spiritually really *sounded* bluesy. . . . They take the melody from a Baptist church hymn, change the words and put it into rock and roll."[52] Born in 1915 in the Arkansas Delta town of Cotton Plant, Tharpe was a child and teen star who began her life on the road early, touring with her mother throughout the 1930s. When they moved to New York, she moved in a more secular direction, and, while juggling live appearances with recording engagements for Decca Records, she frequently appeared at a variety of high-profile venues before both black and white audiences, uptown and downtown. A musical polymath, she was equally at home in blues, swing, gospel, rock, and country. With Marie Knight, Tharpe toured the U.S. South and Midwest to huge audiences and great acclaim. But as gospel star Mahalia Jackson's star rose, Tharpe's waned. Tharpe's career was reborn in the late 1950s, when she began touring to Britain and Continental Europe. She frequently headlined, as she did in *The Blues and Gospel Train*, and her musicianship and performance style had an inestimable influence on the young British rockers who would later become globally famous for their imitations of Tharpe's guitar choreography.

As a performer who toured nearly nonstop for much of her adult life, Tharpe shared a great deal in common with the female tent stars who had preceded her, especially their penchant for elaborate stage shows, costuming, and choreography.[53] Contemporaries and critics frequently compared her to the classic female blues artists, particularly Bessie Smith; like Smith and Gertrude "Ma" Rainey, Tharpe was known to have female lovers.[54] Her wigs and glittering gowns set elegance as the standard for touring performers, and her independence on the tours, particularly with Knight, is reminiscent of the leadership, entrepreneurship, and resourcefulness demonstrated by those women who led their own tours in the teens and twenties. While Tharpe did not usually resemble Smith in vocal style, her 1940s hit, the double entendre-laced "I Want a Tall Skinny Papa," sounded similar to nothing so much as a young Smith singing about her "sweet jelly roll." Though she recorded frequently, she thrived in the live show, relishing the opportunity to appear in wigs, to dance, and to make jokes with her audience. At a time when white audiences of blues preferred to hear the form as an expression of misery, Tharpe was resolutely joyous, her faith in deliverance and salvation infusing all of her performances. Though the masculinization of the form and a rising tide of antitheatricality eventually marginalized Tharpe in the story of the blues revival, her commitment to spectacle and celebration resonated far beyond Cotton Plant as she imported the theatricality of blues and gospel into rock.

Tharpe's participation in the irreverent tradition of theatrical blues comedy arguably set the stage for her long career. Upon arriving in New York, Tharpe became a regular at both the Cotton Club and the Apollo, where her singing was incorporated into skits, revues, and variety acts. She was not always glamorously costumed: a 1944 photograph from *Cue* magazine shows her singing "That's All, Brother, That's All" before a largely white audience at Café Zanzibar, costumed in a checkered shirt, sun hat, and clutching an acoustic guitar, resembling a female Lead Belly (see figure 3.1). But the article that accompanied the photograph describes a quite different Tharpe, one who "has discarded the church robes for a peg-top evening dress, tucked feathers in an upswept hair-do, and looks surprisingly like a plump Gloria Swanson"—a far cry from the Tharpe seen in the photograph.[55] The quick-change tradition of the blues queen endured in Tharpe's appearances before both black and white audiences. When she and Marie Knight toured together, their "Saint and Sinner" routine reveled in the rapid transformation of identity that Smith had played with some decades earlier. While the two women normally appeared in "coordinated gowns or suits," often accessorized with hats, feathers, jewels, and furs, the "Saint and Sinner" routine employed a number of costumes—and showed them all to *be* costume. Tharpe, predictably playing the saint, wore one of her regular gowns and played her guitar. Knight, as the sinner, wore the costume of a sharecropper, much like the one Tharpe had worn at Café Zanzibar—"a big straw hat and jeans and playing a tiny ukulele." As Wald describes, "the contrast between the high-toned, urbane 'saint' and the low-down country bumpkin, with their differently sized instruments" sent the audience into hysterics. At the conclusion of the skit, Knight was the quick-change artist, reappearing on stage in her gown once again, to the great satisfaction of the crowd.[56]

Tharpe, who was raised in the Church of God in Christ, moved with ease between sacred and secular music, as had Thomas Dorsey before her, but her troubling of the boundary between the two worried some of her gospel fans. The difference between sacred and secular may have been more "moral rather than musical," but Tharpe's musical and stylistic hybridity sometimes got her into trouble.[57] Though some did not approve of her performances with Lucky Millinder and His Orchestra, with whom she appeared in the 1940s, the real stir came when Tharpe began to import the theatricality of Pentecostal camp meetings and revivals into her own acts at the Apollo and the Cotton Club. In 1939 and 1940 Tharpe became well known for performing a routine at both venues that recalled a scene from Hurston's *The Great Day* and that *Variety* described in columns as "a holy-roller meeting" and "a camp-meeting number." At the Cotton Club the minstrel comedy was over the top: Tharpe arrived on stage accompanied by a mule, "to the back of which a phone book, suggesting a Bible, [was] strapped." After some business, Tharpe "conduct[ed] her meetin'."[58] At the Apollo the act was no less spectacular, but she exchanged the minstrel-show aesthetics of the Cotton Club routine for "gals dressed in bright-colored old-fashioned dresses on folding chairs around the back of the stage." A group called the Four Alphabets crooned from upstage while comics did "the preacher stuff," a burlesque that climaxed in the appearance of Tharpe herself.[59]

While some were scandalized by the sacrilege, for Tharpe—for whom irreverence was professional and personal currency—there was both homage and critique at work, as well as a recognition that the minstrel show, the variety revue, and the "holy-roller meeting" all pulled from a shared repertoire of manufactured affect and theatrical tricks that enabled the production of sincerity. Her implicit suggestion that blues and gospel performance might share theatrical strategies—or, as Cousin Joe put it, a common supply of "hustling" and "hype"—became a thorny sticking point with her more pious fans.[60] A photograph of the Cotton Club stage that accompanied a profile published by *Life* magazine in 1939 condenses the church and the variety stage—and, by implication, sacred and secular singing—in the figure of Tharpe. Under the alliterative headline "Singer Swings Same Songs in Church and Nightclub," a large black-and-white photograph features Tharpe before a painted backdrop decorated with the markings of windowpanes and reversed lettering that reads "Pentecostal." The backdrop leads the audience to understand that everyone, performers and spectators alike, are inside a Pentecostal church *and* the Cotton Club, where the stage is a church and the church is a stage. The proscenium frame of the stage is decorated with a dancing devil and a childlike representation of Noah's ark, and the threat of eternal damnation gives the impression of an awfully good time, as the stage fills with jitterbugging ensemble members.[61] Tharpe's holy-roller meetings, which were a manifestation of the theatrical sincerity—neither real nor feigned, but something quite other entirely— that governed her career, illuminated the structures that undergirded the production of feeling both on the stage and in the church.

Tharpe's ultimate marriage of sacred and secular, of Christian sincerity with theatrical pageantry, came in the form of her 1951 wedding to Russell Morrison. Held at Griffith Stadium in Washington, DC, the event was witnessed by an audience of approximately twenty thousand people, many of whom came dressed in their Sunday best and bearing gifts for the happy couple. Tharpe and her management conceived of the wedding as a business opportunity at a time when Tharpe was being overshadowed by Jackson—who, unlike Tharpe, kept the sacred-secular binary firmly intact, refusing to perform at the Apollo or any theatrical venue. In spite of (or perhaps because of) the event's calculated intent, sincerity was its overriding affect. To the naysayers who believed the marriage to be a publicity stunt, the Reverend Samuel Kelsey, a well-known Church of God in Christ minister, said of the marriage license in his hand: "You know, somebody said it's a fake! But anytime you see me stand on the floor with a piece of paper in my hand, you may know it's not a fake."[62] Though embedded in a stadium concert that was capped off by fireworks and witnessed by a bridal party of backup singers, Tharpe, Morrison, and Kelsey performed the ceremony with reverent seriousness. The fact that it was Tharpe's third marriage was only vaguely alluded to by Kelsey, who jokingly remarked: "I know how to marry people. I know how to put them together. If they don't stay together, it's not my fault!" But stay together they did (albeit often unhappily), until Tharpe's death. Troubling the line between a theatrical spectacle and a legally binding performative, the wedding was something of a sincere wink. Cultivated through years of practice, Tharpe's earnestly over-the-top ethos defined her performance style, a style that would serve her well when she arrived at an abandoned train depot near Manchester, England, thirteen years after her wedding in a baseball stadium.

THE BLUES AND GOSPEL TRAIN

The stage was filled with a hodgepodge of detritus: posters advertising "wanted" criminals and specious medical cures festooned the exterior of the waiting structure; rocking chairs, hay bales, and rotted-out wooden crates provided seating; hanging shutters, sacks of cotton, a damaged wagon, and a washtub of laundry were scattered about; and the entire scene was crowned by the presence of livestock—roaming chickens and two non-plussed goats, one black, and one white (see figure 3.2). A sign indicating the decidedly British-sounding Wilbraham Road was exchanged for one that Americanized the Manchester suburb of Chorlton to Chorltonville, painted in a Wild West–style typeface. Primarily Southern and agricultural in its panoply of signifiers, Chorltonville was a motley place, its props and typefaces mixing fantasies of the Deep South with the outlaw imagery of the Wild West. Onto this stage stepped a cast of characters: a wandering hobo, a downhome duo, a minstrel clown, and a triumphant queen.

The Blues and Gospel Train, which was taped at Wilbraham Road station on May 7, 1964, and broadcast to twelve to fourteen million British Northerners on August 19 of that same year, repurposed a disused train station in the suburbs of Manchester, decorating one platform so as to "create the Old Southern States feel about it," while an audience of a couple hundred Mancunian teenagers watched from stadium seating on the opposite platform.[63] The event featured Sister Rosetta Tharpe, Sonny Terry and

Rossner

That's Sister Rosetta Tharpe *(above),* singing *That's All, Brother, That's All.* At *right* is glittering-eyed Cab Calloway himself. All at Zanzibar. See below

Mr. Calloway Comes to Town

THE ENTERPRISING Cafe Zanzibar brings Cab Calloway back to the night club scene with a lively show. Mr. Calloway as handsome and prankish as ever adds to the general excitement with his usual quantity of capers. And the Zanzibar show girls are still about the handsomest in town. Besides .some ex-

Arsene

Brownie McGhee, Muddy Waters, and Cousin Joe, among others, who were on tour with the American Folk, Blues, and Gospel Caravan, which traveled through Britain during the spring and summer of 1964.[64] Formed by George Wein; Harold Davison, a British agent; and Joe Boyd, a twenty-two-year-old American manager; the caravan attempted to compete with the American Folk Blues Festival tours while also borrowing a great deal of the theatrical and musical formula that had made the American Folk Blues Festival such a success. Squeezed in between concert dates, the taping of *The Blues and Gospel Train* took one very long day. As Cousin Joe later recalled, "When they brought us for lunch I thought it was all over with, but they said, 'Oh, no. We were just adjusting for sound. Now we're going to do the real *thing*.' And we had to do the whole thing over again."[65]

The Blues and Gospel Train appears to be a spectacular exception to the impulse to shed scenic adornment that governed postwar blues performance at Café Society and other left-leaning venues, particularly in the United States. From that perspective, *The Blues and Gospel Train* seems a peculiar one-night-only event that in its scenic practices, at least, deviated from customary performance conventions. Indeed, many black musical acts in the United States had long been casting off the theatrical trappings of cotton-field backdrops and other racialized fantasies of "the South" that had characterized many of their musical performances before blacks and whites in the early twentieth century. But scenic decoration was still a widespread practice in transatlantic blues concerts; while *The Blues and Gospel Train* is a peerless example, its deployment of theatrical conventions in its staging of blues is by no means unique. An analysis of *The Blues and Gospel Train* sheds light not only on the extraordinary event but also on those performances where the scenic translation of blues for a foreign audience was decidedly more moderate or understated.

Both scenically and architecturally, the decorated Chorltonville train platform evoked multiple spaces and places: train depot, front porch, theatrical stage, Mississippi, and Manchester. The theatricality of *The Blues and Gospel Train* was established by its use of scenery and props and also by its spatial and architectural relations—that is, by its activation of a ready-made proscenium arch. The ironwork features of the train platform—a scalloped iron canopy and classically inspired iron structural support col-

3.1 *(opposite above)* Sister Rosetta Tharpe performs at Café Zanzibar, *Cue*, 1944. Billy Rose Theatre Division, the New York Public Library for the Performing Arts, Astor, Lenox and Tilden Foundations.

3.2 *(opposite below)* Sister Rosetta Tharpe performs on a train-station platform in *The Blues and Gospel Train*, 1964. Reelin' in the Years Productions.

umns—transformed Wilbraham Road into a picture-frame stage. Into this proscenium arch stepped Tharpe, who stood perfectly centered between the two iron columns during her songs. The architectural configuration of nearly identical train platforms facing each other established a thicket of intervisibility, a situation in which spectator and spectacle were regularly reversed, both by the camera, which frequently filmed the audience, and by the performers themselves, who routinely addressed spectators directly. So as to appropriately model musical appreciation for the at-home viewers, the live audience was carefully cast and costumed. The producer, Hamp, who invited students from the University of Manchester to attend, instructed them to wear "denim and sweaters" in order to appear "more modern, more bluesy."[66] He directed half the students to meet at Wilbraham Road; the other half gathered in central Manchester, where a specially hired locomotive with a "Hallelujah" sign on the front brought them and the musicians to the site of the performance.

For a site-specific blues concert, the train station was an obvious choice of venue. The train station amplified the tropes of train tracks, train travel, and train whistles constantly surfacing in blues lyrics, and it also allowed for a reference to one of the most widely disseminated scenarios of blues' discovery: W. C. Handy's 1903 awakening from a nap at the Tutwiler, Mississippi, depot to the sounds of a young man playing "Goin' Where the Southern Cross the Dog" on a slide guitar. For the young audience at Wilbraham Road, watching Waters amble down the railroad ties, carrying a valise, dressed in traveling clothes, and quietly singing "you can't lose what you never had" to himself, reanimated this scenario of discovery of blues in its "natural" environment. Waters's amble down the tracks was essential to creating what Hamp called "the Old Southern States feel"; "this old hobo just walking down," as he put it, reproduced a primal scene of blues travel, using the mobility of its performers to momentarily transport its audience to an imagined Mississippi.[67] What's more, Waters's walk down the tracks reenacted his personal journey from rural, agricultural, acoustic Mississippi to urban, industrial, electrified Chicago, a suggestive transatlantic revisioning of blues' restless fugitivity that conflated migration and the tour under the rubric of an arrival that was also a stage entrance.

SCENIC ALLUSIONS: THE AMERICAN FOLK BLUES FESTIVAL

The stage set of *The Blues and Gospel Train* attempted to create an in situ environment for the musicians, a widespread schema employed by white European and American blues producers during the sixties, and one that would experience a postmodern resurgence in the blues tourism of the 1990s and 2000s. While the material realities of the tour often prevented the transportation of elaborate set pieces, the creation of in situ stage environments did not end with the closure of the Cotton Club. If anything, the creation of these environments intensified, pushed ahead by growing demands for performers, many of them men, to appear rural, impoverished, Southern—that is, "authentic"—to their white middle-class audiences. As Ulrich Adelt describes, elderly musicians at the Newport Folk Festival in 1964 "were forced to stay in a segregated, sparsely furnished white frame building that was dubbed 'blues house.'"[68] An unlikely lodging alternative in a town filled with Gilded Age mansions, the blues house was praised by the blues historian Samuel Charters, who implied direct links between the surroundings and the music produced there: "The rooms were bare, the floors without rugs, the furniture mostly iron cots that had been carried into the house just before the performers began arriving. . . . For many of them it was as though they were back at one of the sukey jumps or cabin buck dances of their youth, and they spent hours playing for each other."[69] Two years later, Alan Lomax re-created a juke joint at Newport, using it as a stage set for a documentary film entitled *Devil Got My Woman: Blues at Newport 1966*, which featured Son House, Bukka White, and Howlin' Wolf. The tendency toward in situ environments—a response to a so-called crisis of displacement generated by the very conditions of the tour itself—was so extensive that Paul Oliver, while ultimately rejecting these simulations, felt the need to address the issue of touring performers' displacement from their regular settings, even when those homes were not in Mississippi but in Chicago or New York. The British Fairfield Hall, Oliver noted in 1964, is "about as far removed from the setting in which the singers normally work as you could get. . . . There is no possibility of reproducing the atmosphere or a Chicago club or a country juke, and any attempt to do so would be fatal to the life of the shows. It is better, therefore, to offer instead the best setting possible in honour of the guests."[70] In spite of Oliver's claim of impossibility, many continued to try to "reproduce[e] the atmosphere" of the juke joint; the American Folk Blues Festival, in particular, frequently attempted to re-create in situ environments, on both the stage and the small screen.

The American Folk, Blues, and Gospel Caravan and *The Blues and Gospel Train* were deeply indebted to four German men who were largely responsible for mapping the visual landscape of blues performance in postwar Europe. In 1962 Horst Lippmann and Fritz Rau enlisted the assistance of the American musician and producer Willie Dixon. Together with Joachim-Ernst Berendt, the host of the German television program *Jazz Gehört und Gesehen* (Jazz heard and seen), they organized the American Folk Blues Festival, a rotating circuit of musicians who embarked on annual European tours between 1962 and 1970. They booked concerts throughout Europe, usually at spaces that hosted classical music, and Berendt made television specials each year that were watched by millions. Lippmann and Rau were particularly interested in black music's potential to aid antiracist causes and denazification in the 1960s. By promoting blues as a progenitor of jazz—itself a musical form with a complicated relationship to the Third Reich—Lippmann and Rau's tours fit within a larger countercultural impulse that grounded romantic ideas in attachments to the cultural and social life of racialized Others.[71] Though the live shows and television specials were advertised as "a documentation of the authentic blues," the producers of the American Folk Blues Festival went to great lengths to produce racial authenticity.[72]

Lippmann, Rau, and Berendt's inclination to "dress up" the blues—even as they tried to squelch the more outrageous performance "gimmicks" of the performers they employed—was enabled by a figure of singular importance in the blues revival: Günther Kieser. Kieser nearly single-handedly established the visual rhetoric of the European blues revival. A designer of elaborate sets for stage shows as well as the annual American Folk Blues Festival's television special *Jazz Heard and Seen*, Kieser also produced the tour's artwork, posters, album covers, and promotional materials.[73] The common scenographic language developed by Kieser governed nearly a decade of blues' stage life in Europe and the United Kingdom. Kieser's sets for the stage performances often included painted backdrops of railroad tracks and agricultural landscapes; the television specials were even more dramatically in situ, as musicians were frequently installed on front porches or in "re-created juke joints, saloons, and nightclubs," complete with "studio props like furniture, barrels, palm trees, and American cars."[74] Taped performances from 1962, for example, show both T-Bone Walker and Sonny Terry and Brownie McGhee performing on a set labeled a "saloon," including shutters and front-porch pillars. For the 1964 television special, singers moved from the front porch to the interior of the building; Willie Dixon sang his short set from a cane chair in a replicated sharecropper's cabin (see figure 3.3)—a setting very similar to the environment Alan Lomax would create a few years later at Newport. In the album cover art and posters for the festival, Kieser often privileged the guitar, as well as images of stagecoaches, trains, and riverboats. The album cover art for the 1963 iteration of the tour featured iconography, both Southern and western, also seen in *The Blues and Gospel Train*, including a horse and cart and a sharecropper's shack. As the years went on and urban unrest in Watts, Detroit, and other American cities headlined news around the world, television-studio environments and Kieser's posters began to add images of urban blight to scenes of front porches and shabby saloons. Iconography familiar to black freedom struggles also began to appear. For the 1965 German television special, the guitarist J. B. Lenoir performed "Alabama Blues," narrating the murder of his siblings, before a backdrop that featured "colored" and "white" water fountains (see figure 3.4).

The visual rhetoric of the American Folk Blues Festival performed a scenic translation of a musical performance that was—at least to its television audience—broadly unfamiliar. Unsurprisingly, it was the 1962 inaugural television special of the American Folk Blues Festival that contained the most explanatory framing material. Drawing on the tradition of the Cotton Club's spectacles and big-band performances of the 1940s, Berendt, Lippmann, and Rau used additional performers to enhance the mise-en-scène of television specials, sometimes illustratively incorporating black dancers into a scene to provide a sense of the viewer's ethnographic discovery. During a performance by Terry and McGhee on the 1962 television special, several young black couples danced in front of the porch, very nearly blocking the camera's view of the musicians. These couples— American soldiers and their wives brought in for the taping from a nearby base—served as the authorizing ground of the duo's performance, offering a supposedly more holistic vision of a blues environment to the European audience.[75] Musicians were called upon to translate the form as well. After a performance of T-Bone Walker's "Call Me When You Need Me," in which a young black woman sat on a front porch, knitting and paying no mind to either Walker or the vocalist Shakey Jake, Walker ambled around the corner. The camera followed him and discovered McGhee and Terry on some front steps, observed from the porch by a young man and a young woman. "Now we'd like to show you something that happens in Louisiana," Walker explained. "The state of Louisiana—the great Deep South—on a Saturday night—what we call a Saturday-night get-together."[76] Terry and McGhee launched into Terry's famous "Hootin' Blues"; at the conclusion of the song, McGhee spoke in quiet, reverential tones to the uninitiated: "Folks, you just heard the blues, in all forms. Blues from the cotton fields, blues from the low lowlands, blues from the big cities, small towns. Blues that's fit for big cities and small towns, like Detroit, Chicago, New York City. People that's born and lived the blues and knows about the blues, blues good, blues bad, blues sad, and sometimes happy. But while you're running around, why don't you take a little time out, and listen to Memphis Slim." The camera then revealed a new scene, this one featuring a behemoth American car and

the sounds of Slim's "The Blues Is Everywhere." As if fulfilling McGhee's portrait of blues' presence in "big cities and small towns," Slim highlighted the ubiquity of the blues, informing his listeners, "I've got the blues, and so have you."

By reproducing images that were familiar to British television audiences because of their proximity to the conventions of the minstrel show, the blues revival translated blues to English audiences by means of familiar theatrical representations of "the South." While blackface had mostly been driven underground in the United States during the postwar period, blackface minstrelsy remained widespread in British television, theater, and radio until the 1970s. Even though blackface "looked old-fashioned and outdated" in the United Kingdom by the 1950s, it experienced a revival of its own, coincident with growing antiblack backlash in response to the influx of Caribbean immigrants, who were known as the *Windrush* generation. Running from 1958 to 1978, the television variety program *The Black and White Minstrel Show* performed "Mississippi tunes and Country and Western songs" before a chart-topping sixteen to eighteen million viewers each week.[77] The program, which featured several male singers in dandyish top hats and blackface and dozens of scantily clad white female chorines who sometimes carried prop banjos, was beloved by British audiences for its spectacularly choreographed renditions of songs such as Stephen Foster's "Camptown Ladies," as well as traditional songs, including "When the Saints Go Marching In" and "Dixie." Multiple live theatrical versions spun off and, capitalizing on the tradition of minstrelsy in British music-hall entertainments, played before tens of thousands between 1960 and 1972.[78] It is difficult to imagine that the performers of *The Blues and Gospel Train*, who were familiar with British popular culture from years of touring there, were unaware of the most popular show on British television. A close look at *The Blues and Gospel Train* shows these artists delicately navigating the minefield of a retrograde mise-en-scène, all while accommodating a very appreciative audience.

Like many before her, including Ledbetter, Rainey, and Bessie Smith, Tharpe underscored her disconnect from the minstrel-show scenario through costume. Tharpe was well known for her spectacular stage appearance, and *The Blues and Gospel Train* was no exception; indeed, she

3.3 *(opposite, above)* Willie Dixon performs on an American Folk Blues Festival set designed to resemble a sharecropper's cabin, 1964. Stephanie Wiesand/Reelin' in the Years Productions.

3.4 *(opposite, below)* J. B. Lenoir performs on an American Folk Blues Festival set depicting "colored" and "white" water fountains, 1965. Stephanie Wiesand/Reelin' in the Years Productions.

was reportedly unhappy at being lumped together with performers who dressed informally and played up their rural bona fides.[79] Dressed for a formal urban affair rather than for the farm, Tharpe, in her high heels and elegant coat with a glittering collar, threw the stereotypical surroundings into sharp relief. Like a bride in a baseball stadium, her glamorous appearance on the broken-down props of the stage set invited a cognitive dissonance that denaturalized the minstrel aesthetic with which she was intimately familiar from her days at the Cotton Club. No longer appearing with her mule and sun hat, as she had at the Club, Tharpe dressed for a concert-hall appearance, sartorially identifying herself with the glamorous entertainers welcomed to European stages in the 1950s and 1960s. Tharpe had made a similar compromise once before: during her 1950 television appearance on Perry Como's *Supper Club*, she "threatened a walkout" when her backup singers, the Rosettes, were told that they would be forced to ride in a hay-filled wagon and to wear bandannas. While Tharpe capitulated to the horse and wagon, the Rosettes were ultimately allowed to wear their regular costumes and hairstyles for the appearance.[80] Tharpe's husband and manager, Russell Morrison, was not at all happy with the uncompensated labor required of Tharpe on *The Blues and Gospel Train*; as Cousin Joe later explained: "He [Morrison] called George Wien, all the way in America, because he wanted to get *paid* for that TV show or he wasn't going to let Rosetta Tharpe come on." But Tharpe and the others, it turned out, were already contractually obligated to appear on the show.[81]

While Tharpe used costume to emphasize her unsuitability for the mise-en-scène offered up by *The Blues and Gospel Train*, camerawork and directorial editing attempted to position the boogie-woogie pianist Cousin Joe as a minstrel clown. As Tharpe sang "Trouble in Mind"—a song with great resonance for those engaged in the black freedom struggle—the camera cut to Cousin Joe in a rocking chair, an onstage spectator and spectacle in one, modeling musical appreciation for the uninitiated in the audience. He mugged a bit for the cameras and clapped in time. The camera lingered on him, emphasizing Cousin Joe's comic persona at the expense of Tharpe's serious song. As far as Cousin Joe's performance is concerned, it was a profoundly ambiguous moment, capable of being read as an accommodationist display of minstrel-show conventions as well as a performance of excess that denaturalized the theatrical conventions of racial authenticity. How the audience understood Cousin Joe's performance remains unknown, but one thing is clear: the pianist was well aware of the requirement to play the role that white audiences expected. Cousin Joe got his start as a ukulele player and tap dancer in New Orleans and spent years performing vaudeville-inspired acts at clubs such as the Grand Terrace and the Gypsy Tea Room. He recalled the act he played at the Famous Door, a whites-only club:

> We had . . . an electric sign of an old man and an old lady. The old white-haired colored fellow had a pipe in his mouth. He was sitting in a rocking chair and rocking. Just a-rocking. The colored lady had a rag around her head and a big old basket like women used to carry on their heads when they worked. . . . We used to have to wear overalls and a blue shirt and a red bandana handkerchief around our neck and a farmer's straw hat, that you'd wear on the farm out in the summer to keep the sun off. We'd sit on this bale of cotton and we'd play. After we'd play a couple of tunes, then we'd get off the bale and we'd go around to the tables. That was the "Southern" exposure.[82]

Cousin Joe made a lot of money wearing overalls and sitting on cotton bales at the Famous Door, and he became adept at performing "Southern exposure" for high-paying whites, cashing in on the dynamics of racial performance and economic reward. On a trip to Texas in 1936, a wealthy white man paid Cousin Joe and his fellow musicians to visit a circuit of Dallas parties; the performer recalled: "He wasn't supposed to give us but thirty dollars but when I got through putting that 'Jim Crow' jive on him, that Southern drawl, he was putting all that money in my pocket. . . . When you're *black* you've got to *act* to make any money off of those people."[83]

JUST ONE STOP: THE LOCAL SIGNIFICANCE OF THE TOUR

An examination of *The Blues and Gospel Train* as a local event offers new dimension to a phenomenon of economic and artistic exchange that is often characterized as generically "transatlantic." Though broadly appealing, the live show's impact in 1964 lay, in part, in its Manchester setting. Examining the local significance of the performance allows for a more precise detailing of the usually more generalized "identification with the socio-economic hardships of African Americans" that, as Neil Wynn notes, was a central component of British affection for black American music.[84] As Wald has noted, almost everywhere, European audiences saw and heard black music as "an index of black suffering as well as innocence"; this interpretation projected European postwar suffering onto an oppressed black American population and tapped into the global drama of the civil rights movement. Wald emphasizes, however, that this British and European embrace of black suffering meant "the revivalists tended to hear blues as the musical expression of misery rather than of perseverance, cultural memory, and heal-ing."[85] While these claims unify broadly felt affective connections to black music, American blues performance was strongly embraced in the North of England, especially in Manchester, for economic, historic, and cultural reasons that, when explicated, enhance our understanding of the perfor-mances themselves and of the blues revival more generally.

Accounts of blues tours to Britain customarily emphasize the music's influence on emergent British blues and rock bands, such as the Yardbirds, the Animals, and Led Zeppelin. Accounts of the American Folk Blues Festi-val performance in Manchester in 1962, for example, invariably emphasize just a few members of the audience—young English blues fans who trav-eled by van from London to hear their idols play. These pilgrims, Mick Jagger, Keith Richards, and Brian Jones, had formed the Rolling Stones only six months earlier and were still six months away from the release of their debut single, a cover of Chuck Berry's "Come On." The attendance of the Rolling Stones at the Free Trade Hall performance in 1962 is one of the ubiquitous legends of British rock, told again and again in liner notes, biographies, and musical histories.[86] These performances thus became pre-cursors to the British invasion—the "return" of black American music to U.S. popular culture, in the form of the Rolling Stones, the Kinks, and the Beatles. Indeed, 1964, the year of *The Blues and Gospel Train*, was arguably the high-water mark of the British invasion, as the Beatles swept through the United States, appearing live and on *The Ed Sullivan Show* to thousands of teenage fans.

The historiographic significance of the tours thus acquires a familiar, if limited, dramaturgy: white British artists, raised on a steady diet of black American music, reshaped and exported blues-inspired rock to the United States, revealing the significance of black vernacular music to an American public that had long since forgotten—or never known—its own cultural heritage. Though black popular forms provided the backbone for Elvis Presley and other American singers, British groups were much more likely to acknowledge blues musicians as direct influences.[87] As Eric Burdon, lead singer for the Animals, chastised in an article for *Ebony*, "Americans for-get their musical roots and in Europe we still study those roots."[88] This model of British refinement of American raw material has its antecedent in nineteenth-century trade and industrial practices, when cotton trav-eled a transatlantic route, first to the North of England and then "back" to the United States in the form of finished goods. But transatlantic blues performances in the British North are significant for reasons beyond hav-ing inspired individual legendary musicians, whose retrospective accounts often fail to register the affiliations, identifications, and misidentifications generated by and exploited in individual, local performances.

While it is impossible to account for the various readings each audience member brought to *The Blues and Gospel Train*, the particular economic, cultural, and historical conditions of 1964—tremendous outmigration from Manchester, increasing disparity in wages between the North and South of England, and growing awareness of racial violence and civil rights protest in both Britain and the United States—temporally and spatially sharpened the performance on the Wilbraham Road stage. In particular, the program's musical and iconographic staging of an imagined American South tapped into contemporary local concerns about the impending collapse of a textile industry that had once been so powerful that it earned Manchester the nickname "The Cottonopolis." This decline was signaled by the most significant set piece: the train. For the Manchester audience, the departure of the train from the long-abandoned station—"The train is gone!" cried Tharpe—tapped into a particularly sensitive state of affairs. In 1963 Richard Beeching, chairman of the newly nationalized British Railways, consolidated the country's rail system by closing scores of lines; like the idled textile factories, disused train stations, including Wilbraham Road, came to be seen as relics of an age of industrial and imperial promise that no longer paid dividends.[89] A point of pride in the nineteenth century, the train lines that had once moved raw cotton and finished textiles back and forth between Liverpool and Manchester now seemed bloated, antiquated, and wasteful—"the most embarrassing of all Britain's Victorian leftovers."[90] The decimation of the railway system upended the imperial symbolism of British trains; as the Commonwealth declined from the Victorian height of its imperial power, the vast transportation networks that built the British Empire were no longer necessary or able to sustain it. If the British train system once symbolized progress and the triumphs of industrial modernity, the 1964 *The Blues and Gospel Train* highlighted the end of industrialization's promise while offering a "look back" to a time when the British North claimed both economic and moral superiority.

Though it lacked the jurisdictive force of the Mason-Dixon Line, Britain's division into "North" and "South" had long permeated local and national consciousness and was felt particularly strongly in the early 1960s. Northerners felt themselves to be part of a marginalized periphery, disenfranchised by the centripetal force of the South. The Cottonopolis was in particular decline; following World War II the textile industry of Manchester, already failing, collapsed. It had been coming for some time: the entire period from 1890 to 1965 saw "the North's waning power and the consequent sense of loss and displacement felt by many of its inhabitants."[91] As a result of the diminishing significance of manufacturing, Northern industrial towns and cities were left behind as the center of British wealth became concentrated in the consumer culture of swinging London. The war's aftermath lingered, amplifying the sense of the regional deprivation; as late as the 1960s, the *Manchester Guardian* was complaining bitterly about the region's glacial pace of postwar reconstruction under the headline "'Man-Made Hell' in South Lancashire." Criticizing the "slow redevelopment" of Manchester, the article quoted physicians who claimed that the bleak and battered surroundings had a detrimental impact on the psychological health of residents, who suffered from increased rates of depression and suicide.[92] More and more, Northern critics accused economic decision makers of victimizing the North for the sake of Southern growth; John Newsom's educational report appealed: "The fat South has to remember the lean North."[93] In a similar vein, a *Manchester Guardian* editorial responding to proposed transit expansion in the Southeast suggested that the planned development of London suburbs came at the expense of the North, Wales, and Scotland.[94]

Often situated on the periphery of national hubs of political, economic, and cultural power, white U.S. Southerners and English Northerners shared not only a profoundly visceral sense of place but also a regional identity developed in contradistinction to a more powerful "center" (the Yankee North, the London South).[95] In the midst of English Northern dissatisfaction and disenfranchisement, many of the region's youths developed an interest in American Southern culture, particularly music. Brian Ward explores the British affection for the Southern "rebel," an affection that manifested in British jazz bands in the 1950s who wore Confederate military costumes for their performances.[96] This turn to Southern music and culture helps explain the appeal of *The Blues and Gospel Train* and proposes new significance to its constant references, particularly in the television program, to "North" and "South." While it would be a mistake to oversimplify parallels between the industrial North of Britain and the agricultural South of the United States, the sheer repetition of the words *North* and *South* in *The Blues and Gospel Train* churns out a dizzying oscillation that demands to be read.

In *The Blues and Gospel Train*, *South* signifies in assorted ways, as a site of possibility and of deprivation, and as a place of the past and a place of the future. As the program begins, the camera follows a giddy group of teenagers as they rush through Manchester's central train station while Terry's "Hootin' Blues" plays, and a serene female voice announces over the station's public address system: "Now boarding, the blues and gospel train, calling at Chorltonville, and all stations south."[97] Ostensibly referring to the U.S. South, the announcement also points to the economically driven outmigration from Manchester to "points south" that was in full swing by the mid-1960s. As deindustrialization transformed Manchester into a service economy, the city experienced rapid population loss; residents relocated to the suburban ring or migrated further afield to London, or to the United States. Particularly hard-hit were those residents who had depended most heavily on the manufacturing sector, especially those employed in the textile mills: the city's population, which had peaked in the 1930s, was in free fall by the 1960s. The black migration that was an essential part of blues music and circulation was amalgamated to the migration of white Mancunian. Still, while *The Blues and Gospel Train* gestured toward an imagined (multiple and mutable) South, the program celebrated the North. Broadcasting to an audience of Northern viewers, Granada Television used its logo to graphically express its regional pride. During the opening credits of *The Blues and Gospel Train*, Granada's official slogan and logo—a large arrow pointing upward, captioned with "From the North"— appeared on the screen, identifying the location of Granada's physical headquarters in Manchester while also illustrating the transmission of Northern consciousness and culture *from* Manchester *to* other parts of Britain. While the specially hired train travels South, *The Blues and Gospel Train* program intently draws its visitors' consciousness *toward* the North, insisting on Northern visibility and audibility in an era of economic decline.

Despite the fact that blues performance in Britain was perceived as modern, it also worked as memory. *The Blues and Gospel Train* revived and restaged nineteenth-century cultural memories and transatlantic sympathies of the British North for the U.S. South. Johnnie Hamp describes the use of the train platform as stage as "a natural thing to do," but contingent historic relations between Manchester and the U.S. South strengthened this "naturalness." Indeed, the program exploited a long-term economic and affective intimacy between the two regions, an intimacy bound up in the arrival and departure of goods.[98] Prior to the American Civil War, Manchester's mills, as well as those throughout the Northern regions of Lancashire, Cheshire, and Derbyshire, received almost all of their raw cotton, which had been handpicked by slaves, from the U.S. South; the mills, in turn, provided local residents with steady employment. Once milling was complete, finished textile goods were exported, many of them to the United States, completing a transatlantic circular movement. The primary purpose of the train in nineteenth-century Britain was not to move people; it was to transport goods and commodities, and it was a commodity—cotton—that served as a key link between one Cottonopolis and another.

The Blues and Gospel Train, then, restaged the scene of the trade circuit that propped up the British Empire, a trade circuit made possible not only by rail transport but also by the unpaid labor of enslaved people. Nineteenth century Mancunian support for emancipation—and the celebratory remembrance of that support that persists even to the present—relied on the assertion of working-class solidarity with enslaved African Americans. Even though the degree of English Northern support for the Union has been widely debated, twentieth-century Mancunians forcefully asserted their stance on the right side of history.[99] By 1860 the U.S. South supplied Britain with more than 80 percent of its raw cotton, but the American Civil War disrupted the well-established trade circuit between the U.S. South and the British North.[100] Many Confederates assumed that they would receive the unequivocal support of Britain, because its industrial economy relied so heavily on the Confederacy's signal resource and bargaining chip, raw cotton. When that backing did not immediately occur, Southern planters proposed a cotton embargo that withheld raw materials from Britain and France in order to induce support born of economic desperation. The Union Navy proceeded to blockade Southern ports; this prevented Lancashire mills from receiving raw materials, which idled factories and resulted in massive unemployment and starvation in the region. The Cotton Famine of Lancashire led to a bitter political and cultural conflict that divided the Northern English population over issues of self-preservation, labor rights, and abolition.

The performance of black American musicians on a Southern-inspired stage set in Manchester in the early 1960s, therefore, reanimated a cherished cultural memory of political affiliation and sympathy with black Southern laborers. Lawrence Grossman notes, "The British, like any people viewing a conflict in another nation, tended to regard the Civil War in terms of their own political interests and their own pre-existing ideological positions rather than in the terms that Americans themselves recognized and fought for."[101] Class status and political positions influenced, but did not determine, which side Britons supported in the American Civil War. Aristocrats and conservatives almost universally supported the Confederacy, while working-class people, Liberals, and Radicals often disagreed among themselves about the merits of the abolitionist cause and the preservation of the Union.[102] Those laborers who did support the Union often expressed solidarity with enslaved people and yoked the trade-union cause to emancipation by comparing the unjust practices of mill owners to those of

Southern planters.[103] An advertisement for a pro-Union meeting in Manchester made these alliances unequivocally clear. Entitled "Southern Slavery Illustrated," the poster depicted a beaten and wounded black man while the text exhorted the "WORKING MEN!" of Manchester: "As you value the rights you already possess, and as you hope for an extension of your own social and political liberties, SUPPORT WITH YOUR BEST SYMPATHIES UNION & EMANCIPATION. This great struggle is essentially a question of REMUNERATED or UNREMUNERATED TOIL—of FREE OR SLAVE LABOUR."[104] While the strategy of creating alliances between Manchester factory workers and African American slaves advanced the trade unions as much as if not more than it supported the emancipation of slaves, these maneuvers had the politically powerful effect of reframing slave labor as unpaid work. As a result, many of Manchester's textile workers supported the Union's blockade, even though their own livelihoods—and lives—were often at stake.

Black American advocacy in Britain leading up to the Civil War laid the groundwork for local support of the Union during the war years. As R. J. M. Blackett has chronicled in *Building an Anti-slavery Wall*, black American activists, such as Frederick Douglass, William Wells Brown, Henry "Box" Brown, and William and Ellen Craft, traveled, lectured, and used the tools of the theater to make their point: they displayed moving panoramas of the American South and reenacted their dramatic escapes from slavery. These travelers, "living refutations of America's boasted freedom," assiduously labored to link their antislavery message to broader working-class concerns, "complementing," rather than competing with, the oppression of British workers.[105] Thousands heard their lectures, in every part of Britain. In addition to informing the public of the horrors of slavery, their own humanity performatively called into being a new respect for black subjectivity. As would later be echoed in the 1960s, these activists' vociferous calls for freedom were conjoined with the rapid spread of mass-media products that depicted the suffering and ingenious escape of American slaves. These slave narratives significantly bolstered the persuasive efforts of the speakers.[106] Though they largely avoided engaging British class conflict, they did not prohibit their British audiences from drawing the (however imperfect) connection between enslaved African Americans and oppressed English workers.[107]

The Blues and Gospel Train was a memorial to the Lancashire Cotton Famine, as well as its support for abolition, and came at a moment when commemorations of the centennial of the American Civil War were in full swing. Renewed interest in the assassination of Abraham Lincoln surged in the months following John F. Kennedy's assassination in November 1963.[108] Lincoln had, in fact, long been a figure of interest in Manchester. In 1919 a statue of Lincoln was erected in Platt Fields Park in Manchester, honoring not only the leader himself but also the city's moral courage in the face of the deprivation and unemployment brought on by the Cotton Famine.[109] In 1986 engraved text was added to the statue to emphasize this point: "This statue commemorates the support that the working people of Manchester gave in the fight for the abolition of slavery during the American Civil War. By supporting the Union under President Lincoln at a time when there was an economic blockade of the Southern states the Lancashire cotton workers were denied access to raw cotton, which caused considerable unemployment throughout the cotton industry." In the 1960s student movements recalled Manchester's sympathy in the nineteenth century for abolition in an attempt to yoke their contemporary causes to American civil rights struggles. Sympathy for trade unions at the University of Manchester ran high, and students sometimes tried to organize their own unions as student laborers. The title of a student newspaper, *Mancunion*, first published in 1964, consolidated local identity and trade-union affiliation.

Paradoxically, *The Blues and Gospel Train*, while dependent on the visual iconography of the Southern pastoral, spoke to racially progressive Mancunian sensibilities amid centennial commemorations of the American Civil War. The contradiction at the heart of *The Blues and Gospel Train*, then, rested in the irreconcilable space between white students' one-way expression of sympathetic identification with African Americans and their enthusiastic consumption of a nostalgic scene that relished the suffering that seemed to produce the blues. Nowhere was this contradiction—a precondition of the "love and theft" that organized the appropriation and reinvention of blues sounds and songs—more unambiguously on display than in the opening sequences of the television program.[110] The program began with a jubilantly integrated train ride, modeling an intimacy between performers and audience. Students danced in the aisle of the carriage to Terry and McGhee's euphoric guitar and harmonica duet; the harmonica echoed the train whistle, and the students got into the rhythm, coordinating their own movements with the music of movement, of transport, of relocation. The musicians, too, performed their delight; Tharpe eagerly looked out the window, clapping her hands together and showing the camera just how pleased she was to be participating in an event that she and the other musicians reportedly greeted with skepticism.[111] For a brief moment, *The Blues and Gospel Train* rendered Northern England as a community living in integrated harmony, a place that offered black American performers respite from their Jim Crow troubles at home. This ideal of interracial intimacy began to break down, however, when the train arrived at "Chorltonville." Waters, who did not immediately decamp for "his" side of the platform, played his first song amid the audience, but the students were torn between appreciating Waters's performance and turning their backs on him to find their assigned seats. After this brief moment of integration, the performers and audience found their pre-assigned marks, with the audience on one side of the tracks and musicians on the other, spectators and spectacle. The tracks, still in use by speeding freight trains, instituted an impressive and dangerous chasm between performers and audience. A Du Boisian color line, the chasm between spectators and spectacle forcefully literalized "the other side of the tracks." If, by some remarkable occurrence, trains were to stop at these stations, audiences would board them for destinations in opposite directions. *The Blues and Gospel Train* thus allegorized an experiment of desegregation of public transportation, ultimately resegregating its participants according to race, and according to nation.

TROUBLE IN MIND: RACE, CIVIL RIGHTS, AND TELEVISION

The dramas of train travel are not race-neutral: the use of a train platform as a stage in 1964 could not help but present the political and cultural drama of desegregation attempts in the American South, where the train and its platform were inflammatory sites of segregation and struggles for equality. Public transportation was among the first public accommodations to be systematically segregated, and its legalized racial hierarchies were legitimated by *Plessy v. Ferguson* in 1896. The action that generated the *Plessy* decision was itself an act of civil disobedience—the plaintiff sat in the whites-only car with the explicit intent of challenging Louisiana's law—and such acts of civil disobedience continued. From bus boycotts to Freedom Rides, the attempts to desegregate transit were globally visible in the 1950s and early 1960s. For black riders who staged social dramas of opposition throughout the midcentury, "public transit had been ritualized as a theatrical setting for performing disharmony and social unrest."[112] Train platforms also accumulated their own racialized dramaturgies. Images of segregated train stations, rife with doubled spaces—from waiting rooms to water fountains to restrooms that, while separate, were certainly not equal—were captured and distributed by Jim Crow–era photographers. These photographs frequently highlighted the symmetrical spaces of segregation, a symmetry that is echoed by the identical train platforms put to use in *The Blues and Gospel Train*. But as Elizabeth Abel points out in her analysis of Jim Crow signs and their photography, "the fiction of symmetrical doorways" suggests a "bedrock and balanced binary" that does not hold up under scrutiny. Like the "separate but equal" waiting rooms, the mirroring of the train platforms produced only the fiction of symmetry, willing an active forgetting of the asymmetrical relations of both the past and the present.[113]

Even though *The Blues and Gospel Train* did not explicitly take up the headlines of the summer of 1964, "the Struggle provided an inescapable context" for many of the songs sung.[114] Since the Birmingham campaign and the March on Washington the previous year, coverage in the United Kingdom of civil rights struggles had been limited. In the summer of 1964, however, news from the American South returned to the headlines with force, and *The Blues and Gospel Train* was but one element of a televisual flow preoccupied by images of protest and congressional hearings. The Manchester music historian C. P. Lee notes: "While we were watching the blues train, we were also seeing on the news Martin Luther King and the civil rights demonstrators being attacked by Alabama police dogs and fire hoses."[115] Tharpe, Waters, Cousin Joe, Terry, and McGhee arrived in England in May, in the midst of a fifty-four-day filibuster launched by the so-called Southern bloc of U.S. senators, who threatened to block the passage of the Civil Rights Act. The long filibuster and eventual passage of the act and the Mississippi Summer Projects (also known as the Freedom Summer) once again directed international media attention to the (still) Jim Crow South. The Manchester press greeted the passage of the Civil Rights Act with optimism, while dismaying at the Republican nomination of Barry Goldwater, citing evidence of white backlash.[116] As the summer went on, British correspondents descended on Mississippi. A short but ominous article appeared in the *Manchester Guardian Weekly* in early July, reporting a search for "three missing civil rights men" in the town of Philadelphia.[117] On August 4, just two weeks before *The Blues and Gospel Train* aired before millions on Granada Television, searchers discovered the bodies of James Chaney, Michael Schwerner, and Andrew Goodman, buried in an earthen dam.

The United States was not the only place to face boycotts and marches; Britain faced its own racial disharmonies in the 1950s and 1960s. The docking of the MV *Empire Windrush* at Tilbury in 1948 was an iconic moment in the wave of black Caribbean and black African migration to Britain in the postwar decades, resulting in a "wholesale reassessment" of British identity.[118] This reassessment was as cultural as it was political and sociological; as Paul Gilroy describes, performances of black diasporic music in Britain in the fifties and sixties were "already articulated by political language, symbols and meanings given by the struggle of social movements for emancipation and equality. Like the cultural forms themselves, this political inheritance had to be dealt with and adapted to British circumstances."[119] Caribbean immigration to Britain peaked between 1955 and 1962; these demographic changes, not unpredictably, witnessed the consolidation of ideologies of white supremacy, culminating in race riots in Notting Hill, London, in 1958. Immigration continued to be an inflammatory issue during the early 1960s in Britain, and black migrants, in particular, encountered daily institutional racism; as the economy declined, and newly independent African nations such as Zanzibar and Ghana troubled the identity of the British Empire, the Commonwealth Immigrants Act of 1962 established limits on migrants. In 1963 Paul Stephenson, a civil rights activist of African and British descent, led a lengthy—and ultimately successful—bus boycott in Bristol, protesting the company's refusal to employ nonwhite drivers.[120]

The Blues and Gospel Train's use of the train platform to stage a scene of blues travel superimposed two coincident "troubles" of 1964: U.S. civil rights violence and Mancunian economic decline. If the failed promises of modernity were evident in the idled factories, abandoned train stations, and the insecure economic conditions of 1960s Manchester, they were equally evident—albeit in a different way—in the 1960s American South. When considered from the point of view of black freedom movements, *The Blues and Gospel Train* exported American culture, but just as powerfully revealed the failed promises of the American experiment; its black performers were cast—willingly or not—as representatives of the failed project of American democracy. It is difficult to know what individual audience members saw or heard as the television screen flipped from news reports that covered civil rights struggles to musicians installed in a pastoral fantasy. Likewise, it is difficult to ascertain whether the performances of *The Blues and Gospel Train* contributed to a greater recognition of black equality, or whether the program's minstrel-show setting further naturalized racialist conceptions of black authenticity. Brian Ward observes, "There has never been any necessary causal connection between white admiration for black cultural forms and performative excellence . . . and more enlightened racial attitudes." As Ward goes on to suggest, however, we might consider how white enthusiasm allowed black performers to consider their work's impact on nonblack, or even non-American, communities: to contemplate how black performers' work might translate to a broader audience and how, in the act of (even one-way) translation, far-reaching support might be enlisted.[121]

Terry's and McGhee's presence on the tour served to link contemporary struggles for black freedom with the causes they had most actively supported in the 1940s, particularly antilynching activism and the right to organize. In fact, it was McGhee who had made the earliest recording of Big Bill Broonzy's "Black Brown and White" in 1947, in which Broonzy made some of the most explicit commentary of his career about the state of racial inequality in the United States:

> If you're black, get back
> If you're brown, stick around
> If you're white, you're all right.

Highlighting the particular injustices faced by those recently returned from war, the last verse of the song proclaimed: "I built this country/I fought for it too." Tharpe also made the black freedom struggle visible and audible, sometimes through comedy, and always through song. Though Tharpe's interludes and banter with the audience were characterized by whimsical insouciance, her forceful performances suggested the violence and danger that haunted the Southern pastoral fantasy. Tharpe's refiguration of black femininity on *The Blues and Gospel Train* stage called to mind not only the blues queens of the 1910s and 1920s but also the fierce women of the civil rights movement—Fannie Lou Hamer, Ella Baker, and Mamie Till-Mobley among them—women who challenged traditional notions of female silence and subservience in the service of the struggle.

Even though Tharpe was unhappy with the set, she did not show it in her performance.[122] Unlike Waters, whose disinterested performance of cool refused the live audience the intimacy it so desperately seemed to crave, Tharpe embraced the crowd as much as they embraced her. Introduced by Cousin Joe as the "inimitable Sister Rosetta Tharpe," she entered the scene as a passenger in a horse-drawn carriage, pulled by a black-and-white paint horse and furnished with a canopy and driver. Described by Hamp as a "surrey with a fringe on top," the carriage alluded to the wildly popular Rodgers and Hammerstein movie musical *Oklahoma!*, a touchstone for British understandings of rural America.[123] Though a fundamentally American horse and buggy, Tharpe's ride was a playful twist on the British carriage that carried nobility and royalty, a not insignificant mode of arrival for a (blues) queen. A third carriage was also invoked by Tharpe's arrival on *The Blues and Gospel Train* stage: Scarlett O'Hara's famous landau from *Gone with the Wind*, a film that played for more than four continuous years in London and was another touchstone for British perceptions of the American South.[124] Playing at the fragile but flinty Scarlett, Tharpe signified on the romance of

Tara on a stage set that was the plantation house's hidden scenography. As the carriage came to a halt, Tharpe graciously acknowledged her top-hatted white driver and disembarked onto the arm of Cousin Joe, who escorted her to the stage. She maneuvered daintily across the wet train platform in her high heels, appearing to enjoy the moment, and she bantered flirtatiously with Cousin Joe. "This is the wonderfulest time of my life!" she exclaimed politely, her Arkansas drawl sneaking in for a moment. Notably, though, Tharpe then turned on a dime, following her performance of genteel and fawning femininity with a surprisingly aggressive—and loud—rock-and-roll take on "Didn't It Rain." In the midst of the song, she paused to rhetorically ask her audience: "Pretty good for a woman, ain't it?" This was a knowing spin on what Sherrie Tucker calls "the ubiquitous *good for girls*" compliment that has historically vexed female musicians.[125]

Though the artists of the American Folk, Blues, and Gospel Caravan rarely spoke publicly about politics, perhaps for fear of alienating the white men who organized their tours and produced their records, the songs they sang on *The Blues and Gospel Train*, as well as at other stops on the European tour, emphasized some key themes of civil rights struggles: suffering and redemption, perseverance, and divine justice. While the performers on the British and European blues tours did not generally choose their concert venues and mise-en-scènes, the artists did have a modicum of control over their repertoires of songs. In spite of the fact that producers often policed the boundaries of genre, set lists were one domain in which the decisions invited some input from the stars themselves—a degree of agency that Terry and McGhee had long been practiced in exploiting, as they had in *Cat on a Hot Tin Roof*. In choosing songs that emphasized struggle and salvation, effort and reward, the musicians—Tharpe in particular—explored a mode of theatrical translation, one that shifted the generic suffering of blues preferred by British audiences to suffering with a purpose, suffering that would be redeemed.

Tharpe's performance of "Trouble in Mind" altered both the lyrics and the timbre of well-known versions of the song, subtly suggesting a response to civil rights-era "trouble." Originally recorded by Thelma La Vizzo in 1924, "Trouble in Mind" was recorded by Tharpe with a big-band sound with Lucky Millinder and His Orchestra in 1941; in the years leading up to *The Blues and Gospel Train*, Dinah Washington had a hit with a torch-song version in 1957, and Nina Simone played it regularly at her live appearances throughout the early 1960s. Tharpe's 1941 recording evinces a jaunty, upbeat relationship to the "trouble"; the lyrics are sung to a danceable accompaniment, and Tharpe delivers the narrator's threat of suicide

("I'm gonna lay my head/On some lonesome railroad line/And let the 2:19 train/Pacify my mind") as a cheerfully and comically defiant solution to brokenhearted agony. As the years went on, a darker message, encoded in the lyrical narrative of unrequited love, began to resound. The song had been speaking to civil rights struggles at least since the playwright Alice Childress claimed the phrase for the movement in 1955. In her play *Trouble in Mind*, a black actress clashes with a white director as the two battle over the representation of race and racism in an antilynching drama—a scenario that, perhaps unintentionally, was echoed by Tharpe's performance within the constraints of a white production team on *The Blues and Gospel Train*. In the 1950s Broonzy, one of the most popular "country blues" singers to tour England and Europe, popularized an acoustic guitar "Trouble in Mind" that removed much of the vaudevillian playfulness from the song and replaced it with deeply felt angst, making the singer's disconsolate determination to "pacify my mind" sound positively inevitable. Since at least 1960, Tharpe's performance of "Trouble in Mind" had been associated with civil unrest; French footage of her performance of the song at the Antibes Jazz Festival in 1960 was intercut with documentary footage of city streets—most likely in Algiers—destroyed by rioting. No longer "laughing just to keep from crying" nor single-mindedly morose, Tharpe made a change to the lyrics of the 1964 version that offered an active alternative to the comically passive self-destructiveness of those facing trouble. Tharpe retained Broonzy's guitar accompaniment, but she took the song electric, incorporating two long solos into her performance on the Chorltonville stage. As opposed to the 1940s blues of comic irony and Broonzy's depressed affect of the 1950s, Tharpe's 1964 "Trouble in Mind" suggested a remedy that went beyond laying one's head on the tracks. In a new final verse, Tharpe's narrator proclaims, "I'm gonna *change* my mind!" Strutting across the stage, she decides to confront her lover:

> I'm going down to New Orleans
> I'm gonna give that old man of mine a call
> I'm gonna give him a piece of my mind
> Because he done me wrong.

By replacing helplessness with action, Tharpe's new final verse sutures the victory of a jilted woman to the victory of all those facing trouble, suggesting an alliance between female self-empowerment and black activist struggle.

Transforming a song that black audiences had enjoyed decades earlier into a civil rights-era appeal for life-affirming action in the face of despair,

Tharpe resurrected a piece of bygone black culture in order to translate contemporary struggles to a transatlantic audience. Modern for Britain, blues was distinctly out-of-date for black American audiences; the European enthusiasm for blues in the 1950s and 1960s was at odds with contemporary black musical tastes in the United States, where Motown, rhythm and blues, and soul—all of which often directly encoded civil rights-era messages into the lyrics—dominated the airwaves. Tharpe refused to museum-ify the blues, reviving an older form to think not about the past but about the future. Tharpe never dwelled for long on the suffering of her songs, choosing instead to focus on the redemption that follows suffering in the Christian worldview. Immediately after she looked up and down the desolate tracks, crying out "the train is gone!" she resolved, "I'm gonna catch the next one!" This bit of dialogue imitated the structure of the "Trouble in Mind" lyric that promised: "I won't be blue always/Cause the sun's gonna shine in my back door someday."

Though blues waned in popularity among black audiences in the 1950s and 1960s, the gospel spiritual remained a living and lively hymn of struggle and praise, the lingua franca of public civil rights events, sung at church, mass meetings, and in jails. It was under the rubric of the "Gospel" component of the American Folk, Blues, and Gospel Caravan that Tharpe sang spirituals to—and with—her English audiences, partially re-creating the revival-meeting atmosphere that had characterized her early career in New York, and enlisting her spectators as co-performers of songs that made up a movement. Linking the struggle for twentieth-century civil rights to a much longer struggle for emancipation, the postwar performance of spirituals in Manchester recalled the tours of the musical groups who had espoused abolition in the nineteenth century. Like her colleague and sometimes competitor Mahalia Jackson, Tharpe exploited gospel's power to uplift, to transform, and to realize the divine plan for justice. Her performances of "Didn't It Rain" and "He's Got the Whole World in His Hands" on *The Blues and Gospel Train* used the familiar form of the spiritual as a means of translating a civil rights struggle to a British audience. Tharpe's interrogative "didn't it rain, children?" on *The Blues and Gospel Train* had the entertaining quality of marrying the representational to the real—and of grounding the iterative touring performance in locally specific facts of the day's weather, as the pouring rain disrupted filming several times. The weather, normally a nonissue in studio performances, now posed a particular challenge for any innovator who wished to film an electrified concert outdoors. Just as *The Blues and Gospel Train* employed innovative tactics and a retrograde stage setting, Tharpe's "Didn't It Rain" simultaneously acknowledged past and future: the long history of the struggle for black freedom and the innovative modern event in which all were participating. Tharpe's visceral and aggressive performance of "Didn't It Rain" emphasized the repetition of struggle—"rain, rain, rain, rain, rain!"—while also suggesting, through the story of Noah and all the performers' perseverance, the possibility of enduring through the flood, through struggle. Amid a setting that imagined a black past, Tharpe sonically weathered the displacement engendered by both migration and the tour, reconstructing black female subjectivity in a state of transit. While acoustic certainly would have been easier—particularly with the rain—Tharpe's insistence on an electric guitar allowed her to revamp old songs for a new musical and social world, one that was incompatible with the broken-down environs of the stage set of *The Blues and Gospel Train*. In Tharpe's performance looking ahead, not back, was what counted: "I'm gonna catch the next one!"

Characterized by acts of translation, the tours of the postwar European blues revival attempted to make black music—and, implicitly, the cultures from which it sprang—intelligible to foreign audiences. Seizing on signifiers of the minstrel show and migration, the producers and directors of the tours rendered a theatrical framework of an imagined black past. And yet, well aware of the opportunity offered by music to build international bridges and solidarity—Terry and McGhee, after all, had performed for years with Robeson, arguably the signal exponent of this strategy—the performers also explained, framed, and cited their work, making it legible to foreign audiences. Through their song choices and repertoires, they linked the train platform to desegregation struggles, in an attempt to harness global empathy for civil rights projects. Ultimately, these acts of translation betrayed a struggle over the representation of African American history. What would triumph: a nostalgic rendering of a bygone pastoral or a technologically and ideologically modern future? Walter Benjamin identifies historical materialism as the production of a past that is shot through "by the presence of the now [*Jetztzeit*]." This "now-time" is of signal importance in productions such as *The Blues and Gospel Train*, which used both the perpetual present *and* the temporal flexibility of the theater to interpenetrate present and past.[126] Bearing in mind the proximity of Benjamin's philosophy of translation to his philosophy of history—both deeply preoccupied by the concerns of the present moment, both conscious of the impossibility of recapturing "original" languages or events—*The Blues and Gospel Train* emerges as a work of both translation and historiography, a look back thoroughly informed by the present's constellation with the past that it produces.

The translation, as Benjamin notes, emerges as the afterlife of the original.[127] *The Blues and Gospel Train*, however—an afterlife without an original—has had numerous afterlives of its own; in the fifty years since it was witnessed by tens of millions of British Northerners, it has enjoyed repeated commemorative screenings in Manchester, and many scenes from the event now circulate on DVDs and on YouTube. A new generation of fans has been recruited by the circulation of these scenes, constituting a revival of the revival. Together they consume afterlives of afterlives, acts of translation that, by virtue of their ubiquity, call into question the original events they purport to represent. When these scenes are enthusiastically consumed by spectators at the beginning of the twenty-first century, what, exactly, is being remembered? The stakes of memory soon began to rise; as the stars of the postwar blues revival passed away in the later decades of the twentieth century, the death of the blues was hastily proclaimed. Such deaths, however, resulted only in the feverish production of ever-more afterlives.

Writing in the 1930s, Walter Benjamin identified the train platform as particularly apt for staging the minidramas of everyday life, a suitability captured in this fragment from his unfinished *Passagen-werk* (*The Arcades Project*): "Today, in the age of the automobile and the airplane, it is only faint atavistic terrors which still lurk within the blackened sheds; and that stale comedy of farewell and reunion, carried on before a background of Pullman cars, turns the railway platform into a provincial stage. Once again we see performed the timeworn Greek melodrama: Orpheus, Eurydice, and Hermes at the station."[1] As a waiting place characterized by the dramas of arrivals and departures, of entrances and exits, the railway platform constitutes its denizens as spectators and spectacle, both witnessing and witnessed by others as they pass time. In 1935 a breathless report in the *New York Herald Tribune* considered the dramaturgy of Huddie Ledbetter (Lead Belly) and Martha Promise's reunion on a train platform in New York City. The columnist cast the event in starkly theatrical terms: "With Lead Belly, as the play begins, is his master and amanuensis, John A. Lomax." Using the present tense to convey the ongoing immediacy of the unfolding scene, the article dramatized the event from the crisis of the lovers' missed encounter, when Promise did not arrive as expected, to their ultimately joyous reunion in the station waiting room. The scene was, as the columnist relayed it, "a comedy of errors, well wrought in accordance with the Aristotelian unities and infused with all the dramatic elements of love, hope, fear, despair, and ultimate jubilation." The two embraced and kissed: a satisfying ending to the show. "The Greek chorus murmur excitedly to themselves," the journalist noted, as the crowd dispersed.[2]

The train platform as stage has cropped up from time to time throughout the decades—most notably in *The Blues and Gospel Train* (1964)—but came into more widespread use in the late twentieth century, when abandoned passenger platforms throughout the Mississippi Delta were repurposed as stages for blues festivals. By framing the migrations of the past and the tourism of the present, these train platform stages remember histories of the blues while simultaneously recuperating them in the hopes of future economic returns. The refitting of these depot platforms as stages by civic authorities attempts to capitalize on the aesthetic and historic significance of blues and trains and revitalize a sign of economic blight. Ever since the self-nominated "Father of the Blues" W. C. Handy told of awakening from a nap at the Tutwiler, Mississippi, depot to the sound of "Goin' Where the Southern Cross the Dog," the train and its station platform have been understood as sites of the emergence of blues. The late twentieth-century reclamation of the train-station platform—along with the front porch, another historic stage for the performance of blues—for free-market enterprises of tourism and civic development is a paradigmatic example of the way contemporary blues tourism turns a profit on blues' theatrical histories and architectures.

Blues tourism is an economic and cultural phenomenon of the late twentieth and early twenty-first centuries that invites leisure tourists to visit and enjoy what Alan Lomax called "the land where the blues began."[3] Blues tourists travel to the Mississippi Delta to hear music and visit museums, as well as to walk—or, more realistically, drive—the roads that served as roots and routes of revered musicians, many of whom rose to international prominence during the blues revival. Some blues tourists travel for thousands of miles, following an extended historical route of black migration that wends its way from New Orleans to Chicago, stopping off in the Mississippi Delta, Memphis, and St. Louis along the way. Those without the available weeks or months required for this lengthy trip choose a more limited tour, driving from Memphis to New Orleans, while some, especially at festival time, head directly for the affective and economic center of the blues-tourism industry, Clarksdale, Mississippi. Clarksdale, historically known as the "Golden Buckle in the Cotton Belt," is the birthplace of Sam Cooke, Ike Turner, and John Lee Hooker, and the death site of Bessie Smith, and it has staked its claim as "ground zero" for blues music and culture. For many blues tourists, coming here represents a trip into the nation's past, but it is also a trip into their personal pasts, and their own youthful memories of discovering blues for the first time. Tourists from locations as varied as California, Australia, London, Indonesia, and Estonia have flocked to the heritage tourism sites of Delta blues for the last twenty years; with a fervor some describe as akin to religious devotion, these pilgrims to the "holy sites" of musical history both consume and produce a genealogy of blues performance.[4]

The popular theatrical history of blues has been largely forgotten by the tourism industry, even though, somewhat incongruously, theatrical practices of reenactment and surrogation are deployed to establish tourist practice and sustain tourist pleasure. By extending the in situ environments of the blues revival's live shows and television specials to an immersive extreme, blues tourism ups the ante of the blues revival's theatricality. No longer do spectators merely *witness* the deployment of a Southern mise-en-scène; in blues tourism they are asked to participate in it. Cast in a theatrical staging of blues' remembrance, tourists immerse themselves in the living presence of a ghostly past, securing an affective, embodied relationship to blues history. While blues tourists enjoy live musical performances, such as those by local favorites Super Chikan and Bobby Rush, musicians are strikingly ancillary to the project of blues tourism. In the contemporary tourist economy for the blues, it is the tourist who takes center stage, as he or she stands in for past and passed performers.

In Clarksdale, an early twentieth-century hub of touring tent and minstrel shows, the theatricality that was expressed in early blues and simultaneously repressed and exploited by folklorists and revivalists finds new articulation in the theatrical trappings of late-capitalist heritage tourism. Blues tourism represents not a break with a supposedly authentic past but a continuation and transformation of the theatrical stagings of blues that I have been exploring throughout this book.[5] The theatrical trappings of blues and the mise-en-scène of the Southern pastoral that appeared on stage in the tent shows, in Ledbetter's performances, and in *The Blues and Gospel Train* migrate offstage in contemporary Clarksdale and into the spaces of daily life, appearing in museums and hotels, at juke joints, and at festivals. Staging a memory of blues that downplays the music's connection to sharecropping, lynching, convict leasing, and Jim Crow, the blues-tourism industry promotes self-conscious, reflexive attractions that enlist *actors*—tourists—to stage (and thus reinforce) a sanitized version of the history of blues. The theatrical tactics and strategies once embodied by blues performers themselves have now been transferred onto the actions and bodies of tourists. As scholars in the field of the new Southern studies have suggested, "the South" has been historically produced by rhetorical strategies, aesthetic interventions, and late-capitalist material culture; the "real South," as Scott Romine puts it, "is full of fakes."[6] Building on this scholarship, this chapter explores the role blues tourism plays in staging "the South" for touristic consumption, particularly as theatrical practices of reenactment and surrogation rewrite the history of the blues through and upon the bodies of a largely white, male, upper-middle-class group.[7]

The Mississippi Delta has been variously and aphoristically defined: as "the most Southern place on earth," as "the land where the blues began," as a place that "begins in the lobby of the Peabody Hotel in Memphis and ends on Catfish Row in Vicksburg," as "goddam."[8] Geographers and civic authorities generally recognize the Delta as composed of seventeen counties in northwestern Mississippi; bordered on the west by the Mississippi River, these counties are largely rural, dotted by a handful of towns and small cities, among them Clarksdale, Greenwood, and Jackson.[9] The infamous Mississippi State Penitentiary (Parchman Farm) is here, as is the Tallahatchie River, where Emmett Till's murdered body was discovered in 1955. The two-century-long black majority in the Mississippi Delta, combined with white planters' demand for a compliant class of agricultural laborers, produced some of the country's harshest Jim Crow legislation and racist vigilantism. These histories of racial terror have produced a state that is also a state of mind: the extraordinary unrest in the midst of the blues revival (including the rioting that accompanied James Meredith's enrollment at the University of Mississippi in 1962, the assassination of Medgar Evers in 1963, and James Chaney's, Michael Schwerner's, and Andrew Goodman's abductions and murders in 1964) cemented the "Mississippi mystique" in the minds of white enthusiasts who allied themselves with the civil rights movement.[10]

In spite of the region's history of nearly indescribable suffering and exploitation, the Delta has been, in Clyde Woods's words, "one of the world's most prolific cultural centers."[11] The Mississippi Delta was a hotbed for tent- and minstrel-show touring entertainments in the early twentieth century; as a site of artistic exchange and innovation, it was also the birthplace or residence of dozens of mostly male blues musicians, many of whom rose to prominence during the revival era, including Muddy Waters, David Honeyboy Edwards, John Lee Hooker, Robert Johnson, Skip James, Robert Nighthawk, and Son House. But contrary to popular representations, blues was not the only genre of music played in the Delta—Sam Cooke and Ike Turner, both from Clarksdale, rose to fame singing rhythm and blues, gospel, and rock and roll. When Alan Lomax, John Work III, and Lewis Jones arrived in Clarksdale in 1941 to conduct a study sponsored by Fisk University, they found nothing but popular hits on the local jukeboxes.

The Mississippi Delta is one part of a larger region that extends along both sides of the southern Mississippi River, stretching from the "boot heel" of Missouri to the Gulf of Mexico. But the Mississippi Delta, some 350 miles north of where the river empties into the gulf, is not, technically speaking, a delta. Like the Arkansas Delta to the west of the river, the Mississippi Delta is an alluvial floodplain, a delta not at the mouth (the end point of the weaving yet linear history that is a river's flow) of a river but off to the side. The position of the Mississippi Delta—which was created by centuries of flooding and the rerouting of oxbows, and only recently managed by a levee system that has frequently strained to maintain the integrity of the river's banks—as "off to the side" corresponds with the sometimes wistful, sometimes pejorative, descriptions of this region as removed from the (main)stream of American culture. The Mississippi Delta is a region first inhabited by Yazoo, Tunica, and Natchez people—a history that is principally remembered in the place names that pepper the Delta—and its reputation as the home of "King Cotton" was only firmly established in the late nineteenth century. Though plantation owners and slaves populated the region throughout the nineteenth century, it was not until the 1880s that a massive agro-industrial project cleared the land of its dense hardwood forests (eradicating many of its large fauna, including panthers and bears), further developed the levee system to manage the river's flooding, and produced the treeless landscape of farmland that is now recognized as essential to the Delta's topographic, economic, and affective identity.[12]

In the postwar era, the Delta, and Clarksdale in particular, became an important center for civil rights organizing and activism.[13] The most well-known movement figure from Clarksdale was Aaron Henry, a pharmacist who owned and ran the Fourth Street Drugstore, an important gathering place for activists, including Freedom Summer volunteers, for decades. Henry was elected president of the Mississippi branch of the NAACP in 1959 and was a central figure in organizing local actions, such as the 1961 boycott of discriminatory Clarksdale businesses, and statewide interventions, such as the 1963 Freedom Vote and the 1964 founding of the Mississippi Freedom Democratic Party. Later in his life, Henry served in the Mississippi State House of Representatives. In spite of Henry's illustrious career, Clarksdale's touristic infrastructure places little emphasis on his life or accomplishments. Only a small marker denotes the site of the former Fourth Street Drugstore; off the touristic beaten path, the acknowledgment of Henry's contribution to the broader civil rights movement, as well as the movement in Clarksdale, is strikingly marginalized. Less well known, but no less significant, were the contributions of Vera Pigee, a beautician and secretary for the local NAACP whose life and work are chronicled by the historian Françoise Hamlin in her local history of the movement, *Crossroads at Clarksdale*. Like Henry's drugstore, Pigee's beauty shop was a gathering place for activists, particularly women, who used the cover of this semiprivate space to communicate, organize, and care for each other. In spite of the concentrated organizing and activist work that took place in Clarksdale, the city does not acknowledge its civil rights history in any formal way, nor does it connect its blues heritage to the dissatisfactions that produced the movement.

Though home to extraordinary wealth concentrated in the hands of a few, the state of Mississippi, and the Delta in particular, suffers from some of the worst poverty in the United States. As of March 2013, 27 percent of Mississippians lived below the federal poverty line, a rate exceeded only by New Mexico and Louisiana; 34 percent of the state's children lived in poverty.[14] With the lowest median annual income and the third-highest incarceration rate in the United States, Mississippi ranks at or near the bottom in nearly every metric measuring health and well-being, including rates of diabetes and obesity, HIV, life expectancy, and low birth weight.[15] Poverty in Mississippi is unequally distributed: 42 percent of black individuals live in poverty, while only 15 percent of whites do, a distribution more unequal than the national average.[16] In the city of Clarksdale, which, according to the 2010 U.S. Census, is nearly 80 percent black, 52 percent of families with children live below the poverty line; for households headed by single women, that number goes up to 66 percent.[17] Jobs are in short supply: in the early 2010s, the unemployment rate in Coahoma County averaged 7–10 percentage points higher than the national average.[18] Clarksdale's most impoverished homes, some of which still lack electricity or running water, brush up against sites of affluence, many of them sustained by and profiting from the burgeoning tourist economy.[19] A few expensive restaurants dot downtown Clarksdale, catering to tourists and to the area's wealthiest residents. Large homes still stand in the downtown district, where the city's white founders once lived, and while there are few elaborate mansions of the kind one might find in Natchez, the "big houses" still architecturally oversee the region's farmland, demonstrating what Woods calls "the resilience of plantation relations" for the region.[20]

As chronicled by Marybeth Hamilton, seekers of the blues have been traveling to the Mississippi Delta since the early twentieth century.[21] White representatives from race-records companies began to descend on the area in the late 1920s, and folklorists and photographers arrived en masse during the Great Depression. Blues-revival enthusiasts, intent on "discovering" long-forgotten or never-known bluesmen, turned up in the 1960s. Beginning in the 1990s, several Mississippi Delta cities and towns, with assistance from state tourism boards and private industry, began to develop their touristic infrastructures, capitalizing on the music-centered tourism that was thriving in cities such as Nashville, Memphis, and New Orleans; indeed, the tourist-friendly redevelopment of Memphis's Beale Street in the 1980s was a key indicator of the economic potential for music tourism in the region.[22] Local chambers of commerce, the Mississippi Delta Tourism Association, and the Mississippi Development Authority began to link their efforts. In a signal shift in 1999, the Delta Blues Museum, previously housed in an unused room of Clarksdale's local library, relocated to the town's historic train-depot building. The early years of the twenty-first century were marked by several high-profile events that bolstered blues tourism: in 2000, the Clinton administration's White House Millennium Council, in partnership with the Department of Transportation, the Rails-to-Trails Conservancy, the American Hiking Society, and the National Endowment for the Arts, selected sixteen National Millennium Trails that, in the words of then–U.S. secretary of transportation Rodney E. Slater, "connect our nation's landscape, heritage, and culture."[23] This initiative spurred interest in fostering tourist experiences by means of trails that connected widely dispersed sites through a common itinerary. Three years later the U.S. Congress, recognizing the centennial anniversary of W. C. Handy's encounter with the blues at the Tutwiler train station, approved a resolution submitted by senators from Mississippi, Arkansas, Tennessee, and Washington. The resolution declared 2003 the "Year of the Blues," and requested that President George W. Bush "issue a proclamation calling on the people of the United States to observe the 'Year of the Blues' with appropriate ceremonies, activities, and educational programs."[24] The most high-profile event that resulted was Martin Scorsese's PBS series *The Blues*: seven films, each made by a different director, that explored various aspects of the history of blues. The series, sponsored by Volkswagen (which cannily exploited the associations between blues and traveling), was accompanied by a website that encouraged visitors to take their own virtual blues road trip. The renewed public interest in blues, as well as in trails as conduits for cultural understanding and touristic consumption, led to the establishment of the Mississippi Blues Commission in 2004 and the development of the Mississippi Blues Trail, which placed its first marker in 2005. The placement of markers continues today, with more than one hundred in place as of the beginning of 2013. The Mississippi Blues Trail now offers an iPhone app, described as "blues for your phone," offering virtual tourists the opportunity to visit the historic sites of the Delta blues without ever leaving home.

While the conventional wisdom has held that increased tourism to the region benefits its residents economically, town and state commissions have undertaken little formal assessment of blues tourism's economic impact. Anecdotally, many Clarksdale residents see blues tourism as economically benefiting only a select few. Woods writes, "In the absence of a tourism agenda that has emerged from community-based decision making, a community's heritage can be turned against it and used to reproduce and expand the existing structures of exploitation."[25] When asked by an interviewer about the "good, big things" that are taking place in the city's tourist economy, George Messenger, proprietor of the oldest black-owned business in Clarksdale, Messenger's Pool Hall, replied: "This is a question that I would rather skip because I don't see it the way you see it."[26]

Who are the blues tourists? Precise demographic details are difficult to determine, largely because neither state nor local officials have attempted to answer this question in a systematic fashion. Some generalizations about the blues tourists are possible, however, and are widely accepted by tourist-industry officials and local residents alike. To a significant extent, blues tourism reflects the contemporary state of blues fandom: the tourists are, for the most part, "baby boomers, well-educated, middle- to upper-middle class whites."[27] Most are men. Female blues tourists frequently travel in the company of men; female blues tourists traveling on their own are rare. Almost all blues tourists are white.[28] International visitors, many of them from the United Kingdom and other parts of Western Europe, make up a significant portion of blues tourists; the Shack Up Inn, one of the most popular lodging options in Clarksdale, reported that one-quarter of its visitors in 2009 were from outside the United States.[29] Though blues tourism is becoming more structured, and the sight of charter buses navigating the narrow streets of the Delta's downtowns is no longer as rare as it once was, most tourists are, according to Stephen King, "noninstitutionalized" travelers. They range, he notes, from the "'explorer' who seeks some autonomy from the tourism industry, to the 'drifter' who 'goes native' by immersing himself or herself in the world of a new host country." These tourists "do not want the Delta region to be transformed into a predictable and protective tourist environment."[30] In short, blues tourists conceive of themselves and their activities as highly individualized, and as capturing the spontaneity and freedom of life on the road associated with the wandering bluesman.

African American tourists also visit the Mississippi Delta, some of them with a long-held affection for blues. More often than not, however, these tourists are drawn less by the region's musical mythos and more by a historical family connection to the area. Many of these visitors, now middle class and living in urban centers in the Northeast and Midwest, come to the Delta to visit the homeland of their elders: sharecropping grandparents and great-grandparents who made the arduous migration northward. While they may not fully embrace the "call to home" that Carol Stack so famously identifies in her 1996 book of the same title, this post-civil rights generation of visitors approach the Delta as a place of familial history and suffering.[31] Their visits often serve the purpose of identifying the distance traveled by a few short generations—the geographic distance of migration, and also the socioeconomic journey from a Southern underclass. At times gathering for large family reunions, African American tourists to the Delta are much more likely to listen to or play music as part of a fife-and-drum hill-country picnic or impromptu sound-system street party rather than at tourist-centered venues, such as Ground Zero Blues Club.[32] The fact remains that, in spite of a small but steady stream of black travelers coming to and through the region, the blues-tourism economy addresses itself primarily to white tourists.

The blues revival of the 1960s is the demographic, economic, and ideological underpinning of blues tourism. In the 1960s revivalists promulgated the mythology of the Mississippi Delta as an undiscovered backwater of blues authenticity; referring to 1920s and 1930s musicians' orientation toward popular music, the blues historian and critic Elijah Wald notes: "If many of [these artists] are unfamiliar to most present-day blues fans, that indicates how much our view of the scene has been influenced by the intervening years, and how little it resembles the views of listeners at the time."[33] Many of the political and affective impulses that drive the blues-tourism industry today mirror those of the revival; if anything, contemporary anxieties about the homogenization of cultural production are more intense in the early years of the twenty-first century than they were in the postwar period. As in the 1960s, the rural emerges as a pastoral alternative for disenchanted suburbanites, a repository of a "simpler" way of life. The logic of the blues revival—the desire to preserve a supposedly disappearing folk form—animates the heritage-tourism industry of the Mississippi Delta, which depends on producing the blues as both disappearing *and* remaining, as both living and dead; the "preservationist impulse" that characterized the revival resembles that of contemporary heritage tourism.[34] The simultaneous invocation and erasure of black suffering is as central to blues tourism as it was to the revival, as is a post-civil rights-era desire for racial reunion and reconciliation. State officials see blues tourism as a strategy for transforming public perception of the state as a racist backwater; still, the constant minimizing of the state-sponsored history of violence toward its black residents ultimately undermines the goal of racial reconciliation that many in Mississippi seek to achieve.[35]

Two modes of heritage tourism predominate in Mississippi: blues tourism and Civil War and plantation tourism. Unlike many other Southern states, Mississippi does not yet have a civil rights tourist infrastructure or a civil rights museum, though one is scheduled open in Jackson in 2017. Plantation tourism has long been a staple of the state's economy; southern Mississippi cities such as Vicksburg and Natchez are the state's touristic centers of antebellum heritage tourism, "white places of honor and romance . . . where the presence of enslaved African Americans is generally elided."[36] Prominent throughout the South, plantation- and antebellum-home tourism is a particular draw for visitors who participate in the annual Natchez Pilgrimage, in which they tour the homes of one of the wealthiest cities in the pre–Civil War South. Described by Jessica Adams as sites where "leisure blends with commerce and motifs of oppression in the rhythmic pulse of postslavery geographies," these preserved eighteenth- and nineteenth-century homes celebrate the wealth, lifestyle, and architectural grandeur of the white, landed antebellum South, placing particular emphasis on white Southern femininity.[37] Exploiting imagery of colonnades and corseted young women in hoop skirts, Natchez markets itself to female tourists; its website encourages "girlfriend getaways" and advertises locations for "weddings and romance."[38] Indeed, the "romance" of Natchez overshadows many of its other historically significant sites, including the Forks of the Road antebellum slave market, historically the most active and profitable in the state. In recent years plantation-tour providers have begun to include slave cabins in their tours of the properties, often to appeal to potential middle-class African American tourists and to Northern whites uncomfortable with the state's slaveholding history.[39] In their study of plantation tourism, Jennifer Eichstedt and Stephen Small criticize the cynicism of these attempts, describing a former slave cabin-turned-restaurant in Louisiana as "'plantation chic'—a framing that stresses romance and relaxation and turns sites of Black suffering into locations for white consumers' pleasure."[40]

Blues tourism appears as the photographic negative of plantation tourism, even as it shares with it a similar orientation toward upper-middle-class white consumers. In contrast to the genteel femininity of plantation tourism, blues tourism is rough-and-ready, is male dominated, and basks in its own lack of luxury: "The Ritz we ain't," the Shack Up Inn proudly announces on its website. The glorification of antebellum wealth in Natchez finds its inverse in blues tourism's romanticizing of poverty, where places such as Clarksdale offer experiences of "poverty tourism."[41] Blues poverty tourism offers travelers the opportunity to visually consume Delta deprivation while also enabling an embodied approximation what it "might have been like" to live in the conditions that produced the blues. Closely linked to dark tourism, which the scholars John Lennon and Malcolm Foley identify as emerging from participants' conflicted experiences of late capitalism, poverty tourism in the Mississippi Delta requires embodied participation; the landscape becomes a stage set onto which tourists step, its key set piece the shotgun shack. For some tourists, however, to enter, or even stay in a "shack" is not to imagine oneself a bluesman but to experience a grandparent's way of life, and to share that experience with a spouse, a child, a friend.

Due to the shaping of the Delta mise-en-scène by documentary photography, blues iconography, and imagery of the blues revival, blues tourists new to the Delta do not step into an unknown place; it is one they and others have already shaped imaginatively. Documentary photography, in particular, has constructed the imagination's stage onto which blues tourists now step. Beginning in the mid-1930s, photographers employed by the Farm Security Administration, including Walker Evans, Dorothea Lange, and Marion Post Wolcott, produced some of the most enduring and widely circulated images of the Mississippi Delta. Under instructions from Roy Stryker, the director of the Farm Security Administration's photography project, to document the struggles of rural life for the sake of generating public support for the administration's aid programs, these photographers—Dorothea Lange in particular—circulated images of sharecroppers' dwellings as persuasive evidence of the region's grueling poverty. These photographs, seen by millions in the pages of *Life* and *Look* magazines, established the template for representations of the Delta that were to follow. Indeed, later photographers, such as those who documented Robert F. Kennedy's visit to Greenville, Mound Bayou, and Clarksdale in 1967, produced many similar images, as if to suggest that little had changed in thirty years. Images of malnourished children living in homes without running water became part of the public persuasion of Kennedy's tour, seared into a generation's consciousness and consciences. Documentary photography of sites of poverty continues throughout the Delta; several organizations hold organized photography workshops in Clarksdale, and independent photographers travel through the region in large numbers. Often showing a preference for rural or abandoned properties over inhabited urban ones, these photographers often present Delta poverty as a thing of the past, its tattered remains animating the landscape, rather than as a harsh condition of the present. As the everyday spaces of the Mississippi Delta become a mise-en-scène and the landscape itself a stage, the place is transformed into a creative space, its participants producing heightened modes of experience, new narratives of history, and charged spaces of encounter.

Clarksdale had a lively early twentieth-century theatrical culture; the city, a popular stop on the chitlin' circuit, had at least two permanent theaters—the Savoy and the Marion—that hosted live entertainment for black audiences. Yet neither of these sites, both of which are still extant, is included in guidebooks or other popular itineraries of Clarksdale.[42] Minstrel shows, both black and white, regularly passed through Clarksdale in the early twentieth century, as did William Cody and Nate Salsbury's Buffalo Bill show, which, in the autumn of 1900, set up on the grounds outside the city and staged a grand procession through the streets of downtown. Touring companies of "straight" plays came through town as well, running for weeks at a time at the Majestic Theatre, whose 1915 season alternated plays with minstrel troupes. Though events for black audiences were rarely covered by the *Clarksdale Register*, the paper occasionally mentioned parties of note, such as a "Ball Masque" (masquerade ball) that took place in the New World District, hosted by "James Anderson, yard boy for W.A. Crawley, and Scotty, Garner and Co.'s delivery driver."[43]

While formal theatrical activity in Clarksdale has slowed, the theatrical spirit that governed the early performances of blues in this region has not disappeared. Though many white blues tourists do not know the name or the music of Bobby Rush (born Emmit Ellis Jr.), he is one of the most well-known of the currently active Mississippi Delta musicians. Known as the king of the chitlin' circuit, Rush plays a high-energy, electrified set of horn-heavy soul blues—a musical repertoire informed by soul, rhythm and blues, and gospel; widely beloved by black audiences, he is mostly unknown to white blues tourists, who prefer the twelve-bar style of acoustic blues. Overstuffed with hip-shaking backup dancers, glittery costumes, double entendres, and lengthy comic monologues, Rush's live shows reveal their indebtedness to his participation in variety and vaudeville blues early in his career, when he performed in Chicago-area clubs with Moms Mabley and Pigmeat Markham. Still, "for some blues tourists, Rush's live performances are the direct antithesis of the 'real blues.'"[44]

But even those performers hailed by blues tourists as the authentic inheritors of a Delta blues tradition betray their connection to a comic theatrical blues tradition. After a long career driving a truck, the Clarksdale musician James "Super Chikan" Johnson, nephew of Big Jack Johnson, established himself as a professional bluesman and has made the most of what he calls his "authentic and old-fashioned" style, which he learned from his grandfather. Unlike Rush, who plays at clubs that attract black audiences, as well as in northwestern Mississippi's casinos, Johnson is a hit on the blues-tourism circuit, regularly playing for majority-white audiences at the Ground Zero Blues Club and the Shack Up Inn. Johnson claims that his music is "a link to the past, and that's what everybody likes and what everybody wants to hear."[45] In interviews and in performances, Johnson emphasizes his connection with the musicians revered by blues revivalists, including Muddy Waters and John Lee Hooker, and he is often photographed in front of sharecropper shacks or in cotton fields. But in performance he, like Rush, also discloses the influence of a popular comic tradition, especially in his frank embrace of "chicken humor," both by means of his name (and the name of his band, the Fighting Cocks) and his rowdy crowing from the stage. He regularly punctuates a song's conclusion with the exclamation "somebody shoot that thang," and in his popular "Tin Top Shack" he describes—with sound effects—how he taught his roosters to sing. Riffing on the animal humor of the minstrel show, Super Chikan signifies on that early twentieth-century tradition while also making light of the derogatory stereotype of the chicken-stealing slave that was widespread in minstrel entertainment. Such gestures, though, are rarely commented on by critics and fans, who focus instead on Johnson's homemade guitars and outsider status, rather than his obvious links to a professional entertainment tradition. "I want to be an entertainer," he explains, simply, while discussing the influence of Chubby Checker and Little Richard on his music.

Contemporary musicians such as Rush and Johnson regularly incorporate some of the lyrical and performance traditions pioneered by blueswomen in the teens and twenties. However, these women and the tent shows that brought them to the Delta are barely present in the histories narrated by the blues-tourism industry, which erects a second generation of male stars as the form's progenitors. This exclusion of blues foremothers and the theatrical culture in which they flourished props up the originality of the male troubadours they influenced. There is one striking exception to this absence of blueswomen from Clarksdalian blues tourism, and that is "Bessie's room" at the Riverside Hotel. Smith, who played in Clarksdale often throughout her career, died in the G. T. Thomas Afro-American Hospital after being injured in an automobile accident outside of town in September 1937. The hospital, the city's only medical facility for black residents, eventually closed and was reopened by Z. L. Hill as the Riverside Hotel in 1944; throughout the 1940s and 1950s, it served as a short-term residence for many black blues travelers, including Ike Turner, Sonny Boy Williamson, and Robert Nighthawk. From 1997 until 2013, the hotel was owned by Frank "Rat" Ratliff, Hill's son, and became a popular lodging option for visiting musicians and tourists.[46] Ratliff gave tours to the curious, always stopping to highlight "Bessie's room," which he declined to rent out, refusing to turn a profit on a space that could claim a very high market value. When asked about the circumstances surrounding Smith's death— was she really refused at a white hospital, costing her precious time and perhaps even her life?—Ratliff was always deliberately indirect, refusing to answer authoritatively about "what really happened," nor taking recourse in published accounts that declare the question settled. Rather than ease visitors' minds and answer their questions, Ratliff kept alive the history and memory of devastating segregation and discrimination, whether or not these had anything to do with the specifics of Smith's death. It *could* have happened that way, he suggested—a hypothetical that was so very important. The irony of the preservation of Bessie's room is that it is a site that commemorates the singer's death rather than her life, or her out-sized influence on the musicians who now draw blues tourists to Clarksdale. Though the influence of Smith's blues theater is not acknowledged, the theatrical practices that characterized the early variety and tent shows are still present in contemporary Clarksdale performances—from those of Rush to performances of tourists themselves.

TOURISM AS PERFORMANCE

Tourism is itself a performance. In his widely read *The Tourist: A New Theory of the Leisure Class*, the sociologist Dean MacCannell outlines the touristic experience as a "stage set," drawing a sharp dividing line between an insider's experience of one's own culture and a formulated version of that culture offered to tourists. Drawing on Erving Goffman's concepts of "front" and "back" regions, MacCannell concludes that the tourist never has access to the supposedly authentic back regions of a culture that is not one's own. John Urry takes MacCannell's argument a step further, suggesting that there is "no authentic tourist experience. . . . There are merely a series of games or texts that can be played."[47] While it is not my intention to distinguish between "authentic" and "inauthentic" touristic experiences, I draw attention to MacCannell's and Urry's positions here to highlight how theatrical language and scenarios (stage sets, games, play) have infiltrated discourse on tourism. MacCannell's and Urry's assessments suggest that tourism is a process of stepping on and off stages, of playing roles, and of observing and being observed. They also point to a recent decisive shift in both touristic experience and tourism studies in recent years, a shift that acknowledges the constructedness of authenticity, even while tourists pursue authentic experiences through playfulness, multiplicity, and flexible historicity. That is to say: millennial tourism is a performance, but one without a "real" referent. Though *authenticity* is still a watchword in Clarksdale's blues-tourism industry (the slogan for the Clarksdale Revitalization Inc. organization is "Keepin' it real!"), blues tourism takes a cheeky approach to the "real" that it purports to preserve.

Rather than eviscerate the concept, blues tourist sites and practices multiply and mobilize the authentic, accessing it through the play of performance. In describing tourism as performance, I am building upon Richard Schechner's oft-cited claim: "Performance means: never for the first time." While there are certainly repeat visitors to any tourist locale—and the Mississippi Delta is filled with such repeat visitors—most tourists *do* understand themselves to be experiencing a place for the first time. But even though a tourist may be new to the place he or she visits, performances of tourism are always, to use Schechner's words, "restored behavior."[48] Despite an oft-professed desire to get off the beaten path, most tourists are, in fact, traveling a well-trod road. Following guidebooks, websites, maps, historical markers, and word-of-mouth recommendations, many tourists consciously and unconsciously retrace the routes of those who have come before them. The supposedly "free" tourist's itinerary is often tightly scripted by infrastructural clues, such as available parking and a certain kind of signage. The tourist, particularly the heritage tourist, not only is a spectator but is cast in a particular role, with his or her behaviors scripted by touristic sites, rhetorics, and practices.

The recent proliferation of heritage trails, which invite tourists to expressly reenact the journeys of others by following in their footsteps, makes the tourism-as-performance paradigm even more explicit. Tourism has always depended on the establishment and maintenance of particular routes, but codified trails, paths, itineraries, and walks have become an integral part of the heritage-tourism industry in the last two decades and a critical strategy for reviving postindustrial economies. "While it looks old," Barbara Kirshenblatt-Gimblett summarizes, "heritage is actually something new. Heritage is a mode of cultural production in the present that has recourse to the past. Heritage thus defined depends on display to give dying economies and dead sites a second life as exhibitions of themselves."[49] Heritage sites, often in cooperation with local chambers of commerce and tourism commissions, have instituted historical walking and driving tours as modes of tourist experience. Jeff Green, of the Rails-to-Trails Conservancy, an organization that transforms disused railroad tracks into multiuse paths for fitness, transportation, and historical preservation, explains the significance of trails to the project of corporeally mapping out American identity: "The migration and trading routes of Native Americans. The epic path drawn by Lewis and Clark. The dusty trails followed by the riders of the Pony Express. The northward treks made by African Americans escaping the bonds of slavery. These journeys all define the cultural identity of America—and they all happened on trails."[50] To walk or drive these trails, Green suggests, is to gain embodied access to the past. Offered an opportunity to travel in the footsteps of those who came before them, tourists are urged to follow these paths as a type of restored behavior. To travel the trail is to enter into a discrete mode of historiography, one that invokes ancestral, genealogical, and national affect.

Contemporary blues tourism is a complex dance of surrogation, one that imprecisely restores and replays black diasporic patterns of blues traveling. Blues tourism functions as both a touring of performance history and a performance practice in and of itself; promoting tourists from spectators to surrogates, it remembers and constructs an "original" of black diaspora, even as it forgets its most salient details. The tourist's experience of the "classic road trip through the cradle of musical innovation in America" on Highway 61 stages "two ways of being out of place," generating an uncomfortable slippage between the leisure tourism of a mostly white, male, older, wealthy group and historical migrations of the rural black poor compelled by economic deprivation and violence.[51] The tourist is cast as a surrogate for the migrant, but, as Joseph Roach underscores in his explication of surrogation, such casting practices never seamlessly map the substitute onto the perceived original. Surrogates step "into the cavities created by loss through death or other forms of departure"; the tourist surrogates of blues tourism, who stand in for those passed away or passed on, reproduce the blues traveler, but they can never get it just right, as they either fall short or exceed the original constructed in retrospect.[52] Such excess or deficiency is a defining characteristic of the surrogate's performance. The substitute and the original are always at variance; it is this gap—the white tourist's inability to fully inhabit a blues-shaped world—that generates the series of compensatory performances that characterize blues tourism.

As a practice that gestures toward reenactment, blues tourism bears an unstable and necessarily theatrical relationship to history and historiography. As with all performances that attempt to apprehend the past through the body, blues tourism resounds in what Rebecca Schneider calls a "temporal crosshatch" with the historical events it remembers—or drags—into the slippery space of the present.[53] Like performances of reenactment and living history, blues tourism puts faith in the body's ability to apprehend material conditions of the past. As Scott Magelssen writes of experiential historical events, "the body becomes a site of knowledge production on equal footing with—or, in the case of living museums, even more powerful than—the book or the archive." But this reordering of epistemic priorities is not without complexity; the "ambiguous historicity of the body itself" becomes decidedly more knotty when the tourist's race, class, or gender does not neatly map onto the bodies of those that he or she seeks to repli-cate.[54] In purposeful pursuits and in wandering, the tourist steps on and off stages of the Mississippi Delta's history, crossing time that crosses across the visitor's body. Because of its status as working-class black cultural his-tory, Mississippi blues have not been understood in detail, nor have they been reverently protected; only in the last twenty years has the ideology of preservation come to the fore, an approach that privileges certain figures while neglecting others. Tourists are invited to touch the past, to intimately apprehend and mold cultural memory. With few discrete events to do over, blues tourists secure a new relationship to history and to memory through participation in a theatrical mise-en-scène of the Delta South. Through the props of the past brought into the present, now meticulously cast (off) as scenic detritus, the tourist becomes a historiographer, scripting a new history of blues that reframes compulsory labor as leisure and poverty as simplicity.

DRIVING THE DELTA

While the mythos of blues train travel reached its apex during the revival, the railroad is no longer the primary mode of transportation in the Missis-sippi Delta: travel throughout the region now requires a car. Most passen-ger trains stopped running decades ago; their tracks are now largely over-grown and their platforms are deserted and idle. Whatever itinerary they choose, blues tourists inevitably travel along U.S. Route 61, the signal route of early and mid-twentieth-century black migration out of the mid-South. Nicknamed "the blues highway," Highway 61 is a fourteen-hundred-mile north-south route, extending the length of the United States from Mis-sissippi to Minnesota, and it has become something of a spiritual locus for blues revivalists and blues tourists. In his autobiography, Bob Dylan—whose pivotal 1965 album *Highway 61 Revisited* integrated blues, folk, and rock—explained the significance of the road to his music, and to his sense of self: "Highway 61, the main thoroughfare of the country blues, begins about where I came from[,] . . . Duluth to be exact. I always felt like I'd started on it, always had been on it and could go anywhere from it, even down into the deep Delta country. It was the same road, full of the same contradictions, the same one-horse towns, the same spiritual ancestors." For Dylan, the highway was both an arterial link between his home and the home of the musicians he idolized and a justifying expression of the continuity between their work and his. Rural blues "was a counterpart of myself," he claimed. Living on Highway 61 meant he "was never too far away from any of it."[55]

Driving Highway 61 takes on its own performative quality, bolstered by fantasies of reenactment, and tourists produce the mythic past they seek. Riffing on a narrative of descent, blues tourists frequently stage black migration in reverse, following the route of Highway 61 from north to south.[56] The tourism industry and tourists themselves carefully manage the histories of the millions who walked these roads: migrants are remembered, even while particular details are forgotten for the sake of touristic pleasure. Because as much as blues tourism is framed as free-spirited, nonconformist, and supremely individualized, it is haunted by the histories of those people whose footsteps pounded out its trails, and whose labor built its railways, highways, and levees. Blues tourism is mimetic of blues travel. In addition it replicates the journeys of the panoply of folklorists, archivists, anthropologists, and archaeologists who have traveled to the Delta as collectors of music, fossils, history, and experience. The *Clarksdale Press Register* rather glibly nominates Hernando de Soto, credited with the first conquest crossing of the Mississippi River in the sixteenth century, as "the first Delta tourist."[57] Steve Cheseborough's guidebook, *Blues Traveling: The Holy Sites of the Delta Blues*, assigns this honor to the Harvard archaeologist Charles Peabody, "who dug up an Indian mound near Clarksdale in 1901–1902."[58] When John and Alan Lomax welded a 350-pound recording machine to the back of their car and traveled throughout the South recording vernacular music in 1933, they were already repeating the journeys of others who came before them, even as they established a template for future tourists, many of whom are inspired by the Lomaxes' story.

Restaging the past through immersion, the blues tourist's road trip is a fantasy of time travel that allows one to traverse—and master—time as well as space. This conquest of time and space is enabled by specifically American mythologies of automobility, described by Cotten Seiler as a set of ideological practices that constitute the modern liberal subject by mobilizing the affect of driving, as well as the qualities of freedom, self-determination, and citizenship supposedly bestowed upon the driver.[59] The modern driver secures autonomy by taking to the open road and, as

Kris Lackey argues, by "fashioning a myth of independence from [industrial] forces, . . . in part by continually reenacting the discovery and early settlement of the country."[60] The American driver's "possessive individualism," however, has historically hinged on the exclusion of those deemed unfit for full citizenship as drivers, primarily women and people of color. In this enduring framework of mobility and containment, such subjects were, in Seiler's words, "denied the elemental self-possession of the autonomous individual, . . . demonstrated in the ability to own and control one's laboring capacity and issue, and to move oneself outward across geographical space or upward through socioeconomic strata."[61] The freedom of the open road is and has been unequally distributed, reinforcing white masculinity as the privileged beneficiary of automobility. One need only look to the representation of blues travel and tourism to see such dynamics at play. Even today, when car access and ownership is far more prominent throughout the working-class South, bluesmen remain represented as walkers or train travelers, while the pickup truck is the preferred accessory of choice for the country musician. Bluesmen are always on the move, but they are not granted the full automobility available to the white tourist, whose "volitional mobility" stands in contrast to the "coerced" or "circumscribed" mobility of "the disabled, racial others . . . , the poor, and women."[62]

The assertion of white masculine automobility in the 1950s, aided in part by the publication of Jack Kerouac's On the Road (1957), continues to shape the affective experience of driving in contemporary blues tourism.[63] During this period of interstate-highway construction, white flight, and suburban expansion, automobility was reshaped in the public imagination in ways that remain salient for contemporary leisure drivers. Driving in the Cold War came to be viewed as "a palliative ideological exercise that was seen to reverse, or at least to arrest, the postwar 'decline of the individual,'" and as a way to secure a model of American heroism in an era of waning expansion.[64] Countering anxieties about cultural conformity, "momism," and the decline of manual labor, driving's reaffirmation of individuality "doubled as a reaffirmation of masculinity."[65] Kerouac's On the Road was the fundamental postwar cultural text of white masculine automobility, signaling the pleasurable convergence that the "contingency and risk" of the open road shares with those living outside middle-class norms, including artists, dropouts, musicians, and drug addicts.

As Hamilton argues, the masculinity of the blues revival is closely linked to that of the Beats: "What united both movements was their almost exclusively male constituency and their romance with outsider manhood, with defiant black men who seemed to scorn the suburban breadwinner's stifling, soul-destroying routine. For revivalists, that model was the country bluesman[,] . . . for Beats it was the black urban jazzman."[66] Promotional materials and guides for blues tourists replicate the Cold War ideology of automobility, foregrounding its freedom and romanticizing the experience of the open road. Through Kerouac, white pleasure taken in black music was laminated onto the pleasures and privileges of driving, a convergence that manifests in contemporary blues tourism. Blues tourists are given the opportunity to reenact the adventures of Sal Paradise and his friends—not only their aimless, free driving but also the infusion of these drives with music. In a place where old, broken-down vehicles are an important part of establishing an anachronistic mise-en-scène, spectating through the windshield becomes a central mode for consuming the Delta. With the de rigueur soundtrack of the blues to accompany them, blues tourists experience the Delta through the proscenium frame or screen of the windshield—a frame through which one can shoot footage of the past while remaining safely protected in the bubble of the present. Indeed, the opening moments of blues films constantly replicate this shot: a passive, timeless, agricultural landscape speeding by the window of a moving car, Muddy Waters on its stereo. It is through this "temporal crosshatch"—the present inside the car spectating the past on the other side of the proscenium—that the theatricality of the Delta is established. When drivers arrive at their destinations, however, they must step out of the car and into an embodied engagement with history.

SCRIPTIVE SITES

The sites of blues tourism script the behavior of heritage tourists, and so too do tourism's itineraries. Through the embodied participation of tourists, blues are imperfectly preserved and mythically restaged across the body. In her performance-centered theorization of how "things" script behavior, Robin Bernstein models a reading of material culture as "promp[ting], inspir[ing], and structur[ing]" human action. Scripting, as Bernstein underscores, implies both a template and the performer's ability to resist, modify, or transform that template. That is, scripting does not deny agency but rather "broadly structures a performance while simultaneously allowing for resistance and unleashing original, live variations that may not be individually predictable."[67] While Bernstein's analysis focuses on "scriptive things"—material objects that script human behavior—I am interested in the utility of her method for analyzing how the itineraries, sites, and architectures of blues tourism "are performative in that they constitute actions: they *think*, or, more accurately, they *are the act of thinking*."[68] Blues tourist sites are not just painterly representations that tourists observe. Rather, tourists *pass through* the theatrical trappings of a staged Delta imaginary, walking the boards and performatively, although imprecisely, revivifying the blues, if not the social and economic conditions in which early blues were performed. As textual templates for human action, guidebooks are the most obvious and literal scripts offered by the blues-tourism industry, prompting touristic behavior by noting attractions to visit, places to sleep and eat, and venues to hear live music. These guidebooks play an important role in establishing the theatricality of the Delta, staging the region for outside visitors and regulating its consumption by tourists. But guidebooks that tell tourists what to do and where to go are not the only "scriptive things" of blues tourism. In the pages that follow, I turn to several scriptive sites of blues tourism, including the Crossroads, the Shack Up Inn, Waters's home, the Delta Blues Museum, and an annual festival in order to examine the varied scriptings of blues memory within the theatrically imagined Delta South. I closely attend to the mundane behaviors, environments, and itineraries that script the enactment of racial histories, all while taking a broader view of how racialization is enacted through performance. The scripts advanced by these sites are neither singular nor integrated. Rather, each site advances its own individual script; taken collectively as a touristic experience, they effect the surrogation of the blues musician by the blues tourist, using the tools of performance to resurrect a supposedly dying form.

ORIGINS

A can't-miss-it roadside structure, a kitsch classic of American vernacular architecture, greets all who drive into Clarksdale. The Graceland-style marker of two guitars stands at the intersection of Highways 49 and 161 (also known as "old 61"). The marker transforms a crossroads into *the* Crossroads—a place of irresolvable multiplicity, one site of many where the most-told tale of the Delta blues might have taken place (see figure 4.1). Stamped with the mark of civic authority and visited by tourists at midnight, it is the place that stands in for all that remains unknown about Robert Johnson, who, more than any other figure in guidebooks and history books, in liner notes and blogs, stands in and stands out as the definitive Delta blues musician. Johnson left behind only three photographs of himself and twenty-nine recorded songs. The scarcity of information about his

4.1 Roadside marker indicating the Crossroads in Clarksdale, Mississippi. Photograph by the author.

life and his death, combined with a successfully marketed box-set release in 1990, prompted what Jim O'Neal of *Living Blues* magazine has called "the mad scramble to find any tangible evidence that Johnson actually existed on this planet."[69] Blues tourism capitalizes on Johnson's posthumous fame; the details of his life story, including a Faustian bargain, a mysterious death, and a seamless blending of European, indigenous American, and West African elements, are sufficiently ambiguous as to require a mythical, rather than factual, telling. Poisoned in the town of Quito, Johnson died in 1938 at the age of twenty-seven somewhere in nearby Greenwood. The precise location of his remains is unknown. At present, no fewer than three headstones mark the possible graves of Johnson—in Morgan City, Quito, and along Money Road, just north of Greenwood. Tourists, hedging their bets, visit all three graves, often leaving offerings—guitar picks, whiskey bottles—at each one. A convenient metonym for Clarksdale's heritage of the blues, the ontological status of the Crossroads is anything but evident. As with Johnson's grave, there are many possible crossroads: roads throughout the Delta have been widened and moved several times, making the feasibility of determining a definitive site—for an event that may not have ever happened—all but impossible.[70]

Like Johnson's grave and the Crossroads, the Delta is filled with sites that multiply the grounds upon which blues tourism stakes its claims of priority. These multiple birthplaces, multiple crossroads, and multiple headstones establish blues' historical sites as transitive or processual, rather than substantive or positivist.[71] It is here that the significance of the tourist as surrogate becomes evident. Positivist substantive sites can exist independently of touristic recognition: the Lorraine Motel remains the site of Martin Luther King Jr.'s assassination whether tourists visit it or not. But transitive sites require the surrogate to constitute them as such, to inscribe history upon a place with one's own body. While sites are scriptive of the behavior of surrogates, the surrogate scripts the site *as* a site. Countering a touristic logic that relies on concepts of origin and self-identicality, the irreducible profusion of transitive sites of blues tourism in the Mississippi Delta sets authenticity in motion, constructing it as always mobile and multiple.

To visit the many possible birthplaces of the blues is to revel in the form's indiscretion. The focus of the tourist becomes the *pursuit* of origins, the collection and embodied production of disparate and contradictory claims, the rep and rev of historiography syncopating with the rep and rev of the twelve-bar form. With relatively few substantive sites to visit, the blues tourist often organizes the experience around the wild goose chase of origins, a road trip throughout the Delta that visits the half dozen or so places that stake a claim as the birthplace of the blues, including Dockery Farms, the home of Charley Patton; the town of Tutwiler, where W. C. Handy first heard blues played; and the Hopson Plantation, where, in 1943, the introduction of the mechanical cotton picker resulted in the economic displacement and migration of tens of thousands of black sharecroppers. Clarksdale is the hometown of some of the most famous names in blues history, but there are few tangible remains of many of these residents' lives there. Instead, brass plaques and historical markers mark absences, identifying an empty lot where a home once stood. Some simply note proximity: Ike Turner's marker explains that the singer was born "less than a mile south-west" from where the tourist stands. In the absence of substantive sites of origin, these provisional locations, legitimated by their trace connections to the lives of those who lived nomadically, have their transitive authority established by the surrogate-tourists who visit, take photographs, and leave offerings. Multiple claims about the origins of blues proliferate and compete in the Delta. But local tourism-development agencies and chambers of commerce, invested in providing a steady stream of attractions that might stretch one night at a hotel into two or three, do little to reconcile these rival assertions. And while there is an economic motivation to the existence of multiple sites, the irreconcilability of these claims of origin—and their peaceful coexistence—also promotes an alternative discourse of tourism, one that embraces the multiplicity and contradictory nature of its sites and offers an alternative framework for seeing the sights and sites of an imagined authentic. This alternative discourse of transitive pursuit aligns with the blues. As Houston Baker Jr. argues, "Like signification itself, blues are always nomadically wandering. Like the freight-hopping hobo, they are ever on the move, ceaselessly summing novel experience."[72] Blues tourists, then, mimic not only the wanderings and migrations of blues travelers but also the blues aesthetic of endless deferral, the constant taking leave of signification.

If there is one site that trumps others in staking its claim as the birthplace of blues, it is not a substantive coordinate but rather the inescapable environment that surrounds the tourist: the land(scape) itself. The blues-tourism industry invites tourists to immerse themselves in the landscape that Alan Lomax gives pride of place in the title of his book *The Land Where the Blues Began*. The industry's emphasis on the land and the landscape allows for a kind of oblique engagement with the social history of sharecropping; at the same time, however, industry rhetoric emphasizes the landscape's "natural" and "scenic" qualities, avoiding any close consideration of slavery, sharecropping, convict labor, Jim Crow, or white privilege. Produced by and productive of generations of compulsory, exploitative labor and shaped by massive concentrations of both wealth and poverty, the contemporary Delta landscape, with its endless rows of planted crops, is the star of the blues-tourism show, frequently represented as haunted by the afterimages of sharecroppers and the sounds of work songs. Local authorities recognize the significance of the land to blues tourism. Indeed, some tourists seem disappointed by a current trend in Delta farming that alters the mise-en-scène of their touristic expectation: instead of farming cotton exclusively, many farmers now plant corn and soybeans. Some tourists have pleaded with the farmers to plant cotton near the road, for enhanced scenic effect.[73]

The constant evocation of blues' relationship to the Delta landscape situates the form as a historical and natural product of the land itself, a point of view clearly articulated in the opening lines of the *Blues and BBQ* guidebook to the region:

> In the land where the blues began, time stands as still as cypress stumps in stagnant water. Dirt-poor, rural, left for the kudzu—that pretty well describes much of the Mississippi Delta. It's an oddly appealing motley of cotton fields, agricultural refuse and early-20th-century towns inclined to lean backwards no matter which way the buildings are tilting. Ongoing economic decline is evident in the rows of abandoned shops and run-down houses and groups of people standing around on street corners. Long-abandoned commissaries and rusted farm equipment pop up along the road, and painted signs fade away on the sides of buildings. In such a place, one can easily imagine that the blues rises from the ground and hangs over everything.[74]

Clarksdale's Delta Blues Museum authorizes the centrality of the landscape to the cultural formation of blues in a long passage of text by Peter Aschoff: "While it cannot be denied that the social and emotional situation in which black Deltans found themselves also contributed to the development of the Delta blues, it was the land itself—a unique geographical setting at just the right point in time—that provided the initial crucible in which African Americans in the Mississippi Delta created the artistic synthesis known as blues."[75] Aschoff's modulation of the "social and emotional situation" of Jim Crow segregation, sharecropping, vigilante violence, and lynching in favor of a deterministic agrarian origin story draws a direct line between the theatrical pastoral scenes of blues prevalent during the revival and contemporary historiographical practice: in both stagings of the blues, contented agricultural labor and black song are "naturally" entwined. Furthermore, as Stephen A. King has noted, identifying blues as a product of the agricultural landscape created a pretext for white people in the Delta to "claim some legitimate ownership" of the form, just as they owned the land, and (historically) those who had labored on it.[76]

Figured as a bountifully fecund site of both nature and culture, the Delta landscape is persistently gendered as a woman by historians and tourism-industry officials alike. As the central point of origin, the land—and not the blueswomen who traversed it—is the mother of the bluesmen celebrated by revivalists and the tourist industry. Alan Lomax's description of Son House in *The Land Where the Blues Began* represents the landscape as female and the bluesman's relationship to it as frankly sexual. House, Lomax rapturously reports, "ripp[ed] apart the surface of the music like his tractor-driven deep plow ripped apart the wet black earth in the springtime, making the sap of the earth song run, while his powerful work-hard hands snatched strange chords out of the steel strings the way they had snatched so many tons of cotton out of brown thorny cotton bolls in the fall."[77] Ascribing sexual prowess to House's musical skill, Lomax imbues the landscape with feminine properties, and he does so in a way that glorifies its exploitation by the bluesman himself, both a product and master of the soil.

HOUSES AND HOMES

From the celebrated tours of antebellum planters' homes in Natchez to the sacred status accorded Rowan Oak, William Faulkner's home and grounds, in Oxford, Mississippi, tourism, including blues tourism, invokes tropes of home, hospitality, and belonging. Travelers crossing into "the hospitality state" are greeted by a road sign that announces a new location and a new state of mind: "Mississippi: It's like coming home." The advertising strategy reassures outsiders that their visit will be a fundamentally comfortable experience: to be at home means to never feel out of place, and to never experience the awkward errors of the tourist. Appearing in promotional materials and on tourist websites, images of Mississippi's plantation homes invite tourists to leave home in order to *come home*.[78] Echoing Waters's "Feel like Going Home," the slogan stirs up the romance and quells any anxieties about the Mississippi road trip, marrying the white aristocratic motif of Southern hospitality to the state's African American cultural heritage. The grammatical oddity of this construction, which situates blues not as *home* or even *like home*, but *like coming* (or going) *home*, suggests that, while blues is constitutive of home, it is never fixed in the way that *home* suggests. Rather, blues is *coming* home, a gerund forever in motion that privileges a home on the road rather than the terminus of arrival. Blues tourism, then, is an enactment of return, of home*coming*.

The rite of return that characterizes blues tourism enacts a version of what Robert Stepto has termed the literary immersion narrative, "a ritualized journey into a symbolic South." Reversing the classic ascent narrative of twentieth-century African American literature, the immersion narrative transforms migration's quest for a better life into tourism's search for roots.[79] Scorsese's *Feel like Going Home*, his directorial contribution to PBS's *The Blues*, follows this narrative structure with precision—and then extends it. Following the journey of the contemporary blues artist Corey Harris, the filmmakers travel first to the Mississippi Delta and then to the West African nation of Mali, searching for the roots of black Atlantic music.[80] Superimposing Harris's journey atop John and Alan Lomax's search for "continuity of culture," the film is an indiscreet palimpsest of Harris's contemporary musical pursuits and Alan Lomax's historic ones; what Lomax did, Scorsese intones, was "one of the most important things anyone could do: . . . preserving the past before it disappeared forever."[81] Harris, who is from Denver, Colorado, is portrayed as fundamentally at home in both Mississippi and Mali: he converses with Ali Farka Touré, his Malian host, in assured French and takes cultural differences, such as Touré's multiple wives, in stride. When the two sit down to play music together, not one moment of improvisational misstep is caught on film. Though the film presents their duet as spontaneous, almost instinctive, their encounter has in fact been honed by years of playing together. Nothing is lost in translation; there are no stops and starts, no stutters of cross-cultural conversation. Rather, the seamlessness of their musical harmonies makes a striking case for the African roots of blues. Touré is the elder voice of authority to Harris's youthful quest, the ancestral father figure both to Harris and to black American music, proclaiming, "when a black American comes to Africa, he should not feel like a foreigner. Because he has left his home and come to his home." Making a strong argument for African retentions, and for African music as "the DNA of the blues," the film suggests that blues tourists who travel to the Delta have not gone far enough.

Consciously or unconsciously, the blues-tourism industry borrows strategies from contemporary African American tourism to West Africa. Described by some as "homeland tourism," these tours primarily visit the slave castle-dungeons of Ghana, but they also visit sites in Senegal and the Gambia and are closely linked to a late twentieth-century resurgence of interest in African Americans' African roots, an exploration enabled by the increased ease of online research, genetic testing, and DNA analysis.[82] Such new methods offer the possibility that African American family histories and memories, forcibly diminished by the slave trade and its aftermath, are, in fact, recoverable, whether through scientific research or through embodied participation in travel. Heritage tourists to Africa frequently find themselves implicated in projects of memory fashioned by the rhetoric of historical sites. Noting the particularly complex nexus of spectatorship and identification that emerges for African American tourists visiting the slave castle-dungeons of Ghana, Sandra Richards observes how African American tourists are cast both as spectators and actors, witnesses to history as well as participants in its revivification. Touching upon the past through the embodied experience of passing through the dungeon's "door of no return," for example, African American tourists are forced to negotiate the tension between history, body, memory, forced diaspora, and the privilege of cosmopolitan travel.[83] Blues tourism is vastly dissimilar to West African homeland tourism: blues tourism's emphasis on pleasure is irreconcilable with the painful truths revealed by the historical sites in Ghana. Most critically, the white visitors to the Delta rarely have direct—or even distant—connections to Mississippi as a place of ancestral origin. But the tourist industry works hard to minimize this fact, and does so by employing some of the methods of the West African touristic sites, which, through embodied participation, invite tourists into a homeland relationship with a foreign place. Both touristic enterprises are actively engaged in the production of homeland, establishing themselves as points of origin and as genetic, musical, and cultural roots.

Though there is a fundamental tension between the rhetoric of Southern hospitality and the reenactment of migration and displacement that blues tourists are invited to perform, the blues-tourism industry ensures that the enactment of return to a Mississippi homeland is available to anyone who wishes to pay for it.[84] State agencies and local businesses have made a concerted effort to rebrand Mississippi, forsaking the racial terrorism of its past and embracing an image of gracious hospitality. Recalling late-nineteenth-century historical desires for post–Civil War reunion and reconciliation, the post-civil rights rhetoric of blues tourism implicitly offers white tourists an opportunity to heal the wounds inflicted by Jim Crow, voter suppression, and racial terrorism.[85] However, whites participating in these rites of return enact not a racial reconciliation but rather a sectional one, whereby Southern whites hospitably welcome Northern whites. Such scenes revisit the post–Civil War reunions between Yankees and Rebels, blues and grays, such as the all-white reunion that took place at Gettysburg in 1913, fifty years after the Emancipation Proclamation. As chronicled by David Blight, this reunion did little to heal the national wounds inflicted by enslavement, Jim Crow, and lynching (then at historic heights), emphasizing instead a sectional reunion between Northern and Southern whites.[86]

Actual houses and homes play a central role in the theatrical crafting of blues historiography, as well as in the industry's rhetorical offering of experiences of reunion, reconciliation, and hospitality; tourists' engagements with these homes allow for their constant revivification as sites of origin of blues music. While the origins of blues are figured variously, actual buildings, such as Waters's cabin or the shacks at the Shack Up Inn, serve as coordinated sites that ground a nomadic form. But it is a site that does *not* exist in the Mississippi Delta—the House of Blues—that arguably sows the seeds of expectation for blues tourists who visit the region and its homes. Founded in Cambridge, Massachusetts, in 1992, this music venue and restaurant (now a national chain) promoted itself by sponsoring concerts that toured the country with Waters's cabin in tow, bringing a piece of the Delta to stages across the United States. Having leased the cabin from the Stovall family, on whose farm Waters had worked as a sharecropper, a team from the House of Blues disassembled the structure in 1996, removed it from its original site, and used it "to spice up stage sets at concerts."[87] From its tours with the House of Blues to its display at the 1996 Olympic Games to its return to the Delta, the many routes of Waters's (mobile) home have been notoriously difficult to track. The cabin's travels, though, capture blues tourism's transformation of actual homes into set dressing of a mise-en-scène of Southern poverty and blues authenticity. The use of Waters's cabin—a hinge between the stage décor of the blues revival and the immersive in situ environments of blues tourism—as stage set was a turning point that suggested the new potential of the shack for the emerging industry of blues tourism.

At the crossroads of commodification and cultural history, the House of Blues produces a now-familiar scene of heritage tourism, musical consumption, and cross-racial and temporal identification. At a House of Blues venue, consumers are architecturally interpellated into fantastical representations of blues performance and physically immersed in a scene of an imagined South that imitates and trades on an environment of Delta hospitality, music, folk art, and foodways. The interior décor of each House of Blues establishment suggests the well-worn charm of a whimsical Southern roadhouse; with massive collections of folk art and wide-plank wood flooring, the House of Blues embraces the juke joint as its inspiration, and its scenography is often mimetic of or directly imported from the interiors and exteriors of those buildings still found in the Mississippi Delta. "Authentic" connections to the Delta are still an important part of the House of Blues: the façade of the West Hollywood venue, for example, incorporates corrugated metal from Clarksdale, and, the company's website notes, "under every stage in the House of Blues is a metal box filled with Delta Mississippi mud. This box is welded to the structure on the stage to ensure that every artist has the roots and the spirit of the South planted beneath their feet."[88] This creation of an immersive Delta blues environment allows for a doubled touristic experience, inviting tourists in Chicago to be tourists of the blues itself and its points of supposed origin in the Mississippi Delta. That is, the pleasure of the House of Blues is that, like the dream worlds of Las Vegas, the venue invites tourists to reimagine where they are and, consequently, who they are, or might be. And while it is not incorrect to describe the

4.2 The Robert Clay Shack at the Shack Up Inn, Clarksdale, Mississippi. Photograph by the author, 2010.

House of Blues as a frivolously consumptive virtual environment that has more in common with Disneyland than with any historically or geographically material Mississippi Delta, it—like documentary photography, like the scenic iconography of the blues revival—has played a significant role in establishing expectations for blues tourists who visit the Delta itself.

The Shack Up Inn carefully and playfully scripts blues tourists into an architectural and affective theatrical scenario of blues history and memory. A popular lodging option located on the grounds of the former Hopson Plantation, just outside Clarksdale, the Shack Up Inn is run by self-described "old hippie" Bill Talbot and his team of "shackmeisters." Originally consisting of about half a dozen "shotgun shacks" formerly inhabited by sharecroppers, tenant farmers, and their descendants who lived throughout the Mississippi Delta, the Shack Up Inn has expanded since its 1998 opening, adding additional cabins and transforming the largest structure original to the site—the cotton gin—into the Cotton Gin Inn, which added six additional rooms ("bins") to the property. The cabins themselves are not original to the site but were originally scattered throughout the Delta (see figure 4.2). Talbot and his partners relocated the cabins to Hopson and pressure washed and updated them with indoor bathrooms, heat, electricity, and running water; the cabins are available to travelers for around seventy-five dollars a night. By inviting tourists to stay in the houses where the blues were "born," the Shack Up Inn casts its visitors as performatively imagining—perhaps even "living"—history by sleeping in history's bed and drinking on history's porch.

But history slips and slides at the Shack Up Inn; it is unclear exactly which historical moment the inn means to evoke. While most of the cabins date from the early twentieth century, the Shack Up Inn places the cabins close to each other, evoking the architectural arrangement of slave quarters in the nineteenth century.[89] Still, the cabins make concessions to the contemporary, not only in their amenities but also in their décor. While the outsides of the cabins have only been slightly altered (some have added screened-in porches), the insides are a far cry from those photographed by Walker Evans in 1936, or the ones Robert F. Kennedy visited in this area in 1967. In contrast to those bare spaces, these shacks are filled—floor to ceiling—with clutter. Each shack is a cabinet of curiosities, filled with kitsch, castoffs, and garbage, thus producing a history of and as detritus. Some of the objects that decorate the space appear to be quite old: family photographs of unknowable families, fans, musical instruments, funeral cards, certificates and awards, and masks adorn the walls. There are also many items that appear to be left behind more recently, such as business cards, tiny bottles of shampoo, CDs, Mardi Gras beads, magazines, books, and empty bottles of bourbon, wine, and beer. The objects filling the cabins invert both the spartan surroundings of the home's prior life and the minimalist aesthetic of the traditional contemporary hotel. Whereas a mainstream hotel invites the visitor to believe that he or she is the room's first occupant, the Shack Up Inn takes the opposite approach, filling its space with detritus so as to allow visitors to imagine that they are stepping into a place characterized by its former tenants. As a pastiche of assorted fantasies of Southern histories, blues music, and various paraphernalia of all kinds of vacation vices, the cabins of the Shack Up Inn revel in and shape the theatricality of Delta blues tourism, their mise-en-scènes establishing and perpetuating the trope of the South as a stage of incomplete history.

The inn, a logical conclusion of the stagings of the South initiated by the blues revival, is a palimpsest of past and present, inviting tourists into an intimate relationship with laborers who once inhabited the cabins. The tourists' presence at the inn, therefore, is indispensable for the surrogation that its historiographic project requires. From the piano to the Mardi Gras beads, from the black and white masks on the walls to the xeroxed pages of Tennessee Williams's *Cat on a Hot Tin Roof* stuffed inside an archive of old newspapers, the Shack Up Inn invites its tourists to perform in both conscious and unconscious ways: indeed, many amateur musicians travel to the inn in order to play on the porches of its cabins. The tourists, it is understood, will transform the cabins by leaving behind objects of their choosing; these calling cards, mementos for future wayfarers, allow tourists to become a permanent part of black musical history. The trash of history that fills each cabin serves as a crucial component of history's rewriting, a way of refocusing and recentering racial history as economic history and economic history as musical history. While histories of black labor are ostensibly at the center of the tourist enterprise of the Shack Up Inn, they are marginalized in order to make room for travelers' leisure. As a tourist destination, the Shack Up Inn gestures to the economies of both the cotton and slave trade, but it also produces a script and mise-en-scène of leisure, dominated by pianos, Mardi Gras beads, and empty liquor bottles. Scripting tourists in a surrogate relationship of pleasure rather than suffering, the inn (which refers to itself as a "B & B—Bed & Beer") swaps terror for pleasure; the tourist's enjoyment serves, retrospectively, as a justification for the sharecropper system.[90]

By amalgamating contemporary leisure and histories of unremunerated labor, the Shack Up Inn works hard to make white tourists feel at home, even as they revel in feeling out of place. Whereas other environments in Clarksdale, such as the Riverside Hotel and Red's (a juke joint), bring black and white locals and tourists together, demanding that all reckon with the productive dis-ease born of the historical truths of Clarksdale's painful past, tourists staying at the Shack Up Inn stand a relatively good chance of experiencing the "birthplace of the blues" surrounded entirely by Euro-Americans and Western Europeans. Even the mise-en-scène participates in this whitening of blues history. In the Robert Clay Shack, for example, the photograph of Clay, a sharecropper who lived in this unheated home until his death in 1998, is amended by a tintype of white man inserted carelessly into the corner of its frame. As with plantation tourism, the Shack Up Inn elides histories of enslavement, even as silences accrue in the interstices of historical revisions. This whitening of blues history and performance marginalizes the significance of race and racism, pointing instead to poverty as blues' determining characteristic, even as it circumvents the historical truths that made—and make—poverty's distribution fundamentally unequal.

Styling itself as a counterpoint to luxury tourism, the Shack Up Inn inverts the domestic settings and the logic of antebellum plantation tourism, casting its visitors as standing at a distance from the wealth of the planter class. If the plantation is the home of the genteel, aristocratic, and feminized South, the Shack Up Inn stages itself as all that the antebellum home is not: ramshackle, masculine, and unrefined. Trumpeting the lack of luxury while also managing expectations of tourists who might not know what they're in for, the inn's website provides a detailed explanation of amenities *not* offered—thread counts, wake-up calls—and celebrates the hotel's rough edges with its motto: "The Ritz we ain't." Whereas the docents of antebellum plantation houses celebrate the romance and the romantic relationships of the white antebellum aristocrats who once lived there, the inn pays tribute to "shacking up"—sex without marriage.

Some tourists at the inn believe that poor Mississippi whites lived in these cabins too, a belief that opens up another role that tourists might play: "white trash." The appeal of white trash, a social imaginary memorably described by Matt Wray as "not quite white," provides a possible answer to the lingering question: what accounts for the wild popularity of the Shack Up Inn? How is it that Robert F. Kennedy's tour of these Delta homes highlighted the failure of the United States to care for its most vulnerable citizens while tourists now enthusiastically pay for the privilege of poverty tourism? Do visitors fail to see that these cabins represent the Mississippi Delta's present as much as they represent its past? If these incongruities are observed, they are trumped by tourists' desire to construct a different, extradaily relationship to capital, to get away from mass (re)produced lodging, to disavow one's own privilege, and to enjoy the pleasures of "simple" living. One Internet forum poster enthusiastically describes the inn as "the ultimate white trash motel!"[91] Other online reviews of the inn are almost universally positive, praising the "magical" environment while criticizing travelers who would "moan about the fact that the shower curtain had a ring missing."[92] Though historically a slur against poor Southern whites, "white trash" is recuperated here as a point of pride, transforming the heretofore negative qualities ascribed to those who lived on the margins, who crossed color lines with both black and American Indian populations, and who barely scratched out a subsistence living.[93] In the New South someone designated as "white trash" holds a special chip: that person's ancestors likely did not own slaves and may have even worked as sharecroppers themselves. Using embodied heritage, the Shack Up Inn casts the tourist as a person without (slave) property and offers absolution from histories and economies of property and pleasure. While Jessica Adams suggests that "in the new plantation economy, tourists can view themselves as slaves but also as masters," the Shack Up Inn offers tourists the opportunity to view themselves as insiders, but innocent.[94]

Though its primary purpose is lodging, the Shack Up Inn's owners see themselves as preservationists of a recent Southern past; the website invites you to "immerse yourself in the living history you will find at Hopson," where "you will glimpse plantation life as it existed only a few short years ago." But tourists are invited to do far more than "glimpse," especially as they cast their own bodies into the domestic spaces of sharecropper life. By shacking up in Jim Crow–era cabins, the tourist experiences the transgressive thrill of touching the past, across and through the body of an imagined Other. Though not a museum, the inn's theatrical environments of "living history" share a great deal in common with the logic of museum display. To those who approach them as historical preservations of the past, the cabins of the Shack Up Inn function as in situ displays, "mimetic re-creations" of (imagined) sharecropper life that recall those of the 1960s stage and television settings. If, as Kirshenblatt-Gimblett argues, "live displays, and specifically the display of humans, are central to the completeness of *in situ* exhibitions," then tourists themselves realize the curatorial process, stepping into the human-shaped spaces, occupying beds and chairs, completing—and revising—re-creations of the past.[95] The Delta Blues Museum, also located in Clarksdale, utilizes similar in situ aesthetics and uses effigial display to "hold open a place in memory" that visitors are invited to fill through imaginative surrogation.[96] And while the Delta Blues Museum's purchase on historical fact may seem to stand at a significant distance from the questionable account of the past presented by the Shack Up Inn, the museum, like the inn, employs various strategies to conjure the absent blues musician and to script the behavior of its visitors. In that scripting, the museum secures a particular relationship between the tourist, blues musicians, and a Delta past.

Though the Delta Blues Museum generally resists making declarative statements about the origins of blues, its structured itinerary and ground plan make an argument of their own. Upon entering the museum, one immediately encounters the wall text by Aschoff, cited earlier, that emphasizes the deterministic power of the Delta landscape and the supposedly culturally isolated nature of early twentieth-century Delta life, a claim this book refutes. A long, narrow hallway that leads to a more open gallery space presents different possible points of origin. West African instruments are displayed and linked to the diddley bow and the guitar; though the accompanying text does not make any direct claims regarding African retentions, the inclusion of these West African instruments suggests blues' orientation within a black Atlantic vernacular, and, however ambiguously, blues' connections to the slave trade. The museum then introduces its first portrait:

Handy. Though the content of the wall text undermines the singularity of his "father of the blues" claim, the comparatively large amount of space devoted to Handy—only Waters gets more square footage—emphasizes his position of priority in blues history. The cross-purposes at which Handy functions in the Delta Blues Museum—founder but not, father but not— are unintentionally (and humorously) underscored by a "certificate of authenticity" displayed beneath Handy's photograph and a piece of paper that bears his signature.

Like other representations of blues in contemporary Delta tourism, the history of the blues presented by the Delta Blues Museum is almost exclusively male. Notably, this hall of origins does not mention traveling tent and minstrel shows, nor the women who popularized the blues on that circuit; only elsewhere, in displays commemorating Big Joe Williams and Waters, are organizations such as the Rabbit Foot Minstrels and Silas Green from New Orleans mentioned, and then only in passing. The visitor continues along the path suggested by the museum's design, encountering a procession of great bluesmen in roughly chronological order: John Lee Hooker, Charley Patton, and Son House represent the past, while Charlie Musselwhite and Super Chikan represent the present.

The Delta Blues Museum evokes the absent bodies of the blues musicians it commemorates through its display of objects—not props but prosthetics. One of the great challenges of any museum that works to preserve and represent the intangible acts of performance is its choice of material objects: what things best represent and gesture to histories that are fundamentally embodied? A more recent addition to the heritage tourism circuit in Clarksdale, the Rock and Blues Museum, has chosen records: inert when separated from a phonograph, the museum's records stand in as the material symbol of the performer's commercial success. The Delta Blues Museum, however, makes little use of records; the ones that are shown are often displayed only for the sake of showcasing the cover art. Instead, the museum gives preferential treatment to objects that have touched the body of the musician, such as instruments. Costumes are also critical to the representation of the past in the Delta Blues Museum, which displays them in such a way as to communicate the size and shape of the men and women who wore them in performance. Big George Brock's red suits, Little Milton's sequined top, Eddy "the Chief" Clearwater's vest, and the spangled evening gowns of Denise La Salle and Dorothy Moore all showcase the care these singers put into their appearance on stage—and are significantly at odds with the overalls and work boots worn by many of the musicians who perform for white tourists at contemporary festivals. For the most part, these costumes are not displayed flat, nor worn by lifelike mannequins, but draped and hung as if outlining an invisible, absent body. Displayed as an effigy, the costume invites the museum visitor to corporeally engage with the past and passed body of the musician: was that person taller, shorter, thinner, fatter, than I? Notably, the cross casting invited here is one in which size—and not race—matters.

These displays of blues musicians' theatrical prosthetics—instruments and costumes—prepare the museum visitor for the pièce de résistance: a life-sized sculpture of Waters, ensconced in the rear of the museum, enclosed within a Mississippi-cypress cabin. The sound of a short looped movie echoes throughout the museum, drawing the visitor further and further into the gallery until arriving at a four-walled cypress enclosure: this room is a partial remnant of Waters's home on the Stovall plantation, the very same one that toured with the House of Blues corporation. Waters seems to have moved back in.[97] Dressed formally and playing electric, the scene depicts the urban—and famous—Waters in his old shack, himself a Delta tourist, home for a visit. The Delaware artists Ray and Mary Daub crafted the wax sculpture of Waters; dressed in Waters's own suit and hat, the sculpture not only produces an uncanny resemblance but also blurs the distinction between body and effigy, between prop and actor. At nearly six feet, the sculpture is scaled to Waters's height, but seated on a slightly raised platform, he appears larger than life. Waters is cut down to mortal size, however, by a marker placed nearby; made out of granite and engraved with his given name, McKinley Morganfield, the marker resembles a gravestone. Installed as a museum exhibit, the cabin's life on the road is now, apparently, complete. Still, its history as an enormous set piece means that it can never be completely returned to its role as artifact. Instead, it exists in the unstable space between artifact and prop, between domestic architecture and theatrical stage. Transformed from a traveling sight to a site of travel, Waters's house retains its iconic status and confers iconic status upon similar dwellings, such as those of the Shack Up Inn. This small room invites viewers to project themselves into the scene, to measure their own size against Waters's, and to wonder about his wandering.

THE FESTIVAL

During festival time, Clarksdale scripts tourists' movements throughout the city, manipulating their relationship to civic life and history. Festivals celebrating blues, barbecue, or both are a major draw for Delta tourists and a central element of the region's tourist economy. Most tourists plan their visits around festivals, which allow for a concentrated consumption of musical performance in a majority-white environment, as well as other diversions and entertainments not available during the rest of the year. The two largest music festivals of the year, the Juke Joint Festival, held in April, and the Sunflower River Blues and Gospel Festival, held in August, make ample use of all of the city's permanent, formalized performance spaces, among them Red's, Ground Zero, the New Roxy, the Clarksdale Civic Auditorium, and the Bluesberry Café. But the sheer quantity of performances during festival time overflows these spaces, and informal stages proliferate, many set up on the street, in front of inhabited or abandoned storefronts. Though these found spaces are sometimes just a raised platform or a few carpets laid down on the asphalt, their designation as stages (the Delta Furniture Stage, Wade Walton Barbershop Stage, and so on) mark the performances upon them as set apart from daily life, inventing and instituting a theatrical frame where one did not previously exist. Spectators play their role in constituting these stages as such: by setting up their camping chairs in orderly rows, they inevitably physically distance themselves from the featured performers. Additionally, both front porches and train-station platforms are transformed into stages throughout the Delta during festival time. Reversing Zora Neale Hurston's "proscenium box for a born first-nighter," Clarksdale's front porches transform from observation boxes to sites of spectacle; blues festivals find many professional and amateur musicians playing on front porches around the city. In both Clarksdale and Helena, Arkansas, disused passenger-train platforms now double as stages for the Sunflower River Blues and Gospel Festival and the King Biscuit Blues Festival, respectively (see figure 4.3). After the festivals conclude, these stage sites are returned to their daily functions as parking spaces and patios, porches and abandoned depots; the memories of the performers remain, however, infusing the city's public spaces with stages.

The Shack Up Inn invites tourists into the homes of the blues, casting visitors as both guests and ghosts, resurrecting and reanimating the absent body of the sharecropper; the Juke Joint Festival scales this model up, stretching the parameters of the stage to enclose entire neighborhoods and the people that live and labor in them. For a few days each spring, "an ethnographic bell jar drops over the terrain," transforming the town into an enormous in situ exhibit, where "the museum effect, rendering the quotidian spectacular, becomes ubiquitous."[98] Marketed as "half blues fest, half small-town fair, and all about the Delta!" the Juke Joint Festival draws several thousand visitors and offers attendees the opportunity to sample blues performance in its most heralded site: the juke (or "jook") joint.[99] The

4.3 Clarksdale's train platform repurposed as a stage during the Sunflower Blues and Gospel Festival. Photograph by the author, 2010.

high point of the festival, which is a weekend-long bacchanal of barbecue, beer, and retro-rural entertainments such as pig races, is Saturday night, when dozens of musical performances take place around town; attendance at multiple venues is encouraged by an all-inclusive cover charge and a shuttle bus that circulates among the New Roxy, Red's, Messenger's Pool Hall, Ground Zero, and other downtown venues. The Shack Up Inn hosts bands in both the Juke Joint Chapel and the Commissary and provides a specially hired train to transport guests to and from downtown. The Juke Joint Festival offers white tourists a rare opportunity to travel as a group to the other side of the tracks and walk through the New World District, which served as the original home for most of the city's blues venues. The density of performances presented by the Juke Joint Festival squeezes several weeks' worth of musical performances into a single weekend, "offering in a concentrated form, at a designated time and place, what the tourist would otherwise search out in the diffuseness of everyday life, with no guarantee of ever finding it."[100]

Like blues tourism more generally, the festival enacts an ambivalent relationship to the theatrical history of blues, an ambivalence that manifests in its apparent aversion to theatrical spectacle, even while it deploys its devices. Like the Smithsonian Folklife Festival, which serve as a template for many heritage-tourism sites and events, Juke Joint Festival performances contain "a suppression of *representation* markers and a foregrounding of *presentation* markers, an avoidance of the suggestion of 'theater' and an attempt to achieve the quality of pure presence, of a slice of life."[101] The first night of the 2011 festival made this tension between theatrical representation and "slice of life" presentation abundantly clear. While most festival performances involve little more than setting up a few chairs and a strip of carpet in a juke joint or on a found outdoor stage, the weekend kicked off on the stage of a movie theater, the Delta Cinema, where the North Mississippi String Band played a set of old-time music that mixed blues, bluegrass, country, and ragtime. The red-velvet-curtain backdrop, the makeshift lighting ("courtesy of Walmart," the band leader joked), and the patter between songs lent the event a variety feel, a "unique" aspect of the evening that several audience members commented on after the show. While a fiddler and bassist wore street clothes, the front men Jimbo Mathus, who is white, and Alvin Youngblood Hart, who is black, costumed themselves in overalls; Mathus wore a straw hat and Hart an engineer's cap. And even though Mathus seemed to relish his role as the hillbilly, he appeared in quite a different costume a few nights later while playing with another of his bands, KnockDown South, with his blond curls loose around his face and his black tank top rock-star tight.[102] Through venue and costuming, the evening made the theatrical history of the string band and blues performance present, even while not directly commenting on this historical connection.

The star of the festival every year is the juke joint itself. Roger Stolle describes, "Unlike traditional, big-stage music festivals, Juke Joint Festival seeks to highlight not only the blues musicians, but also the venues where their music grew from and where they feel most comfortable—the juke joints. *For the Mississippi Delta, the juke joint is like the frame around the picture.*"[103] Though rarely turning much of a profit, juke joints still exist in Clarksdale; some, such as Red's, flourish. Others, such as the New Roxy, a recently repurposed building that was once a black movie theater, open only at festival time. Still other juke joints—often unnamed—are located off the festival map, and are rarely, if ever, visited by white outsiders. A few rural jukes remain; one, Po' Monkey's Lounge in Merigold, has enjoyed widespread publicity in recent years thanks to a feature article in the *New York Times* and its designation as a historic site by the Mississippi Blues Commission in 2009. Though the lounge's distance from Clarksdale precludes its presence on the official itinerary of the Juke Joint Festival, it is a popular destination for more intrepid tourists on festival weekends. The most active juke joint in town, though, is a new venue that looks old, a site where the frame often overtakes the picture: the Ground Zero Blues Club, a restaurant and club with juke-joint aspirations, opened in 2001 by the local attorney and politician Bill Luckett and the actor Morgan Freeman.

The juke joint is one of contemporary blues' most significant theatrical historical remains. The historical relationship to popular black theater began with the touring tent and minstrel shows; after these shows were completed, many black performers and audience members would repair to the juke joint for after-hours entertainment, music, and dancing.[104] It wasn't long before artists began to experiment with putting the juke joint on stage. Hurston was one of the first to recognize the theatrical possibilities of the juke, a site she explored in her ethnographic research, her essays, and her stage productions. As the single day of *The Great Day* came to an end, a leisurely scene in the juke joint replaced the scenes of labor that had dominated the early part of the show. In addition to showing New York audiences the songs and dances of black Southern life—and the social institutions, such as the juke joint, that shaped expressive culture—Hurston was the first scholar to attempt to definitively record the characteristics of a juke joint, which she mentions in *Mules and Men* and catalogs more thoroughly in her essay "Characteristics of Negro Expression" (1934). "Jook is the word for a Negro pleasure house," she explains. "It may mean a bawdy house. It may mean the house set apart on public works where the men and women dance, drink and gamble. Often it is a combination of all these." She underscores the juke's cultural significance: "Musically speaking, the Jook is the most important place in America." Like the traveling tent show, the spaces of the juke joints were sites of mobile transmission, where "the songs grow by incremental repetition as they travel from mouth to mouth and from Jook to Jook for years before they reach outside ears. Hence the great variety of subject-matter in each song."[105] In both her essay and in *The Great Day*, Hurston used the scene of the juke joint to criticize black-cast theatrical productions that originated in New York, cast light-skinned performers, and catered to white audiences:

> The Negro theatre, as built up by the Negro, is based on Jook situations, with women, gambling, fighting, drinking. Shows like "Dixie to Broadway" are only Negro in cast, and could just as well have come from pre-Soviet Russia. . . . To those who want to institute the Negro theatre, let me say it is already established. It is lacking in wealth, so it is not seen in the high places. A creature with a white head and Negro feet struts the Metropolitan boards. The real Negro theatre is in the Jooks and the cabarets. Self-conscious individuals may turn away the eye and say, "Let us search elsewhere for our dramatic art." Let 'em search. They certainly

won't find it. Butter Beans and Susie, Bo-Jangles and Snake Hips are the only performers of the real Negro school it has ever been my pleasure to behold in New York.[106]

For Hurston, the juke joint is the stage of the "real Negro theatre," a site of black dramatic expression in the everyday and the cradle of the popular, vaudeville-influenced performers—Butterbeans and Susie, Bill "Bojangles" Robinson, and Snake Hips—whom she champions.

Though black-owned and black-patronized juke joints were intended as private places, floating worlds that temporarily allowed for an escape from the subjugating force of the plantation and the sharecropping economies, white visits to them are almost as old as the institution itself. In the 1930s such visits were undertaken in the name of documentary: Marion Post Wolcott, a contemporary of both Hurston and Alan Lomax, produced the first widespread photographic representation of Florida juke joints for the Works Progress Administration.[107] The tradition of juke-joint photography continues today; well-known art photographers, from Birney Imes to Annie Leibovitz, have photographed juke joints, including Po' Monkey's.[108] Their example has inspired a cottage industry of professional and amateur photographers, many of whom travel to the Mississippi Delta in large groups to document a cultural site thought to be disappearing. Jostling the largely black Thursday-night crowd at Po' Monkey's, these photographers, most of whom are white, make Southern black life picturesque, restaging a familiar scene that casts locals "as 'foreigners,' strangers at home."[109] Temporarily remapping and restaging Clarksdale's historic downtown, the Juke Joint Festival invites tourists to freely walk the stages of the "jook situation," as Hurston puts it. Crossing the tracks and traveling en masse throughout the historically black New World District, festival attendees, most of whom are white, visit juke joints in neighborhoods white people largely avoid the rest of the year. In suggesting that such divisions were never all that hard and fast in the first place, the festival stages a civic drama of racial reconciliation by means of the blues.

Points of origin, houses and homes, and festival performance in Clarksdale all remember the blues by scripting the itineraries and behaviors of blues tourists. Invited to step into the role of the black migrant, the tourist enacts both the travels of the past and the silences of the present. For what is most notable about blues tourism in the Delta is what is not said or included in its itineraries: detailed histories of slavery and sharecropping, the contributions of women to blues innovation, and accounts of civil rights boycotts, Freedom Rides, and desegregation. Attentive visitors might be able to spot the architectural remnants of the segregated spaces of the Greyhound bus station, but this repurposed building, now the Information Station, provides only selective statements about Clarksdale's history. Furthermore, there is a surprising marginalization of musical performance itself. Robert Palmer, an authority on the history and musicology of blues, claimed of the Delta in 1982: "The area is no longer a source of musical innovation and hasn't been since the plantations automated." But many genres of contemporary music that are not blues are performed throughout the region, namely Delta rap and hip hop, a lively scene explored by Ali Colleen Neff in her critical ethnography *Let the World Listen Right*.[110] Largely unappreciated by tourists, who prefer the music that provided fuel for the blues revival and British invasion of their youths, Clarksdale rappers remain largely invisible to the blues-tourism industry even though, like early blues, their rhymes register as a cry of protest against overcrowded housing, the de facto segregation of public schools, and the socioeconomic challenges of the black working class of the "dirty South." In spite of all these silences, however, a community of black elders in Clarksdale continues to speak to whomever will listen about the histories of the region that are frequently effaced and sanitized by the touristic rhetoric of blues. George Messenger, Frank "Rat" Ratliff, and James "Super Chikan" Johnson are a few of these elders who, though participants in a blues-tourism economy, produce their own vivid countermemories as ballasts against any easy nostalgia for a pastoral Mississippi. Telling the history of "second-class citizenship" (Messenger) and the widespread black disavowal of Mississippi (Johnson), these men are outspoken about the ways in which they have chosen to "get along" with a largely white-operated tourist economy, often as paid entertainers. As Johnson puts it, "[The smile] is a tool, it's a weapon, it's a pass, it's a green card, it's anything you want it to be."[111]

KILLING YOURSELF TO LIVE

"Robert [Johnson]'s more popular because he died," Honeyboy Edwards observes in his autobiography *The World Don't Owe Me Nothing*.[112] The death of an elderly bluesman is often big news in Clarksdale, and beyond.[113] When a Delta bluesman dies, the mainstream press and blogosphere habitually mourn the passing of a way of life and proclaim the end of an era. When Edwards died at the age of ninety-six, the man who once said that "blues ain't never going anywhere" was mourned as the last living link to Johnson and a Delta past—the death of a man equated with the death of an entire genre of music.[114] Indeed, concerns about the mortality of blues are nearly as old as the form itself: the Lomaxes bemoaned vernacular folk music's disappearance as early as the 1930s. The very terminology of the blues *revival* was premised on the fact that blues was already dead. And the logic of blues tourism, whereby the tourist stands in for the migrant, implies that such embodied prophylactics are vital to blues' continued survival. Given that blues tourism is steeped in a logic of revival, the death of the blues must be constantly invoked, its loss the necessary precondition to resurrection. The insistence on the disappearance of blues, rather than its remaining and reinvention, feeds an economy of scarcity, providing rhetorical incentives for tourists to consume the blues while they still have the (short-lived) opportunity.

But reports of the death of the blues have been greatly exaggerated. The rhetoric of a dead or dying musical culture may entice some tourists to undertake journeys that the Clarksdale resident and blues promoter Roger Stolle described to me as the "dead man blues tour." Yet these same tourists are sometimes surprised to find—thanks in large part to the booking and publicity efforts of Stolle himself—that "live" blues still thrives in the Delta. In his regular newsletter and Facebook posts, Stolle walks a fine line between respecting the past and resisting the thrall to disappearance. Turning readers' attention to the continued reinvention of blues, Stolle implicitly suggests an approach to blues aligned with Schneider's explication on the fundamental embodiedness of performance "not as that which disappears . . . but as both the *act* of remaining and as a means of reappearance."[115] The Delta Blues Education Fund, an organization that works with children, similarly emphasizes blues' present and future, though not at the expense of its past. Founded by the musician Johnnie Billington, the organization both teaches blues' musical repertoire and passes its performance conventions (including collaborative musicianship and professional conduct) to a younger generation. It is in this "passing on" that blues has always remained, whether its sites of transfer have been the classroom, the juke joint, or the traveling tent show.

The Mississippi Delta blues first achieved widespread public recognition in a state of revival. The postwar classification and shaping of the Delta blues largely severed the form's relationship with the popular theater, and with the women who were its primary innovators. But these links, while frayed, continue to remain in contemporary performance, from the soul blues of Bobby Rush to the antic riffs of Super Chikan and the Fighting Cocks, as well as in the urban landscape. Such remains, however, are not always acknowledged: on my fourth trip to Clarksdale, half a dozen years after I had begun my research, I stumbled across the ruins of an old build-

4.4 Remains of the Savoy Theater, Clarksdale, Mississippi. Photograph by the author, 2013.

ing. Unmarked, it occupies a vacant lot in the New World District, the heart of Clarksdale's historic blues scene that goes largely unexplored by tourists. Concrete supports and rusted electrical wiring are all that remains of the Savoy Theater, a key stop on the black circuit, where Clarksdalians gathered for decades for blues, drinking, dancing, and comedy (see figure 4.4). On a sunny Sunday morning in the spring, the Savoy is quiet. There are no tourists, no historical markers. The churchgoers at the end of the block pay no mind. A ruin not yet made pastoral, the Savoy stands as testimony to the theatrical heritage of early twentieth-century blues and the performers who played here, and in hundreds of venues like it. Like the Savoy itself, theatrical blues is "forgotten but not gone," its heritage and history occasionally manifesting itself as a reappearance of both Mississippian racial terror and the celebratory, resilient leisure of blueswomen and men on a Saturday night.[116]

INTRODUCTION   BEALE ON BROADWAY

1. Chris King, "Curator for the Blues," *St. Louis Magazine*, April 2007, 242; Alan Lomax, *The Land Where the Blues Began* (New York: Pantheon Books, 1993).

2. Kim Massie, interview with the author, May 28, 2012, Fairview Heights, Illinois.

3. Brooks McNamara's chapter "Popular Entertainment" (378–408) in *The Cambridge History of American Theater, Volume 2*, edited by Don B. Wilmeth and Christopher Bigsby (Cambridge: Cambridge University Press, 1999), provides an excellent overview of various nineteenth- and twentieth-century popular entertainments, including circus, carnival, Wild West shows, blackface minstrelsy, and the medicine show. An excellent bibliography prepared by editor Don B. Wilmeth appears at the conclusion of the chapter (408–10). See also McNamara's authoritative *Step Right Up*, a history of the medicine show (Jackson: University Press of Mississippi, 1995).

4. I borrow the term *possessive investment* from George Lipsitz's influential *The Possessive Investment in Whiteness* (Philadelphia: Temple University Press, 1998). Other scholars whose work explores performances in and of the South include Jessica Adams, Michael Bibler, and Cécile Accilien, eds., *Just below South: Intercultural Performance in the Caribbean and the U.S. South* (Charlottesville: University of Virginia Press, 2007); Jessica Adams, *Wounds of Returning: Intercultural Performance in the Caribbean and the U.S. South* (Charlottesville: University of Virginia Press, 2007); and Tara McPherson, *Reconstructing Dixie: Race, Gender, and Nostalgia in the Imagined South* (Durham, NC: Duke University Press, 2003).

5. My use of the term *scenario* is indebted to Diana Taylor, who defines the concept as "a paradigmatic setup that relies on supposedly live participants." While Taylor often focuses on the scenario as emplotted, it is equally notable for its scenic elements: "Theatricality makes that scenario alive and compelling." The scenario, unlike its narrative equivalent, the trope, does not prioritize literary, textual, or lyrical content. Rather, it "demands that we also pay attention to milieux and corporeal behaviors such as gestures, attitudes, and tones not reducible to language." Diana Taylor, *The Archive and the Repertoire: Performing Cultural Memory in the Americas* (Durham, NC: Duke University Press, 2003), 13, 13, 28.

6. *Oxford English Dictionary Online*. December 2013. Oxford University Press. Accessed January 27, 2014.

7. William Faulkner, *Absalom, Absalom!* (New York: Vintage, 1987), 271.

8. Jennifer Greeson, *Our South: Geographic Fantasy and the Rise of National Literature* (Cambridge, MA: Harvard University Press, 2010), 1.

9. Saidiya Hartman, *Scenes of Subjection: Terror, Slavery, and Self-Making in Nineteenth-Century America* (New York: Oxford University Press, 1997), 42.

10. Paul Oliver, *Bessie Smith* (London: Cassell Press, 1959), 3–5.

11. Jayna Brown, *Babylon Girls: Black Women Performers and the Shaping of the Modern* (Durham, NC: Duke University Press, 2008), 5.

12. The concept of the "hidden transcript" is James C. Scott's. See his *Domination and the Arts of Resistance* (New Haven, CT: Yale University Press, 1990). Both Hartman's *Scenes of Subjection* and Daphne A. Brooks's *Bodies in Dissent: Spectacular Performances of Race and Freedom, 1850–1910* (Durham, NC: Duke University Press, 2003) have explored the resistant potential—and limits—of black performance and everyday practices.

13. Benjamin Filene, *Romancing the Folk: Public Memory and American Roots Music* (Chapel Hill: University of North Carolina Press, 2000), 49.

14. Lynn Abbott and Doug Seroff, *Ragged but Right: Black Traveling Shows, "Coon Songs," and the Dark Pathway to Blues and Jazz* (Oxford: University Press of Mississippi, 2007), 25.

15. Gayle Wald, *Shout, Sister, Shout! The Untold Story of Rock-and-Roll Trailblazer Sister Rosetta Tharpe* (Boston: Beacon Press, 2007), 178.

16. Paul Oliver, "Festival Blues: The American Blues Festival, 1964," *Jazz Monthly*, December 1964, 4.

17. Jonas Barish's *The Antitheatrical Prejudice* (Berkeley: University of California Press, 1981) is the signal work on antitheatricalism. Thomas Postlewait and Tracy C. Davis's "Theatricality: An Introduction" in their edited collection *Theatricality* (Cambridge, UK: Cambridge University Press, 2003) provides a useful overview of histories of antitheatricality.

18. W. C. Handy, *Father of the Blues: An Autobiography* (New York: Macmillan, 1941), 10.

19. See Giles Oakley, *The Devil's Music: A History of the Blues* (Cambridge, MA: Da Capo Press, 1997).

20. Lawrence Levine, *Black Culture and Black Consciousness* (New York: Oxford University Press, 1978), 179.

21. Quoted in Jim O'Neal and Amy van Singel, *The Voice of the Blues: Classic Interviews from Living Blues Magazine* (New York: Routledge, 2001), 3.

22. Houston A. Baker Jr., *Modernism and the Harlem Renaissance* (Chicago: University of Chicago Press, 1987), 22. For Baker, Afro-modernism was constituted first and foremost at the intersection of "race," minstrelsy, and postemancipation forms of black performance.

23. Baker, *Modernism and the Harlem Renaissance*, 50.

24. Kevin Gaines, *Uplifting the Race: Black Leadership, Politics, and Culture in the Twentieth Century* (Chapel Hill: University of North Carolina Press, 1996), 93.

25. I borrow the phrase *uplifting the race* from Gaines's book of the same title. See David Krasner's *A Beautiful Pageant: African American Theater, Drama, and Performance in the Harlem Renaissance, 1910–1927* (New York: Palgrave Macmillan, 2002) and *Resistance, Parody, and Double Consciousness, 1895–1910* (New York: St. Martin's Press, 1997) for his recentering of theater and performance within the critical and artistic legacy of the Harlem Renaissance.

26. Gaines, *Uplifting the Race*, 68.

27. I thank Jonathan Holloway for suggesting that I consider the framework of uplift as a script.

28. Gaines, *Uplifting the Race*, 3.

29. Indeed, Du Bois's speech—delivered shortly after Booker T. Washington's famous "Atlanta Compromise" speech—at a school dedicated to the instruction of African American teachers might be understood as a fascinating contribution to the ongoing conversation between Henry Lyman Morehouse, Washington, and Du Bois about black education and leadership. See Henry Louis Gates Jr., "Who Really Invented the 'Talented Tenth'?," *The Root*, February 18, 2013, accessed May 12, 2013. http://www.theroot.com/views/who-really-invented-talented-tenth.

30. W. E. B. Du Bois, "The Problem of Amusement," in *Du Bois on Religion*, edited by Phil Zuckerman (New York: AltaMira Press, 2000), 19.

31. W. E. B. Du Bois, "Krigwa Players Little Negro Theatre: The Story of a Little Theatre Movement," *Crisis* 32, no. 3 (1926): 135.

32. W. E. B. Du Bois, *The Souls of Black Folk* (New York: Dover Publications, 1994), 110; Alain Locke, "The Negro Spirituals," in *The New Negro: Voices of the Harlem Renaissance*, edited by Alain Locke (New York: Simon and Schuster, 1992), 199.

33. Du Bois, *The Souls of Black Folk*, 112.

34. James Weldon Johnson, *Black Manhattan* (New York: Da Capo Press, 1991), 95, 171–72.

35. J. Johnson, *Black Manhattan*, 124–25.

36. James Weldon Johnson, "Now We Have the Blues," *Saturday Review of Literature*, June 19, 1926, 848.

37. Gaines, *Uplifting the Race*, 93.

38. See Shane Vogel's *The Scene of Harlem Cabaret: Race, Sexuality, Performance* (Chicago: University of Chicago Press, 2009) for his analysis of the mobilization of blues by the Cabaret School "against uplift."

39. Langston Hughes, "The Negro Artist and the Racial Mountain," *The Nation*, June 23, 1926. Hughes was critical of one place, though: the Cotton Club. The club, he explained, "was a Jim Crow club for gangsters and monied whites." As expressed in the "Spectacles in Color" chapter of *The Big Sea: An Autobiography* (New York: Hill and Wang, 1940), Harlem was a site of both onstage and offstage theatricality—from drag balls to spectacular weddings and funerals. By and large, Hughes experienced the theatricality of Harlem as expressing "a positive relation between artifice and nature, performance and feeling." The theatricality of the Harlem Renaissance was, for Hughes, only a problem when Harlemites themselves became an object of white spectatorial curiosity at "cabarets and bars . . . where strangers were given the best ringside tables to sit and stare at the Negro customers—like amusing animals in a zoo" (225).

40. Wallace Thurman, "Negro Artists and the Negro," *The New Republic*, August 31, 1927, 37.

41. Zora Neale Hurston, "My People! My People!," in *Folklore, Memoirs, and Other Writings* (New York: Library of America, 1995), 730.

42. Zora Neale Hurston, *Dust Tracks on a Road*, in *Folklore, Memoirs, and Other Writings* (New York: Library of America, 1995), 806.

43. Jeff Todd Titon, *Early Downhome Blues: A Musical and Cultural Analysis* (Chapel Hill: University of North Carolina Press, 1994), 22.

44. Though there are countless books on blues and its histories, a few stand out for their attention to blues' earliest theatrical manifestations in tent shows and on the

TOBA circuit: Paul Oliver's *Conversation with the Blues* (Cambridge, UK: Cambridge University Press, 1965) reproduces transcripts of interviews with musicians, many of whom describe the theatrical circuit; his *Barrelhouse Blues: Location Recording and the Early Traditions of the Blues* (New York: Basic Civitas Books, 2009); *Blues Fell This Morning: Meaning in the Blues* (Cambridge, UK: Cambridge University Press, 1960); and *Songsters and Saints: Vocal Traditions on Race Records* (Cambridge, UK: Cambridge University Press, 1984) have all stood the test of time and acknowledge the role of theatrical traditions in early twentieth-century Southern music. Both Elijah Wald's *Escaping the Delta: Robert Johnson and the Invention of the Blues* (New York: HarperCollins, 2004) and Peter Muir's *Long Lost Blues: Popular Blues in America, 1850–1920* (Champaign: University of Illinois Press, 2010) work to dismantle the "folk-popular" binary that has governed a great deal of the music's assessment. *Blues People: Negro Music in White America* (New York: Harper Perennial, 1963) by LeRoi Jones (Amiri Baraka) was an early model for all scholars of blues performance and remains a foundational text that places African American vernacular musical production in social, political, and cultural context.

45. Rebecca Schneider, *Performing Remains: Art and War in Times of Theatrical Reenactment* (Oxon, UK: Routledge, 2011), 102.

46. Joseph Roach, *Cities of the Dead: Circum-Atlantic Performance* (New York: Columbia University Press, 1996), 3.

47. Roach, *Cities of the Dead*, 6.

48. Richard Schechner, *Between Theater and Anthropology* (Philadelphia: University of Pennsylvania Press, 1985), 36. Literary critic Henry Louis Gates Jr. and playwright Suzan-Lori Parks have explicated the significance of repetition and revision for African American literature, music, and performance. "How," Parks asks, "does this Rep & Rev— a literal incorporation of the past—impact on the creation of a theatrical experience?" Suzan-Lori Parks, "From Elements of Style," in *The America Play, and Other Works* (New York: Theatre Communications Group, 1995), 10. See also Gates, *The Signifying Monkey: A Theory of African American Literary Criticism* (New York: Oxford University Press, 1989).

49. Foucault famously advocated for genealogical historiography, which, he claimed, "does not pretend to go back in time to restore an unbroken continuity that operates beyond the dispersion of forgotten things." Michel Foucault, "Nietzsche, Genealogy, History," in *Language, Counter-memory, Practice: Selected Essays and Interviews*, edited by D. F. Bouchard (Ithaca, NY: Cornell University Press, 1977), 146.

50. Foucault, "Nietzsche, Genealogy, History," 139.

51. Foucault, "Nietzsche, Genealogy, History," 147. Muddy Waters, who appears repeatedly—though often as a supporting player—throughout this book, is a vibrant example of descent in action. A likely spectator of the tent shows in the Clarksdale area, Waters was, briefly, a performer with the Silas Green from New Orleans tent show; Alan Lomax later "discovered" and recorded Waters on the front porch of his Mississippi home, a cabin on the Stovall Plantation. Waters was a transatlantic traveler on the Blues and Gospel Train musical tour. His home was removed from its original location in the 1990s by the House of Blues franchise; the Delta Blues Museum in Clarksdale later recovered the home for display, where Waters reappears, returned to the Delta as an effigy—a waxy museum-ified attraction in the economies of contemporary blues tourism. Waters's route is just one subterranean current that runs throughout this book; his is just one performing body to which narratives of descent attach, though we can imagine others.

52. Christopher Small, *Musicking: The Meanings of Performance and Listening* (Middletown, CT: Wesleyan University Press, 1998), 2.

53. E. Wald, *Escaping the Delta*. See also Karl Hagstrom Miller, *Segregating Sound: Inventing Folk and Pop Music in the Age of Jim Crow* (Durham, NC: Duke University Press, 2010), which explores the way Southern music was segmented into discrete "white" (country, hillbilly) and "black" (blues, jazz) genres in the early twentieth century.

54. Abbott and Seroff, *Ragged but Right*, 207.

55. My work is indebted to Philip Auslander's *Liveness: Performance in a Mediatized Culture* (London: Routledge, 1999) and *Performing Glam Rock: Gender and Theatricality in Popular Music* (Ann Arbor: University of Michigan Press, 2006), which have persuasively bridged performance studies and popular-music studies. In *Liveness* Auslander works to untangle the live-mediated binary and explains how recordings sever the "aural experience of music from its visual experience," and he identifies the securing of musical "authenticity" that takes place at a live performance (85; see 61–111).

56. Small, *Musicking*, 8.

57. Lynn Abbott and Doug Seroff, "'They Cert'ly Sound Good to Me': Sheet Music, Southern Vaudeville, and the Commercial Ascendancy of the Blues," *American Music* 14, no. 4 (1996): 413.

58. "Memphis Blues" and "Crazy Blues," respectively.

59. Abbott and Seroff, *Ragged but Right*, 22. Abbott and Seroff's précis of ragtime's explosion at the turn of the twentieth century is particularly thorough. See also M. Alison Kibler, *Rank Ladies: Gender and Cultural Hierarchy in American Vaudeville* (Chapel Hill: University of North Carolina Press, 1999).

60. Daphne A. Brooks, "'This Voice Which Is Not One': Amy Winehouse Sings the Ballad of Sonic Blue(s)face Culture," *Women and Performance: A Journal of Feminist Theory* 20, no. 1 (2010): 40. Brooks persuasively constructs a genealogy of women's racial mimicry, blackface, and blues, a practice that begins with Tucker and Rainey and extends, she argues, to Amy Winehouse.

61. Abbott and Seroff, *Ragged but Right*, 4.

62. There is, intriguingly, a 1929 recording of "Voice Throwin' Blues" by Walter "Buddy Boy" Hawkins in which he sings a country blues in two different voices, presumably his and the dummy's.

63. The layout of William Barlow's wide-ranging and informative regional history, *Looking Up at Down: The Emergence of Blues Culture* (Philadelphia: Temple University Press, 1980), provides an instructive example. Barlow's opening chapters discuss a number of Delta bluesmen born in the late nineteenth century: Big Bill Broonzy (born 1893), Charley Patton (born 1891), Son House (born 1902), and others. Barlow charts the development of both the musical structures (the blue notes, the A–A–B poetic form, and the changing social conditions (greater mobility, either forced or chosen, for African American men) that enabled the emergence of the culture of blues performance. More than one hundred pages into the book, Barlow turns to what he calls "urban blues." Only then does he mention the female contemporaries of these male innovators: Rainey (born 1886), Bessie Smith (born 1894), and Ida Cox (born 1896), many of whom were born earlier, began performing and recording earlier, and achieved fame sooner than did their male counterparts.

64. E. Wald, *Escaping the Delta*, 69.

65. Barlow, *Looking Up at Down*, 77.

66. Hazel V. Carby, *Cultures in Babylon: Black Britain and African America* (New York: Verso, 1999), 36. Angela Y. Davis calls this the "masculinist bias" of blues cultural studies in *Blues Legacies and Black Feminism: Gertrude "Ma" Rainey, Bessie Smith, and Billie Holiday* (New York: Vintage, 1999), 44. See also Daphne Duval Harrison, *Black Pearls: Blues Queens of the 1920s* (New Brunswick, NJ: Rutgers University Press, 1988).

67. "Classic" frequently appears in quotation marks, as if to undercut any claims to priority or originality.

68. Titon, *Early Downhome Blues*, 21.

69. Titon, *Early Downhome Blues*, 261–81.

70. Of course, "diaspora" is not a unitary phenomenon, and, as James Clifford warns, diaspora "cannot become a master trope or 'figure' for modern, complex, or positional identities." James Clifford, "Diasporas," *Cultural Anthropology* 9, no. 3 (1994): 319. Rather, as Brent Hayes Edwards has argued in *The Practice of Diaspora: Literature, Translation, and the Rise of Black Internationalism* (Cambridge, MA: Harvard University Press, 2003), diaspora is best described as a set of practices: communiqués, migrations, and encounters that shape the development not of a monolithic diaspora but of diasporic consciousness and relations that are historically and culturally particular. While the black Atlantic diaspora is by definition transnational and supranational, my analysis considers the intranational practices of migration as integral to these circum-Atlantic flows.

71. Jean Baudrillard, *America* (London: Verso Press, 1988), 1.

72. Kris Lackey, *Road Frames: The American Highway Narrative* (Lincoln: University of Nebraska Press, 1997), ix.

73. Sandra Lieb, *Mother of the Blues: A Study of Ma Rainey* (Amherst: University of Massachusetts Press, 1981), 7.

ONE   REAL PERSONALITY

1. Chris Albertson, *Bessie* (New Haven, CT: Yale University Press, 2003), 114.

2. Erika Brady, *A Spiral Way: How the Phonograph Changed Ethnography* (Jackson: University Press of Mississippi, 1999), 27–51.

3. Some have interpreted the shiny wood platform underneath the dog as the surface of a coffin. Jonathan Sterne, *The Audible Past: Cultural Origins of Sound Reproduction* (Durham, NC: Duke University Press, 2003), 300–307.

4. For an account of Brown's escape and performance career, and his connection with various spiritualist and mesmerist practices, see Daphne A. Brooks, *Bodies in Dissent: Spectacular Performances of Race and Freedom, 1850–1910* (Durham, NC: Duke University Press, 2003), 66–130. See also John Ernest, "Introduction: The Emergence of Henry 'Box' Brown," in *Narrative of Henry Box Brown, Written by Himself* (Chapel Hill: University of North Carolina Press, 2008) for its description of Brown's near-instant and widespread fame following his escape.

5. John W. Work, *American Negro Songs: 230 Folk Songs and Spirituals, Religious and Secular* (Mineola, NY: Dover Publications, 1998), 32.

6. Lynn Abbott and Doug Seroff, *Ragged but Right: Black Traveling Shows, "Coon Songs," and the Dark Pathway to Blues and Jazz* (Jackson: University Press of Mississippi, 2007);

and Peter Muir, *Long Lost Blues: Popular Blues in America, 1850–1920* (Champaign: University of Illinois Press, 2010).

7. David Savran, *Highbrow/Lowdown: Theater, Jazz, and the Making of the New Middle Class* (Ann Arbor: University of Michigan Press, 2009), 110–13.

8. Abbott and Seroff, *Ragged but Right*, 6.

9. Savran, *Highbrow/Lowdown*, 15. Savran chronicles the generic fracturing between popular theater and popular music in the early decades of the twentieth century. The decline of the road show, aesthetic- and class-based debates about "legitimacy," the development of the art theater movement, and the rise of the Hollywood studio system, Savran argues, segregated a new kind of art theater from (black and black-influenced) popular music.

10. Savran, *Highbrow/Lowdown*, 18, 43.

11. Paula Lockheart, "A History of Early Microphone Singing, 1925–1939: American Mainstream Popular Singing at the Advent of Electronic Microphone Amplification," *Popular Music and Society* 26, no. 3 (2003): 376.

12. Thomas A. Dorsey quoted in Jim O'Neal and Amy van Singel, *The Voice of the Blues: Classic Interviews from Living Blues Magazine* (New York: Routledge, 2001), 15.

13. As Carby puts it, "Historians and demographers seem to agree that what is now called the Great Migration needs to be viewed in the context of these earlier migratory patterns and in light of the fact that black people were becoming increasingly urbanized before they left for northern cities." Hazel V. Carby, *Cultures in Babylon: Black Britain and African America* (New York: Verso, 1999), 22.

14. Historical Census Browser, University of Virginia Library, accessed August 3, 2013. http://mapserver.lib.virginia.edu/.

15. Angela Y. Davis, *Blues Legacies and Black Feminism: Gertrude "Ma" Rainey, Bessie Smith, and Billie Holiday* (New York: Vintage, 1999), 72.

16. Ma Rainey quoted in Thomas Fulbright, "Ma Rainey and I," *Jazz Journal*, March 1956; cited in Sandra Lieb, *Mother of the Blues: A Study of Ma Rainey* (Amherst: University of Massachusetts Press, 1981), 46.

17. In her early days as a touring star, Bessie Smith sang "Standin' in the Rain Blues": "Standin' in the rain and ain't a drop fell on me (x 2)/My clothes is all wet, but my flesh is as dry as can be/. . . I've got my raincoat, hat, umbrella, boots, and shoes." And she sang not in the climate-controlled sterility of the recording studio (as she eventually would) but in the open-air setting of the tent-show environment. This merging of the real and the representational may have become even more palpable if Smith sang her rain-themed song *in* the rain, as Rosetta Tharpe would, some years later, when she belted out "Didn't It Rain" on a train platform stage in rainy Manchester, England.

18. Carby, *Cultures in Babylon*, 14.

19. Carby, *Cultures in Babylon*, 34.

20. Elijah Wald, *Escaping the Delta: Robert Johnson and the Invention of the Blues* (New York: HarperCollins, 2004), 33. Black vaudevillians—especially those in the North who battled their way to acceptance in the "white circuits" of Keith and Albee—saw themselves as workers deserving of organized labor's protection. Excluded from the White Rats, a protounion of white vaudeville performers founded in 1900, black vaudevillians formed their own fraternal organization, the Frogs, in 1908 and the Colored Vaudeville Benevolent Organization in 1909. In the South traveling entertainers formed kinship

networks as an attempt to secure similar protection from management; Rainey, for example, was known for the band of children that she had adopted and who traveled with her under her protection. Self-management was also sometimes an option for the wealthier and more powerful stars.

21. My argument about the circulation and dissemination of cultural forms is indebted to Jayna Brown's *Babylon Girls: Black Women Performers and the Shaping of the Modern* (Durham, NC: Duke University Press, 2008), particularly its "challenge" to "the tendency within studies of vernacular culture and its circulation to trace itself solely along the routes of male labor" (3).

22. E. Wald, *Escaping the Delta*, 85.

23. Abbott and Seroff, *Ragged but Right*.

24. Max C. Elliott, "The Stage," *Indianapolis Freeman*, October 27, 1927. Census Data for Year 1910, Historical Census Browser, University of Virginia Library, accessed August 3, 2013, http://mapserver.lib.virginia.edu/php/start.php?year=V1910. Select "total population," "Mississippi," "County-Level Data."

25. Quoted in Abbott and Seroff, *Ragged but Right*, 216.

26. Abbott and Seroff, *Ragged but Right*, 214–17.

27. Jeff Todd Titon, *Early Downhome Blues: A Musical and Cultural Analysis* (Chapel Hill: University of North Carolina Press, 1994), 204.

28. Tent shows in the Delta were regularly followed by all-black dances. In the Delta Metropolis column of the *Indianapolis Freeman*, published on September 16, 1916, Lee A. Motley Jr. reported from Greenwood: "The Big 6 Orchestra put on a dance after the show for the bunch, and a big bunch of boys and girls from Clarksdale, Miss., and we all had a nice time. Another big dance next Monday night after Mahoney's Mobile Minstrels." Though their details may remain unknown to us, these dances are suggestive sites of transmission, encounter, pleasure, and play. Likely all-black events, they created a space of release and relaxation for performers and audience alike after the tent show, which usually played before a racially mixed audience. Sandra Lieb's influential biography of Rainey—the only extant biography to date—describes Rainey's attendance (and possible performance) at these postshow dances. Lieb cites an interview with Sam Chatmon (of the Mississippi Sheiks) and explains that "after the show was over, [Rainey] would go to a dance at the local black café behind a gas station, to entertain and socialize with her own people." Lieb, *Mother of the Blues*, 12.

29. Adam Gussow's *Seems like Murder Here: Southern Violence and the Blues Tradition* (Chicago: University of Chicago Press, 2002) chronicles the textual tradition of blues as a reckoning with Jim Crow violence.

30. Revisionist accounts of Jürgen Habermas's conceptualization of the public sphere by Nancy Fraser and Michael Warner, among others, have trained an eye and ear on cultures of mass media and entertainment and their role in the establishment of the "counterpublics" of those minoritized subjects who were excluded from the (white, male) bourgeois public sphere; the argument that mass cultural products play a role in shaping publics pushes back against a hard-line Frankfurt School argument, especially the suspicions of mass culture shared by Max Horkheimer and Theodor Adorno. Michael Warner, "The Mass Public and the Mass Subject," in *Habermas and the Public Sphere*, edited by Craig Calhoun (Cambridge, MA: MIT Press, 1992), 380–81. See also Elsa Barkley Brown's article "Negotiating and Transforming the Public Sphere: African American Political Life

in the Transition from Slavery to Freedom," *Public Culture* 7 (1994), for her assessment of the black church's role in the development of a postbellum black public sphere.

31. Benedict Anderson, *Imagined Communities: Reflections on the Origin and Spread of Nationalism* (London: Verso, 1983).

32. In a contemporaneous parallel project, the Chautauqua circuit morally shaped a white Christian audience through its traveling performances of lecture entertainments.

33. Farah Jasmine Griffin, "When Malindy Sings: A Meditation on Black Women's Vocality," in *Uptown Conversation: The New Jazz Studies*, edited by Robert G. O'Meally, Brent Hayes Edwards, and Farah Jasmine Griffin (New York: Columbia University Press, 2004), 104.

34. Sterling A. Brown, "Ma Rainey," in *The Collected Poems of Sterling A. Brown*, edited by Michael S. Harper (Evanston, IL: TriQuarterly Books, 1980).

35. See Joanne V. Gabbin, *Sterling A. Brown: Building the Black Aesthetic Tradition* (Charlottesville: University of Virginia Press, 1994).

36. See Benston, "Listen Br'er Sterling: The Critic as Liar [A Pre(r)amble to Essays on Sterling Brown]," *Callaloo* 21, no. 4 (1998); Nicole Furlonge, "An Instrument Blues-Tinged: Listening, Language, and the Everyday in Sterling Brown's 'Ma Rainey,'" *Callaloo* 21, no. 4 (1998); and Robert Stepto, "'When de Saint Go Ma'chin' Home': Sterling Brown's Blueprint for a New Negro Poetry," *Callaloo* 21, no. 4 (1998).

37. Indeed, Brown concludes the poem on a note of forced displacement, as Rainey sings Bessie Smith's "Backwater Blues," a song that quickly became associated with the catastrophic 1927 flood of the Mississippi River.

38. Philip Auslander's "Musical Personae" persuasively argues "what musicians perform first and foremost is not music, but their own identities as musicians, their musical personae." He defines the persona as "neither an overtly fictional character nor simply equivalent to the performer's 'real' identity." Philip Auslander, "Musical Personae," *TDR* 50, no. 1 (2006): 102.

39. Richard Schechner, *Between Theater and Anthropology* (Philadelphia: University of Pennsylvania Press, 1985), 123. Schechner memorably describes the "not/not not" in terms of Laurence Olivier's performance as Hamlet; the phenomenological doubleness of the performance, where Olivier is "not Hamlet," but "not not Hamlet," is characteristic of the theater. Of the man who performs Narad-muni in India, Schechner says: "He performs in the field between a negative and a double-negative, a field of limitless potential, free as it is from both the person (not) and the person impersonated (not not)." Schechner, *Between Theater and Anthropology*, 123.

40. See David Krasner's chronicling of the emergence of long form musical comedy in New York in *A Beautiful Pageant: African American Theater, Drama, and Performance in the Harlem Renaissance, 1910–1927* (New York: Palgrave Macmillan, 2002) and *Resistance, Parody, and Double Consciousness in African American Theater, 1895–1910* (New York: St. Martin's Press, 1997).

41. Abbott and Seroff, *Ragged but Right*, 261.

42. J. Brown, *Babylon Girls*, 140.

43. Journalistic scrutiny of the touring female was inflamed by the French actress Sarah Bernhardt, whose 1915 American tour cemented the sexual—and cultural (though raised Catholic, Bernhardt's father was Jewish)—difference of the traveling actress in the public imagination. Bernhardt was cast as Salome in the original production of

Wilde's 1892 play. The production was censored and canceled before it could open, but "for a moment, this British theatrical scandal linked the figures of Salome and Sarah Bernhardt." Sander Gilman, "Salome, Syphilis, Sarah Bernhardt, and the 'Modern Jewess,'" *German Quarterly* 66, no. 2 (1993): 203.

44. Sylvester Russell, "Sylvester Russell's Review," *Pittsburgh Courier*, July 2, 1927.

45. A. Davis, *Blues Legacies and Black Feminism*, 73.

46. In *Bodies in Dissent* Brooks tracks late nineteenth- and early twentieth-century iterations of this performative reconciliation; see, especially, her analysis of the career of Aida Overton Walker, 281–342.

47. Brooks, *Bodies in Dissent*, 282, 287.

48. Aida Overton Walker, "Colored Men and Women on the American Stage," *Colored American Magazine*, October 1905.

49. Sylvester Russell, "The Husband? Makes a Hit," *Indianapolis Freeman*, September 14, 1907.

50. Russell, "The Husband? Makes a Hit."

51. Sylvester Russell, "An Examination in Musical Comedy," *Indianapolis Freeman*, November 2, 1907.

52. Sylvester Russell, "Annual Review," *Indianapolis Freeman*, January 5, 1907.

53. While actresses in the West had historically been equated with disrepute, the actresses of the early twentieth century faced the strong correlations between acting and prostitution that emerged in the Victorian era, an equation examined in detail by Tracy C. Davis, whose analysis demonstrates that, in nineteenth-century England, "the actress was inseparable from the whore and synonymous with sex." Tracy C. Davis, *Actresses as Working Women: Their Social Identity in Victorian Culture* (New York: Routledge, 1991), 107.

54. I borrow the term *matrixed* from Michael Kirby, who uses *matrixed* and *non-matrixed* to describe modes of nonacting—that is, performance without the representation of fictional characters. Michael Kirby, "The New Theatre," *Tulane Drama Review* 10, no. 2 (1965).

55. I see non-matrixed performance as related to, but distinct from, performances of "Afro-alienation," described by Brooks as strategies of disruption of hypervisibility in the postbellum era. Brooks, *Bodies in Dissent*, 4–6.

56. J. Brown, *Babylon Girls*, 5–6.

57. A. Davis, *Blues Legacies and Black Feminism*, 13.

58. A. Davis, *Blues Legacies and Black Feminism*, 13.

59. Lieb, *Mother of the Blues*, 18.

60. J. Brown, *Babylon Girls*, 50.

61. Transcript of interview between Clyde Bernhardt and Sandra Lieb, Sandra Lieb Collection, Blues Archive, the Department of Archives and Special Collections, J.D. Williams Library, University of Mississippi, Oxford, MS. Box 1, Folder 1. Bernhardt described the tents as "'round about two by 75—two hundred feet long and 75 feet wide—big tents that had big stages on there, had big drops, you know. It was bigger than, you know, some medium-sized theaters."

62. Albertson, *Bessie*, 42–43.

63. Clyde Bernhardt, as told to Sheldon Harris, *I Remember: Eighty Years of Black Entertainment, Big Bands, and the Blues; An Autobiography* (Philadelphia: University of Pennsylvania Press, 1986), 26; emphasis added. Bernhardt also recalled a tent show from around 1909 where an anonymous singer appeared similarly dressed: "This fat, black

woman was out front, all painted with bright red on her cheeks and thick black eyelashes sticking out. Had a wide hat with long, pretty feathers coming out the top. Glittering spots all over her tight dress, all jiggling, and her waist was pulled in very very tight by a big belt" (8).

64. See Lindon Barrett's *Blackness and Value: Seeing Double* (Cambridge, UK: Cambridge University Press, 1999) for its extensive literary and philosophical meditation on these questions of value and valuation. Stephen Calt and Gayle Dean Wardlow, "The Buying and Selling of Paramounts, Part 3," *78 Quarterly* 5 (1990): 10.

65. Monica Miller, *Slaves to Fashion: Black Dandyism and the Styling of Black Diasporic Identity* (Durham, NC: Duke University Press, 2009), 3. See also Shane White and Graham J. White, *Stylin': African American Expressive Culture from Its Beginnings to the Zoot Suit* (Ithaca, NY: Cornell University Press, 1998).

66. Robin D. G. Kelley, *Race Rebels: Culture, Politics, and the Black Working Class* (New York: Simon and Schuster, 1996), 50.

67. Zora Neale Hurston, "Characteristics of Negro Expression," in *Sweat*, edited by Cheryl Wall (New Brunswick, NJ: Rutgers University Press, 1997), 59.

68. Bernhardt, *I Remember*, 24.

69. See Titon's *Early Downhome Blues* for an analysis of these hand-drawn advertisements (218–60).

70. Alex van der Tuuk, *Paramount's Rise and Fall: A History of the Wisconsin Chair Company and Its Recording Activities* (Littleton, CO: Mainspring Press, 2003), 81. In the 1930s Burley moved to New York and became the theater editor at the *Amsterdam News*.

71. Brooks, *Bodies in Dissent*, 337. See Brooks, *Bodies in Dissent*, 330–42; and J. Brown, *Babylon Girls*, 178–84, for their influential analyses of the adoption of Salome by black women performers.

72. Gaylyn Studlar, "'Out Salome-ing Salome': Dance, the New Woman, and Fan Magazine Orientalism," in *Visions of the East: Orientalism in Film*, edited by Matthew Bernstein and Gaylyn Studlar (New Brunswick, NJ: Rutgers University Press, 1997), 100.

73. "Ballets Russes (Diaghilev), American tour, 1915–1916," program, New York Public Library Digital Gallery, New York Public Library for the Performing Arts, Jerome Robbins Dance Division. Search Image ID: 160201 at digitalgallery.nypl.org, accessed August 3, 2013.

74. Melani McAlister, *Epic Encounters: Culture, Media, and U.S. Interests in the Middle East since 1945* (Berkeley: University of California Press, 2005), 21–22.

75. Studlar, "'Out Salome-ing Salome': Dance, the New Woman, and Fan Magazine Orientalism," 114. See also Peter Wollen, "Fashion/Orientalism/the Body," *New Formations* 1 (1987) 5-33. Marlis Schweitzer's *When Broadway Was the Runway: Theater, Fashion, and American Culture* (Philadelphia: University of Pennsylvania Press, 2009) discusses Poiret's influence on American theatrical practice in the teens.

76. Mary Davis, *Classic Chic: Music, Fashion, Modernism* (Berkeley: University of California Press, 2008), 24–25.

77. Lesley M. M. Blume, "How Josephine Baker Helped Save Post-war French Fashion," *Huffington Post*, June 7, 2010, accessed August 3, 2013, http://www.huffingtonpost.com/lesley-m-m-blume/josephine-baker-fashion-h_b_601072.html. While one might consider that the tent-show stars were trying to be Baker, or at least to capitalize on her success, her celebrated Revue Negre came somewhat at the tail end of the heyday of the tent-show acts.

78. A photograph of Rainey wearing her headdress can be seen at the Mainspring Press website: http://www.mainspringpress.com/blues_bobRainey.html (accessed August 3, 2013). The photograph is from *The Paramount Book of the Blues*, 2nd ed. (Port Washington, WI: New York Recording Laboratories, 1927), 9.

79. Brooks, *Bodies in Dissent*, 340.

80. Emily Apter, "Acting Out Orientalism: Sapphic Theatricality in Turn-of-the-Century Paris," in *Performance and Cultural Politics*, edited by Elin Diamond (London: Routledge, 1996), 19–20.

81. Patricia White, "Nazimova's Veils: Salome at the Intersection of Film Histories," in *A Feminist Reader in Early Cinema*, edited by Jennifer M. Bean and Diane Negra (Durham, NC: Duke University Press, 2002), 71.

82. Alixa Naff, *Becoming American: The Early Arab Immigrant Experience* (Carbondale: Southern Illinois University Press, 1985), 163. I am indebted to James G. Thomas for much of the material in this section, and I am grateful to him for sharing his thesis with me: "Mississippi *Mahjar*: The History of Lebanese Immigration to the Mississippi Delta and the Role of the Group within a Traditionally Black-and-White Social System," master's thesis, University of Mississippi, 2007.

83. Most immigrants from came from the Mount Lebanon region of what was then called Syria, which included contemporary Lebanon, Israel, Palestine, and Jordan. When Lebanon achieved independence in 1943 most of these Mississippi residents began referring to themselves as Lebanese. Though they occupied a uniquely liminal ethnic position in the racially binarized South, the racial logic of Jim Crow routinely aggregated Italians, Arabs, Southeast Asians, Jews, Greeks, and Mexicans under a rubric of nonwhiteness, even blackness.

84. Thomas, "Mississippi *Mahjar*," 10–11.

85. Contact between black people and Arab immigrants was not limited to countryside peddling, however, as many Syrians lived in African American neighborhoods in town, largely in harmony. Many of these peddlers eventually opened shops in town—and these were also patronized by black shoppers, who found the Syrian-owned shops to be less hostile to them than the white-owned businesses. Thomas, "Mississippi *Mahjar*," 82.

86. Lu Ann Jones, *Mama Learned Us to Work: Farm Women in the New South* (Chapel Hill: University of North Carolina Press, 2002), 35.

87. Thomas Pridgett, "The Life of Ma Rainey, by Her Brother Thomas Pridgett," *Jazz Information*, September 6, 1940.

88. St. Clair Bourne, "Blues—Swing: Death of Bessie Smith Marks Close of 'Blues' Era," *New York Amsterdam News*, October 16, 1937.

89. Harry Fiddler, "Bessie Smith, Blues Singer, Auto Victim," *Chicago Defender*, October 2, 1937.

90. Fiddler, "Bessie Smith, Blues Singer, Auto Victim," *Chicago Defender*, October 2, 1937.

91. "'Queen of Blues' Auto Crash Casualty," *Philadelphia Tribune*, September 30, 1937.

92. Albertson, *Bessie*, vii.

93. For all we know, Smith may have published an autobiography similar to Waters's *His Eye Is on the Sparrow: An Autobiography* (Cambridge, MA: Da Capo Press, 1992) (originally published in 1951) were it not for the untimely nature of her death.

94. Carl Van Vechten, "Memories of Bessie Smith," *Jazz Record*, September 1947, 6.

95. Van Vechten used a 35 mm Leica for these and his other photographs; its portable size and fast shutter speed facilitated the creation of more "candid," less posed photographs.

96. Carl Van Vechten, "Memories of Bessie Smith." *Jazz Record*, September 1947, 7.

97. See Keith Davis, *The Passionate Observer: Photographs by Carl Van Vechten* (Albuquerque: University of New Mexico Press, 1993); and James Smalls, *The Homoerotic Photography of Carl Van Vechten* (Philadelphia: Temple University Press, 2006).

98. Bert O. States, "Phenomenology of the Curtain Call," *Hudson Review* 34, no. 3 (1981): 373.

99. "7,000 Attend Funeral of Bessie Smith," *Afro-American*, October 9, 1937.

100. Theodore A. Stanford, "Bessie Smith: Her Life Story," *Philadelphia Tribune*, September 30, 1937. The accident that took Smith's life was actually in Clarksdale, Mississippi.

101. Lillian Johnson, "Entertainers Find Perils along the Road," *Afro-American*, December 11, 1937.

102. Edward Albee, The Sandbox *and* The Death of Bessie Smith (New York: Penguin, 1988).

103. August Wilson, *Ma Rainey's Black Bottom* (New York: Penguin Books, 1981).

TWO   THEATER FOLK

1. James Weldon Johnson, "Race Prejudice and the Negro Artist," *Harper's Magazine*, November 1928, 769–70. *The Original Vision* is the title of the 1989 Smithsonian Folkways album. This album, which inaugurated the label, consists of songs sung by Lead Belly and Woody Guthrie, taken from original Folkways masters.

2. James Weldon Johnson, *Along This Way: The Autobiography of James Weldon Johnson* (New York: Da Capo Press, 1933), 326.

3. As newly available, less expensive, and more portable technologies of sound recording transformed both the race-records industry and the folklorists' enterprises, so too did technologies of mass media transform the Southern tent show and popular theater scenes in which early blues had developed and thrived. As movie palaces dotted the landscape and the fiscal meltdowns of the Great Depression bankrupted small theaters, the tent shows and vaudeville tours, while not dying out, markedly decreased in number.

4. My understanding of the constructed and contested category of "the folk" is informed by J. M. Favor's *Authentic Blackness: The Folk in the New Negro Renaissance* (Durham, NC: Duke University Press, 1999); Benjamin Filene's *Romancing the Folk: Public Memory and American Roots Music* (Chapel Hill: University of North Carolina Press, 2000); Robin D. G. Kelley's "Notes on Deconstructing 'the Folk,'" *American Historical Review* 97, no. 5 (1992): 1400–1408; Anthea Kraut's *Choreographing the Folk: The Dance Stagings of Zora Neale Hurston* (Minneapolis: University of Minnesota Press, 2008); and Sonnet Retman's *Real Folks: Race and Genre in the Great Depression* (Durham, NC: Duke University Press, 2011). Deployed by different communities for differing ends, concepts of "the folk" and "folk authenticity" have been bound up in each other since the late nineteenth century. While early twentieth-century black intellectuals such as James Weldon Johnson and Sterling A. Brown celebrated black folk culture as a unique cultural contribution, New Deal–era white artists frequently romanticized (poor, South-

ern, black) folk as repositories of "lost" cultural traditions, supposedly untainted by urban life, popular culture, and other capitalist iterations of the modern. Though she does not take on the Lomaxes' and Ledbetter's work specifically, Retman has insightfully identified how "folklore constituted a particularly performative kind of authentic fiction" (161).

5. Michael Ann Williams, *Staging Tradition: John Lair and Sarah Gertrude Knott* (Champaign: University of Illinois Press, 2006), x.

6. See Hazel V. Carby, *Race Men* (Cambridge, MA: Harvard University Press, 1998); Nolan Porterfield, *Last Cavalier: The Life and Times of John A. Lomax, 1857–1948* (Champaign: University of Illinois Press, 2001); John Szwed, *Alan Lomax: The Man Who Recorded the World* (New York: Penguin, 2011); and Charles Wolfe and Kip Lornell, *The Life and Legend of Leadbelly* (New York: HarperCollins, 1992) for accounts of the relationship between Ledbetter and the Lomaxes.

7. James C. Scott, *Domination and the Arts of Resistance* (New Haven, CT: Yale University Press, 1990), 4–5.

8. Ross Russell, "Illuminating the Lead Belly Legend," *Down Beat* 37, no. 15 (1970), 12.

9. Wolfe and Lornell, *The Life and Legend of Leadbelly*, 53. I am indebted to Wolfe and Lornell for their thorough description of Ledbetter's early life.

10. R. Russell, "Illuminating the Lead Belly Legend," 33.

11. Sean Killeen, *Lead Belly Letter* 5–6, nos. 4 and 1 (1996): 11.

12. Sean Killeen, *Lead Belly Letter* 2, nos. 2 and 3 (1992): 5.

13. R. Russell, "Illuminating the Lead Belly Legend," 13.

14. The stationery and its photographs can be found on the website for the American Folklife Center at the Library of Congress (accessed July 20, 2013): http://www.loc.gov/folklife/guide/images/LedbetterLetter0037_450.jpg.

15. Viewers familiar with the Southern tent show may have had a unique association of Ledbetter with the character of Toby, the familiar "country bumpkin" figure from the tent shows who managed to "outwit and confuse the city slickers who tried to take advantage of him." These Toby characters "always appeared the same—redhaired, freckled, with blacked-out tooth and farm clothes." Charles Reagan Wilson, "Traveling Shows," in *Encyclopedia of Southern Culture*, edited by Charles Reagan Wilson, William Ferris, and Ann J. Adadie (Chapel Hill: University of North Carolina Press, 1989), 1249.

16. Sean Killeen, "Lead Belly: More Than a Name," in *Lead Belly: A Life in Pictures*, edited by Tiny Robinson and John Reynolds (London: Steidl Photography International, 2008), 20.

17. Both John and Alan Lomax have been criticized for misleading the public about the authorship and ownership over the songs they collected. See Porterfield, *The Last Cavalier*, 326; and Szwed, *Alan Lomax*, 292–96.

18. Ledbetter also loved to sing country music, and he longed for a career like that of Gene Autry, the "Singing Cowboy." Karl Hagstrom Miller's *Segregating Sound: Inventing Folk and Pop Music in the Age of Jim Crow* (Durham, NC: Duke University Press, 2010) is instructive regarding the segregation of Southern music enacted by collectors and race-records producers: country from blues, black from white.

19. Miller, *Segregating Sound*; E. Wald, *Escaping the Delta*, 14–42.

20. R. Russell, "Illuminating the Lead Belly Legend," 14. Zora Neale Hurston, *Dust Tracks on a Road*, in *Folklore, Memoirs, and Other Writings* (New York: Library of Amer-

ica, 1995), 807. I have chosen the term "revue" here for descriptive specificity. Hurston, though, always called *The Great Day* a "concert"; this naming may have been an effort to distinguish the event from certain trends in black performance (especially on Broadway) that she believed were denigrating to black artists.

21. Pete Seeger, "Lead Belly," in *Lead Belly: A Life in Pictures*, edited by Tiny Robinson and John Reynolds (London: Steidl Photography International, 2008), 11.

22. Szwed, *Alan Lomax*, 352.

23. Porterfield, *Last Cavalier*, 350.

24. The Black Bottom was a dance that "traveled from rent parties and nightclubs to the theatrical stage and back again" and "involved slapping your hips and hopping forward and back, touching the ground and letting your backbone slide from side to side." Thomas DeFrantz, "Popular Dance of the 1920s and Early '30s," in *Ain't Nothing Like the Real Thing: The Apollo Theater and American Entertainment*, edited by Richard Carlin and Kinshasha Holman Conwill (Washington, DC: Smithsonian Books, 2010), 68.

25. John Avery Lomax Family Papers, 1842 and 1853–1986, Dolph Briscoe Center for American History, University of Texas, Austin (hereafter JAL Papers).

26. Lead Belly, *Lead Belly's Last Sessions*, Smithsonian Folkways Recordings, recorded in 1948, released in 1994, four discs, CD, archived at Smithsonian Center for Folklife and Cultural Heritage, liner notes by Sean Killeen.

27. Ledbetter thus extended the fin de siècle cakewalk craze, described by Jayna Brown in *Babylon Girls: Black Women Performers and the Shaping of the Modern* (Durham, NC: Duke University Press, 2008), 128.

28. J. Brown, *Babylon Girls*, 139, 159.

29. J. W. Johnson, "Race Prejudice and the Negro Artist," 770.

30. Wolfe and Lornell, *The Life and Legend of Leadbelly*, 85.

31. Wolfe and Lornell, *The Life and Legend of Leadbelly*, 86.

32. Wolfe and Lornell, *The Life and Legend of Leadbelly*, 85.

33. Saidiya Hartman, *Scenes of Subjection: Terror, Slavery, and Self-Making in Nineteenth-Century America* (New York: Oxford University Press, 1997), 56.

34. Caleb Smith, *The Prison and the American Imagination* (New Haven, CT: Yale University Press, 2009), 153.

35. Wolfe and Lornell, *The Life and Legend of Leadbelly*, 87.

36. William Stott's *Documentary Expression and Thirties America* (New York: Oxford University Press, 1973) is a central text that explores the documentary impulse of New Deal–era artists, journalists, and activists. Patricia Ybarra develops "theatrical thinking" in "Mexican Theater History and Its Discontents: Politics, Performance, and History in Mexico," *Modern Language Quarterly* 70, no. 1 (2009).

37. Hurston, in addition to receiving support from Columbia, private foundations, and her patron "godmother," Charlotte Osgood Mason, worked for both the Federal Writers' Project and the Federal Theater Project. In addition to serving as curator of the Archive of American Folk Song, John Lomax, as part of the Federal Writers' Project, supervised the gathering and recording of thousands of interviews with formerly enslaved Americans.

38. In their foreword to Joanne V. Gabbin's *Sterling A. Brown: Building the Black Aesthetic Tradition* (Charlottesville: University of Virginia Press, 1994), John Blassingame and Henry Louis Gates Jr. chronicle the shifting attitudes toward "the folk" over time.

39. Sterling A. Brown quoted in Jerrold Hirsch, *Portrait of America: A Cultural History of the Federal Writers' Project* (Chapel Hill: University of North Carolina Press, 2006), 109.

40. Hirsch, *Portrait of America*, 117.

41. Sterling A. Brown, Negro Poetry and Drama *and* The Negro in American Fiction (New York: Atheneum, 1972), 139.

42. James Weldon Johnson, *Black Manhattan* (New York: Da Capo Press, 1991), 218.

43. Judith Weisenfeld's overview of the reception of *The Green Pastures* is particularly useful. See *Hollywood Be Thy Name: African American Religion in American Film, 1929–1949* (Berkeley: University of California Press, 2007), 52–87.

44. S. A. Brown, Negro Poetry and Drama *and* The Negro in American Fiction, 119.

45. J. W. Johnson, *Black Manhattan*, xxviii.

46. Wolfe and Lornell, *The Life and Legend of Leadbelly*, 229.

47. Langston Hughes, "Trouble with the Angels," in *The American Stage: Writing on Theater from Washington Irving to Tony Kushner*, edited by Laurence Senelick (New York: Library of America, 2010), 423–24.

48. Zora Neale Hurston quoted in Valerie Boyd, *Wrapped in Rainbows: The Life of Zora Neale Hurston* (New York: Scribner, 2003), 220.

49. Hurston, *Dust Tracks on a Road*, 701.

50. Hurston's commitment to paradox, signifying, and parody, deftly explored elsewhere by Retman, helps account, somewhat, for the fact that Hurston's own writings—and her position vis-à-vis her subjects—were frequently contradictory. Her own stated desire to present authentic Southern folk culture was bound up in her drive for commercial success. In her widely circulated essay "The Politics of Fiction, Anthropology, and the Folk," Carby shines a light on Hurston's "romantic" and "colonial" attitude, and her production of a timeless rural past. Hazel V. Carby, *Cultures in Babylon: Black Britain and African America* (New York: Verso, 1999), 168–87. As one who "complained bitterly" about mass media and mass culture, particularly their impact on folk songs, Hurston at times reproduces a folk-commercial binary discussed in the introduction—a binary that the Lomaxes were also deeply invested in. Bolstering both Hurston's and the Lomaxes' theatrical approach to vernacular performance was an implicit—and sometimes explicit—belief in an inherent penchant for performance among black people. This approach is upheld by Hurston in her essay "Characteristics of Negro Expression" (1934), which she opens by claiming that "the Negro's universal mimicry is not so much a thing in itself as an evidence of something that permeates his entire self. And that thing is drama." Zora Neale Hurston, "Characteristics of Negro Expression," in *Sweat*, edited by Cheryl Wall (New Brunswick, NJ: Rutgers University Press, 1997), 55.

51. Hurston, *Dust Tracks on a Road*, 648–49; emphasis added.

52. Hurston wrote these words in her Rosenwald application. Robert E. Hemenway, *Zora Neale Hurston: A Literary Biography* (Champaign: University of Illinois Press, 1977), 207.

53. Hurston, *Dust Tracks on a Road*, 589; Zora Neale Hurston, "How It Feels to Be Colored Me," in *I Love Myself When I Am Laughing . . . and Then Again: A Zora Neale Hurston Reader*, edited by Alice Walker (New York: Feminist Press at the City University of New York, 1979), 826; Zora Neale Hurston, *Mules and Men* (New York: HarperCollins, 1990), 9.

54. For a description of *The Great Day*, see V. Boyd, *Wrapped in Rainbows*, 228–33; Brooks, "'Sister, Can You Line It Out?': Zora Neale Hurston and the Sound of Angular

Black Womanhood," *Amerikastudien/American Studies* 55, no. 4 (2010); and Kraut, *Choreographing the Folk*, 91–118. Hurston was not the only public figure advocating the theater's suitability for presenting black vernacular life. As Michael Ann Williams puts it, folk material was not "source material for theatrical presentation" but "a form of theatrical presentation" itself. Williams, *Staging Tradition*, 16. Sarah Gertrude Knott, with whom Hurston worked, inaugurated the National Folk Festival in 1934 in St. Louis. Though she was interested in folk music and performance, Knott's entry into the folk-festival world was through theater. Inspired by Frederick Koch and Paul Green, with whom she studied, she established the National Folk Festival as a "dramatic offshoot of the pageantry movement" (Williams, *Staging Tradition*, 13). The festival incorporated musical performances by ensembles from the Carolinas, the Ozarks, the Southwest, and New England. Hurston performed in the inaugural festival and served on the advisory board for many years after that. Both Lomaxes, however, were conspicuously absent from an advisory board that had on its roster nearly every distinguished public folklorist of the period.

55. V. Boyd, *Wrapped in Rainbows*, 151. Hurston describes how after the first half of the concert, the performer Lee Whipper pushed her out onto the stage, where she found herself in the position of having to improvise an explanatory lecture: "I explained why I had done it. That music without motion was unnatural with Negroes, and what I had tried to do was to present Negro singing in a natural way—with action." Hurston, *Dust Tracks on a Road*, 807.

56. See the final chapter of Kraut's *Choreographing the Folk*, "Black Authenticity, White Artistry," 173–212.

57. Alan Lomax's 1938 plan for the 1939 New York World's Fair, while never executed, indicates the young folklorist's indebtedness to Hurston's *The Great Day*. Lomax proposed a series of musical environments, complete with labor re-creations and music sung in situ.

58. Carla Kaplan, ed., *Zora Neale Hurston: A Life in Letters* (New York: Anchor Books, 2002), 332–33.

59. Alan Lomax, "Zora Neale Hurston—A Life of Negro Folklore," *Sing Out!* 10 (October/November 1960): 12.

60. Carby, *Cultures in Babylon,* 176.

61. John Lomax's autobiography, *Adventures of a Ballad Hunter* (New York: Macmillan, 1947), and Porterfield's biography, *Last Cavalier*, are both instructive guides to this period in Lomax's life.

62. Lomax was not the first folklorist to do this: an article from the *Los Angeles Daily Times*, dated October 25, 1913, "'Not One Dern,' Prof. Warbles," describes the singing and lecturing of the cowboy scholar N. O. Shepard of the University of Southern California. Lomax kept a clipping of this article, which can be found in the JAL Papers, box 3D167s.

63. Roger D. Abrahams, "Mr. Lomax Meets Professor Kittredge," *Journal of Folklore Research* 37, no. 2 (2000): 102.

64. Charlotte Canning, "The Platform versus the Stage: Circuit Chautauqua's Antitheatrical Theater," *Theater Journal* 50, no. 3 (1998): 304.

65. Szwed, *Alan Lomax*, 13; circular circa 1933, JAL Papers, box 3D172. Lomax's circular advertised five different programs: "1. The Songs of the Cowboy, 2. Cowboy Verse, 3. Some Types of the American Ballad, 4. Negro Spirituals, 5. Songs of the Worl'ly Negro." The cowboy songs were by far the most popular, though he began to perform more

"Negro songs" as the years wore on, in part because he was playing many return engagements where the cowboy songs had already been heard.

66. Such practices live on: Barbara Kirshenblatt-Gimblett describes the "ascetic approach to staging" that characterizes the Smithsonian Institute's Festival of American Folklife as "an 'ethnographic' way of marking the authenticity of what appears on the stage." Barbara Kirshenblatt-Gimblett, *Destination Culture: Tourism, Museums, and Heritage* (Berkeley: University of California Press, 1998), 216.

67. Shannon Jackson, *Professing Performance: Theatre in the Academy from Philology to Performativity* (Cambridge, UK: Cambridge University Press, 2004), 42.

68. Jackson, *Professing Performance*, 45.

69. Jackson, *Professing Performance*, 48.

70. Josette Féral, "Theatricality: The Specificity of Theatrical Language," translated by Ronald P. Bermingham, *SubStance* 31, no. 2 (2002): 97. See also Mary Louise Pratt's *Imperial Eyes: Travel and Transculturation* (New York: Routledge, 1992), which describes histories and practices of travel that follow a colonial logic, staging the Other as such.

71. Letter from John Lomax to Ruby Terrill, August 10, 1933, JAL Papers, box 3D149.

72. Letter from John Lomax to Ruby Terrill, December 8, 1933, JAL Papers, box 3D149.

73. Letter from John Lomax to Ruby Terrill, April 17, 1934, JAL Papers, box 3D149.

74. Letter from Ruby Terrill to John Lomax, March 21, 1934, JAL Papers, box 3D149.

75. As a spectator, John Lomax was forever "framing," which, Féral argues, engenders the transaction that is theatricality. Lomax's framing was often architectural; he frequently imposed a traditional proscenium arch between him and quotidian performances. In a letter to Terrill, Lomax described a Cajun singer's performance, which took place within a found frame of a doorway: "While Alan and I sat on an old branch underneath the tree he framed himself in the doorway where the rays of the setting sun, filtering through the mass, shone forth on him. He played and sang on and on, old Cajun love songs. The lines on his bronzed, dark brown face became softened and his eyes brightened from the music perhaps, more likely from the early memories (he was an *old* bachelor). The sun went down. A mockingbird sang. [He] played more softly. Caught up in the spell of the surrounding beauty, the music, the swaying mass, the quiet of a dying day, and [his] shining face, I was only conscious of you. I was submerged in your love, all the dear pictures I carry of you in special moments of our association became more vivid." Letter from John Lomax to Ruby Terrill, June 23, 1934, JAL Papers, box 3D150.

76. Circular circa 1933, JAL Papers. I draw on Benedict Anderson's *Imagined Communities: Reflections on the Origin and Spread of Nationalism* (London: Verso, 1983) here; just as Anderson invoked the circulation of newspapers as critical to the stitching together of a national imaginary, the Lomaxes both implicitly and explicitly acknowledged the role of song. John A. and Alan Lomax, eds., *Our Singing Country: Folk Songs and Ballads* (Mineola, NY: Dover Publications, 2000).

77. In large part, Ledbetter was such a potent migratory figure because of the sociological and demographic fact of mass migration. While the early 1930s are often recognized as a lull in the Great Migration, millions were still on the move: black and white migrant farmworkers of the Great Plains fled drought and ruined harvests, moving west and southwest in search of fertile land. Black Southerners had already been on the move for decades, relocating from rural tenant farms to northeastern and Midwestern urban centers as the threat of lynching and the replacement of manual agricultural labor with

machines made life untenable for many. See James A. Gregory, *American Exodus: The Dust Bowl Migration and Okie Culture in California* (New York: Oxford University Press, 1989); and, especially, James A. Gregory, *The Southern Diaspora: How the Great Migrations of White and Black Southerners Transformed America* (Chapel Hill: University of North Carolina Press, 2005).

78. I have written extensively elsewhere about the "magic of song" staged by Ledbetter during his tours with the Lomaxes. See Paige A. McGinley, "'The Magic of Song!' John Lomax, Huddie Ledbetter, and the Staging of Circulation," in *Performance in the Borderlands*, edited by Ramón Rivera-Servera and Harvey Young (Chippenham, UK: Palgrave Macmillan, 2010).

79. John Lomax, quoted in Carl Engel, *Archive of American Folk Song: A History*, Alan Lomax Collection, American Folklife Collection, Library of Congress, Washington, DC (hereafter AL Collection).

80. Letter from John Lomax to Oliver Strunk, October 1, 1934, AL Collection.

81. Profits from Ledbetter's stage, screen, and recording-studio performances were split three ways, two-thirds to the Lomaxes, one-third to Ledbetter—an economically exploitative relationship that was perversely legitimized by the obscuring of Ledbetter's professional past. Szwed, *Alan Lomax*, 75.

82. Porterfield, *Last Cavalier*, 343.

83. Floyd J. Calvin, "Around the World," *New York Amsterdam News*, February 27, 1937.

84. Kenton Jackson, "Two Time Dixie Murderer Sings Way to Freedom," *Philadelphia Independent*, January 6, 1935, JAL Papers, box 3D200.

85. Caleb Smith, in his assessment of Parchman Prison recordings, identifies prison song's supposedly rehabilitative effects; singing offered the opportunity to "open the walls of the cellular soul so that the self escapes, merging with the chorus." C. Smith, *The Prison and the American Imagination*, 167.

86. See Carby, *Cultures in Babylon*; Filene, *Romancing the Folk*; Porterfield, *Last Cavalier*; and Wolfe and Lornell, *The Life and Legend of Leadbelly*.

87. Alan Lomax, *Alan Lomax: Selected Writings, 1934–1997*, edited by Ronald Cohen (New York: Routledge, 2003), 198.

88. Letter from John Lomax to Oliver Strunk, October 1, 1934, AL Collection.

89. See Filene, *Romancing the Folk*, 58; and Porterfield, *Last Cavalier*, 331.

90. John Lomax and Alan Lomax, *Negro Folk Songs as Sung by Lead Belly* (New York: Macmillan, 1936), 33; letter from John Lomax to Ruby Terrill, September 24, 1934, JAL Papers, box 3D150.

91. "Lomax Arrives with Lead Belly, Negro Minstrel; Sweet Singer of the Swamplands Here to Do a Few Tunes Between Homicides," *New York Herald Tribune*, January 3, 1935.

92. Lawrence Gellert, "Lawrence Gellert's Reply," *New Masses*, December 11, 1934, 21–22.

93. There has been a great deal of controversy about whether or not John Lomax forced Ledbetter to wear his prison clothes on stage. Ledbetter was indeed required to perform in the work clothes (overalls) that were common for twentieth-century Southern prisoners, though, as Lomax noted in *Negro Folk Songs as Sung by Lead Belly*, Ledbetter "always hated to wear them" (36). He did not regularly wear stripes on stage, but he wore them in the *March of Time* newsreel and in the Harlem reenactment that followed. Szwed points out that prison stripes were often associated with stage comedy: "When

convicts were characters in stage shows, usually as part of early novelty acts, they were always in striped clothes." Szwed, *Alan Lomax*, 73.

94. Hurston, *Mules and Men*, 10.

95. Letter from John Lomax to Ruby Terrill, August 13, 1933, JAL Papers, box 3D149. Alan Lomax also discusses these practices in the 1990 film *The Land Where the Blues Began*. In the film we see him staging a similar re-creation with a group of men who are building a railroad.

96. Letter from John Lomax to Ruby Terrill, September 26, 1934, JAL Papers, box 3D150.

97. Raymond Fielding, *The March of Time: 1935–1951* (New York: Oxford University Press, 1978), 41.

98. Some of these impersonations were, in fact, *too* perfect. Fielding recounts President Franklin Roosevelt's displeasure with the program's impersonations of his voice, as statements made by "President Roosevelt" on the program were frequently attributed to Roosevelt himself. Fielding, *The March of Time*, 15.

99. Eric Barnouw, *Documentary: A History of the Non-fiction Film* (New York: Oxford University Press, 1974), 121.

100. Wolfe and Lornell, *The Life and Legend of Leadbelly*, 164.

101. Porterfield, *Last Cavalier*, 357.

102. Harlem's nightlife is chronicled in rich detail by Langston Hughes in *The Big Sea: An Autobiography* (New York: Hill and Wang, 1940), as well as in more contemporary works, such as those by George Chauncey (*Gay New York: Gender, Urban Culture, and the Making of the Gay Male World, 1890–1940* [New York: Basic Books, 1994]) and Shane Vogel (*The Scene of Harlem Cabaret: Race, Sexuality, Performance* [Chicago: University of Chicago Press, 2009]).

103. Pigmeat Markham, "Interview with Tony Bruno," *Artist and Influence* 13 (April 18, 1972): 154.

104. Tuliza Fleming, "It's Showtime! The Birth of the Apollo Theater," in *Ain't Nothing Like the Real Thing: The Apollo Theater and American Entertainment*, edited by Richard Carlin and Kinshasha Holman Conwill (Washington, DC: Smithsonian Books, 2010), 75.

105. Lonnie Bunch III, "The Apollo: A Place of Possibility," in *Ain't Nothing Like the Real Thing: The Apollo Theater and American Entertainment*, edited by Richard Carlin and Kinshasha Holman Conwill (Washington, DC: Smithsonian Books, 2010), 16.

106. Ted Fox, *Showtime at the Apollo: The Story of Harlem's World Famous Theater* (Cambridge, MA: Da Capo Press, 2003), 13.

107. Fox, *Showtime at the Apollo*, 17.

108. Fox, *Showtime at the Apollo*, 67.

109. Bobby Schiffman quoted in Fox, *Showtime at the Apollo*, 18.

110. *New York Age* quoted in Fox, *Showtime at the Apollo*, 74.

111. The amplification of the Apollo established a certain kind of preferred sound. From the beginning, the Apollo advertised itself as a leader in new amplification technologies; an ad in the *New York Age* announced the opening of the theater: "Dear Friends and Patrons, The opening of the 125th Street Apollo Theatre next Friday night will mark a revolutionary step in the presentation of stage shows. . . . Courtesy and consideration will be the watchword of the management, truly a resort for the better people. High-Fidelity RCA sound equipment, the same as used by Radio City Music Hall, and an in-

novation in public address systems, has been installed." Chris Albertson, *Bessie* (New Haven, CT: Yale University Press, 2003), 233.

112. Willie the Lion Smith with George Hoefer, *Music on My Mind* (London: MacGibbon and Kee, 1965), 101.

113. Jack Schiffman, *Harlem Heyday* (New York: Prometheus Books, 1984), 54.

114. Schiffman quoted in Herb Boyd, "The Apollo and Civil Rights," in *Ain't Nothin' Like the Real Thing: The Apollo Theater and American Entertainment*, edited by Richard Carlin and Kinshasha Holman Conwill (Washington, DC: Smithsonian Books, 2010), 170.

115. Quoted in Wolfe and Lornell, *The Life and Legend of Leadbelly*, 189.

116. R. Russell, "Illuminating the Leadbelly Legend,"12.

117. The James Weldon Johnson and Grace Nail Papers, box 82, folder 614. Beinecke Rare Book and Manuscript Library, Yale University, New Haven, CT.

118. Michael Denning, *The Cultural Front: The Laboring of American Culture in the Twentieth Century* (New York: Verso, 1997), xvi.

119. Denning, *The Cultural Front*, 360. Denning goes on to identify jazz and Tin Pan Alley as the representative sounds of cultural-front life, an observation that links the musical life of the Apollo with that of the stages and cabarets that hosted numerous benefits to support the Spanish Civil War and various relief efforts.

120. Alfred Brennan, no title, *TAC* (March 1939): 19.

121. Wolfe and Lornell, *The Life and Legend of Leadbelly*, 205.

122. Wolfe and Lornell, *The Life and Legend of Leadbelly*, 206.

123. In reorienting Ledbetter's political point of view, I take my cue from Denning's assessment of Billie Holiday who, "unlike many political artists, . . . was not an intellectual." Denning goes on to observe that the tendency to ascribe the label of "political artist" only to those who also presented themselves as public intellectuals is misguided: "Most of the people who made up the Popular Front social movement were not intellectuals, and their political convictions and activities grew out of the political formations in their neighborhoods and workplaces" (*The Cultural Front*, 328). Like many of his contemporaries, including Holiday, Count Basie, Duke Ellington, and Paul Robeson, Ledbetter performed at dozens of Popular Front events, not as simply another gig, but as a lending of his energies and star power to a dynamic social movement. As Denning concludes, "The benefit concerts and the letterheads of the various ad hoc musicians' committees are not simply the ephemera of cultural history, but the traces of the intangible relationship between a popular star, the star's audience, and a political movement" (*The Cultural Front*, 333).

124. Huddie Ledbetter quoted in Wolfe and Lornell, *The Life and Legend of Leadbelly*, 210.

125. Richard Wright, "Huddie Ledbetter, Famous Negro Folk Artist, Sings the Songs of Scottsboro and His People," *Daily Worker*, August 12, 1937.

126. See Adam Gussow's *Seems Like Murder Here: Southern Violence and the Blues Tradition* (Chicago: University of Chicago Press, 2002) for his analysis of blues lyrics' pervasive references to lynching.

127. See Glenda Gilmore, *Defying Dixie: The Radical Roots of Civil Rights, 1919–1950* (New York: W. W. Norton, 2009).

128. Stephen Biel, *Down with the Old Canoe: A Cultural History of the Titanic Disaster* (New York: W. W. Norton, 1996), 115.

129. Wright, "Huddie Ledbetter, Famous Negro Folk Artist, Sings the Songs of Scottsboro and His People," August 12, 1937.

130. For a rich account of the cultural activities of the National Negro Congress during World War II, see Erik Gellman, *Death Blow to Jim Crow: The National Negro Congress and the Rise of Militant Civil Rights* (Chapel Hill: University of North Carolina Press, 2011), 165–212.

131. Celeste Bernier, *African American Visual Arts: From Slavery to the Present* (Chapel Hill: University of North Carolina Press, 2008), 130–31.

132. *Christian Science Monitor*, February 28, 1939.

133. "Program to Aid 'Okies,'" *New York Times*, February 28, 1940, 22.

134. Wolfe and Lornell, *The Life and Legend of Leadbelly*, 216.

135. "Program to Aid 'Okies,'" *New York Times*, February 28, 1940, 22.

136. Joe Klein, *Woody Guthrie: A Life* (New York: Random House, 1980), 146.

137. Ledbetter can be thought of as a central player in what Denning has named "migrant narratives," the sometimes satirical, sometimes deeply earnest representations of people on the move during the Great Depression. Denning, *The Cultural Front*, 259–82.

THREE SOUTHERN EXPOSURE

1. C. P. Lee, *From Manchester to the Mississippi*, BBC 4 Radio Documentary, first broadcast November 13, 2008.

2. Philip Auslander, *Liveness: Performance in a Mediatized Culture* (London: Routledge, 1999).

3. Walter Benjamin, "The Task of the Translator," in *Illuminations: Essays and Reflections*, edited by Hannah Arendt, translated by Harry Zohn (New York: Schocken Books, 1968), 70.

4. I thank Brent Hayes Edwards, Emily Coates, and Lacina Coulibaly for this insight.

5. Benjamin, "The Task of the Translator," 70.

6. Benjamin, "The Task of the Translator," 78.

7. Benjamin, "The Task of the Translator," 72.

8. Benjamin, "The Task of the Translator," 76; brackets in the original.

9. Tejaswini Niranjana, *Siting Translation: History, Post-structuralism, and the Colonial Context* (Berkeley: University of California Press, 1992), 3. Johannes Fabian's *Time and the Other: How Anthropology Makes Its Object* (New York: Columbia University Press, 1983) usefully outlines the process by which colonized or subjugated peoples are accorded a premodern or primitive temporal identity.

10. Dizzy Gillespie quoted in Penny Von Eschen, *Satchmo Blows Up the World: Jazz Ambassadors Play the Cold War* (Cambridge, MA: Harvard University Press, 2004), 34.

11. Antitheatrical sentiment governed the State Department tours as well, where theatricality stood at odds with high art modernism. Von Eschen notes that Katherine Dunham was excluded from the tours because her dances were considered by one official to be too "theatrical in the cheapest sense." Von Eschen, *Satchmo Blows Up the World*, 22.

12. Von Eschen, *Satchmo Blows Up the World*, 8.

13. Von Eschen, *Satchmo Blows Up the World*, 187–88.

14. In his introduction to *Cross the Water Blues*, Neil Wynn identifies several nineteenth-century touring groups, including Major Dumbledon's Ethiopian Serenaders

(1848), Georgia Minstrels (1866), and Fisk Jubilee Singers (1870s and beyond). Neil Wynn, "'Why I Sing the Blues': African American Music in the Transatlantic World," *Cross the Water Blues: African American Music in Europe*, edited by Neil Wynn (Jackson: University Press of Mississippi, 2007), 11. For a history of the minstrel show in nineteenth-century Britain, see Stephen Johnson's online database, The Juba Project: Early Blackface Minstrelsy in Britain, 1842–1852, http://www.utm.utoronto.ca/~w3minstr/index.html; and Michael Pickering, *Blackface Minstrelsy in Britain* (Aldershot, UK: Ashgate, 2008).

15. Roberta Freund Schwartz, *How Britain Got the Blues: The Transmission and Reception of American Blues Style in the United Kingdom* (Aldershot, UK: Ashgate, 2007), 2–9.

16. Paul Oliver's book, *Blues Fell This Morning: Meaning in the Blues* (Cambridge, UK: Cambridge University Press, 1960), appeared in 1960, while Samuel B. Charters's *The Country Blues* (New York: Da Capo Press, 1959), was published in 1959.

17. Ulrich Adelt, *Blues Music in the Sixties: A Story in Black and White* (New Brunswick, NJ: Rutgers University Press, 2010), 96.

18. Adelt, *Blues Music in the Sixties*, 1.

19. Skiffle likely derived its name from Dan Burley and His Skiffle Boys, an American folk blues ensemble headed by Dan Burley, the young *Chicago Defender* sportswriter who took some of the early publicity photographs of Paramount's classic blues artists. The ensemble, which included Brownie McGhee, played throughout Chicago in the 1940s.

20. Hamp had already introduced northern English audiences to many new musical groups—including Freddie and the Dreamers, the Hollies, Little Richard, the Beatles, and the Dakotas—on his news-magazine program *Scene at 6:30*. Many significant blues television programs were taped in Manchester, most with live audiences; the year before *The Blues and Gospel Train*, Hamp produced *I Hear the Blues*, also for Granada. Also featuring a live audience, though this time in studio, *I Hear the Blues* showcased Sonny Boy Williamson, Muddy Waters, Memphis Slim, Willie Dixon, and Victoria Spivey.

21. Paul Oliver, "Festival Blues: The American Blues Festival, 1964," *Jazz Monthly*, December 1964, 4.

22. Adelt, *Blues Music in the Sixties*, 63–64.

23. Adelt, *Blues Music in the Sixties*, 88.

24. Adelt, *Blues Music in the Sixties*, 40. The only time dance was encouraged on the tours was in the television studio, and then only as ethnographic adornment to the scenes of Southern pastoral staged by programs such as *Jazz Heard and Seen*.

25. Oliver, "Festival Blues," 4.

26. Brownie McGhee, interview with Anthony Connors and Robert Neff, audio cassette, Robert Neff and Anthony Connors Blues Collection, Oral History of American Music, Yale University, New Haven, CT.

27. Schwartz, *How Britain Got the Blues*, 100, 111.

28. Sherrie Tucker, *Swing Shift: "All-Girl" Bands of the 1940s* (Durham, NC: Duke University Press, 2000).

29. John Postgate, "Random Reflections," *Jazz Journal* 10, no. 2 (April 1964): 2.

30. Charles Wolfe and Kip Lornell, *The Life and Legend of Leadbelly* (New York: HarperCollins, 1992), 227.

31. Francis Davis, *The History of the Blues: The Roots, the Music, the People* (Cambridge, MA: Da Capo Press, 1993), 172.

32. McGhee, interview with Neff and Connors.

33. McGhee, interview with Neff and Connors.

34. Michael Denning, *The Cultural Front: The Laboring of American Culture in the Twentieth Century* (New York: Verso, 1997), 325.

35. Langston Hughes, *The Ballad of the Man Who Went to War*. Typescript. Langston Hughes Papers. James Weldon Johnson Collection in the Yale Collection of American Literature, Beinecke Rare Book and Manuscript Library, Yale University, New Haven, CT, box 273, folder 4482.

36. John Szwed, *Alan Lomax: The Man Who Recorded the World* (New York: Penguin, 2011), 206.

37. Langston Hughes, *The Ballad of the Man Who Went to War*.

38. Langston Hughes, *The Ballad of the Man Who Went to War*.

39. Langston Hughes, *The Ballad of the Man Who Went to War*.

40. "Blues with Big Bill Broonzy, Sonny Terry, Brownie McGhee," interviewed by Studs Terkel. Recorded 1957, Folkways Records.

41. Brooks Atkinson, "New Play," *New York Times*, November 1, 1947.

42. E. Y. Harburg and Fred Saidy, *Finian's Rainbow: A Musical Satire*, music by Burton Lane (New York: Random House, 1947), 3, 13.

43. Izzy, "Reviewer Tabs 'Finian's Rainbow' Big Hit in N.Y.," *Pittsburgh Courier*, January 18, 1947. One dissenting note was offered prior to the production's opening by Lou Swarz of the *Baltimore Afro-American*, who opined: "Speaking of a mixed cast, the wise thing (my belief) is for Canada Lee (made up as white in a show), to just play the parts, no makeup, since he is a great actor anyway. Do Amos and Andy make up to play colored characters?" Lou Swarz, "Lou Swarz' Breezy Items," *Baltimore Afro-American*, October 12, 1946.

44. The Irish actor Albert Sharpe, who traveled to the United States to play the role of Finian, was similarly positioned as an authenticating agent of the satirical musical.

45. Langston Hughes and David Martin, *Simply Heavenly: A Comedy with Music* (New York: Dramatists Play Service, 1959), 6.

46. Hughes and Martin, *Simply Heavenly*, 6.

47. A representative tale appears in Francis Davis's *The History of the Blues*: "A funny story: Brownie and Sonny were given roles as strolling blues singers in the original Broadway production of Tennessee Williams's *Cat on a Hot Tin Roof*. It was explained to them that since their songs served as cues to the actors, they would have to sing them the same way every night. They said they couldn't possibly do that, then quickly changed their minds when they found out how much they would be paid for sticking to the script" (172).

48. Brooks Atkinson, "Theatre: Tennessee Williams' *Cat*," *New York Times*, March 25, 1955; Eric Bentley, "Theatre," *The New Republic* (April 11, 1955), 132.

49. "Cat on a Hot Tin Roof Hits Loop with a Bang," *Chicago Defender*, May 18, 1957, 8.

50. Tennessee Williams, *Cat on a Hot Tin Roof* (New York: New Directions, 2004), 15.

51. Gayle Wald, *Shout, Sister, Shout! The Untold Story of Rock-and-Roll Trailblazer Sister Rosetta Tharpe* (Boston: Beacon Press, 2007), 171. I am particularly indebted to Wald's biography of Tharpe, from which I draw much of the information presented here.

52. Pleasant "Cousin Joe" Joseph and Harriet J. Ottenheimer, *Cousin Joe: Blues from New Orleans* (Chicago: University of Chicago Press, 1987), 8–10.

53. G. Wald, *Shout, Sister, Shout!*, 45.

54. G. Wald, *Shout, Sister, Shout!*, 38, 91, 154.

55. *Cue*, 1944, clippings file, Billy Rose Theatre Division, New York Public Library for the Performing Arts, New York.

56. G. Wald, *Shout, Sister, Shout!*, 82–85.

57. G. Wald, *Shout, Sister, Shout!*, 141.

58. "Cotton Club, N.Y.," *Variety*, May 8, 1940, clippings file, Billy Rose Theatre Division, New York Public Library for the Performing Arts, New York.

59. "Apollo, N.Y.," *Variety*, July 19, 1939, clippings file, Billy Rose Theatre Division, New York Public Library for the Performing Arts, New York.

60. Joseph and Ottenheimer, *Cousin Joe*, 8–9.

61. "Singer Swings Same Songs in Church and Night Club," *Life*, August 28, 1939, clippings file, Billy Rose Theatre Division, New York Public Library for the Performing Arts, New York.

62. Sister Rosetta Tharpe, "Bonus Track: The Wedding," *Sister Rosetta Tharpe: The One and Only Queen of Hot Gospel*. CD released by Upbeat Recordings, 2011.

63. Johnnie Hamp, interview with the author. June 1, 2010. Manchester, UK.

64. Granada was an early contractor of Independent Television (ITV), the first commercial television network in Britain.

65. Joseph and Ottenheimer, *Cousin Joe*, 165.

66. Hamp, interview with the author.

67. Hamp, interview with the author.

68. Adelt, *Blues Music in the Sixties*, 49.

69. Samuel Charters quoted in Adelt, *Blues Music in the Sixties*, 49.

70. Oliver, "Festival Blues," 4.

71. Adelt, *Blues Music in the Sixties*, 78–79.

72. Adelt, *Blues Music in the Sixties*, 85.

73. Adelt, *Blues Music in the Sixties*, 89.

74. Adelt, *Blues Music in the Sixties*, 91.

75. Adelt, *Blues Music in the Sixties*, 91.

76. All quotations from televised events are my own transcription.

77. Sarita Malik, *Representing Black Britain: Black and Asian Images on Television* (London: Sage Publications, 2002), 113.

78. Stephen Bourne, *Black in the British Frame: The Black Experience in British Film and Television* (London: Continuum Press, 2001), 4.

79. G. Wald, *Shout, Sister, Shout!*, 187.

80. G. Wald, *Shout, Sister, Shout!*, 105–6.

81. Joseph and Ottenheimer, *Cousin Joe*, 165.

82. Joseph and Ottenheimer, *Cousin Joe*, 84.

83. Joseph and Ottenheimer, *Cousin Joe*, 92–93.

84. Wynn, "'Why I Sing the Blues,'" 15.

85. G. Wald, *Shout, Sister, Shout!*, 161.

86. See David Williams, *First Time We Met the Blues: A Journey of Discovery with Jimmy Page, Brian Jones, Mick Jagger, and Keith Richards* (York, UK: Music Mentor Books, 2009); as well as the liner notes by Mike Rowe from *American Folk Blues Festival, 1962–1966*, vols. 1–4, produced by David Peck, Jon Kanis, Janie Hendrix, and John McDermott (San Diego: Reelin' In the Years Productions and Experience Hendrix, 2003), DVDs.

87. Brian Ward, *Just My Soul Responding: Rhythm and Blues, Black Consciousness, and Race Relations* (Berkeley: University of California Press, 1998), 175.

88. Eric Burdon, "An 'Animal' Views America," *Ebony*, December 1966, 161.

89. I thank Joel Anderson for calling my attention to the possible implications of the Beeching Report and railway "reform."

90. Anthony Sampson, *Anatomy of Britain Today* (New York: Harper and Row, 1965), 580.

91. Dave Russell, "Music and Northern Identity, 1890–c.1965," in *Northern Identities: Historical Interpretations of "The North" and "Northernness,"* edited by Neville Kirk (Aldershot, UK: Ashgate, 2000), 24.

92. "'Man-Made Hell' in South Lancashire," *Manchester Guardian*, January 9, 1964.

93. "The Fat South and the Lean North," *Manchester Guardian*, January 2, 1964.

94. "The South-east versus the Rest," *Manchester Guardian*, March 20, 1964.

95. Despite Helen Jewell's persuasive illustration of the medieval roots of the English North-South divide, most histories of the divide identify the industrial nineteenth century as the key moment in the growth of regional sensibilities throughout the island nation. See Helen Jewell, *The North-South Divide: The Origins of Northern Consciousness in England* (Manchester, UK: Manchester University Press, 1994).

96. Brian Ward, "By Elvis and All the Saints: Images of the American South in the World of 1950s British Popular Music," in *Britain and the American South: From Colonialism to Rock and Roll*, edited by Joseph P. Ward (Jackson: University Press of Mississippi, 2003), 187–213. See Helen Taylor's *Circling Dixie: Contemporary Southern Culture through a Transatlantic Lens* (New Brunswick, NJ: Rutgers University Press, 2001) and Joseph P. Ward's edited collection *Britain and the American South: From Colonialism to Rock and Roll* (Jackson: University Press of Mississippi, 2003) for accounts of mutual affiliations between British Northern and American Southern people and cultural institutions.

97. All transcriptions from *The Blues and Gospel Train* are my own.

98. Hamp, interview with the author.

99. While many previous scholars had accepted working-class solidarity between industrial British workers and black Southerners as given truth, Peter d'A Jones dismisses this position as a "myth" in the epilogue of Mary Ellison's *Support for Secession*, which tackled the widely held opinion that British Northerners supported emancipation and the Union. Jones attributed the myth to "the English Radical-Liberals . . . , Marx and Engels . . . , and Americans." Peter d'A Jones, "The History of a Myth," epilogue to *Support for Secession: Lancashire and the American Civil War*, by Mary Ellison (Chicago: University of Chicago Press, 1972), 200. In recent years, however, R. J. M. Blackett has articulated a more moderate position in his *Divided Hearts: Britain and the American Civil War* (Baton Rouge: Louisiana State University Press, 2001). Blackett depicts Northern England as contested ground, a place where supporters of both the Union and the Confederacy successfully solicited people's attachments and identifications. Blackett challenges Ellison's argument that Lancashire cotton workers were universally supportive of the Confederacy because of their own economic self-interest. He also works against analyses that suggest that support for the Union or Confederacy was exclusively and universally determined by class. Blackett and Ellison agree when it comes to their assessment of Manchester: when measured against other towns and cities of the North, Manchester had comparatively more vocal supporters of the Union in its midst, and city residents saw themselves as supporters of the Union and of emancipation; this self-perception

enabled Mancunians to distance themselves from rival cities, especially Liverpool, which Ellison calls "the most Southern of cities." Mary Ellison, *Support for Secession: Lancashire and the American Civil War* (Chicago: University of Chicago Press, 1972), 47. See also Duncan Andrew Campbell's *English Public Opinion and the American Civil War* (Suffolk, UK: Boydell Press, 2003) for a nuanced analysis of attitudes toward British neutrality. Frank Owsley's *King Cotton Diplomacy: Foreign Relations of the Confederate States of America* (Chicago: University of Chicago Press, 1936) remains an important, if disputed, source.

100. Stephen Yafa, *Cotton: The Biography of A Revolutionary Fiber* (New York: Penguin, 2006), 130.

101. Lawrence Grossman, "'A Total Misconception': Lincoln, the Civil War, and the British, 1860–1865," in *The Global Lincoln*, edited by Richard Carwardine and Jay Sexton (New York: Oxford University Press, 2011), 107.

102. Blackett, *Divided Hearts*, 17.

103. Blackett, *Divided Hearts*, 105.

104. Poster appears as plate in Blackett, *Divided Hearts*.

105. R. J. M. Blackett, *Building an Anti-slavery Wall* (Baton Rouge: Louisiana State University Press, 1983), 5, 23.

106. Blackett, *Building an Anti-slavery Wall*, 177–78.

107. Blackett, *Building an Anti-slavery Wall*, 202.

108. Adam I. P. Smith, "'The Stuff Our Dreams Are Made Of': Lincoln in the English Imagination," in *The Global Lincoln*, edited by Richard Carwardine and Jay Sexton (New York: Oxford University Press, 2011), 133.

109. The statue, sculpted by George Gray Barnard and donated by the Cincinnati residents Charles Phelps Taft and his wife, was originally meant to stand outside London's Parliament but was so disliked that it went to Manchester. Critics excoriated the depiction of Lincoln as less than heroic, "a shambling figure with apparently distended hands crossed in front of his abdomen, alarmingly large feet and strangely sloping shoulders." Adam I. P. Smith, "'The Stuff Our Dreams Are Made Of,'" 132.

110. I borrow the phrase *love and theft* from Eric Lott, *Love and Theft: Blackface Minstrelsy and the American Working Class* (New York: Oxford University Press, 1995).

111. Hamp, interview with the author.

112. Nicole Fleetwood, "'Busing It' in the City: Black Youth, Performance, and Public Transit," *TDR* 48, no. 2 (2004): 36. Robin D. G. Kelley has seized on the metaphor of "moving theaters" to describe Birmingham's buses during World War II, playing on a double meaning of *theater* as both "a site of performance and . . . a site of military conflict." Robin D. G. Kelley, *Race Rebels: Culture, Politics, and the Black Working Class* (New York: Simon and Schuster, 1996), 55–57.

113. Elizabeth Abel, *Signs of the Times: The Visual Politics of Jim Crow* (Berkeley: University of California Press, 2010), 2.

114. Guido van Rijn, "'Climbing the Mountain Top': African American Blues and Gospel Songs from the Civil Rights Years," in *Media, Culture, and the Modern African American Freedom Struggle*, edited by Brian Ward (Gainesville: University Press of Florida, 2001), 123.

115. C. P. Lee, *From Manchester to the Mississippi*.

116. This front-page story excoriated the Republican platform and the nomination of Goldwater for "embodying almost all the worst aspects of a certain strain of American thought." "A Packet of Misinformation," *Guardian*, July 14, 1964, 1.

117. Hella Pick, "Hope of Finding Vanished Civil Rights Men Fading," *Manchester Guardian Weekly*, July 2, 1964.

118. Mike Phillips and Trevor Phillips, *Windrush: The Irresistible Rise of Multi-racial Britain* (Toronto: HarperCollins Canada, 1998), 6.

119. Paul Gilroy, *"There Ain't No Black in the Union Jack": Cultural Politics of Race and Nation* (London: Routledge, 1992), 172.

120. Phillips and Phillips's *Windrush: The Irresistible Rise of Multi-racial Britain* provides a useful overview of the experience of Caribbean immigrants to the United Kingdom.

121. Brian Ward, "Forgotten Wails and Master Narratives: Media, Culture, and Memories of the African American Freedom Struggle," in *Media, Culture, and the Modern African American Freedom Struggle*, edited by Brian Ward (Gainesville: University Press of Florida, 2001), 5.

122. Hamp, interview with the author.

123. Hamp, interview with the author.

124. Melon the Librarian, *"Gone With the Wind—A Wartime PR Success,"* *Melon the Librarian* (blog), February 9, 2012, accessed July 3, 2013. http://melonthelibrarian.wordpress.com/2012/02/09/gone-with-the-wind-a-wartime-pr-success/.

125. Tucker, *Swing Shift*, 6.

126. Walter Benjamin, "Theses on the Philosophy of History," in *Illuminations: Essays and Reflections*, edited by Hannah Arendt, translated by Harry Zohn (New York: Schocken Books, 1968), 261.

127. Benjamin, "The Task of the Translator," 71.

FOUR   HIGHWAY 61 REVISITED

1. Walter Benjamin, *The Arcades Project*, edited by Rolf Teidemann, translated by Howard Eiland and Kevin McLaughlin (Cambridge, MA: Harvard University Press, 1999), 406.

2. *New York Herald Tribune*, January 14, 1935.

3. Alan Lomax, *The Land Where the Blues Began* (New York: Pantheon Books, 1993).

4. The title of Steve Cheseborough's popular guide, *Blues Traveling: The Holy Sites of the Delta Blues* (Jackson: University Press of Mississippi, 2001), for example, conflates the tour and the pilgrimage.

5. There have been few scholarly inquiries into blues tourism; the most sustained and significant is Stephen A. King's *I'm Feeling the Blues Right Now: Blues Tourism and the Mississippi Delta* (Jackson: University Press of Mississippi, 2011).

6. Scott Romine, *Real South: Southern Narrative in the Age of Cultural Reproduction* (Baton Rouge: Louisiana State University Press, 2008), 2. See also Tara McPherson's *Reconstructing Dixie: Race, Gender, and Nostalgia in the Imagined South* (Durham, NC: Duke University Press, 2003) for its analysis of the late twentieth-century circulation of the cultural signs and symbols of "the South."

7. Since 2005 I have made several visits to Clarksdale; while there I attended musical performances and festivals; interviewed musicians, residents, tourists, and tourist-industry officials; and analyzed a variety of touristic sites, such as historic markers, hotels, tourist literature and ephemera, museums, and performance venues.

8. James C. Cobb, *The Most Southern Place on Earth: The Mississippi Delta and the Roots of Regional Identity* (New York: Oxford University Press, 1992); Alan Lomax, *The Land Where the Blues Began* (New York: Pantheon Books, 1993); David Lewis Cohn, *Where I Was Born and Raised* (Cambridge, MA: Houghton Mifflin, 1948), 12; Nina Simone, "Mississippi Goddam," *Nina Simone in Concert*, Philips Records, recorded 1964, CD.

9. For background on the Mississippi Delta and its musical histories, see Cobb, *The Most Southern Place on Earth*; Ted Gioia, *Delta Blues* (New York: W. W. Norton, 2008); Nicholas Lemann, *The Promised Land: The Great Black Migration and How It Changed America* (New York: Vintage Press, 1992); Elijah Wald, *Escaping the Delta: Robert Johnson and the Invention of the Blues* (New York: HarperCollins, 2004); and Clyde Woods, *Development Arrested: Race, Power, and the Blues in the Mississippi Delta* (New York: Verso, 1996).

10. Bill Talbot, interview with the author, September 11, 2005. Clarksdale, MS.

11. Woods, *Development Arrested*, 2.

12. See Cobb, *The Most Southern Place on Earth*; and Woods, *Development Arrested*, for geologic and indigenous histories of the Delta region prior to its nineteenth-century settlement by planters and loggers from the east.

13. See John Dittmer, *Local People: The Struggle for Civil Rights in Mississippi* (Champaign: University of Illinois Press, 1995); Françoise Hamlin, *Crossroads at Clarksdale: The Black Freedom Struggle in the Mississippi Delta after World War II* (Chapel Hill: University of North Carolina Press, 2012); Aaron Henry and Constance Curry, *Aaron Henry: The Fire Ever Burning* (Jackson: University Press of Mississippi, 2000); and Charles M. Payne, *I've Got the Light of Freedom: The Organizing Tradition and the Mississippi Freedom Struggle* (Berkeley: University of California Press, 2007).

14. "Distribution of Total Population by Federal Poverty Level," Henry J. Kaiser Family Foundation, accessed August 3, 2013, http://www.statehealthfacts.org/compare maptable.jsp?ind=9&cat=1&sub=2&yr=274&typ=2; "Poverty Rate by Age," Henry J. Kaiser Family Foundation, accessed August 3, 2013, http://kff.org/other/state-indicator/ poverty-rate-by-age/.

15. See "Estimated Numbers of HIV Diagnoses, Adults and Adolescents," Henry J. Kaiser Family Foundation, accessed August 3, 2013, http://kff.org/hivaids/state-indicator/ estimated-numbers-of-hiv-diagnoses-adults-and-adolescents/; "Incarceration Rate per 100,000 Men, by State and Race / Ethnicity, 2008," Henry J. Kaiser Family Foundation, accessed August 3, 2013, http://kff.org/disparities-policy/state-indicator/incarceration -rate/; "Life Expectancy at Birth (in Years)," Henry J. Kaiser Family Foundation, accessed August 3, 2013, http://kff.org/other/state-indicator/life-expectancy/; "Median Annual Household Income," Henry J. Kaiser Family Foundation, accessed August 3, 2013, http://kff.org/other/state-indicator/median-annual-income/; "Percent of Adults Who Are Overweight or Obese," Henry J. Kaiser Family Foundation, accessed August 3, 2013, http://kff.org/other/state-indicator/adult-overweightobesity-rate/; "Percent of Adults Who Have Ever Been Told by a Doctor That They Have Diabetes," Henry J. Kaiser Family Foundation, accessed August 3, 2013, http://kff.org/other/state-indicator/adults -with-diabetes/#table; and "Percent of Live Births That Are Low-Birthweight, by State and Race/Ethnicity, 2003–2005," Henry J. Kaiser Family Foundation, accessed August 3, 2013, http://kff.org/disparities-policy/state-indicator/low-birthweight-infants/.

16. "Poverty Rate by Race/Ethnicity," Henry J. Kaiser Family Foundation, accessed August 3, 2013, http://kff.org/other/state-indicator/poverty-rate-by-raceethnicity/.

While the majority of Clarksdale residents identify as African American or white, the region is much more ethnically diverse than is generally recognized. Chinese immigrants arrived in Mississippi after the Civil War, serving, for a time, as replacement laborers for planters forced to release African American slaves. Descendants of Italian, Lebanese, Mexican, Jewish, and German immigrants live in Clarksdale. The organizing black-white binaries of Jim Crow have historically produced a delicate negotiation of racial and ethnic identities and relations, as immigrants attempted to secure a position of "whiteness" in the segregated South.

17. "American FactFinder—Results," U.S. Census Data and American Community Survey results, accessed February 8, 2014, http://factfinder2.census.gov/faces/tableservices/jsf/pages/productview.xhtml?pid=ACS_12_5YR_DP03.

18. "Local Area Unemployment Statistics Map," U.S. Department of Labor, Bureau of Labor Statistics, accessed August 3, 2013, http://data.bls.gov/map/MapToolServlet?survey=la&map=county&seasonal=u. Search terms: Mississippi, Coahoma County.

19. Ali Colleen Neff, *Let the World Listen Right: The Mississippi Delta Hip-Hop Story* (Jackson: University Press of Mississippi, 2009), 6.

20. Woods, *Development Arrested*, 4.

21. Marybeth Hamilton, *In Search of the Blues* (New York: Basic Books, 2008).

22. S. King, *I'm Feeling the Blues Right Now*, 59.

23. "First Lady Hillary Rodham Clinton, U.S. Transportation Secretary Slater Announce 16 National Millennium Trails," White House Millennium Council, accessed January 29, 2014, http://clinton2.nara.gov/Initiatives/Millennium/trails_doc.html.

24. A Bill Designating the Year Beginning February 1, 2003, as the "Year of the Blues," S. Res. 316, 107th Cong., 2d sess. (2002).

25. Woods, *Development Arrested*, 261.

26. Charlotte Buchen and Ria Nurrachman, "Messenger's," produced, directed, and edited by Charlotte Buchen and Ria Nurrachman, 2005, accessed July 9, 2013, www.vimeo.com/m/7068430.

27. S. King, *I'm Feeling the Blues Right Now*, 12.

28. While promoters of local tourism rarely fail to mention the multiracial makeup of the tourist population, I met few black tourists during my many visits to Clarksdale over multiple years.

29. Becky Gillette, "Banking on the Blues," *Delta Business Journal*, July 2010, reprinted on the website of the B.B. King Museum and Delta Interpretive Center, accessed August 3, 2013, http://www.bbkingmuseum.org/banking-on-the-blues.

30. S. King, *I'm Feeling the Blues Right Now*, 11–12. On the other hand, package tours have begun to spring up. Nashville's Sweet Magnolia company, for example, offers a ten-day extended bus tour from Nashville to New Orleans that passes through Memphis and the Mississippi Delta.

31. Carol Stack, *Call to Home: African Americans Reclaim the Rural South* (New York: Basic Books, 1996).

32. Adam Fisher, "Blues Travelers," *New York Times Style Magazine*, May 17, 2012, accessed August 3, 2013, http://www.nytimes.com/2012/05/18/t-magazine/mississippi-blues-travelers.html?pagewanted=all&_r=1&.

33. E. Wald, *Escaping the Delta*, 41.

34. S. King, *I'm Feeling the Blues Right Now*, 39.

35. S. King, *I'm Feeling the Blues Right Now*, 145–49.

36. Jennifer L Eichstedt and Stephen Small, *Representations of Slavery: Race and Ideology in Southern Plantation Museums* (Washington, DC: Smithsonian Institution Press, 2002), 101.

37. Jessica Adams, *Wounds of Returning: Race, Memory, and Property on the Post-slavery Plantation* (Chapel Hill: University of North Carolina Press, 2007), 20.

38. "Weddings and Romance," accessed February 8, 2014, http://www.visitnatchez.com/custom/webpage.cfm?content=content&id=145&cat=WeddingsRomance; "Getaways for Girlfriends," accessed February 8, 2014, http://www.visitnatchez.com/custom/webpage.cfm?content=content&id=201&cat=GetawaysForGirlfriends.

39. Adams, *Wounds of Returning*, 64.

40. Eichstedt and Small, *Representations of Slavery*, 129–30.

41. The term *poverty tourism* gained traction in the early twenty-first century as a way to describe wealthy tourists' visits to developing countries. Closely linked to *dark tourism*, which promotes visits to sites of tragedy, terror, and other forms of suffering, poverty tourism has been championed for raising awareness and funneling money into needy local economies and criticized for exploiting impoverishment without contributing any lasting change. See John Lennon and Malcolm Foley, *Dark Tourism: The Attraction of Death and Disaster* (London: Continuum, 2000).

42. The only time I have ever witnessed these buildings' inclusion on a tourist itinerary was when they were pointed out during a historical bus tour led by Robert Birdsong during the 2010 Juke Joint Festival.

43. *Clarksdale Register*, March 24, 1915.

44. S. King, *I'm Feeling the Blues Right Now*, 109.

45. Neal Moore, "Livin' the Blues with James 'Super Chikan' Johnson—II," CNN iReport, October 29, 2009, accessed August 3, 2013, http://ireport.cnn.com/docs/DOC-347817.

46. After his death, Ratliff's daughter Zelena Ratliff became the hotel's proprietor.

47. Dean MacCannell, *The Tourist: A New Theory of the Leisure Class* (New York: Schocken Books, 1976), 100; John Urry, *The Tourist Gaze* (London: Sage Publications, 2002), 11. Erving Goffman, *The Presentation of Self in Everyday Life* (New York: Doubleday, 1959), 106–40.

48. Schechner defines performance as, alternately "restored behavior" and "twice-behaved behavior." While both terms imply a kind of doubleness or repetition, "twice-behaved behavior" implies a doubleness localized to one actor: the actor in rehearsal and then in performance, for example, or the teacher who introduces herself anew at the beginning of each semester. I use "restored behavior," here, however, because it gestures toward a repetition that is not limited to a single actor; it suggests a cultural or collective repetition. In this way, historical reenactors can "perform" a history they have never directly experienced. Richard Schechner, *Between Theater and Anthropology* (Philadelphia: University of Pennsylvania Press, 1985), 36.

49. Barbara Kirshenblatt-Gimblett, *Destination Culture: Tourism, Museums, and Heritage* (Berkeley: University of California Press, 1998), 7.

50. Jeff Green, "Historic Preservation and Community Identity," PDF Fact Sheet located at "Benefits of Rail-Trails," Rails-to-Trails Conservancy, accessed August 3, 2013, http://www.railstotrails.org/ourWork/trailBasics/benefits.html#preservation.

51. Richard Knight, *The Blues Highway: New Orleans to Chicago* (Surrey, UK: Trailblazer Productions, 2003), back cover; MacCannell, *The Tourist*, 5. Though primarily concerned with the status of the tourist, MacCannell suggests a dialectical relationship between tourism and diaspora, while arguing that "it would be theoretically and morally wrong to equate the forced nomadism and homelessness of the refugee and the impoverished with the supercilious voluntaristic Abercrombie and Fitch tourist or other soldiers of fortune" (xxiii).

52. Joseph Roach, *Cities of the Dead: Circum-Atlantic Performance* (New York: Columbia University Press, 1996), 2.

53. Rebecca Schneider, *Performing Remains: Art and War in Times of Theatrical Reenactment* (Oxon, UK: Routledge, 2011), 27.

54. Scott Magelssen, "'This Is a Drama. You Are Characters': The Tourist as Fugitive Slave in Conner Prairie's 'Follow the North Star,'" *Theatre Topics* 16, no. 1 (2006): 21.

55. Bob Dylan, *Chronicles*, vol. 1 (New York: Simon and Schuster, 2004), 240–41.

56. The term *narrative of descent* is from Robert Stepto's *From Behind the Veil: A Study of Afro-American Narrative* (Champaign: University of Illinois Press, 1979).

57. "What to See and Do," *Clarksdale Press Register*, November 16, 2000, accessed February 8, 2014, http://www.pressregister.com/article_ce905987-6f69-5d0c-842a-362217b5d5f1.html.

58. Cheseborough, *Blues Traveling*, 3.

59. Cotten Seiler, *Republic of Drivers: A Cultural History of Automobility in America* (Chicago: University of Chicago Press, 2008).

60. Kris Lackey, *Road Frames: The American Highway Narrative* (Lincoln: University of Nebraska Press, 1997), 42.

61. Seiler, *Republic of Drivers*, 18–19.

62. Seiler, *Republic of Drivers*, 23.

63. Jack Kerouac, *On the Road* (New York: Viking Press, 1957).

64. Seiler, *Republic of Drivers*, 72.

65. Seiler, *Republic of Drivers*, 78–79.

66. Hamilton, *In Search of the Blues*, 241.

67. Robin Bernstein, "Dances with Things: Material Culture and the Performance of Race," *Social Text* 27, no. 4 (2009): 68–69.

68. Bernstein, "Dances with Things," 69–70.

69. Jim O'Neal, *Delta Blues Map Kit* (Kansas City, MO: Bluesoterica, 2004), unpaginated. Two excellent accounts of the circulation of the Johnson myth are Patricia Schroeder's *Robert Johnson, Mythmaking, and Contemporary American Culture* (Champaign: University of Illinois Press, 2004); and Elijah Wald's *Escaping the Delta*.

70. Describing the Beulah crossroads, where the 1986 *Crossroads* was filmed, the guidebook author Cheseborough betrays the Möbius-strip relationship between tales of the crossroads and grounds of touristic authenticity: "Since it was really the movie *Crossroads* that popularized the whole crossroads-devil-blues concept, the movie's crossroads could be considered the 'real' one." Cheseborough, *Blues Traveling*, 106.

71. I borrow the distinction between substantive and transitive from Nick Kaye. In his study *Site-Specific Art: Performance, Place, and Documentation* (New York: Routledge, 2000), Kaye distinguishes between "substantive" (positivist) and "transitive" (mobile,

processual) approaches to sites, arguing that it is performance that works to destabilize substantive understandings of site.

72. Houston A. Baker Jr., *Blues, Ideology, and Afro-American Literature: A Vernacular Theory* (Chicago: University of Chicago Press, 1984), 8.

73. Clifford Krauss, "Mississippi Farmers Trade Cotton Plantings for Corn," *New York Times*, May 6, 2009.

74. Tom Downs, *Blues and BBQ* (Melbourne, Australia: Lonely Planet Publications, 2005), 4.

75. Peter Aschoff, wall text, 2010, Delta Blues Museum, Clarksdale, MS.

76. S. King, *I'm Feeling the Blues Right Now*, 90.

77. A. Lomax, *The Land Where the Blues Began*, 18.

78. See Tara McPherson's trenchant critique in *Reconstructing Dixie* of Southern hospitality as masquerade; as with femininity, she notes, it is "conscious and compulsory" and rests on fictional imaginings of antebellum race relations (157).

79. Stepto, *From Behind the Veil*, 167.

80. *Feel Like Going Home, The Blues*, season 1, episode 1, directed by Martin Scorsese, written by Peter Guralnick, produced by Sam Pollard, aired on PBS on September 28, 2003.

81. The film's hagiography of the Lomaxes is illustrated, ironically, with a still from the *March of Time* newsreel, shot with Lead Belly clad in prison stripes. At no point is it acknowledged that this image is a constructed reenactment, not a historic representation.

82. Henry Louis Gates Jr.'s *African American Lives* television series played a crucial role in stimulating this renewed interest in African origins, as did Oprah Winfrey's 2005 revelation that she had taken a DNA test that determined her origins to be Zulu. See Alondra Nelson's "Bio Science: Genetic Genealogy Testing and the Pursuit of African Ancestry," *Social Studies of Science* 38, no. 5 (2008), for its incisive assessment not only of new paradigms in genetic testing but also the extent to which self-fashioning and "genealogical aspirations" inform such practices.

83. See Sandra Richards, "What Is to Be Remembered? Tourism to Ghana's Slave Castle-Dungeons," *Theatre Journal* 57 (2005): 617–37.

84. In addition to soliciting tourists' return "home," performances of homecoming regularly grace the stages of Clarksdale blues tourism. From the year 2000 until his death in 2011, Joe Willie "Pinetop" Perkins, a boogie-woogie blues piano star, returned to the Hopson Plantation—now the site of the Shack Up Inn—for the Pinetop Perkins Homecoming, celebrating his birthday at a self-nominated birthplace of the blues. Perkins lived and worked at Hopson until the 1940s; he is the plantation's most famous former resident. When Perkins passed away in 2011 at the age of ninety-seven, a local resident described to me the memorial service for Perkins as "Pinetop's final homecoming."

85. See Nina Silber, *The Romance of Reunion: Northerners and the South, 1865–1900* (Chapel Hill: University of North Carolina Press, 1993).

86. David Blight, *Race and Reunion: The Civil War in American Memory* (Cambridge, MA: Harvard University Press, 2001), 1–12.

87. Knight, *The Blues Highway*, 132.

88. "About House of Blues," House of Blues, accessed August 3, 2013, http://www.houseofblues.com/aboutHOB/.

89. Bill Talbot, interview with the author. September 11, 2005, Clarksdale, MS. In fact, this relocation of sharecropper cabins to a nineteenth-century arrangement was, as Charles Aiken notes, common practice in the mid-twentieth century and beyond, designed to clear the way for mechanized labor. Charles Aiken, *The Cotton Plantation South since the Civil War* (Baltimore, MD: Johns Hopkins University Press, 1998), 110.

90. Drinking is a significant part of the blues tourism industry in Clarksdale; many of the events emphasize the celebratory nature of the blues and the close connection between blues performance and illicit alcohol consumption during the era of Prohibition.

91. APRILRAZZ, "I found the ultimate white trash motel!," forum post on Pirate4x4 .com, October 27, 2007, accessed August 3, 2013, http://www.pirate4x4.com/forum/ general-chit-chat/625439-i-found-ultimate-white-trash-motel.html.

92. a1000yardstare, "Magical Experience," forum post on TripAdvisor.com, January 2, 2013, accessed August 3, 2013, http://www.tripadvisor.com/ShowUserReviews-g43722-d267750-r148581035-Shack_Up_Inn-Clarksdale_Mississippi.html.

93. Matt Wray, *Not Quite White: White Trash and the Boundaries of Whiteness* (Durham, NC: Duke University Press, 2006), 135.

94. Adams, *Wounds of Returning*, 59.

95. Kirshenblatt-Gimblett, *Destination Culture*, 4.

96. Roach, *Cities of the Dead*, 36.

97. In fact, Waters's original home on the Stovall plantation had four rooms. The reconstruction of only a singular room, especially in a way that so closely resembles the "shacks" of the Shack Up Inn, suggests a more impoverished setting than the one in which Waters actually lived.

98. Kirshenblatt-Gimblett, *Destination Culture*, 54.

99. While spelled *jook* by Zora Neale Hurston and others in the early twentieth century, *juke* is now more commonly used. The Juke Joint Festival invites tourists to visit the Southern sites that inspired the urban House of Blues venues, and its stated aims are commemorative and economic, both "educat[ing] and enlight[ing] native Deltans and blues tourists alike through a series of performances, exhibits, and presentations involving music, art, storytelling, film, and children's events" and "mix[ing] visitors with locals and showcas[ing] the economic power of cultural tourism, turning average Deltans into ambassadors for the region." "About Us: Juke Joint Festival; 2013—10th Annual Edition of Juke Joint Festival & Related Events!," Juke Joint Festival, accessed August 3, 2013, http://www.jukejointfestival.com/about.php. Clarksdale Downtown Development Association, composed of Roger Stolle, Goldie Hirsberg, and Nan Hughes, is the organizing body of the Juke Joint Festival.

100. Kirshenblatt-Gimblett, *Destination Culture*, 59.

101. Kirshenblatt-Gimblett, *Destination Culture*, 74.

102. Perhaps not coincidentally, Mathus, a former band member of the Squirrel Nut Zippers and Clarksdale's favorite son, has recently undertaken a foray into musical theater—his 2010 revue *Mosquitoville* also played on the Delta Cinema stage.

103. Roger Stolle quoted in Matt Marshall, "Juke Joint Festival in Mississippi Kicks Off Blues Festival Season," *American Blues Scene*, April 8, 2011, accessed August 3, 2013, http://www.americanbluesscene.com/2011/04/juke-joint-festival-in-mississippi-kicks -off-blues-festival-season/; emphasis added.

104. Harlem rent parties, common during the twenties and thirties, were Northern, urban renditions of the jook-joint festivities. See Valerie Boyd, *Wrapped in Rainbows: The Life of Zora Neale Hurston* (New York: Scribner, 2003), 95; and Katrina Hazzard-Gordon, *Jookin': The Rise of Social Dance Formations in African American Culture* (Philadelphia: Temple University Press, 1990).

105. Zora Neale Hurston, "Characteristics of Negro Expression," in *Sweat*, edited by Cheryl Wall (New Brunswick, NJ: Rutgers University Press, 1997), 67.

106. Hurston, "Characteristics of Negro Expression," 67, 70–71.

107. See Juliet Gorman's website "Jukin' It Out: Contested Visions of Florida in New Deal Narratives," May 2001, accessed August 3, 2013, http://www.oberlin.edu/library/papers/honorshistory/2001-Gorman/, which examines Marion Post Wolcott's photographs and the documentary work of the Works Progress Administration. Gorman connects Wolcott's early photography of the Group Theatre with the theatricality of her juke-joint photographic compositions.

108. See Ken Murphy and Scott Barretta, *Mississippi: State of the Blues* (Bay St. Louis, MS: Proteus/Ken Murphy Publishing, 2010). The book is a collaboration between the photographer Murphy and the blues writer Barretta, and its photographs composed a special exhibit in the Delta Blues Museum in the spring of 2011.

109. Adams, *Wounds of Returning*, 6.

110. Robert Palmer, *Deep Blues* (New York: Penguin, 1982), 253. Neff, *Let the World Listen Right*.

111. Buchen and Nurrachman, "Messenger's." Moore, "Livin' the Blues with James 'Super Chikan' Johnson."

112. I draw the title of this section from Chuck Klosterman's book *Killing Yourself to Live: 85% of a True Story* (New York: Scribner, 2005). Why, Klosterman asks, is a spectacular death the greatest career move for a musician? See David Honeyboy Edwards, as told to Janis Martinson and Michael Frank, *The World Don't Owe Me Nothing* (Chicago: Chicago Review Press, 1997), 105.

113. Such events seem to happening ever more frequently; many well-known musicians—Pinetop Perkins, Sam Carr, Big Jack Johnson, Mr. Tater the Music Maker, T-Model Ford, and Honeyboy Edwards—passed away between 2009 and 2013.

114. Caryn Rousseau, "David 'Honeyboy' Edwards Dead at 96," *Huffington Post*, August 29, 2011, accessed August 3, 2013, http://www.huffingtonpost.com/2011/08/29/david-honey-boy-edwards-d_n_941203.html.

115. Schneider, *Performing Remains*, 101.

116. Roach, *Cities of the Dead*, 31.

ARCHIVAL COLLECTIONS CONSULTED

Alan Lomax Collection, American Folklife Collection, Library of Congress, Washington, DC.

Billy Rose Theatre Division, New York Public Library for the Performing Arts, New York.

James Weldon Johnson and Grace Nail Johnson Papers, Beinecke Rare Book and Manuscript Library, Yale University, New Haven, CT.

James Weldon Johnson Collection, Yale Collection of American Literature, Beinecke Rare Book and Manuscript Library, Yale University, New Haven, CT.

John Avery Lomax Family Papers, 1842 and 1853–1986, Dolph Briscoe Center for American History, University of Texas, Austin.

Sandra Lieb Collection, Blues Archive, the Department of Archives and Special Collections, J.D. Williams Library, University of Mississippi, Oxford.

NEWSPAPERS AND PERIODICALS CONSULTED

Baltimore Afro-American
Chicago Defender
Clarksdale Banner
Clarksdale Challenge
Clarksdale Daily Register
Indianapolis Freeman
Jazz Journal
Jazz Monthly
Manchester Guardian
Manchester Guardian Weekly
New York Amsterdam News
New York Times
Philadelphia Tribune
Pittsburgh Courier
Sing Out!

BOOKS AND ARTICLES

Abbott, Lynn, and Doug Seroff. *Ragged but Right: Black Traveling Shows, "Coon Songs," and the Dark Pathway to Blues and Jazz*. Jackson: University Press of Mississippi, 2007.

———. "'They Cert'ly Sound Good to Me': Sheet Music, Southern Vaudeville, and the Commercial Ascendancy of the Blues." *American Music* 14, no. 4 (1996): 402–54.

Abel, Elizabeth. *Signs of the Times: The Visual Politics of Jim Crow*. Berkeley: University of California Press, 2010.

Abrahams, Roger D. "Mr. Lomax Meets Professor Kittredge." *Journal of Folklore Research* 37, no. 2 (2000): 99–118.

Adams, Jessica. *Wounds of Returning: Race, Memory, and Property on the Post-slavery Plantation*. Chapel Hill: University of North Carolina Press, 2007.

Adams, Jessica, Michael Bibler, and Cécile Accilien, eds. *Just below South: Intercultural Performance in the Caribbean and the U.S. South*. Charlottesville: University of Virginia Press, 2007.

Adelt, Ulrich. *Blues Music in the Sixties: A Story in Black and White*. New Brunswick, NJ: Rutgers University Press, 2010.

Aiken, Charles. *The Cotton Plantation South since the Civil War*. Baltimore, MD: Johns Hopkins University Press, 1998.

Albee, Edward. The Sandbox *and* The Death of Bessie Smith. New York: Penguin, 1988.

Albertson, Chris. *Bessie*. New Haven, CT: Yale University Press, 2003.

Anderson, Benedict. *Imagined Communities: Reflections on the Origin and Spread of Nationalism*. London: Verso, 1983.

Apter, Emily. "Acting Out Orientalism: Sapphic Theatricality in Turn-of-the-Century Paris." In *Performance and Cultural Politics*, edited by Elin Diamond, 15–34. London: Routledge, 1996.

Auslander, Philip. *Liveness: Performance in a Mediatized Culture*. London: Routledge, 1999.

———. "Musical Personae." TDR 50, no. 1 (2006): 100–119.

———. *Performing Glam Rock: Gender and Theatricality in Popular Music*. Ann Arbor: University of Michigan Press, 2006.

Baker, Houston A., Jr. *Blues, Ideology, and Afro-American Literature: A Vernacular Theory*. Chicago: University of Chicago Press, 1984.

———. *Modernism and the Harlem Renaissance*. Chicago: University of Chicago Press, 1987.

Barish, Jonas. *The Antitheatrical Prejudice*. Berkeley: University of California Press, 1981.

Barlow, William. *Looking Up at Down: The Emergence of Blues Culture*. Philadelphia: Temple University Press, 1980.

Barnouw, Eric. *Documentary: A History of the Non-fiction Film*. New York: Oxford University Press, 1974.

Barrett, Lindon. *Blackness and Value: Seeing Double*. Cambridge, UK: Cambridge University Press, 1999.

Baudrillard, Jean. *America*. London: Verso Press, 1988.

Benjamin, Walter. *The Arcades Project*. Edited by Rolf Teidemann. Translated by Howard Eiland and Kevin McLaughlin. Cambridge, MA: Harvard University Press, 1999.

———. "The Task of the Translator." In *Illuminations: Essays and Reflections*, edited by Hannah Arendt, translated by Harry Zohn, 69–82. New York: Schocken Books, 1968.

———. "Theses on the Philosophy of History." In *Illuminations: Essays and Reflections*, edited by Hannah Arendt, translated by Harry Zohn, 253–64. New York: Schocken Books, 1968.

Benston, Kimberly. "Listen Br'er Sterling: The Critic as Liar [A Pre(r)amble to Essays on Sterling Brown]." *Callaloo* 21, no. 4 (1998): 837–45.

Bernhardt, Clyde, as told to Sheldon Harris. *I Remember: Eighty Years of Black Entertainment, Big Bands, and the Blues; An Autobiography*. Philadelphia: University of Pennsylvania Press, 1986.

Bernier, Celeste. *African American Visual Arts: From Slavery to the Present*. Chapel Hill: University of North Carolina Press, 2008.

Bernstein, Robin. "Dances with Things: Material Culture and the Performance of Race." *Social Text* 27, no. 4 (2009): 67–94.

Biel, Stephen. *Down with the Old Canoe: A Cultural History of the Titanic Disaster*. New York: W. W. Norton, 1996.

Blackett, R. J. M. *Building an Anti-slavery Wall*. Baton Rouge: Louisiana State University Press, 1983.

———. *Divided Hearts: Britain and the American Civil War*. Baton Rouge: Louisiana State University Press, 2001.

Blassingame, John, and Henry Louis Gates Jr. Foreword to *Sterling A. Brown: Building the Black Aesthetic Tradition*, by Joanne V. Gabbin, ix–xiii. Charlottesville: University of Virginia Press, 1994.

Blight, David. *Race and Reunion: The Civil War in American Memory*. Cambridge, MA: Harvard University Press, 2001.

Bourne, Stephen. *Black in the British Frame: The Black Experience in British Film and Television*. London: Continuum Press, 2001.

Boyd, Herb. "The Apollo and Civil Rights." In *Ain't Nothin' Like the Real Thing: The Apollo Theater and American Entertainment*, edited by Richard Carlin and Kinshasha Holman Conwill, 170–73. Washington, DC: Smithsonian Books, 2010.

Boyd, Valerie. *Wrapped in Rainbows: The Life of Zora Neale Hurston*. New York: Scribner, 2003.

Brady, Erika. *A Spiral Way: How the Phonograph Changed Ethnography*. Jackson: University Press of Mississippi, 1999.

Brooks, Daphne A. *Bodies in Dissent: Spectacular Performances of Race and Freedom, 1850–1910*. Durham, NC: Duke University Press, 2003.

———. "'Sister, Can You Line It Out?' Zora Neale Hurston and the Sound of Angular Black Womanhood." *Amerikastudien/American Studies* 55, no. 4 (2010): 617–27.

———. "'This Voice Which Is Not One': Amy Winehouse Sings the Ballad of Sonic Blue(s)face Culture." *Women and Performance: A Journal of Feminist Theory* 20, no. 1 (2010): 37–60.

Brown, Elsa Barkley. "Negotiating and Transforming the Public Sphere: African American Political Life in the Transition from Slavery to Freedom." *Public Culture* 7 (1994): 107–46.

Brown, Jayna. *Babylon Girls: Black Women Performers and the Shaping of the Modern*. Durham, NC: Duke University Press, 2008.

Brown, Sterling A. "Ma Rainey." In *The Collected Poems of Sterling A. Brown*, edited by Michael S. Harper, 62–63. Evanston, IL: TriQuarterly Books, 1980.

———. *Negro Poetry and Drama and* The Negro in American Fiction. New York: Atheneum, 1972.

Bunch, Lonnie, III. "The Apollo: A Place of Possibility." In *Ain't Nothing Like the Real Thing: The Apollo Theater and American Entertainment*, edited by Richard Carlin and Kinshasha Holman Conwill, 14–17. Washington, DC: Smithsonian Books, 2010.

Burdon, Eric. "An 'Animal' Views America." *Ebony*, December 1966, 161–70.

Calt, Stephen, and Gayle Dean Wardlow. "The Buying and Selling of Paramounts, Part 3." *78 Quarterly* 5 (1990): 7–24.

Campbell, Duncan Andrew. *English Public Opinion and the American Civil War*. Suffolk, UK: Boydell Press, 2003.

Canning, Charlotte. "The Platform versus the Stage: Circuit Chautauqua's Antitheatrical Theater." *Theater Journal* 50, no. 3 (1998): 303–18.

Carby, Hazel V. *Cultures in Babylon: Black Britain and African America*. New York: Verso, 1999.

———. *Race Men*. Cambridge, MA: Harvard University Press, 1998.

Charters, Samuel B. *The Country Blues*. New York: Da Capo Press, 1959.

Chauncey, George. *Gay New York: Gender, Urban Culture, and the Making of the Gay Male World, 1890–1940*. New York: Basic Books, 1994.

Cheseborough, Steve. *Blues Traveling: The Holy Sites of the Delta Blues*. Jackson: University of Mississippi Press, 2001.

Clifford, James. "Diasporas." *Cultural Anthropology* 9, no. 3 (1994): 302–38.

Cobb, James C. *The Most Southern Place on Earth: The Mississippi Delta and the Roots of Regional Identity*. New York: Oxford University Press, 1992.

Cohn, David Lewis. *Where I Was Born and Raised*. Cambridge, MA: Houghton Mifflin, 1948.

Davis, Angela Y. *Blues Legacies and Black Feminism: Gertrude "Ma" Rainey, Bessie Smith, and Billie Holiday*. New York: Vintage, 1999.

Davis, Francis. *The History of the Blues: The Roots, the Music, the People*. Cambridge, MA: Da Capo Press, 1993.

Davis, Keith. *The Passionate Observer: Photographs by Carl Van Vechten*. Albuquerque: University of New Mexico Press, 1993.

Davis, Mary. *Classic Chic: Music, Fashion, Modernism*. Berkeley: University of California Press, 2008.

Davis, Tracy C. *Actresses as Working Women: Their Social Identity in Victorian Culture*. New York: Routledge, 1991.

DeFrantz, Thomas. "Popular Dance of the 1920s and Early '30s." In *Ain't Nothing Like the Real Thing: The Apollo Theater and American Entertainment*, edited by Richard Carlin and Kinshasha Holman Conwill, 66–70. Washington, DC: Smithsonian Books, 2010.

Denning, Michael. *The Cultural Front: The Laboring of American Culture in the Twentieth Century*. New York: Verso, 1997.

Dittmer, John. *Local People: The Struggle for Civil Rights in Mississippi*. Champaign: University of Illinois Press, 1995.

Downs, Tom. *Blues and BBQ*. Melbourne, Australia: Lonely Planet Publications, 2005.

Du Bois, W. E. B. "Krigwa Players Little Negro Theatre: The Story of a Little Theatre Movement." *Crisis* 32, no. 3 (1926): 134–36.

———. "The Problem of Amusement." In *Du Bois on Religion*, edited by Phil Zuckerman, 19–28. New York: AltaMira Press, 2000.

———. *The Souls of Black Folk*. New York: Dover Publications, 1994.

Dylan, Bob. *Chronicles*. Vol. 1. New York: Simon and Schuster, 2004.

Edwards, Brent Hayes. *The Practice of Diaspora: Literature, Translation, and the Rise of Black Internationalism*. Cambridge, MA: Harvard University Press, 2003.

Edwards, David Honeyboy, as told to Janis Martinson and Michael Frank. *The World Don't Owe Me Nothing*. Chicago: Chicago Review Press, 1997.

Eichstedt, Jennifer L., and Stephen Small. *Representations of Slavery: Race and Ideology in Southern Plantation Museums*. Washington, DC: Smithsonian Institution Press, 2002.

Ellison, Mary. *Support for Secession: Lancashire and the American Civil War*. Chicago: University of Chicago Press, 1972.

Ernest, John. "Introduction: The Emergence of Henry 'Box' Brown." In *Narrative of Henry Box Brown, Written by Himself*, edited by John Ernest, 1–38. Chapel Hill: University of North Carolina Press, 2008.

Fabian, Johannes. *Time and the Other: How Anthropology Makes Its Object*. New York: Columbia University Press, 1983.

Faulkner, William. *Absalom, Absalom!* New York: Vintage, 1987.

Favor, J. M. *Authentic Blackness: The Folk in the New Negro Renaissance*. Durham, NC: Duke University Press, 1999.

Féral, Josette. "Theatricality: The Specificity of Theatrical Language." Translated by Ronald P. Bermingham. *SubStance* 31, no. 2 (2002): 94–108.

Fielding, Raymond. *The March of Time: 1935–1951*. New York: Oxford University Press, 1978.

Filene, Benjamin. *Romancing the Folk: Public Memory and American Roots Music*. Chapel Hill: University of North Carolina Press, 2000.

Fleetwood, Nicole. "'Busing It' in the City: Black Youth, Performance, and Public Transit." *TDR* 48, no. 2 (2004): 33–48.

Fleming, Tuliza. "It's Showtime! The Birth of the Apollo Theater." In *Ain't Nothing Like the Real Thing: The Apollo Theater and American Entertainment*, edited by Richard Carlin and Kinshasha Holman Conwill, 72–83. Washington, DC: Smithsonian Books, 2010.

Foucault, Michel. "Nietzsche, Genealogy, History." In *Language, Counter-memory, Practice: Selected Essays and Interviews*, edited by D. F. Bouchard, 139–64. Ithaca, NY: Cornell University Press, 1977.

Fox, Ted. *Showtime at the Apollo: The Story of Harlem's World Famous Theater*. Cambridge, MA: Da Capo Press, 2003.

Fulbright, Thomas. "Ma Rainey and I." *Jazz Journal* 9, no. 3 (March 1956): 1–2, 26.

Furlonge, Nicole. "An Instrument Blues-Tinged: Listening, Language, and the Everyday in Sterling Brown's 'Ma Rainey.'" *Callaloo* 21, no. 4 (1998): 969–84.

Gabbin, Joanne V. *Sterling A. Brown: Building the Black Aesthetic Tradition*. Charlottesville: University of Virginia Press, 1994.

Gaines, Kevin. *Uplifting the Race: Black Leadership, Politics, and Culture in the Twentieth Century*. Chapel Hill: University of North Carolina Press, 1996.

Gates, Henry Louis, Jr. *The Signifying Monkey: A Theory of African American Literary Criticism*. New York: Oxford University Press, 1989.

Gellman, Erik. *Death Blow to Jim Crow: The National Negro Congress and the Rise of Militant Civil Rights*. Chapel Hill: University of North Carolina Press, 2011.

Gilman, Sander. "Salome, Syphilis, Sarah Bernhardt, and the 'Modern Jewess.'" *German Quarterly* 66, no. 2 (1993): 195–211.

Gilmore, Glenda. *Defying Dixie: The Radical Roots of Civil Rights, 1919–1950*. New York: W. W. Norton, 2009.

Gilroy, Paul. *"There Ain't No Black in the Union Jack": Cultural Politics of Race and Nation*. London: Routledge, 1992.

Gioia, Ted. *Delta Blues*. New York: W. W. Norton, 2008.

Goffman, Erving. *The Presentation of Self in Everyday Life*. New York: Doubleday, 1959.

Greeson, Jennifer. *Our South: Geographic Fantasy and the Rise of National Literature*. Cambridge, MA: Harvard University Press, 2010.

Gregory, James A. *American Exodus: The Dust Bowl Migration and Okie Culture in California*. New York: Oxford University Press, 1989.

———. *The Southern Diaspora: How the Great Migrations of White and Black Southerners Transformed America*. Chapel Hill: University of North Carolina Press, 2005.

Griffin, Farah Jasmine. "When Malindy Sings: A Meditation on Black Women's Vocality." In *Uptown Conversation: The New Jazz Studies*, edited by Robert G. O'Meally, Brent Hayes Edwards, and Farah Jasmine Griffin, 102–25. New York: Columbia University Press, 2004.

Grossman, Lawrence. "'A Total Misconception': Lincoln, the Civil War, and the British, 1860–1865." In *The Global Lincoln*, edited by Richard Carwardine and Jay Sexton, 107–22. New York: Oxford University Press, 2011.

Gussow, Adam. *Seems Like Murder Here: Southern Violence and the Blues Tradition*. Chicago: University of Chicago Press, 2002.

Hamilton, Marybeth. *In Search of the Blues*. New York: Basic Books, 2008.

Hamlin, Françoise. *Crossroads at Clarksdale: The Black Freedom Struggle in the Mississippi Delta after World War II*. Chapel Hill: University of North Carolina Press, 2012.

Handy, W. C. *Father of the Blues: An Autobiography*. New York: Macmillan, 1941.

Harburg, E. Y., and Fred Saidy. *Finian's Rainbow: A Musical Satire*. Music by Burton Lane. New York: Random House, 1947.

Harrison, Daphne Duval. *Black Pearls: Blues Queens of the 1920s*. New Brunswick, NJ: Rutgers University Press, 1988.

Hartman, Saidiya. *Scenes of Subjection: Terror, Slavery, and Self-Making in Nineteenth-Century America*. New York: Oxford University Press, 1997.

Hazzard-Gordon, Katrina. *Jookin': The Rise of Social Dance Formations in African American Culture*. Philadelphia: Temple University Press, 1990.

Hemenway, Robert E. *Zora Neale Hurston: A Literary Biography*. Champaign: University of Illinois Press, 1977.

Henry, Aaron, and Constance Curry. *Aaron Henry: The Fire Ever Burning*. Jackson: University Press of Mississippi, 2000.

Hirsch, Jerrold. *Portrait of America: A Cultural History of the Federal Writers' Project*. Chapel Hill: University of North Carolina Press, 2006.

Hughes, Langston. *The Big Sea: An Autobiography*. New York: Hill and Wang, 1940.

———. "The Negro Artist and the Racial Mountain." *The Nation*, June 23, 1926, 692–94.

———. "Trouble with the Angels." In *The American Stage: Writing on Theater from Washington Irving to Tony Kushner*, edited by Laurence Senelick, 419–24. New York: Library of America, 2010.

Hughes, Langston, and David Martin. *Simply Heavenly: A Comedy with Music*. New York: Dramatists Play Service, 1959.

Hurston, Zora Neale. "Characteristics of Negro Expression." In *Sweat*, edited by Cheryl Wall, 55–72. New Brunswick, NJ: Rutgers University Press, 1997.

———. *Dust Tracks on a Road*. In *Folklore, Memoirs, and Other Writings*, 557–808. New York: Library of America, 1995.

———. "How It Feels to Be Colored Me." In *I Love Myself When I Am Laughing . . . and Then Again: A Zora Neale Hurston Reader*, edited by Alice Walker, 152–55. New York: Feminist Press at the City University of New York, 1979.

———. *Mules and Men*. New York: HarperCollins, 1990.

———. "My People! My People!" In *Folklore, Memoirs, and Other Writings*, 719–33. New York: Library of America, 1995.

Jackson, Shannon. *Professing Performance: Theatre in the Academy from Philology to Performativity*. Cambridge, UK: Cambridge University Press, 2004.

Jewell, Helen. *The North-South Divide: The Origins of Northern Consciousness in England*. Manchester, UK: Manchester University Press, 1994.

Johnson, James Weldon. *Along This Way: The Autobiography of James Weldon Johnson*. New York: Da Capo Press, 1933.

———. *Black Manhattan*. New York: Da Capo Press, 1991.

———. "Now We Have the Blues." *Saturday Review of Literature*, June 19, 1926, 848.

———. "Race Prejudice and the Negro Artist." *Harper's Magazine*, November 1928, 769–76.

Jones, LeRoi. *Blues People: Negro Music in White America*. New York: Harper Perennial, 1963.

Jones, Lu Ann. *Mama Learned Us to Work: Farm Women in the New South*. Chapel Hill: University of North Carolina Press, 2002.

Jones, Peter d'A. "The History of a Myth." Epilogue to *Support for Secession: Lancashire and the American Civil War*, by Mary Ellison, 199–219. Chicago: University of Chicago Press, 1972.

Joseph, Pleasant "Cousin Joe," and Harriet J. Ottenheimer. *Cousin Joe: Blues from New Orleans*. Chicago: University of Chicago Press, 1987.

Kaplan, Carla, ed. *Zora Neale Hurston: A Life in Letters*. New York: Anchor Books, 2002.

Kaye, Nick. *Site-Specific Art: Performance, Place, and Documentation*. New York: Routledge, 2000.

Kelley, Robin D. G. "Notes on Deconstructing 'the Folk.'" *American Historical Review* 97, no. 5 (1992): 1400–1408.

———. *Race Rebels: Culture, Politics, and the Black Working Class*. New York: Simon and Schuster, 1996.

Kerouac, Jack. *On the Road*. New York: Viking Press, 1957.

Kibler, M. Alison. *Rank Ladies: Gender and Cultural Hierarchy in American Vaudeville*. Chapel Hill: University of North Carolina Press, 1999.

Killeen, Sean. "Lead Belly: More Than a Name." In *Lead Belly: A Life in Pictures*, edited by Tiny Robinson and John Reynolds, 19–20. London: Steidl Photography International, 2008.

King, Chris. "Curator for the Blues." *St. Louis Magazine*, April 2007, 242.

King, Stephen A. *I'm Feeling the Blues Right Now: Blues Tourism and the Mississippi Delta*. Jackson: University Press of Mississippi, 2011.

Kirby, Michael. "The New Theater." *Tulane Drama Review* 10, no. 2 (1965): 23–43.

Kirshenblatt-Gimblett, Barbara. *Destination Culture: Tourism, Museums, and Heritage*. Berkeley: University of California Press, 1998.

Klein, Joe. *Woody Guthrie: A Life*. New York: Random House, 1980.

Klosterman, Chuck. *Killing Yourself to Live: 85% of a True Story*. New York: Scribner, 2005.

Knight, Richard. *The Blues Highway: New Orleans to Chicago*. Surrey, UK: Trailblazer Productions, 2003.

Krasner, David. *A Beautiful Pageant: African American Theater, Drama, and Performance in the Harlem Renaissance, 1910–1927*. New York: Palgrave Macmillan, 2002.

———. *Resistance, Parody, and Double Consciousness in African American Theater, 1895–1910*. New York: St. Martin's Press, 1997.

Kraut, Anthea. *Choreographing the Folk: The Dance Stagings of Zora Neale Hurston*. Minneapolis: University of Minnesota Press, 2008.

Lackey, Kris. *Road Frames: The American Highway Narrative*. Lincoln: University of Nebraska Press, 1997.

Lemann, Nicholas. *The Promised Land: The Great Black Migration and How It Changed America*. New York: Vintage Press, 1992.

Lennon, John, and Malcolm Foley. *Dark Tourism: The Attraction of Death and Disaster*. London: Continuum, 2000.

Levine, Lawrence. *Black Culture and Black Consciousness*. New York: Oxford University Press, 1978.

Lieb, Sandra. *Mother of the Blues: A Study of Ma Rainey*. Amherst: University of Massachusetts Press, 1981.

Lipsitz, George. *The Possessive Investment in Whiteness*. Philadelphia: Temple University Press, 1998.

Locke, Alain. "The Negro Spirituals." In *The New Negro: Voices of the Harlem Renaissance*, edited by Alain Locke, 199–213. New York: Simon and Schuster, 1992.

Lockheart, Paula. "A History of Early Microphone Singing, 1925–1939: American Mainstream Popular Singing at the Advent of Electronic Microphone Amplification." *Popular Music and Society* 26, no. 3 (2003): 367–85.

Lomax, Alan. *Alan Lomax: Selected Writings, 1934–1997*. Edited by Ronald Cohen. New York: Routledge, 2003.

———. *The Land Where the Blues Began*. New York: Pantheon Books, 1993.

———. "Zora Neale Hurston—A Life of Negro Folklore." *Sing Out!* 10 (October/November 1960): 12.

Lomax, John A. *Adventures of a Ballad Hunter*. New York: Macmillan, 1947.

Lomax, John A. and Alan Lomax. *Negro Folk Songs as Sung by Lead Belly*. New York: Macmillan, 1936.

———, eds. *Our Singing Country: Folk Songs and Ballads*. Mineola, NY: Dover Publications, 2000.

Lott, Eric. *Love and Theft: Blackface Minstrelsy and the American Working Class*. New York: Oxford University Press, 1995.

MacCannell, Dean. *The Tourist: A New Theory of the Leisure Class*. New York: Schocken Books, 1976.

Magelssen, Scott. "'This Is a Drama. You Are Characters': The Tourist as Fugitive Slave in Conner Prairie's 'Follow the North Star.'" *Theatre Topics* 16, no. 1 (2006): 19–34.

Malik, Sarita. *Representing Black Britain: Black and Asian Images on Television*. London: Sage Publications, 2002.

Markham, Pigmeat. "Interview with Tony Bruno." *Artist and Influence* 13 (April 18, 1972): 152–62.

McAlister, Melani. *Epic Encounters: Culture, Media, and U.S. Interests in the Middle East since 1945*. Berkeley: University of California Press, 2005.

McGinley, Paige A. "'The Magic of Song!' John Lomax, Huddie Lebetter, and the Staging of Circulation." In *Performance in the Borderlands*, edited by Ramón Rivera-Servera and Harvey Young, 128–46. Chippenham, UK: Palgrave Macmillan, 2011.

McNamara, Brooks. "Popular Entertainment." In *The Cambridge History of American Theater, Volume 2*, edited by Don B. Wilmeth and Christopher Bigsby, 378–408. Cambridge: Cambridge University Press, 1999.

———. *Step Right Up*. Jackson: University Press of Mississippi, 1995.

McPherson, Tara. *Reconstructing Dixie: Race, Gender, and Nostalgia in the Imagined South*. Durham, NC: Duke University Press, 2003.

Miller, Karl Hagstrom. *Segregating Sound: Inventing Folk and Pop Music in the Age of Jim Crow*. Durham, NC: Duke University Press, 2010.

Miller, Monica. *Slaves to Fashion: Black Dandyism and the Styling of Black Diasporic Identity*. Durham, NC: Duke University Press, 2009.

Muir, Peter. *Long Lost Blues: Popular Blues in America, 1850–1920*. Champaign: University of Illinois Press, 2010.

Murphy, Ken, and Scott Barretta. *Mississippi: State of the Blues*. Bay St. Louis, MS: Proteus/Ken Murphy Publishing, 2010.

Naff, Alixa. *Becoming American: The Early Arab Immigrant Experience*. Carbondale: Southern Illinois University Press, 1985.

Neff, Ali Colleen. *Let the World Listen Right: The Mississippi Delta Hip-Hop Story*. Jackson: University Press of Mississippi, 2009.

Nelson, Alondra. "Bio Science: Genetic Genealogy Testing and the Pursuit of African Ancestry." *Social Studies of Science* 38, no. 5 (2008): 759–83.

Niranjana, Tejaswini. *Siting Translation: History, Post-structuralism, and the Colonial Context*. Berkeley: University of California Press, 1992.

Oakley, Giles. *The Devil's Music: A History of the Blues*. Cambridge, MA: Da Capo Press, 1997.

Oliver, Paul. *Barrelhouse Blues: Location Recording and the Early Traditions of the Blues*. New York: BasicCivitas Books, 2009.

———. *Bessie Smith*. London: Cassell Press, 1959.

———. *Blues Fell This Morning: Meaning in the Blues*. Cambridge, UK: Cambridge University Press, 1960.

———. *Conversation with the Blues*. Cambridge, UK: Cambridge University Press, 1965.

———. "Festival Blues: The American Blues Festival, 1964." *Jazz Monthly*, December 1964, 4.

———. *Songsters and Saints: Vocal Traditions on Race Records*. Cambridge, UK: Cambridge University Press, 1984.

O'Neal, Jim. *Delta Blues Map Kit*. Kansas City, MO: Bluesoterica, 2004.

O'Neal, Jim, and Amy van Singel. *The Voice of the Blues: Classic Interviews from Living Blues Magazine*. New York: Routledge, 2001.

Owsley, Frank. *King Cotton Diplomacy: Foreign Relations of the Confederate States of America*. Chicago: University of Chicago Press, 1936.

Palmer, Robert. *Deep Blues*. New York: Penguin, 1982.

Parks, Suzan-Lori. "From Elements of Style." In *The America Play, and Other Works*, 6–18. New York: Theatre Communications Group, 1995.

Payne, Charles M. *I've Got the Light of Freedom: The Organizing Tradition and the Mississippi Freedom Struggle*. Berkeley: University of California Press, 2007.

Phillips, Mike, and Trevor Phillips. *Windrush: The Irresistible Rise of Multi-racial Britain*. Toronto: HarperCollins Canada, 1998.

Pickering, Michael. *Blackface Minstrelsy in Britain*. Aldershot, UK: Ashgate, 2008.

Porterfield, Nolan. *Last Cavalier: The Life and Times of John A. Lomax, 1857–1948*. Champaign: University of Illinois Press, 2001.

Postgate, John. "Random Reflections." *Jazz Journal* 10, no. 2 (April 1964): 2.

Postlewait, Thomas, and Tracy C. Davis. "Theatricality: An Introduction." In *Theatricality*, edited by Tracy C. Davis and Thomas Postlewait, 1–39. Cambridge, UK: Cambridge University Press, 2003.

Pratt, Mary Louise. *Imperial Eyes: Travel and Transculturation*. New York: Routledge, 1992.

Pridgett, Thomas. "The Life of Ma Rainey, by Her Brother Thomas Pridgett." *Jazz Information*, September 6, 1940.

Retman, Sonnet. *Real Folks: Race and Genre in the Great Depression*. Durham, NC: Duke University Press, 2011.

Richards, Sandra. "What Is to Be Remembered? Tourism to Ghana's Slave Castle-Dungeons." *Theatre Journal* 57 (2005): 617–37.

Rijn, Guido van. "'Climbing the Mountain Top': African American Blues and Gospel Songs from the Civil Rights Years." In *Media, Culture, and the Modern African American Freedom Struggle*, edited by Brian Ward, 122–44. Gainesville: University Press of Florida, 2001.

Roach, Joseph. *Cities of the Dead: Circum-Atlantic Performance*. New York: Columbia University Press, 1996.

Romine, Scott. *Real South: Southern Narrative in the Age of Cultural Reproduction*. Baton Rouge: Louisiana State University Press, 2008.

Russell, Dave. "Music and Northern Identity, 1890–c. 1965." In *Northern Identities: Historical Interpretations of "The North" and "Northernness,"* edited by Neville Kirk, 23–46. Aldershot, UK: Ashgate, 2000.

Russell, Ross. "Illuminating the Lead Belly Legend." *Down Beat* 37, no. 15 (1970): 12–14, 33.

Sampson, Anthony. *Anatomy of Britain Today*. New York: Harper and Row, 1965.

Savran, David. *Highbrow/Lowdown: Theater, Jazz, and the Making of the New Middle Class*. Ann Arbor: University of Michigan Press, 2009.

Schechner, Richard. *Between Theater and Anthropology*. Philadelphia: University of Pennsylvania Press, 1985.

Schiffman, Jack. *Harlem Heyday*. New York: Prometheus Books, 1984.

Schneider, Rebecca. *Performing Remains: Art and War in Times of Theatrical Reenactment*. Oxon, UK: Routledge, 2011.

Schroeder, Patricia. *Robert Johnson, Mythmaking, and Contemporary American Culture*. Champaign: University of Illinois Press, 2004.

Schwartz, Roberta Freund. *How Britain Got the Blues: The Transmission and Reception of American Blues Style in the United Kingdom*. Aldershot, UK: Ashgate, 2007.

Schweitzer, Marlis. *When Broadway Was the Runway: Theater, Fashion, and American Culture*. Philadelphia: University of Pennsylvania Press, 2009.

Scott, James C. *Domination and the Arts of Resistance*. New Haven, CT: Yale University Press, 1990.

Seeger, Pete. "Lead Belly." In *Lead Belly: A Life in Pictures*, edited by Tiny Robinson and John Reynolds, 11–12. London: Steidl Photography International, 2008.

Seiler, Cotten. *Republic of Drivers: A Cultural History of Automobility in America*. Chicago: University of Chicago Press, 2008.

Silber, Nina. *The Romance of Reunion: Northerners and the South, 1865–1900*. Chapel Hill: University of North Carolina Press, 1993.

Small, Christopher. *Musicking: The Meanings of Performance and Listening*. Middletown, CT: Wesleyan University Press, 1998.

Smalls, James. *The Homoerotic Photography of Carl Van Vechten*. Philadelphia: Temple University Press, 2006.

Smith, Adam I. P. "'The Stuff Our Dreams Are Made Of': Lincoln in the English Imagination." In *The Global Lincoln*, edited by Richard Carwardine and Jay Sexton, 123–38. New York: Oxford University Press, 2011.

Smith, Caleb. *The Prison and the American Imagination*. New Haven, CT: Yale University Press, 2009.

Smith, Willie the Lion, with George Hoefer. *Music on My Mind*. London: MacGibbon and Kee, 1965.

Stack, Carol. *Call to Home: African Americans Reclaim the Rural South*. New York: Basic Books, 1996.

States, Bert O. "Phenomenology of the Curtain Call." *Hudson Review* 34, no. 3 (1981): 371–80.

Stepto, Robert. *From Behind the Veil: A Study of Afro-American Narrative*. Champaign: University of Illinois Press, 1979.

———. "'When de Saint Go Ma'chin' Home': Sterling Brown's Blueprint for a New Negro Poetry." *Callaloo* 21, no. 4 (1998): 940–49.

Sterne, Jonathan. *The Audible Past: Cultural Origins of Sound Reproduction*. Durham, NC: Duke University Press, 2003.

Stott, William. *Documentary Expression and Thirties America*. New York: Oxford University Press, 1973.

Studlar, Gaylyn. "'Out Salome-ing Salome': Dance, the New Woman, and Fan Magazine Orientalism." In *Visions of the East: Orientalism in Film*, edited by Matthew Bernstein and Gaylyn Studlar, 99–129. New Brunswick, NJ: Rutgers University Press, 1997.

Szwed, John. *Alan Lomax: The Man Who Recorded the World*. New York: Penguin, 2011.

Taylor, Diana. *The Archive and the Repertoire: Performing Cultural Memory in the Americas*. Durham, NC: Duke University Press, 2003.

Taylor, Helen. *Circling Dixie: Contemporary Southern Culture through a Transatlantic Lens*. New Brunswick, NJ: Rutgers University Press, 2001.

Thomas, James G. "Mississippi *Mahjar*: The History of Lebanese Immigration to the Mississippi Delta and the Role of the Group within a Traditionally Black-and-White Social System." Masters thesis, University of Mississippi, 2007.

Thurman, Wallace. "Negro Artists and the Negro." *The New Republic*, August 31, 1927: 37–39.

Titon, Jeff Todd. *Early Downhome Blues: A Musical and Cultural Analysis*. Chapel Hill: University of North Carolina Press, 1994.

Tucker, Sherrie. *Swing Shift: "All-Girl" Bands of the 1940s*. Durham, NC: Duke University Press, 2000.

Tuuk, Alex van der. *Paramount's Rise and Fall: A History of the Wisconsin Chair Company and Its Recording Activities*. Littleton, CO: Mainspring Press, 2003.

Urry, John. *The Tourist Gaze*. London: Sage Publications, 2002.

Van Vechten, Carl. "Memories of Bessie Smith." *Jazz Record* (September 1947): 6–7, 29.

Vogel, Shane. *The Scene of Harlem Cabaret: Race, Sexuality, Performance*. Chicago: University of Chicago Press, 2009.

Von Eschen, Penny. *Satchmo Blows Up the World: Jazz Ambassadors Play the Cold War*. Cambridge, MA: Harvard University Press, 2004.

Wald, Elijah. *Escaping the Delta: Robert Johnson and the Invention of the Blues*. New York: HarperCollins, 2004.

Wald, Gayle. *Shout, Sister, Shout! The Untold Story of Rock-and-Roll Trailblazer Sister Rosetta Tharpe*. Boston: Beacon Press, 2007.

Ward, Brian. "By Elvis and All the Saints: Images of the American South in the World of 1950s British Popular Music." In *Britain and the American South: From Colonialism to Rock and Roll*, edited by Joseph P. Ward, 187–214. Jackson: University Press of Mississippi, 2003.

———. "Forgotten Wails and Master Narratives: Media, Culture, and Memories of the African American Freedom Struggle." In *Media, Culture, and the Modern African American Freedom Struggle*, edited by Brian Ward, 1–15. Gainesville: University Press of Florida, 2001.

———. *Just My Soul Responding: Rhythm and Blues, Black Consciousness, and Race Relations*. Berkeley: University of California Press, 1998.

Ward, Joseph P., ed. *Britain and the American South: From Colonialism to Rock and Roll*. Jackson: University Press of Mississippi, 2003.

Warner, Michael. "The Mass Public and the Mass Subject." In *Habermas and the Public Sphere*, edited by Craig Calhoun, 377–401. Cambridge, MA: MIT Press, 1992.

Waters, Ethel, with Charles Samuels. *His Eye Is on the Sparrow: An Autobiography*. Cambridge, MA: Da Capo Press, 1992.

Weisenfeld, Judith. *Hollywood Be Thy Name: African American Religion in American Film, 1929–1949*. Berkeley: University of California Press, 2007.

White, Patricia. "Nazimova's Veils: Salome at the Intersection of Film Histories." In *A Feminist Reader in Early Cinema*, edited by Jennifer M. Bean and Diane Negra, 60–87. Durham, NC: Duke University Press, 2002.

White, Shane, and Graham J. White. *Stylin': African American Expressive Culture from Its Beginnings to the Zoot Suit*. Ithaca, NY: Cornell University Press, 1998.

Williams, David. *First Time We Met the Blues: A Journey of Discovery with Jimmy Page, Brian Jones, Mick Jagger, and Keith Richards*. York, UK: Music Mentor Books, 2009.

Williams, Michael Ann. *Staging Tradition: John Lair and Sarah Gertrude Knott*. Champaign: University of Illinois Press, 2006.

Williams, Tennessee. *Cat on a Hot Tin Roof*. New York: New Directions, 2004.

Wilson, August. *Ma Rainey's Black Bottom*. New York: Penguin Books, 1981.

Wilson, Charles Reagan. "Traveling Shows." In *Encyclopedia of Southern Culture*, edited by Charles Reagan Wilson, William Ferris, and Ann J. Adadie, 1249. Chapel Hill: University of North Carolina Press, 1989.

Wolfe, Charles, and Kip Lornell. *The Life and Legend of Leadbelly*. New York: HarperCollins, 1992.

Wollen, Peter. "Fashion/Orientalism/the Body." *New Formations* 1 (1987): 5–33.

Woods, Clyde. *Development Arrested: Race, Power, and the Blues in the Mississippi Delta*. New York: Verso, 1996.

Work, John W. *American Negro Songs: 230 Folk Songs and Spirituals, Religious and Secular*. Mineola, NY: Dover Publications, 1998.

Wray, Matt. *Not Quite White: White Trash and the Boundaries of Whiteness*. Durham, NC: Duke University Press, 2006.

Wynn, Neil. "'Why I Sing the Blues': African American Music in the Transatlantic World." In *Cross the Water Blues: African American Music in Europe*, edited by Neil Wynn, 3–22. Jackson: University Press of Mississippi, 2007.

Yafa, Stephen. *Cotton: The Biography of A Revolutionary Fiber*. New York: Penguin, 2006.

Ybarra, Patricia. "Mexican Theater History and Its Discontents: Politics, Performance, and History in Mexico." *Modern Language Quarterly* 70, no. 1 (2009): 133–45.

Index

Page numbers followed by f indicate a picture.

Abbott, Lynn, 8, 19, 34, 40
Abel, Elizabeth, 167–68
abolition movement, 92, 133, 164–66, 173
Abrahams, Roger D., 101–2
Absalom, Absalom! (Faulkner), 5
Abyssinia (musical), 34
acting. *See* theatrical blues performance
Adams, Jessica, 186, 209
Adelt, Ulrich, 135, 153
Adorno, Theodor, 228n30
Adventures of a Ballad Hunter (J. Lomax), 237n61
African American Lives series, 253n82
"Aggravatin' Papa," 88
"Alabama Blues," 155
Albee, Edward, 79
Albertson, Chris, 71
Allan, Maud, 59, 63
"All Coons Look Alike to Me," 46
Allen, O. K., 108
American Folk, Blues, and Gospel Caravan, 133–34, 136, 173
American Folk Blues Festival, 133–36, 139, 151; influence on rock and roll of, 160; sets and tour artwork for, 153–57
The American Guide Series, 94–95
American Negro Blues Festival, 137
Ammons, Albert, 124
Anderson, Benedict, 42, 238n76
Anderson, Marian, 120, 123, 124
the Animals, 160
antebellum heritage tourism, 185–86, 202
antitheatricalism, 8–9, 70, 84; in blues scholarship, 9, 223n44; in European staging of blues, 136–39, 242n11, 243n24; of John Lomax, 101–4; in "pictorial journalism," 110–11
Aphrodite, 61

Apollo Theater, 112–19; Amateur Night at, 114; aspirational middle-class aesthetic of, 114–19, 240n111; urban sounds at, 115; variety show format of, 113–14
Apter, Emily, 63, 64f
Arab peddlers, 68, 232n85, 232n87
The Arcades Project (Benjamin), 177
Archie Savage Dancers, 124
Archive of American Folk Songs at the Library of Congress, 100, 111, 235n37
Armstrong, Louis, 134–35
Armstrong, T. A., 102–3
Asch, Moe, 135
Aschoff, Peter, 201
As Thousands Cheer, 22
Atkinson, Brooks, 142, 145
Auslander, Philip, 131, 225n55, 229n38
authenticity, 7–8, 238n66; African roots and, 202–4, 210–11; antitheatricality in, 101–4, 136–39, 242n11, 243n24; blues tourism and, 185, 190–93, 197–212; Ledbetter and, 82, 111; onstage dramatic personas and, 21–25, 51–54, 77, 229n38, 230n47; realism discourses and, 47; revival period emphasis on, 28–29, 82–84, 185; white audience expectations of, 130. *See also* staging the South
automobile travel, 193–96

backdrops. *See* sets and backdrops

Baker, Ella, 170

Baker, Houston, Jr., 12, 20, 222n22

Baker, Josephine, 62–63, 135, 231n79

Bakst, Leon, 60

Ballets Russes, 59–60

Bandanna Land (musical), 54, 59

Bara, Theda, 63, 64*f*

Baraka, Amiri (LeRoi Jones), 17, 223n44

Barish, Jonas, 11

Barlow, William, 17, 23, 225n63

Barraud, Francis, 31–32

Baudrillard, Jean, 25

Beale on Broadway, 1–4

Beale Street Sheiks, 68

the Beatles, 160

the Beats, 195–96

Beck, Jeff, 7

Beeching, Richard, 161

Benjamin, Walter: on historical materialism, 174; on train platforms, 177; on
translation, 132–33, 174–75

Bentley, Gladys, 83

Berendt, Joachim-Ernst, 153–55

Bernhardt, Clyde, 54–55, 230n63

Bernhardt, Sarah, 58, 62, 229n44

Bernier, Celeste, 124

Bernstein, Robin, 196–97

Berry, Chuck, 160

Billington, Johnnie, 219

binary classifications of blues, 23–25, 102,
114, 234n18, 236n50

The Birth of a Nation (Griffith), 46, 52

Black America (McClain and Salsbury), 47

The Black and White Minstrel Show, 157

the Black Bottom, 89, 235n24

"Black Brown and White," 170

Blackett, R. J. M., 165, 245n99

blackface minstrelsy, 7, 11–12, 157, 180; in
Clarksdale, 188–89; mammy figures in,
51–54; mimicry and mistaken identity
in, 21–25; satire in *Finian's Rainbow* of,
142–44; shouted coon songs in, 21–22,
225n62; in Southern tent shows, 27,
46–47; in urban musical comedies,
45–46; white composers in, 15

Black Manhattan (Johnson), 15

Black Patti Troubadours, 86

black theater, 13–15, 227n9; moral character of actresses in, 49–54; move to Harlem of, 14, 15, 222n25, 223n39; uplift
and, 27–28, 34, 50; vernacular forms
in, 15, 95–99, 105; white audiences of,
96–97. *See also* musical comedy

black women: sexual slander against, 49;
uplift and, 48–54. *See also* female blues
singers

Blake, Eubie, 45–46

Blight, David, 204

Blitzstein, Marc, 126

The Blues (Scorsese/PBS), 183, 202–3,
253nn80–81

The Blues and Gospel Train, 22, 28–29,
130–31, 139, 149–75, 224n51; civil
rights movement context of, 133,
167–75; commemorative screenings
of, 175; costumed live audience of,
152, 162–63, 166; local reception of,
131; Manchester's civic identity and,
133, 159–67; performers on, 140–49,
149–51; television broadcast of, 130,
131, 136, 149; theatricality of, 139; train
station venue of, 130, 149–52, 161–64,
166–68, 177; visual rhetoric of, 131,
151–53, 157–59

Blues People (L. Jones [Baraka]), 223n44

blues tourism, 27, 29, 177–220, 224n51;
Delta landscape in, 200–202; demographics of, 184–85, 189, 195, 204–5,
250n28; documentary photography
and, 187–88; driving Route 61 in,
193–96, 252n56; economic impact of,
184, 213; festivals in, 177–78, 212–18;
guidebooks for, 197; immersion experiences in, 204–10, 253n78, 253n84;
omissions from, 217–18; pastoral
aesthetics of, 179, 185, 215; performers for, 188–90, 195–96, 211, 218; as
poverty tourism, 186–88, 209, 251n41;
pursuit of origins in, 197–202, 210–11,
252n69, 252n71; racial history in, 204;
repurposed train station platforms in,
177–78, 213, 214*f*; as restored behavior,
191–95, 199, 204, 207–8, 210, 251n48;
routes and sites of, 180, 183, 191–218,
250n30, 252n56; theatrical perfor-

mance in, 179, 188–93, 214–15. *See also* Clarksdale, Mississippi

Blues Traveling: The Holy Sites of the Delta Blues (Cheseborough), 194

"Boll Weevil Blues," 87

"Bourgeois Blues," 122–23

Bourne, St. Clair, 70

Boyd, Joe, 151

Brecher, Leo, 112

Brecht, Bertolt, 120

Brennan, Alfred, 120

Britain, 2, 7, 130, 160; affective connections to African Americans in, 159–67; American Civil War and, 164–66, 245n99; antitheatricalism of blues performance in, 136–39; black anti-slavery activism in, 165; black Caribbean immigrants in, 157, 168–69; blackface minstrelsy in, 157–58; blues influence on music in, 146, 160–61; jazz ban in, 135; *The Man Who Went to War* radio play in, 141–42; North-South divide in, 162, 245n95; skiffle in, 135–36, 243n19; televised blues performances in, 136; waning industrialization in, 161–64; white audiences in, 135–37. See also *The Blues and Gospel Train*; Manchester, England; transatlantic stagings of the blues

British invasion, 160–61, 218

British Railway, 161–64

Broadway blues performance, 142–45

Brock, George, 211

Brooks, Daphne A., 21–22; on Hurston, 97; on racial uplift, 49, 230n48, 230n57; on Salome, 59, 63

Brooks, Lori, 47

Broonzy, Big Bill, 23, 225n63; European popularity of, 135, 172; on U.S. racism, 170

Brown, Henry "Box," 32, 165

Brown, Jayna, 6, 47, 228n21; on black vernacular dance, 91; on Salome, 59

Brown, Sterling A.: on black folk culture, 233n4; on *The Green Pastures*, 93–94; on "Ma" Rainey, 42–44, 229n37; on theatricality in folk music, 13, 84, 93–94

Brown, William Wells, 165

Brubeck, Dave, 134

Building an Anti-slavery Wall (Blackett), 165

Bunch, Lonnie, 114

Burdon, Eric, 160

Burley, Dan, 57, 72, 231n72

Butterbeans and Susie, 113, 116, 217

cabaret, 2, 83, 227n9. *See also* vaudeville tradition

cakewalk, 83, 90–91, 235n27

Caldwell, Erskine, 126

"Call Me When You Need Me," 155

Calloway, Cab, 115, 150*f*

Calvin, Floyd J., 107

"Camptown Ladies," 157

Canning, Charlotte, 102

Carby, Hazel: on blues masculinity, 23–24; on female blues singers, 39, 44; on Hurston's romanticism, 236n50

Carr, Sam, 255n114

Cat on a Hot Tin Roof (Williams), 22, 144–45, 171, 207–8, 244n47

"C'est Bon, Les Oeufs (Scrambled Egg Song)," 129–30

Chaney, James, 168, 180

"Characteristics of Negro Expression" (Hurston), 216–17, 236n50

Charters, Samuel, 135, 153

Chatmon, Sam, 228n28

Chautauqua performances, 102–3, 229n32

Cheseborough, Steve, 194, 252n70

Childress, Alice, 172

Civil Rights Act of 1964, 168

civil rights movement: Freedom Summer of, 168, 180, 181; iconography of, 155; in the Mississippi Delta, 181–82; Mississippi's tourist infrastructure and, 185–86; musical anthems of, 141; public transportation's role in, 167, 247n112; transatlantic blues promotion and, 133–34, 167–75

Civil War: all-white reunions after, 204; Britain's position during, 164–65, 245n99; centennial commemorations of, 164–66

Clapton, Eric, 7, 135

Clarksdale, Mississippi: Bessie Smith's death in, 189–90; black hospital of, 78–79; blues tourism in, 29, 178, 184–91, 197–218, 224n51; civil rights movement in, 181–82; the Crossroads of, 197–99, 252n70; Delta Blues Museum in, 29, 183, 201, 210–12, 224n51; juke joints in, 215–16; Muddy Waters in, 224n51; music festivals in, 212–18, 254n100; performance spaces in, 213; poverty tourism in, 186–88, 209; rap and hip-hop in, 218; Riverside Hotel of, 189–90, 208; Rock and Blues Museum of, 211; Savoy and Marion theaters of, 188, 219–20, 251n42; Shack Up Inn of, 29, 184, 206–10, 214, 254n90; theatrical culture in, 40, 78, 188–89

classic blues, 2, 3, 23–24, 114, 226n67; acting roles in, 26; in authenticity debates, 138–39; ending of, 81; professionalism of performers in, 39–40, 227n20; theatrical background in, 33–37, 146; vaudeville sites of, 27–28. See also female blues singers

Clay, Robert, 206f, 208

Clifford, James, 226n70

Coahoma County, Mississippi, 38. See also Mississippi Delta

Cobain, Kurt, 81

Cody, William, 188

Cole, Bob, 14–15, 45–46

Colored American magazine, 49

Colored Vaudeville Benevolent Organization, 227n20

Commonwealth Immigrants Act of 1962, 169

communism, 120–21, 241n123

Connelly, Marc, 96

The Contribution of the Negro to American Democracy (White), 123–24, 125f

Conversation with the Blues (Oliver), 223n44

Cook, Will Marion, 46

Cooke, Sam, 178, 180

coon shouters, 21–22, 225n62

coon songs, 46

Cooper, Ralph, 113

costumes: dramatic personas and, 53–56, 230n65; Orientalist style in, 61–65;

Poiret's designs of, 61–63; as representation of wealth, 55–56

Count Basie Orchestra, 115, 241n123

counterpublics, 228n30

country blues, 23–24, 114, 180; blues tourism and, 188–90, 211; European performances of, 130; masculinity in, 24, 91, 103–4, 138–39, 195–96, 226n66; musician photographs in, 57; primacy in blues scholarship of, 24, 70, 79. See also male blues singers; staging the South

Cousin Joe (Pleasant Joseph), 12, 28, 130; on The Blues and Gospel Train, 151, 158–59, 171; on gospel music, 145–46, 148; on performing for white audiences, 159

Cox, Ida, 86, 225n63

The Cradle Will Rock (Blitzstein), 126

Craft, Ellen, 165

Craft, William, 165

Creole Show (musical), 15

"Criteria for Negro Art" (Du Bois), 16

the Crossroads, 197–99

Crossroads at Clarksdale (Hamlin), 181–82

Crossroads film, 252n70

Cross the Water Blues (Wynn), 242n14

cult of authenticity. See authenticity

cultural front, 119–27; jazz and Tin Pan Alley in, 241n119; pageant of Negro music and, 124; performance aesthetics of, 119–20; political causes of, 120; relief concerts of, 126–27, 242n137; White's The Contribution of the Negro mural in, 123–24, 125f

Dafora, Asadata, 124

Daily Worker, 120–21, 123

dance, 37; in European blues performance, 138, 243n24; Ledbetter's performance of, 88–93, 235n24, 235n27; multivocality in performance of, 91–93

the Dancing Sheiks, 53, 68

dark tourism, 251n41

Davis, Angela Y., 44, 48, 226n66

Davis, Tracy C., 230n48

Davison, Harold, 151

"Death Letter Blues," 86

The Death of Bessie Smith (Albee), 79
death of the blues, 81, 117, 218–20, 255n114
Delta blues, 23–24, 218–20; in authenticity debates, 138–39; deaths of bluesmen and, 218–19, 255n114; historic sites of, 178; male laborers of, 22–23. *See also* blues tourism
Delta Blues Education Fund, 219
Delta Blues Museum, 29, 183, 201–2, 210–12, 224n51, 254n98
Delta rap, 218
Denning, Michael, 119, 120, 241n119, 241n123
desegregation. *See* civil rights movement
Devil Got My Woman: Blues at Newport 1966 (A. Lomax), 153
"devil's music," 9–17
Diaghilev, Sergei, 59
diaspora, 226n70. *See also* migration and travel
"Diasporas" (Clifford), 226n70
"Didn't It Rain," 171, 173–74, 227n17
Dixon, Willie, 139, 153–55, 156f
DNA analysis, 203, 253n82
Dockery Farms, 199
documentary impulse, 94, 235n36
documentary photography, 187–88
Don't You Want to Be Free? (Hughes), 124
Dorsey, Thomas A., 10–11, 37, 114
Douglass, Frederick, 165
Du Bois, W. E. B.: on black popular entertainment, 13–14, 223n29; on Christian aversion to popular performance, 11; critical challenges to, 16; musical-historical pageant of, 124
Dunbar, Paul, 46
Dunham, Katherine, 89, 94
Dust Tracks on a Road (Hurston), 97–98
Dylan, Bob, 193–94

Early Downhome Blues (Titon), 24
"East Coast Blues" (Hurston), 99
Edwards, Brent Hayes, 226n70
Edwards, David Honeyboy, 180, 218–19, 255n113
Eichstedt, Jennifer, 186

Ellington, Duke, 134–35, 241n123
Elliott, Max C., 40
Ellison, Mary, 246n99
"Equality for Negros," 121–22
Escaping the Delta (Wald), 223n44
European performances. *See* transatlantic stagings of the blues
Evans, Walker, 187, 207
Evers, Medgar, 180

Famous Door, 140, 159
"Fannin Street," 86, 87
"Far Away Blues," 39
Father of the Blues (Handy), 9–10, 15
Faulkner, William, 202
Feel Like Going Home (Scorsese), 202–3, 253nn80–81
"Feel Like Going Home," 202
female blues singers: acting experience of, 22, 31–37; blues tourism and, 189–90, 211–12; classic blues tradition of, 23–25, 225n63; costumes of, 53–56, 230n65; critical marginalization of, 24, 70, 79, 104, 138; first-person confessional modes of, 44–45, 48, 71–72; influence on Ledbetter by, 86, 88; onstage dramatic personas of, 6, 21–25, 51–54, 77, 229n38, 230n47; professionalism of, 39–40, 227n20; resistance to racism by, 6, 51, 53, 222n12; respectability narratives and, 48–54, 230n48, 230n55; travel and labor migration of, 38–44, 39–41, 227n17. *See also* Rainey, Gertrude "Ma"; Smith, Bessie; theatrical blues performance
Féral, Josette, 104, 238n75
Fiddler, Harry, 70
Filene, Benjamin, 7, 108
Fine Clothes for the Jew (Hughes), 16
Finian's Rainbow (musical), 142–44, 244nn43–44
Fire!! literary journal, 16
first-person narration, 22, 44–45, 48, 71–72
Fitzgerald, Ella, 114, 115
Florida Blossom Minstrel Show, 113
Foley, Malcolm, 187
folk (as term), 233n4

folklorists, 8, 93–99, 182; binary classifications by, 23–25, 102, 114, 234n18, 236n50; field recording of, 7–8, 70, 99, 100, 224n51, 233n3, 235nn37–38; staging of the blues by, 28, 82, 84; study of dance by, 89; theatrical thinking of, 104–6; WPA programs for, 94–95. *See also* Hurston, Zora Neale; Lomax, Alan; Lomax, John; scholarship of the blues

folk music: authenticity debates about, 7–8, 28–29, 82–84; classification of blues as, 23, 81; cultural front performance of, 119–27; left-leaning leaders of, 114; postwar revival period of, 7–8, 28–29, 81–82; theatrical thinking and, 83–84, 94–99, 104–6. *See also* Ledbetter, Huddie

folk-popular binary, 17, 28, 88, 102, 223n44

Foster, Stephen, 4, 46, 157

Foucault, Michel, 224n49

Franklin, Aretha, 1

Fraser, Nancy, 228n30

Freedom Summer, 168, 180, 181

Freeman, Morgan, 216

the Frogs, 227n20

"From Spirituals to Swing" concert, 124, 136

front porch settings, 98, 126–27, 131, 151, 213

Gaines, Kevin, 12

"Gallows Pole," 81, 122

Gates, Henry Louis, Jr., 224n48, 253n82

Gee, Jack, 70

Geer, Will, 126, 143

Gellert, Lawrence, 108

gendering of blues, 21–25; blues tourism and, 179, 184–85, 195, 208–9; of classic blues, 23–25, 225n63; of coon shouters, 21–22, 225n62; of country blues, 24, 91, 103–4, 138–39, 226n66

genetic genealogy testing, 203, 253n82

genre of blues, 23–25

Georgia Smart Set Minstrels, 33, 41, 54–55

Gettysburg reunion, 204

Gillespie, Dizzy, 133, 134, 135

Gilroy, Paul, 168–69

Glanville, Maxwell, 145

Goffman, Erving, 190

"Goin' Where the Southern Cross the Dog," 152, 177

Goldwater, Barry, 168, 247n116

Goodman, Andrew, 168, 180

"Goodnight, Irene," 81, 85, 111

Gordon, Robert H., 124

gospel music, 8, 10–11, 145–46, 173–74, 180, 188

"Governor Pat Neff," 92

Granada Television, 136, 163, 245n64

Granny Maumee (Torrence), 14–15

"*Grapes of Wrath* evening," 126–27, 242n137

The Great Day (Hurston), 17, 141, 237n57; explanatory lecture in, 101, 237n55; Hurston's rationale for, 88, 97–99, 234n20; juke joint in, 216–17; work-song performance in, 109

Great Migration, 26–28, 37, 178, 227n13, 237n77

Green, Jeff, 191–92

Green, Paul, 236n54

The Green Pastures (musical), 15, 95–97, 105

Greeson, Jennifer, 5

Greiss, Abe, 90

Griffin, Farah Jasmine, 31

Griffith, D. W., 46

Grossman, Lawrence, 164

"Ground Hog Blues," 86

Ground Zero Blues Club, 184–85, 189, 215–16

Guthrie, Woody, 82, 126–27, 143, 233n1

Habermas, Jürgen, 228n30

Hall Johnson Choir, 96, 141

Hamer, Fannie Lou, 170, 243n20

Hamilton, Marybeth, 182, 195–96

Hamlin, Françoise, 181–82

Hammond, John, 78–79, 124, 136

Hamp, Johnnie, 136, 139, 152, 163, 170. See also *The Blues and Gospel Train*

Handy, W. C., 15; compositions by, 20, 21; on "devil's music," 9–10; role in blues history of, 211; in Tutwiler train station, 152, 178, 183, 199

Harlem: black migration to, 15–16; black theater in, 14, 15, 222n25; black vernacular entertainment in, 112–14; Cotton Club of, 132, 146–48, 153, 165, 223n39; Ledbetter's Apollo Theater concerts in, 112–13, 116–19; praise of the blues in, 15; rent parties in, 255n105; theatrical presentation of "folk" in, 95–99; white spectators in, 112, 223n39

Harlem Renaissance, 81, 95

Harris, Corey, 202–3

Harrison, Daphne Duval, 44

Harrison, Richard, 96–97

Hart, Alvin Youngblood, 215

Hartman, Saidiya, 11

Harvard folklore studies, 100, 103–4

Haverly's American-European Mastodon Minstrels, 85

"Hawaiian Song," 88

Hawley, Monte, 116

Hegamin, Lucille, 88, 113

Helena, Arkansas, 213

Henry, Aaron, 181

heritage tourism, 191–92; House of Blues and, 204–6; to plantations, 185–86, 202; to West Africa, 203–4. *See also* blues tourism

"He's Got the Whole World in His Hands," 173

"Hesitation Blues," 88

Highway 61, 78, 192, 193–96, 252n56

Highway 61 Revisited (Dylan), 193–94

His Eye Is on the Sparrow: An Autobiography (Waters), 232n95

His Master's Voice (Barraud), 31–32, 226n3

The History of the Blues (Davis), 244n44

Hogan, Ernest, 15, 46

Holiday, Billie, 114, 115, 241n123

homeland tourism, 203–4

Hooker, John Lee, 29, 178, 180, 189, 211

"Hootin' Blues," 143, 155, 162, 166

Hopson Plantation, 199, 206, 253n84. *See also* Shack Up Inn

Horkheimer, Max, 228n30

Horne, Lena, 115

"Hot Dogs," 89

House, Son, 23, 153, 180, 201–2, 211, 225n63

House of Blues chain, 4, 204–6, 212, 224n51, 254n100

Houston, Whitney, 1

"How It Feels to Be Colored Me" (Hurston), 98

Howlin' Wolf, 8–9, 114, 138, 153

Hughes, Langston, 16, 83, 223n39; on *The Green Pastures*, 96–97; musical-historical pageant of, 124; radio play of, 141–42

Hunter, Alberta, 22, 46, 83, 88

Hurston, Zora Neale, 16–17, 93–94; on blues and dance, 88–89; on clothing and appearance, 55; concerts and plays by, 97–99, 101, 109, 141, 234n20, 236n50, 237n55, 237n57; field work of, 94, 235n37; front porch of, 98, 127, 213; on *The Green Pastures*, 94–99; on juke joints, 216–17, 254n100; on theatricality of folk music, 84, 94–99, 236n54

The Husband?, 50

"I Don't Feel No Ways Tired," 141

"If the Man in the Moon Were a Coon," 46

I Hear the Blues, 139

"I Like You 'Cause You Got Such Lovin' Ways," 113

imagined community, 42, 238n76

Imes, Birney, 217

"I'm Gonna Hold It in Her," 88

immersion narratives, 202–3

Immigration Act of 1924, 68

"I'm On My Last Go Round," 87

In Dahomey (musical), 46

Indianapolis Freeman, 12, 20, 21, 23; blues debates in, 27–28; on Rainey's career, 33; Russell on moral character of actresses in, 49–52; on touring performers, 39, 40

International Jazz Festival (Paris), 130

International Ladies' Garment Workers' Union (ILGWU), 124, 142

Irwin, May, 21–22

"I've Been Mistreated and I Don't Like It," 53

"I Want a Tall Skinny Papa," 146

Jackson, Aunt Molly, 126
Jackson, Mahalia, 146, 148, 173
Jackson, Shannon, 103–4
Jagger, Mick, 7, 135, 160
James, Etta, 1
jazz, 35–36; international tours of, 133, 134–35, 139; in Paris clubs, 135; Third Reich and, 154
Jazz Heard and Seen (Jazz Gehört und Gesehen), 153–55
Jefferson, Blind Lemon, 70, 86, 89
Jim Crow. *See* racism and racial violence
"Jim Crow," 122
"John Henry," 141, 145
Johnson, Jack, 122, 255n114
Johnson, James "Super Chikan," 188–89, 211, 218, 219
Johnson, James Weldon, 13; on black folk culture, 233n4; *Black Manhattan* of, 14–15; on death of the blues, 81, 117; on *The Green Pastures*, 96; on Ledbetter's beat balancing, 118–19; on multivocality of performance, 91–92; musical comedy work of, 14, 45–46; on theatricality of folk music, 95
Johnson, J. Rosamond, 14–15, 45–46
Johnson, Robert, 10, 41, 180, 197–99, 218, 252n69
Johnson, Walter P., 124
John Steinbeck Committee to Aid Agricultural Organization, 126–27
Jones, Brian, 160
Jones, LeRoi (Amiri Baraka), 17, 223n44
Jones, Lewis, 173
Jones, Lu Ann, 69
Jones, Peter d'A., 245n99
Jones, Sissieretta, 49, 58, 86
Joplin, Janis, 82
Joseph, Pleasant. *See* Cousin Joe
Juke Joint Festival, 213–18, 254n100
juke joints, 215–17, 254n100

Kaye, Nick, 252n71
Kazan, Elia, 144–45
Keil, Charles, 17
Keith, Benjamin Franklin, 35, 36, 42, 227n20
Kelley, Robin D. G., 55

Kellner, Bruce, 72
Kelsey, Samuel, 149
Kennedy, John F., 166
Kennedy, Robert F., 187, 207, 209
Kerouac, Jack, 195–96
Kieser, Günther, 154–55
King, Martin Luther, Jr., 168, 199
King, Stephen A., 184, 201, 248n5
King Biscuit Blues Festival, 213
the Kinks, 160
Kirby, Michael, 230n56
Kirshenblatt-Gimblett, Barbara, 191, 238n66
"Kitchen Man," 45
Kittredge, George Lyman, 100, 104
Klosterman, Chuck, 255n113
Knight, Marie, 146, 147
KnockDown South, 215
Knott, Sarah Gertrude, 236n54
Koch, Frederick, 236n54
Kraut, Anthea, 97, 99
"Krigwa Players Little Negro Theatre" (Du Bois), 13–14

Lackey, Kris, 195
Lancashire Cotton Famine, 164–66
The Land Where Blues Began (A. Lomax), 200, 201–2
The Land Where the Blues Began film, 240n95
Lange, Dorothea, 187
Last Cavalier (Porterfield), 237n61
Last Sessions (Ledbetter), 88
La Vizzo, Thelma, 171
Ledbetter, Huddie, 6, 12, 28, 81–93, 177; Apollo Theater concert of, 112–13, 116–19; authenticity debates on, 82, 111; awards and honors of, 82; contribution and impact of, 81–84, 140, 233n1; copyright of songs by, 88, 234n17; creative agency of, 82, 84–88; criminal reputation of, 90; cultural front performances of, 119–27, 242n137; dancing skills of, 88–93, 235n24, 235n27; European performances of, 127, 129–30, 133; female blues singers and, 86, 88; folklorist recording of, 70; on the "Lead Belly"

myth, 113–14; Lomaxes' presentation of, 28, 82, 84, 86–87, 90, 91, 94–95, 106–12, 237n81; musical diversity of, 88; political engagement of, 120–24, 241n123; publicity photographs of, 86–87; stage name of, 22, 82, 87–88; tempo swings and beat balancing by, 117–19, 129–30; theatrical experience of, 85–93, 234n15; theatrical thinking of, 26–27, 82, 83–84; white audience of, 82

Led Zeppelin, 1–2, 81, 160

Lee, Canada, 141, 244n43

Lee, C. P., 130, 168

Leibovitz, Annie, 217

Lennon, John, 187

Lenoir, J. B., 155, 156f

Let the World Listen Right (Neff), 218

Levine, Lawrence, 10, 17

Lewis, Meade Lux, 124

Lieb, Sandra, 228n28, 230n63

Lincoln, Abraham, 164–66, 247n109

Lippmann, Horst, 137–38, 153–55

Lipsitz, George, 221n4

Little Henry (ventriloquist dummy), 21

Liveness: Performance in a Mediatized Culture (Auslander), 225n55

Locke, Alain, 14, 15, 17

Lomax, Alan, 1, 93–94, 135; copyright of Ledbetter's songs by, 88, 234n17; field recordings by, 7–8, 99, 100, 109, 173, 194, 203, 224n51; Hurston's influence on, 99; on Ledbetter, 108, 123; Ledbetter's management by, 28, 82, 84, 86–87, 94–95, 237n81; on the Mississippi Delta, 200, 201–2; Newport Folk Festival blues documentary by, 153, 154; New York World's Fair plans of, 237n55; participation in *The Man Who Went to War*, 141; performance career of, 83; study of dance by, 89

Lomax, John, 93–94, 100–112; autobiography of, 237n61; awards and honors of, 101, 107; on blues as folk music, 23; copyright of Ledbetter's songs by, 88, 234n17; field work of, 100, 107, 194, 203, 235n37; Hurston's influence on, 99; lecture-performances of, 100–106,

237n62, 237n65; on Ledbetter's dancing, 89, 91; Ledbetter's management by, 28, 82, 84, 86–87, 90, 91, 94–95, 99, 106–12, 237n81, 237n93; on prison populations, 106–7; prison staging by, 109, 239n93; rhetorical antitheatricality of, 101–4; theatrical thinking of, 104–6, 126–27, 236n50, 238n66, 238n75

Long Lost Blues (Muir), 34, 223n44

Looking Up at Down (Barlow), 225n63

Lornell, Kip, 90, 120

Luce, Henry, 110

Luckett, Bill, 216

Lucky Millinder and His Orchestra, 147, 171

Mabley, Jackie Moms, 113, 116, 188

MacCannell, Dean, 190–91, 252n51

Magelssen, Scott, 193

male blues singers, 180; blues tourism and, 189–90, 195–96, 211–12; country blues of, 24, 70, 130; folklorist collection of, 24, 70, 79, 84, 93–99; masculinized portrayals of, 24, 91, 103–4, 138–39, 195–96, 211, 226n66; public personas of, 84–88; revival period of, 81–84; work songs of, 17, 22–23, 109. *See also* Ledbetter, Huddie

mammy figures, 51–54

Manchester, England, 28–29, 131, 175; American Civil War and, 164–66, 173, 246n99; civic identity of, 133, 159–67; decline of the textile industry of, 161–64, 169; statue of Lincoln in, 166, 247n109. See also *The Blues and Gospel Train*

The Man Who Went to War radio play, 141–42

"Ma Rainey" (Brown), 42–44

Ma Rainey's Black Bottom (Wilson), 79

The March of Time newsreels, 110–12, 116–17, 239n93, 240n98

Markham, Dewey Pigmeat, 113, 114, 188

Massie, Kim, 1–3, 10

Mathus, Jimbo, 215, 254n103

matrixed performance, 51–52, 230nn56–57

McAlister, Melani, 60

McClain, Billy, 47

McGhee, Brownie, 22, 28, 119, 130, 140–45; acting career of, 22, 142–45, 171, 244n43, 244n47; in *The Blues and Gospel Train*, 149–51, 166, 170; on entertainers vs. musicians, 138; in *Jazz Heard and Seen* television special, 154–57; in *The Man Who Went to War* radio play, 141–42; musical diversity of, 140; political engagement of, 170, 171, 174; recording of "Black Brown and White" by, 170; in *Simply Heaven*, 144

McNamara, Brooks, 221n3

McPherson, Tara, 253n78

Memphis Minnie, 24

Memphis Slim, 155–57

Meredith, James, 180

Messenger, George, 184, 218

migration and travel, 25–29, 38–44, 133, 226n70; of Arab peddlers, 68–69, 232n85, 232n87; by automobile, 194–95; as black public sphere, 40, 41–42, 228n30; from Britain's deindustrializing north, 163; of dust-bowl laborers, 126–27; as focus of theatrical performance, 38–39, 41–44, 151–52, 227n17; of folklorists, 101; on Highway 61, 78, 192, 193–96, 252n56; of the 1930s, 237n77; racism and, 35–36, 38, 47–48, 78–79, 190; shadow texts of, 26; within the South, 37, 227n13; trails and routes for, 191–96; uplift and respectability narratives of, 48–54, 229n44, 230n48; of working performers, 33–37, 39–44. *See also* blues tourism; transatlantic stagings of the blues

Miller, Karl Hagstrom, 88, 225n53, 234n18

Miller, Monica, 55

Mills, Florence, 15, 46

minstrelsy tradition. *See* blackface minstrelsy

mise-en-scène. *See* sets and backdrops

Mississippi Blues Commission, 183, 215

Mississippi Blues Trail, 183

Mississippi Delta, 3, 23, 26, 180–83; Arab (Syrian) peddlers of, 68–69, 232n85, 232n87; black population of, 38; blues tourism in, 29, 178–80, 183–90, 224n51; in *Cat on a Hot Tin Roof*, 145; civil rights movement in, 181–82; documentary photography of, 187–88; ethnic diversity of, 68, 249n16; Great Migration from, 26–28; Jim Crow legislation in, 180; landscape of, 200–202; mobility of population of, 40; musical diversity of, 180, 218; poverty in, 182, 209; repurposed train platforms of, 177–78, 213, 214f; Robert F. Kennedy's visit to, 187, 207, 209; traveling entertainment in, 33–37, 40–44, 180, 188–89. *See also* classic blues; Delta blues

the Mississippi Sheiks, 68

Mississippi Summer Projects. *See* Freedom Summer

mobility. *See* migration and travel

Modern Language Association, 101, 107–8

"Moonshine Blues," 31–33, 37, 42

Morganfield, McKinley. *See* Waters, Muddy

Morrison, Russell, 148–49, 158

Motown music, 173

Muir, Peter, 34, 223n44, 226n6

Mules and Men (Hurston), 109, 216

musical comedy, 14–15, 34–35, 45–46

musical-historical pageants, 14, 120, 124

"Musical Personae" (Auslander), 229n38

Music on My Mind (W. Smith), 115

Musselwhite, Charlie, 211

NAACP, 181

Natchez tourism, 186, 202

National Folk Festival, 236n54

National Millennium Trails, 183

National Negro Congress, 123–24

Nazimova, Alla, 63, 64f

Neff, Ali Colleen, 218

Neff, Pat, 92–93

"The Negro Artist and the Racial Mountain" (Hughes), 16

"Negro Artists and the Negro" (Thurman), 16

Negro Folk Songs as Sung by Leadbelly (Lomax and Lomax), 86–87, 107, 118–19, 239n93

Negro Poetry and Negro Drama (S. Brown), 95

New Masses, 108
Newport Folk Festival, 134, 135–36, 153, 154
Nighthawk, Robert, 180
Nirañjana, Tejasini, 132
"Nobody in This World Is Better Than Us," 121–22
nonmatrixed performance, 51–52, 230nn56–57
North Mississippi String Band, 215

Okeh Records, 21
Oklahoma! (musical), 170
Oliver, Paul, 6, 17, 135; antitheatricalism of, 8–9, 137–38; on in situ environments, 153; on theatrical traditions, 223n44; on Williamson, 24
O'Neal, Jim, 198
O'Neill, Eugene, 35
On the Road (Kerouac), 195–96
Orientalism: in black popular music, 68–69; in fashion and costuming, 58–64; lesbianism and, 64–66
The Original Vision album, 233n1
origin debates, 17–21; blues tourism and, 197–202, 210–11, 252n69, 252n71; folk-popular binary in, 17, 28, 223n44

Page, Jimmy, 7
Palmer, Robert, 218
Parks, Suzan-Lori, 18, 224n48
pastoral aesthetic: blues tourism and, 185; responses of female stars to, 57, 170; in staging of the South, 4–5, 95
Patton, Charley, 23, 41, 199, 211, 225n63
performers. *See* female blues singers; male blues singers
Performing Glam Rock (Auslander), 225n55
Perkins, Pinetop, 29, 253n84, 255n114
Petard, Gilles, 77
The Philadelphia Negro (Du Bois), 16
phonographs. *See* recording industry
photography: documentary projects in, 110–12, 116–17, 187–88, 217, 239n93, 240n98, 255nn108–9; of male country blues musicians, 57; for publicity, 56–58, 72, 86–87; by Van Vechten (of Smith), 70–77, 87, 233n97
"Pick a Bale of Cotton," 92, 118, 145

pickaninny choruses, 52–53
pictorial journalism, 110–12, 116–17, 239n93, 240n98
Pigee, Vera, 181–82
Pinetop Perkins Homecoming, 253n84
Pins and Needles musical, 124, 142
Plant, Robert, 2
plantation musicals, 4, 46, 54–55
plantation tourism, 185–86, 202
Plessy v. Ferguson, 167
Poiret, Paul, 61–63
Po' Monkey's Lounge, 215, 217
Popular Front, 119–21, 140, 142, 241n123
Porterfield, Nolan, 108, 237n61
Postgate, John, 139
postwar blues revival. *See* revival period
poverty tourism, 186–88, 209, 251n41
The Practice of Diaspora (Edwards), 226n70
Pratt, Mary Louise, 104
Pridgett, Thomas, Jr., 69–70
prison blues, 17, 22–23, 84; Ledbetter's performance of, 106–12, 117, 237n77; Lomax staging of, 109, 237n93
"The Problem of Amusement" (Du Bois), 13, 223n29
"Program to Aid 'Okies,'" 126–27, 242n137
Prohibition, 254n91
Promise, Martha, 111, 121, 140, 177
"Prove It on Me Blues," 65–66, 67f

Rabbit's Foot Minstrels, 33, 35, 40–41, 78, 211
race records. *See* recording industry
racial assumptions: in blackface minstrelsy performance, 11–12; in segmenting of musical genres, 19, 225n53; in staging the South, 4–6, 46, 221nn4–5
racism and racial violence: Arab immigrants and, 68, 232n85, 232n87; black economic migration and, 35–36; black prison labor and, 17, 84, 106–12, 117, 237n77, 237n85; black World War II soldiers and, 142, 170; blues tourism and, 204; Ledbetter's songs on, 121–24; lynchings and, 54; in the Mississippi Delta, 180, 186; paradox of jazz and blues promotion and, 133–34, 167–75;

racism and racial violence (*continued*)
performer resistance to, 6, 51, 53,
222n12; role of white womanhood in,
54, 92; segregation and, 8, 167–68;
traveling blues performer experiences
of, 38, 47–48, 78–79, 190. *See also*
blackface minstrelsy

Ragged but Right (Abbott and Seroff),
34, 40

Rainey, Gertrude "Ma," 2, 6, 27, 115; acting skill of, 33–34, 70; adopted children
of, 52–53, 227n20; as Afro-Oriental
character, 63–68; Brown's poem
about, 42–44, 229n37; costumes and
appearance of, 54–58, 232n80; death
and obituary of, 69–70; Dorsey's work
with, 10, 37; early blues singing by,
21, 23, 225n63; first-person confessional mode of, 44–45, 48; influence
of, 8, 146; Lieb's biography of, 228n28;
minstrelsy traditions of, 46–47; nonnormative sexual portrayals by, 65–66,
67f; onstage dramatic persona of,
51–54; publicity photographs of, 56f,
57–58; recording by, 19, 23, 36; "Stormy
Sea Blues" of, 37; travel and mobility
of, 47–48; "Traveling Blues" of, 38–39;
as "up-to-date coon shouter," 22;
Victrola act of, 31–33, 37, 42; Wilson's
play about, 79

Rainey, Pa, 35, 39, 46

Ratliff, Frank "Rat," 189–90, 218

Rau, Fritz, 153–55

realism, 47. *See also* authenticity

Reconstructing Dixie (McPherson), 253n78

recording industry, 18–21; mass production focus of, 37; portable technology of, 233n3; race records of, 35, 94,
234n18; studio contexts of, 36

recording the blues: by folklorists,
7–8, 70, 99, 100, 233n3; phonograph
technology and, 18–21; of the revival
period, 83; social contexts of, 19

*The Resurrection of Henry Box Brown at
Philadelphia* (Rowse), 32, 33f

Retman, Sonnet, 233n4, 236n50

revival period, 28–29, 135, 219–20;
antitheatricalism in, 84, 101–4;

authenticity rhetoric of, 7–8, 83, 185;
blues tourism and, 184–85; cultural
front performance of, 119–27; folklorist staging of the blues in, 28, 82–84;
"*Grapes of Wrath* evening" in, 126–27;
Ledbetter's contribution to, 81–84; in
the Mississippi Delta, 182; National
Folk Festival and, 236n54; primacy
of male blues singers in, 24, 70, 79,
84, 93–99; prison as site of blues
in, 84, 106–12, 117, 237n77, 237n85;
theatrical thinking of, 26–27, 82–84,
94–99, 104–6, 126–27, 236n50, 237n62,
238n66, 238n75. *See also* folklorists;
Ledbetter, Huddie; transatlantic stagings of the blues

Revue Negre, 231n79

rhythm and blues, 173, 180, 188

Richards, Keith, 135, 160

Richards, Sandra, 203–4

The Rider of Dreams (Torrence), 14–15

Riverside Hotel, 189–90, 208

Roach, Joseph, 18, 192

Robert Clay Shack, 206f, 208

Robeson, Paul, 123, 124; European
performances of, 133; international
bridge-building by, 174; in *The Man
Who Went to War* radio play, 141–42;
public political activism of, 120–21,
241n123

Robinson, Bill "Bojangles," 116, 217

Rock and Blues Museum, 211

rock and roll, 8, 130, 145, 180

Rock and Roll Hall of Fame, 82

the Rolling Stones, 160

Romine, Scott, 179

Route 61. *See* Highway 61

Rowse, Samuel, 32, 33f

Rush, Bobby, 188–89, 219

Russell, Ross, 117–18

Russell, Sylvester, 12, 27–28; on moral
character of actresses, 49–52, 54; on
Salome performances, 63

Salome (character), 58–69; black diasporic consciousness and, 67–69; headdresses of, 63, 64f, 232n80; Orientalist
vogue and, 58–63; sexuality associated

with, 63–66, 229n44; Walker's performance of, 54, 59, 60*f*, 63, 68; white portrayals of, 59, 68, 229n44
Salome (Wilde), 58, 229n44
Salsbury, Nate, 47, 188
Savran, David, 35, 36, 227n9
Scarlett O'Hara (character), 170–71
scenery and props. *See* sets and backdrops
Schechner, Richard, 45, 191, 230n47
Scheherazade, 59–60
Schiffman, Bobby, 114–15
Schiffman, Frank, 112
Schiffman, Jack, 116
Schneider, Rebecca, 17, 192, 219
scholarship of the blues: binary classifications in, 23–25, 102, 114, 234n18, 236n50; in Britain, 135; on dance, 91; on historical reproduction of the South, 179; marginalization of female blues singers in, 24, 70, 79, 104, 138–39; marginalization of theatricality in, 9, 101–4, 223n44; positivist methodology in, 104; primacy of male blues singers in, 24, 70, 79, 84, 138–39; primacy of recordings in, 19–20, 225n55; theatrical thinking and, 104–6. *See also* folklorists; Lomax, Alan; Lomax, John
Schwartz, Roberta Freund, 135
Schwerner, Michael, 168, 180
Scorsese, Martin, 183, 202–3, 253nn80–81
Scott, Esther Mae "Mother," 86
Scott, James C., 85
Scottsboro Nine case, 120–21, 123
Seeger, Pete, 120, 126
"See See Rider," 113
Segregating Sound (Miller), 225n53
segregation. *See* racism and racial violence
Seiler, Cotten, 194
Seroff, Doug, 8, 19, 34, 40
sets and backdrops, 54; of the American Folk Blues Festival, 153–57; of *The Blues and Gospel Train*, 151–53, 157–59; front porch settings, 98, 126–27, 131, 151, 213; minstrelsy traditions in, 154–58; pastoral aesthetics of, 132, 179; referencing black freedom struggles in,

155; in situ environments in, 153; visual rhetoric of, 154–55
sexuality: actress associations with, 230n55; in double-entendres in song lyrics, 2, 45, 65, 88; Jim Crow perspectives of white women's, 54, 92; lesbianism, homosexuality, and bisexuality of female blues performers, 63–66; in portrayals of Salome, 58–69; in slander against black women, 49, 55; in uplift and respectability narratives, 48–54, 63, 229n44, 230n48
Shack Up Inn, 29, 184, 186, 189, 206–10, 214, 254n90
The Sheik, 59
"The Sheik of Desplaines Street," 68
Showboat (musical), 22
Silas Green from New Orleans tent show, 33, 41, 211, 224n51
Simone, Nina, 171
Simon the Cyrenian (Torrence), 14–15
Sissle, Noble, 45–46
Siting Translation (Nirañjana), 132
skiffle, 135–36, 243n19
Small, Christopher, 19, 20
Small, Stephen, 186
Smith, Bessie, 6, 12, 27, 37, 39; acting skill of, 22, 33–34, 70, 73–77; Albee's play about, 79; Apollo Theater performances by, 114, 115; costumes and appearance of, 55–58; death of, 48, 70–71, 77–79, 178, 189–90, 233n102; early blues singing by, 23, 225n63; first-person confessional mode of, 45, 48, 71–72; influence of, 8, 86, 88, 146; minstrelsy traditions of, 46–47; nonnormative sexual portrayals by, 65–66; onstage dramatic persona of, 51–54, 77; as Oriental character, 62*f*, 63–68; privacy of, 71, 78–79, 232n95; publicity photographs of, 56*f*, 57–58, 72; recording by, 23; travel of, 41–42, 227n17; as "up-to-date coon shouter," 22; Van Vechten's photographs of, 70–77, 87, 233n97
Smith, Caleb, 237n85
Smith, Clara, 86
Smith, Eva Vaughn, 145

Smith, Mamie, 21
Smith, Ruby, 124
Smith, Willie "the Lion," 115
Smithsonian Folklife Festival, 214–15, 238n66
Smithsonian Folkways series, 233n1
songspiel, 120
Sonny Terry and Brownie McGhee. *See* McGhee, Brownie; Terry, Sonny
soul music, 173, 188
The Souls of Black Folk (Du Bois), 14
The South before the War (musical), 46
Southern Enchantment (musical), 46
Southern Road (S. Brown), 95
spirituals, 14, 15, 95–96, 99, 141, 173
Stack, Carol, 185
staging the South, 4–6, 221n5; in European performances, 127, 134–39, 151–59; minstrelsy traditions in, 154–58; pastoral aesthetics in, 132, 179, 185, 215; performers' hidden transcripts in, 6, 222n12; in prison recordings, 109; rhetoric of authenticity in, 47; sets and backdrops for, 54–55, 131, 132; in urban musical comedies, 45–46; white possessive investment in, 4, 6, 221n4. *See also* authenticity; blues tourism; racism and racial violence; transatlantic stagings of the blues
"Standin' in the Rain Blues," 227n17
The Star of Ethiopia (Du Bois), 13–14, 124
States, Bert O., 77
Stepto, Robert, 202
Stolle, Roger, 215, 219
"Stormy Sea Blues," 37
Stott, William, 235n36
Stovall Plantation, 212, 224n51, 254n98
Strauss, Richard, 59
Strunk, Oliver, 106
Stryker, Roy, 187
Studlar, Gaylyn, 59
subjectivity of black female singers, 44–47
Sugar Land Shuffle, 92–93
Sunflower River Blues and Gospel Festival, 29, 213, 214f
Super Chikan and the Fighting Cocks, 188–89, 211, 218, 219

surrogation, 192–93
"Sweet Mary," 92
Syrjala, S., 124
Szwed, John, 141, 239n93

"'T'Ain't Nobody's Bizness If I Do," 66
Talbot, Bill, 206, 254n90
"The Task of the Translator" (Benjamin), 132–33, 174–75
Taylor, Diana, 221n5
tent shows, 7, 18, 34–36, 38, 180, 227n9; Arab peddlers and, 68–69; blackface minstrelsy of, 11, 27, 46–47; dances held after, 228n28; diversity of genres in, 24–25; friendly rivalries among, 41; Toby figure in, 234n15; variety show format of, 46–47, 85
Terrill, Ruby, 104–5. *See also* Lomax, John
Terry, Sonny, 22, 28, 119, 130, 140–45; acting career of, 22, 142–45, 171, 244n43, 244n47; on *The Blues and Gospel Train*, 149–51, 166, 170; in *Finian's Rainbow*, 142–44, 244n43; on *Jazz Heard and Seen* television special, 154–57; in *The Man Who Went to War* radio play, 141–42; musical diversity of, 140; political engagement of, 170, 171, 174
Tharpe, Sister Rosetta, 6, 28, 130, 135, 145–49, 227n17; blending of sacred and secular by, 147–49; on *The Blues and Gospel Train*, 149–52, 157–59, 161, 166, 170–74; gospel singing of, 10, 145–46, 173–74; musical diversity of, 146; New York performances of, 114, 146–48, 150f; on racism and the civil rights movement, 170–74; stadium marriage ceremony of, 148–49; theatrical performance style of, 8–9, 146–49, 157–59, 170–71
"That's All Right, Brother, That's All," 147
Theater Arts Committee (TAC), 120, 126, 140; *Pins and Needles* of, 124, 142; Popular Front cabarets of, 142
Theater Owners Booking Association (TOBA), 27, 34–35, 117, 223n44; Ledbetter's work with, 86; rural South performances of, 38; variety show format of, 85, 113

theatrical blues performance, 22, 31–37; blues tourism and, 179, 188–93, 214–15; costumes in, 53–56, 230n65; dance and choreography in, 37, 88–93, 235n24, 235n27; decline of, 83; diversity of genres in, 24–25, 35–36, 234n18; first-person confessional modes in, 22, 44–45, 48, 71–72; genealogy of, 3–9, 18–21, 46, 221n3, 224n49; ideals of femininity and, 53–54; of Ledbetter, 82, 85–93, 104; as mimesis and repetition, 17–18, 191, 224n48; mise-en-scène of, 37, 126–27; in the Mississippi Delta, 33–37, 40–44, 180, 188–89; onstage dramatic personas in, 51–54, 229n38, 230n47; Orientalist vogue in, 54, 58–69; publicity photography in, 56–58; Rainey's Victrola act and, 31–33, 37; representing the South in, 34, 45–47; television and, 136; as threat to "legitimate" music and theater, 35–36; of traveling troupes, 33–37, 40–44; uplift narratives and, 48–54, 63, 230n48, 230n55; in urban settings, 83. See also female blues singers

theatrical thinking, 94–99; definition of, 104; of Hurston, 236n50; of John Lomax, 104–6, 126–27, 237n62, 238n66, 238n75; of Ledbetter, 26–27, 82, 83–84

Thomas, James G., 232n84

Thurman, Wallace, 16

Till, Emmett, 180

Till-Mobley, Mamie, 170

"Tin Top Shack" (Super Chikan), 189

Titon, Jeff Todd, 17, 24, 41

Tobacco Road stage set, 126–27

Toby figures, 234n15

Tolliver's Smart Set, 35, 36

Tom shows, 4, 46, 51–52, 55

Topsy figures, 51–52

Torrence, Ridgely, 14–15

Touré, Ali Farka, 203

tourism. See blues tourism

The Tourist: A New Theory of the Leisure Class (MacCannell), 190–91, 252n51

train stations/platforms: in The Blues and Gospel Train, 130, 149–52, 161–64, 166–68, 177; in blues festivals, 177–78, 213, 214f; Delta Blues Museum in, 224n51

transatlantic stagings of the blues, 27, 28–29, 129–75; affective connections in, 133, 159–67; authenticity and antitheatricality debates in, 136–39, 242n11, 243n24; civil rights movement context of, 133; Cold War context of, 133–34; educational component of, 136; festival/variety show format of, 136; influence on rock and roll of, 160–61; Ledbetter in, 129–30; paradox of U.S. racial violence and, 133–34, 167–75; references to Jim Crow in, 142; staging the South in, 127, 134–39, 151–59, 242n14; televised performances in, 136; translation and contextualization in, 131–33, 141–42, 155–57, 174–75, 242n9; venues for, 139–40; white audiences of, 135–36, 139–40, 158–59. See also The Blues and Gospel Train; Britain; Manchester, England

translation, 131–33, 141–42, 155–57, 174–75, 242n9

travel. See migration and travel

"Traveling Blues," 38–39

Trouble in Mind (Childress), 172

"Trouble in Mind," 171–73

"Trouble with the Angels" (Hughes), 96–97

Tucker, Sherrie, 139, 171

Tucker, Sophie, 21–22, 88

Turner, Ike, 178, 180, 199

Turner, Nat, 124

Tutwiler, Mississippi, 152, 178, 183, 199

United Kingdom. See Britain

uplift ideology, 13–14, 16–17, 222n25; black theatrical portrayals of, 27–28, 34, 50; female respectability in, 48–54, 63, 230n48, 230n55; realism discourses in, 47

Urry, John, 190–91

Valentino, Rudolph, 59

Vance, Claire, 21–22

Van Vechten, Carl: photographs of Bessie Smith by, 70–77, 87, 233n97; use of theatrical iconography by, 74–77 vaudeville tradition, 2, 7, 34–36, 227n9; black fraternal organizations in, 227n20; Great Migration and, 27–28; Keith and Albee circuits in, 35, 36, 42; moral character of actresses in, 49–54; publicity photography in, 58; ventriloquism in, 21–22, 225n62

ventriloquist acts, 21–22, 225n62

vernacular (popular) theater/music, 35, 227n9. *See also* classic blues; country blues; tent shows; vaudeville tradition

the Victrola, 31–33, 226n3

visual rhetoric. *See* sets and backdrops

von Eschen, Penny, 134

Wald, Elijah, 19, 22; on folk-popular binary, 88, 223n44; on professionalism of musicians, 39–40

Wald, Gayle, 145, 147, 159–60

Walker, Aida Overton, 14–15, 27–28, 71; musical comedy work of, 46; on respectability of theatrical life, 49–51, 54, 59; as Salome, 54, 59, 60*f*, 63, 68

Walker, George, 34, 45–46

Walker, Ruby, 31, 53

Ward, Brian, 162, 169

Warner, Michael, 228n30

Washington, Booker T., 12, 223n29

Washington, Dinah, 1, 171

Waters, Ethel, 15, 71, 86; acting career of, 22; Apollo theater performances by, 115; autobiography of, 232n95; cabaret performance of, 83; in *The Man Who Went to War* radio play, 141; musical comedy work of, 46

Waters, Muddy, 28, 41, 114, 180, 224n51; on *The Blues and Gospel Train*, 151–52, 167; blues tourism and, 189; cabin of, 212, 254n98; Delta Blues Museum focus on, 211, 212; European performances

of, 130, 135; given name of, 212; House of Blues chain and, 204–5, 212

The Weary Blues (Hughes), 16

the Weavers, 81

Weill, Kurt, 120

Wein, George, 134, 151

Wendell, Barrett, 100, 104

"We're in the Same Boat Brother," 123

West Africa, 202–4, 210–11

"What You Gonna Do with Your Long Tall Daddy," 88

"When Malindy Sings" (Griffin), 31

"Where Did You Sleep Last Night?," 81

White, Charles, 123–24, 125*f*

White, Georgia, 1, 2

White, Josh, 119, 120, 140, 141

Wildcats Jazz Band, 31, 37

Wilde, Oscar, 58, 63, 229n44

Williams, Bert, 14–15, 34, 45–46

Williams, Big Joe, 211

Williams, Michael Ann, 84, 236n54

Williamson, Sonny Boy, 8, 24, 137

Wilson, August, 79

Wolcott, Marion Post, 187, 217, 255n108

Wolfe, Charles, 90, 120

Woods, Clyde, 180, 184

Woods, Johnnie, 21, 24

Work, John, III, 173

"Working on the Railroad," 109

work songs, 17, 22–23, 109

Works Progress Administration (WPA), 94–95, 187, 235n37, 255n108

Wray, Matt, 209

Wright, Richard, 119, 121, 123

Wynn, Neil, 159, 242n14

the Yardbirds, 28, 160

Ybarra, Patricia, 235n36

the Year of the Blues, 183

Yergan, Max, 124